Tao: The Pathless Path

Talks on the Mystic Lieh Tzu

OSHO FROM FULL CIRCLE

- Gita Darshan (Vol-II)
- Gita Darshan (Vol-I)
- Tao: The Pathless Path
- Inner War and Peace
- Die O' Yogi Die
- Behind A Thousand Names
- Freedom from the Past
- Ah This!
- The Way of the Sufi
- The Silence of the Heart
- The True Name
- The Secret
- Truth Simply Is
- In Search of Celebration
- From Sex to Superconsciousness
- Never Born, Never Died
- Walk without feet, Fly without wings...
- Won't you Join the Dance?
- Priests & Politicians – The Mafia of the Soul
- My Diamond Days with Osho
- Tantra – The Supreme Understanding
- The Goose is Out
- Sex, Money and Power
- The Rebel
- A New Vision of Women's Liberation
- I Teach Religiousness Not Religion
- Words From A Man of No Words
- First In The Morning
- Last In The Evening

OSHO

Tao: The Pathless Path

Talks on the Mystic Lieh Tzu

FULL CIRCLE

TAO: THE PATHLESS PATH

First Edition, 2011
This Reprint, June 2019

ISBN 978-81-7621-220-5

For Sale in India only

FULL CIRCLE

Published by **FULL CIRCLE PUBLISHING** *PVT LTD*
J-40, Jorbagh Lane, New Delhi-110003
Tel: +011-24621011
E-mail: contact@fullcirclebooks.in *website:* www.fullcirclebooks.in

Originally published in English under the title: Tao: The Pathless Path Vol. 2

Typesetting: SCANSET
J-40, Jorbagh Lane, New Delhi-110003

Printed at Yash Printographics, C-37, Sector-58, Noida-201301 U.P.

PRINTED IN INDIA

Contents

CHAPTER 1

The Ultimate Synthesis

Hui Ang visited King K'ang of Sung. The king stamped his foot, coughed and said fiercely, "What pleases me is courage and strength. I take no pleasure in men who preach morality. What have you to teach me?"

"Suppose that I have a way to make anyone, however brave and strong, miss when he stabs or strikes at you. Wouldn't Your Majesty be interested?"

"Excellent! This is the sort of thing I like to hear."

"But even if a stab or blow misses, it is still humiliating for you. Suppose that I have a way to prevent anyone, however brave and strong, from daring to stab or strike you. But a man who does not dare to harm you may still have the will to harm you. Suppose that I have a way to ensure that men have absolutely no will to harm you. But a man who has no will to harm you may still have no thought of loving or benefiting you. Suppose that I have a way to make every single man and woman in the world joyfully desire to love and benefit you. This is three degrees better than courage and strength. Isn't Your Majesty interested?"

"This is the sort of way I should like to find."

"The teaching of Confucius and Mo Tzu is what I have in

mind. Confucius and Mo Tzu became princes without owning territory, became leaders without holding office. Every man and woman in the world craned his neck and stood on tiptoe in his eagerness for their safety and benefit. Now Your Majesty is the Lord of ten thousand chariots. If you were indeed to share the aims of these two men, everyone within your four borders would enjoy the benefit. You would be far greater than Confucius and Mo Tzu."

Hui Ang hurried out. And the king said to his courtiers, "Clever, the way he talked me round with his argument!"

Tao means transcendence – transcendence of all duality, transcendence of all polarity, transcendence of all opposites. Tao is the ultimate synthesis – the synthesis of man and woman, of positive and negative, life and death, day and night, summer and winter.

But how does this synthesis become possible? How has one to grow into that ultimate synthesis? A few things have to be understood....

First, the principle of yin, the principle of femininity, is like a ladder – a ladder between hell and heaven. You can go to hell through it and you can go to heaven through it; the direction will differ but the ladder will be the same. That ladder is the principle of yin, the principle of femininity. Nothing happens without the woman. The energy of the woman is the ladder of the lowest and of the highest, of the darkest valley and of the lightest peak. This is one of the fundamental principles of Tao. It has to be understood in detail. Once it gets rooted in your heart things will become very simple.

It will be good to go into the symbol of Adam and Eve.

The world does not start with Adam, it starts with Eve. It is through Eve that the serpent persuades Adam to disobey. The serpent could not persuade Adam directly – it is as if there is no direct way to the man. If you want to reach the man you have to go through the woman. The woman functioned as a medium for the evil.

Then again, when Christ is born, he is born out of the Virgin Mary. The Christ Child is born out of virgin femininity, out of virgin yin. The highest enters through the woman.

The lowest and the highest have both been through the woman.

Adam means earth, clay – exactly red earth. God made Adam out of red earth. Adam is the principle of dust unto dust. Man is the outer principle, the principle of extraversion: man is the physical body.

Try to understand these symbols. Man is the physic body and God created Eve out of man's physical body. It was something higher. First man had to be created, then woman. It was something subtler, something more refined, something of a greater synthesis. Eve was created out of a rib, Eve could not be created directly from the earth.

For example: you cannot eat mud but you can eat apples – apples are on a higher plane. They come out of the mud. The tree grows out of the mud, so the apple is nothing but earth transformed. You can eat the apple and you can digest it but if you try to eat the earth you will die. The apple is from the earth but it is a superior synthesis – better, more digestible.

God created Adam and the way man has taken it is that because God created man first he is first. No, man is created first because he is very close to the earth. Then the woman is created – she is not as close to the earth, she is created out of Adam, she is a higher synthesis.

The name of Eve is also very significant. It means the heart. Adam means the earth and Eve means the heart. God told Adam to name things, so he named everything. When he came to name Eve he simply said loudly, "She is my heart, Eve." That became Eve's name. Eva or Eve means the heart. Translated into modern jargon it would mean the psyche. Man is the body principle, woman is the psyche. Man is body, woman is mind. Everything happens through the mind.

If you do bad, your mind has to be convinced about it first;

if you do good, your mind has to be convinced about it first. Everything happens first as all idea then it can be actualized. Your body cannot be persuaded to do something unless your mind is ready. Even if illness enters your body it enters through the mind. Anything that ever happens, happens through the mind. That is the meaning of the whole parable: the serpent persuaded Eve. Only mind can be persuaded, convinced, seduced, and then the mind can persuade the body very easily. In fact, the body follows the mind like a shadow. Once your mind has got a thought it is bound to be translated into actuality.

Through Eve, Adam fell. Through Eve, he was expelled from the garden of God. Through Eve came this great adventure we call the world. Through Eve, he disobeyed.

I have heard:

A man was brought to a court and the policeman said, "Either he is mad or he is completely drunk, because he was just standing in the middle of the road. I told him many times to move but he would not. I was surprised because I didn't think that he was drunk and I didn't think that he was mad. He seemed to be sane in every way and I smelled his mouth and he had not been drinking. But he would not move from the middle of the road."

The magistrate said, "Tell me. Why were you standing there? Why didn't you move when the policeman was telling you to again and again?"

The man was a very tiny man, very weak and thin. He said, "Sir, I had to choose between the law of the government and the law of my wife."

The magistrate said, "What do you mean?"

He said, "My wife told me to meet her at exactly that spot at twelve o'clock. So I had to choose. Naturally I chose the law of my wife."

The magistrate laughed, "That has been always the case. You go home. If that is the problem then one has to choose the law of the wife."

Since Adam it has been so. The woman is the principle of the inner – not, certainly, of the innermost, but of the inner. She is just in the middle. The innermost you call the soul, the outermost you call the body, and just between the two is the psyche, the mind.

Adam followed Eve on this adventure into the world.

Then again, the parable about Jesus is the same. Jesus is born out of the Virgin Mary. Why virgin? Because if you understand rightly, virgin means a mind which is absolutely pure, uncontaminated by thought. Thoughts are represented by the serpent, because the ways of thoughts are very serpentine. If you watch your thoughts you will understand why they have been represented by the serpent. They are very serpentine, they walk without legs just like serpents, they wriggle within you. And they are very cunning and very clever and very deceptive – like the serpent. They hide in dark holes in your unconscious and whenever they have an opportunity they jump upon you. In the night, in the dark night, they come out; in the daylight they hide. When you are a little alert those thoughts disappear; when you are not so alert they come out, they start influencing you.

The Virgin Mary means a mind in meditation; Eve means a mind full of thoughts, full of serpents. Jesus enters again into the world through the Virgin Mary, through purity, through innocence. Thought is cunning; thoughtlessness is innocent.

If you understand these beautiful parables you will be surprised. We have not done justice to them. They are not historical facts, they are great metaphors of the inner being of man. Through Eve, Adam fell, and through the Virgin Mary, Jesus rose and entered again into the world of God.

One thing more. It is said that the sin of Adam was disobedience. God had said not to eat the fruit of a certain tree, the Tree of Knowledge – but the serpent persuaded Eve and Eve persuaded Adam. It was disobedience.

You will be surprised to know that the Hebrew meaning of "Mary" means rebellion. The Hebrew word is *mariam*. It means rebellion. Through disobedience Adam fell and through rebellion Jesus rose. Disobedience means a reaction, going against, against God; rebellion means negating the negative, going against the world, going against the serpents. Eve listened to the serpents and went against God; Jesus rebelled against the serpents and listened to God.

Disobedience is political; rebellion is religious. Disobedience only brings disorder; rebellion, real rebellion, brings a radical change in your being – a hundred-and-eighty-degree turn, a conversion.

But both Adam and Jesus happened through the feminine principle. In Taoist language the feminine principle is called yin and the male principle is called yang. Yang is ambition, yang is aggression, yang is desire and projection, yang is political – yin is religious. Whenever you are ambitious it is impossible for you to be religious; whenever you are religious it is impossible for you to be political. They don't go together. They don't mix. They cannot mix. Their very nature is like trying to mix water and oil.

Ambition and meditation never mix, they cannot mix. The politician functions through the male principle and the sage functions through the feminine principle. That's why the sages become so soft, so feminine, so round, so beautiful. A certain grace surrounds them. And the beauty is certainly not only of the body – sometimes it happens that the body may not be beautiful at all.

In early Christianity there was a principle that Jesus was the ugliest person in the world. By and by Christians dropped that idea, they didn't like it. But it has something beautiful in it. It said that the body was ugly but still, when you came across Jesus, you would be suddenly surprised, overtaken, possessed, overwhelmed by his beauty. His body was ugly. If you had seen a picture you would see only his ugliness but if you had come to him, entered his actual presence, you would forget all about his ugliness because so much beauty was flowing, so much beauty was pouring out, raining. You would not even remember that he was ugly. So those who had not seen him used to think that he was ugly and those who had seen him used to say that he was the most beautiful person.

The body is not the question. The sage does not live in the body or as the body – he lives through the body. The politician is nothing but the body, the extrovert. The body is extrovert, the psyche is introvert, and when you transcend both, Tao arises. When you are neither extrovert nor introvert, when you are not going into the outer nor into the inner, when you are not going anywhere, there is tremendous stillness, no movement because there is no motivation. Your inner flame is no longer wavering because there is no direction to go in, there is no purpose to fulfill. There is nowhere to be and nobody else to be, you are absolutely content with the moment. Then you have transcended man and woman and the polarity. In that transcendence is Tao.

This transcendence has been taught in different ways all over the world. Different terms have been used. I would like to explain one term to you because it will help. The term is *Israel.* It is not the name of a certain race – certainly not of the Jews – and it is not a name of a certain individual. "Israel" is exactly what Tao is.

Try to understand. The word *Israel* is made of three symbols: is-ra-el. *Is* means the feminine principle. *Is* comes from the Egyptian word *isis*. Isis means the moon goddess the moon is the feminine principle. Remember the word *moon* because in Hindu metaphors also the moon is the symbol of the feminine.

In Yoga they say there are three passages in the human being: the moon, the sun, and the transcendental. Through one nostril you breathe the moon energy, through another nostril you breathe the sun energy. And deep inside, when both breathings stop, then you transcend. That is called *sushumna ida, pingala, sushumna.*

"Israel" is made of three symbols. *Is* comes from *isis* the Egyptian goddess of the moon or the Babylonian goddess *ishtar* who is also the moon goddess. This is the principle of yin, the feminine. *Ra* comes from the Egyptian sun god. It represents the masculine principle, yang. And *el* comes from *elohim* from which same root the Mohammedans derive *Allah.* The Hebrew word for God is *elohim; el* comes from there. It represents the meeting of the feminine and the masculine and their transcendence too. "Israel" means Tao exactly.

If you are dominated by the sun you will be aggressive, madly aggressive, ambitious, political, hot, burning will, desire and passion. If you are dominated by the moon you will be cool, non-ambitious, non-aggressive, receptive, peaceful, silent. But both have to be transcended because both are lop-sided. One has to come to a moment when one can say, "I am neither man nor woman." That's when a man becomes a Buddha or a man becomes a Christ or a man becomes a Krishna when he is neither man nor woman, neither moon nor sun, neither "is" nor "ra," neither yin nor yang. He simply is, purely is. All formulations have disappeared.

But this happening happens only by and by. First you have to drop the principle of "ra" – the principle of the sun, the male energy – and you have to move into the feminine, into the female. And from there you have to move into the beyond.

Everything happens through the feminine principle, remember it, always remember it. It is the middle principle, so whether you are going beyond or you are going below makes no difference – it is the ladder.

With the body, with the sun energy, with the male, you become a rapist, you rape life. You are not a lover. Science comes out of sun energy; science is male-oriented. That's why the East could not develop it. The East has lived through the moon principle – passive, silent, easy-going, not trying to conquer, in deep love with nature, not trying to fight. The East has never been a rapist, the West has raped nature. Hence the problem of ecology has arisen: all nature is being destroyed.

With the feminine principle, with the moon principle, there is love. You love but you don't rape. Sometimes the physical act may look the same, but the innermost quality is different.

I have heard about a woman who was complaining against a

man in the court. The magistrate asked, "Again and again you say that this man raped you. When did he rape you?"

And the woman said, "When? January, February, March, April, May, June, July, August, September, October, November, December. The whole year – rape and rape and rape and nothing else."

The magistrate was surprised. He said, "How could he rape you the whole year?"

The woman said, "He is my husband."

"But then why do you call it rape? Legally it is not rape."

The woman said, "It is still rape. He did not love me."

You can rape even your wife if you don't love her. The physical act of making love to or raping a woman may be the same, but the inner quality differs.

With the sun energy, science is born: it is the rape of nature. With the moon energy, poetry, art, painting, dance, music are born: it is love playing with nature. The East has lived through art, through music, dance, drama. The West has been trying to use male energy too much. The West has lost balance, but so has the East; no society has yet evolved which can be called "Israel," which can be called Tao, which has transcended both or synthesized both in such harmony that the antagonism has disappeared.

Tao is the goal: to create a human being who is fully integrated, totally integrated, and also to create a human society which is totally integrated.

Now this story. These few things I have told you will help you to understand it.

> Hui Ang visited King K'ang of Sung. The king stamped his foot, coughed and said fiercely, "What pleases me is courage and strength. I take no pleasure in men who preach morality. What have you to teach me?"

Now look at the attitude. This is not an attitude of somebody who wants to learn – it is the attitude of the rapist who wants to snatch.

> The king stamped his foot, coughed and said fiercely, "What pleases me is courage and strength. I take no pleasure in men who preach morality. What have you to teach me?"

This is no way to learn. This is insulting. No master would agree to teach this man. In fact, no master would visit the palace of such a man. This man is unworthy even of being talked to.

But this Hui Ang is a Confucian. Disciples of Confucius used to go to the courts. Their whole effort was to persuade the politicians, the ministers, the kings, the princes. They thought that if you could persuade the king, you could change the whole society. It is the oldest illusion, the ancient-most illusion – that if you can persuade the politician it will be easy to change the society; or, if you can change the politician it will be easy to change the society; or, if you change the ruling party it will be easy to change the society. It has never happened.

You can change the politician, you can even convince the politician about beautiful things, but deep down the politician remains the politician. He understands only one language: the language of ambition, the language of greed, the language of the world. He is outgoing, extrovert.

> He coughed, stamped his foot and said fiercely, "What pleases me is courage and strength."

The moment you say that, you have some prejudice. The moment you say that this pleases you and this does not please you, you can never learn what truth is because truth has no need to fit in with your pleasure. Truth has no obligation to fit in with what pleases you and what does not please you. You have to fit with truth, truth has not to fit with you.

It is said that there are two categories of men in the world: one who would like truth to stand by their side and the other who would like to stand by the side of truth. The first category is that of the politician – the aggressive, the sun-energy, the ambitious. The second category is that of the religious the moon principle, the non-aggressive, the receptive. Remember this: never want truth to stand by your side because whatsoever stands by your side, is ready to stand by your side, cannot be truth. It will be a lie. Only lies are ready to stand by your side, truth never. You will have to stand by the side of truth. If you have that much courage – courage to drop your old prejudices, likes and dislikes, only then can you go into truth, otherwise not.

Now what does this man say? Look at his gesture.

> He stamped his foot, coughed and said fiercely, "What pleases me is courage and strength. I take no pleasure in men who preach morality."

Yes, how can a politician take any interest in morality? Morality comes from the feminine principle. Look, all the great-teachers in the world have created more femininity in the world – Buddha, Christ, Krishna. They have all created more and more of the feminine, the soft.

Friedrich Nietzsche has criticized both Buddha and Jesus – he said they were not real men. And he is right. He says that they have destroyed manliness. And he is right – right for wrong reasons but still right. Buddha, Mahavira, Christ, certainly have taught something which will make you less aggressive, which will make you less violent. And if you listen to them totally you will become absolutely non-violent.

Naturally Nietzsche cannot like it. He says that the most beautiful thing in the world is the soldier and the greatest music is war music. He says, "In my whole life's experience the moment that I remember again and again, the moment I call the most beautiful moment, was when a group of soldiers were marching on the road – their legs, their feet falling in tune, their boots making a rhythmic noise, their swords shining in the sun, erect, powerful, aggressive, ambitious. When I saw this group of soldiers marching in the sun it was the greatest moment of beauty that I know."

If such a man comes across Buddha he will wonder how Buddha can be beautiful. Sitting under the tree he is so silent that you can almost forget about him. He is almost absent. His music is that of silence. His music is that of receptivity. He is just a cool phenomenon – no heat, no passion, no desire. Sitting there silently he is almost like a tree; flowering there he is almost like a tree. And in the East, particularly in India, we have thought of a buddha as a lotus flower which has bloomed fully – a one-thousand-petalled lotus flower. Yes, he is almost like a tree.

For five hundred years in India a statue of Buddha was not made. Instead of a statue of Buddha, people worshipped a tree. Many statues were made of the tree, many pictures were made of the tree, many paintings were made of the tree, many temples were built, but there was no statue of Buddha, just the Bodhi tree. Because Buddha was almost absent – he had become formless, he had become as if he was not. His music is that of silence. Nietzsche would not recognize the beauty of it, no politician would recognize the beauty of it.

This king said, *"I take no pleasure in men who preach morality."* The basis of all morality is to love and the basis of all politics is to hate. The moralist says, "Love even your enemy," and the politician says, "Hate even your friend." If you want to see a contrast you can read Jesus and Machiavelli. Or, the Indian parallel, you can read Buddha and Chanakya. It is not just a coincidence that the part of Delhi where Indian politicians live is called Chanakyapuri – it is named after Chanakya, the Indian Machiavelli. Machiavelli says, "Don't even trust your friend. Don't say anything to your friend which you would not like to say to your enemy." Why? "Because," he says, "who knows? Your friend may become your enemy tomorrow. So don't say anything that you would not like to say to an enemy."

And look at Jesus. He says, "Even if somebody slaps you on one cheek, give him the other too. Love your enemy as yourself."

Naturally politicians cannot be ready to listen to the teachings of morality. Morality means love and politics means hate, hatred. Politicians may smile but hidden behind that smile is a horrible face. They may show a beautiful face but behind it they are preparing for hell. They may talk about peace but they prepare for war. Their whole life depends on destruction. Love is creation; hate is destruction.

Naturally the king was not interested in any kind of morality. He said, "What pleases me is courage and strength." Why courage and strength? Why strength?

Jesus says, "Blessed are the meek" not "Blessed are the strong," no. "Blessed are the meek, blessed are the humble, blessed are the poor in spirit." Not the strong, not the strong-headed but those who have soft hearts; not people like rocks but people like flowers – they are blessed.

Jesus is right, but no politician will want to listen to this. This is nonsense. The politician cannot understand this language. He has his own language: the language of cunningness, calculation, hatred, domination, destruction. The politician lives on evil. How can he listen to morality?

Remember, the language of politics is not the language of religion and the language of religion is not the language of politics. In fact, they are so far apart that they cannot even be translated into each other. Impossible. They are not only two languages, they are two different planes, two different worlds, two separate realities.

In a way the king is sincere, he is showing his real face. *The king stamped his foot, coughed and said fiercely, "What pleases me is courage and strength."* Why courage? Why have people talked so much about courage? – to kill people and to be killed? Why has strength been praised so much? – because without strength it is difficult to rape nature, it is difficult to rape other people, it is difficult to conquer, dominate, it is difficult to destroy.

When a religious person talks of courage, his courage has a different meaning, remember. And when he talks of strength, his strength has a totally different meaning, remember. When a religious person calls something courageous he does not mean the same thing as the politician. For the religious, courage means to be creative; courage means to be oneself; courage means to be sincere, authentic; courage means not to yield to lies; courage means not to allow corruption to set in, in one's own being; courage means to resist all temptations of going astray. Courage does not mean the capability to kill and be killed, no; courage means the capacity to live and to live your own life according to your own heart.

And strength does not mean the capacity of violence, strength means the capacity to understand, the capacity to know, the capacity to love, the capacity to be open. When somebody hits you it is not strength to hit him back, it is very simple, anybody can do it. Even a child can do it. But when somebody hits you and you don't hit back, it is strength.

When Jesus was crucified and he prayed to God, "Father, forgive these people because they don't know what they are doing," it is strength – the strength of the meek, the power of the humble.

Remember, the same word, if used by different people, becomes different. In fact, there should be different dictionaries: religious dictionaries, political dictionaries. There should be different dictionaries. In a better world there will be – because the same words cannot mean the same.

A diner in a restaurant rushed over to a man who was standing just near the door. "I've been robbed!" he screamed. "I turned my head and someone stole my brown topcoat. It had buttons on the sleeves and a fur collar!"

"Hmmmmmmm," murmured the stranger who was standing at the door. "Come to think of it, I saw a man walking out of here just a few minutes ago wearing that very coat!"

"Quick, quick!" demanded the customer. "What did the guy look like?"

"Terrible," the man sighed. "The sleeves were much too short for him!"

Then seeing the surprised look on the robbed man's face he added immediately, "You see, I'm a tailor."

Your language is your language. The words have no meaning in themselves, the meaning is brought by the person who uses them.

A rancher applied for a loan at a bank.

"How much do you want to borrow?" asked the loan interviewer.

"Twenty-five thousand dollars."

"All right, but you'll have to show security. How many bulls do you have on your ranch?"

"Two hundred."

"That should be enough security. The loan is approved."

Several months later the rancher returned to the bank to repay the loan.

"Here's your money," he declared, peeling off bills from a huge bankroll.

"Well, sir, let me congratulate you on your sudden prosperity," said the interviewer, eyeing the bankroll. And for safety's sake, may I suggest you deposit that extra money in our bank?'

Staring at him coldly, the rancher asked, How many bulls do *you* have?'

Everybody has his own language. The politician has a very subtle language, a definite language and morality is certainly not part of it. By any means or methods, deception, immorality – one has to fulfill one's ambition. So even if a politician uses morality, he uses it only as a means. Sometimes a politician may look very moral if it fulfills his purpose.

Mahatma Gandhi was a politician, not a religious man at all. When India was fighting with the Britishers, non-violence was fulfilling a purpose. When India became free then the ideology of non-violence became defunct, then it was not of much use. Even Gandhi approved of an Indian military army. And when it was getting ready to attack Pakistan he blessed it. When he saw airplanes flying over Delhi towards Pakistan he said, "Good. With my blessings."

Now what has happened? This is the same man who was against all violence but then violence was not possible, India was not in a situation to fight the British violently. So non-violence was in favor, and Gandhi used it. But when India became independent, then he forgot all his talk about non-violence. He did not then say, "Dissolve the army now. Dissolve the police force. Let the country be ruled by love." He forgot all about non-violence.

That's why I say he was a politician. If he had been a religious person then this was a real opportunity to be non-violent. The country has become free, now he should have dissolved the military, the army, the police force. In fact, he should have dropped government itself because a government is a violent organization. But he kept mum.

A politician can use morality when it serves *his* purpose. He can say that "Honesty is the best policy" but remember, it is a policy. It serves the purpose. Policy means politics. And when dishonesty is the best policy, then? When it serves the purpose then it is perfectly okay. A politician is like a whore. He can change. He is opportunistic. Whatsoever serves his purpose becomes his ideal and his principle. Deep down there is only one principle: that is his ambition has to be fulfilled.

The king was in a way sincere.

> "I take no pleasure in men who preach morality. What have you to teach me?"
>
> "Suppose," said Hui Ang, "that I have a way to make anyone, however brave and strong, miss when he stabs or strikes at you. Wouldn't Your Majesty be interested?"

Now, no Taoist would do this. First, the Taoist would not go to the king, the king would have to come to the Taoist. And even then he may not see the king, because he knows that the politician is the worst man possible.

In Buddhist classifications they have divided man into three categories. The first they call *adampurush*, the lowest, the worst man. The second they call madhyampurush, the middle man, and the third they call *mahapurush*, the great man. *Mahapurush* is one who lives naturally, religiously, without any ambition and without any mind. He is just a part of this cosmos, not fighting, not struggling. He is just floating with it, flowing with it. He is in a deep let-go. That *is mahapurush*, the great man.

Then next to him comes the middle man who is not totally in the flow but sometimes there are moments when he flows. Sometimes there are moments when he freezes, sometimes he starts fighting, and sometimes he relaxes. He has a double bind. He is in the middle. Sometimes he moves to the lower, sometimes to the higher. He is still wavering. He has not yet become decisive. His integration is not complete yet.

And then comes the third, the lowest, *adampurush*, the worst. He is settled at the lowest and he does not want to move from there.

The politician is *adampurush*, the worst; the artist is the *madhyampurush*, the middle man; and the religious is the *mahapurush*, the great man. And beyond the three is the fourth, *turiya* – one who has gone beyond all categories, the non-categorized. He is in Tao. He is beyond politics, he is beyond art, he is even beyond religion. He is simply beyond.

No Taoist will go to teach a king. That is foolish, stupid. The disciple has to come to the master. Why? Because unless the disciple comes and seeks, he is not ready to learn.

The disciple has to be humble. If a disciple stamps his foot, coughs and says fiercely, “What do you have to teach me?” then it is better not to teach him. He is incurable.

But there is the difference between the Confucian and the Taoist. Confucius and his followers were constantly going to the kings and the ministers and the powerful people and trying to convert them, trying to convince them. They thought that that seemed to be the easiest way to change the world. It has always been thought that if you want to change humanity the best way is to go to the capital. No, it has proved to be wrong, absolutely wrong.

For five thousand years at least, we know well that the way to transform man does not go through the capital; it goes through the heart not through the capital. And you can only change a person who is ready to be changed, who is willing to be changed, who is cooperative, who is ready to learn and bow down and surrender, to receive.

But Hui Ang tried. He said,

> "Suppose that I have a way to make anyone, however brave and strong, miss when he stabs or strikes at you. Wouldn't Your Majesty be interested?"

Now he is trying to persuade the king in his own language. Never do that, because when you bring religion to the level of the worst man, religion is destroyed.

Tao cannot be translated into the language of greed although this is what Hui Ang is doing. He is trying to translate desirelessness into greed.

The king became interested. He said, "Excellent!" Look at the change. Just a moment before he was stamping his foot, coughing and was saying fiercely, "What do you have to teach me? I don't want to listen to anything about morality."

> "Excellent!" he said. "This is the sort of thing I like to hear."

Now this comes close. It is not going to change him because religion has come down to adjust to him, he has not gone up to adjust to religion. This is very irreligious. To do such a thing is irreligious. This man, Hui Ang, is falling into the trap of the politician rather than helping the politician to come out of his imprisonment. He himself is falling into the trap – to persuade the king he is bringing truth to almost the level of a lie.

What does he say? He says he can make someone... *"however brave and strong, miss when he stabs or strikes at you."* This seems good to the ego, the greedy ego – because if this can be done then it will become unconquerable. This is worth something. Now this comes close to ambition. This becomes a policy, this becomes a strategy.

"Excellent! This is the sort of thing I like to hear."

Remember always, the sort of thing that you like to hear is always wrong because being the sort of man you are, how can you like to hear the right thing? It is very difficult to be ready to hear the truth. It shatters, it confuses, it uproots, it shocks, it dismantles, it destroys your prejudices, it hits you hard. In fact, it tries to kill you as you have existed up to now. That's why very rare people are ready to hear the truth.

If I were to talk in terms of lies you would find millions of people around here. I was talking to thousands and thousands of people, great crowds used to gather. But then by and by I recognized the fact that they gathered not to hear what I had to say, they gathered to hear what they wanted to hear. They were not there to be transformed, they were there to be consoled, they were there to be convinced. Wherever they were and whatsoever they were, they wanted to know that they were right. The moment I started saying the truth they started disappearing. Now only rarely will a few people be coming to me – because I don't make any compromise. I will say only that which is true. If you want to agree with it, good, but if you want it to agree with you then this is not the place for you.

"But even if a stab or blow misses, it is still humiliating for you."

Now he persuades more. He says, "I can teach a certain art so nobody can stab you, or, even if he does, he will miss." Now he sees that the king is ready, persuaded. The king says, *"Excellent!*

This is the sort of thing I like to hear." Now he moves ahead. He says, *"But even if a stab or blow misses it is still humiliating for you.* If somebody tries to kill you. even though he misses, the effort on your life is humiliating. I can do something for that too."

"Suppose that I have a way to prevent anyone, however brave and strong, from daring to stab or strike you. I can do something more. I call create such a situation that he will not even dare to stab or make an effort on your life. What about it, sir?"

> "But a man who does not dare to harm you may still have the will to harm you."

"He may not dare to harm you but he has the idea, it is humiliating that somebody even thinks of destroying you."

> "Suppose I have a way to ensure that men have absolutely no will to harm you. But a man who has no will to harm you may still have no thought of loving or benefiting you."

"A man may have no thought to harm you but that does not make it sure that he wants to benefit you or has a loving attitude towards you."

> "Suppose that I have a way to make every single man and woman in the world joyfully desire to love and benefit you. This is three degrees better than courage and strength. Isn't Your Majesty interested?"
>
> "This is the sort of way I should like to find,"

said the king.

Now truth is brought to the level of the *adampurush*, the lowest man. In bringing truth to the lowest man, truth loses its quality of being true. It becomes a falsehood. Now it is a lie. Now it is clever argument. It is no longer a statement of truth, it is a cunning device. It is sophistry. Yes, that is exactly the word for it. This man is not a sage, he is a sophist.

You must have heard about sophists. They existed in Athens in Greece. Before Socrates there was great power in the hands of the sophists. They traveled all over the country. They convinced everybody, they were greatest arguers but they had no principles. Whatsoever you wanted to be convinced about they would convince you. It was a sort of prostitution. They were paid and they became very affluent because they were ready to support anything. "Just you tell me what you want to be convinced of" they would say. And they would convince you, they would give you beautiful arguments. They had schools to teach people argumentation.

Because of Socrates they disappeared from the world. Socrates had a great impact on the Greek mind and he destroyed that whole prostitution.

Bertrand Russell used to tell a small story again and again. I don't know where he got it from but the story is beautiful so there is no need to worry about it.

He used to say again and again that one day a sophist came to see Socrates. He had a beautiful dog with him and Socrates looked at him and asked, "Is this your dog?"

And the sophist said, "Yes."

Socrates said, "Is the dog male or female?"

And the sophist said, "A female."

Socrates asked, "Is the dog a mother or not yet a mother?"

And the sophist said, "Yes, the dog is a mother."

Socrates laughed and said, "You are the son of it, you son of a bitch."

I don't know where Bertrand Russell got it from but sophists were that type of people. They had no principles, they had no truth, they were opportunists. And they were ready to argue for anything – wrong or right was not the question. They simply enjoyed argumentation. They were like lawyers. You go to the lawyer and it does not matter whether you are wrong or right, he is ready to support you, he is ready to fight for you.

Mulla Nasruddin went to a lawyer and told him the whole story. The lawyer said, "Don't be worried, your victory is absolutely certain, a hundred per cent certain. You trust me. You leave it to me. You are going to win."

But Mulla Nasruddin got up and started to leave the office. The lawyer said, "Where are you going? You have not said anything."

Mulla replied, "There is no need I have told you the other man's story, the other side's story. Now there is no need to fight."

But this is no way to judge. You tell any story and the lawyer says, "Yes, you are going to win." And he will support you and he will argue for you. He has no interest in truths: his only interest is if he is paid rightly – then everything is okay. Then whom is he serving? Truth or untruth? It does not matter, it is immaterial. He serves money, prestige, power, respectability. If these things come he is ready to support anybody. He is not against crime; he is ready to protect crime if that is the way money comes.

Now this man is a sophist, he is not a sage, he is not a master – he is not even a teacher, not even an honest teacher. He is a sophist. But he has persuaded the king – *"This is the sort of way I would like to find."* But there is nothing to find.

"The teachings of Confucius and Mo Tzu are what I have in mind."

Hui Ang is a disciple of Confucius and Mo Tzu. Mo Tzu is a disciple of Confucius. Just as Lao Tzu and Chuang Tzu were the two top-most Taoists, so Confucius and Mo Tzu were the two top-most Confucianists.

"Confucius and Mo Tzu became princes without owning territory.... "

Now he flatters the king even more, he buttresses him more.

"The teachings of Confucius and Mo Tzu are what I have in mind. Confucius and Mo Tzu became princes without owning

> territory, became leaders without holding office. Every man and woman in the world craned his neck and stood on tiptoe in his eagerness for their safety and benefit. Now Your Majesty is the Lord of ten thousand chariots. If you were indeed to share the aims of these two men, everyone within your four borders would enjoy the benefit. You would be far greater than Confucius and Mo Tzu."

Now he is buttressing the ego of the king as much as possible. He says, "Look! Confucius and Mo Tzu were not kings but they were almost like uncrowned kings. They had no territory but they were treated everywhere as great kings. They were men of character, morality, knowledge. They were respected everywhere. They became leaders without holding office."

> "Every man and woman in the world craned his neck and stood on tiptoe in his eagerness for their safety and benefit."

But if that is true then why was Jesus crucified? If that is true then why was Socrates poisoned? If that is true then why was Mansoor al-Hillaj killed? No, Confucius and Mo Tzu are not real masters. They were men of character, great discipline, but a man of character is nothing but a man who follows the rules and regulations of the society. He is not rebellious, he is a conformist. The society certainly respects him but it is because he respects the rules of the society.

Jesus had to be crucified because he rebelled. Mansoor had to be killed because he rebelled. The society takes revenge if you don't follow the rules of the society, if you start talking in ways which sabotage the foolish rules of the society. The rules are stupid, they are meaningless, but millions of people believe in them. Once a man like Jesus or Socrates or Mansoor is there and he starts talking about truth and that truth goes against the so-called truths of the society, they are bound to take revenge.

But Confucius was respected. He was not a man of rebellion, he was just a conformist, traditional. He followed the neurotic rules of the society; the stupid ways of society he followed to the very letter. Yes, he was moral, but he was not religious. A religious man has found his own law. If it fits with the society, good. If it doesn't fit with the society, then he still lives his own law. A religious man is free; a religious man is freedom. He lives through his innermost core. He has no outer imposed discipline on himself, he lives in no cage. He lives like a free being – whatsoever the cost. Even if his life has to be paid for it he is ready to pay but he is not ready to curtail his freedom. Freedom is his utmost value, his ultimate value. He can lose everything, but not freedom.

A traditional man is ready to lose freedom for cheap things: respectability, social honor. Yes, Confucius and Mo Tzu were honored, they were really honored, but the honor was because they were not free men, not men of Tao.

> "Now Your Majesty is the Lord of ten thousand chariots. If you were indeed to share the aims of these two men, everyone within your four borders would enjoy the benefit. You would be far greater than Confucius and Mo Tzu."

Now he is saying, "You can become the greatest man in the world – because Confucius is the last word, you can become even greater than Confucius."

Look…that is the way society persuades everybody. A child is born and the parents start telling him: be moral, have character, do this and that and you will be respected and the whole society will respect you. You will become a great man, famous, well-known and well-respected. What are they doing? They are creating the ego, they are helping to create the ego in the child.

The ego is the principle of immorality and your so-called morality hangs on the principle of ego. It is based on immorality. But you have been taught to be this way – be the way society wants you to be and society will respect you. If you want the respect, never rebel; if you want the respect, bow down to the order of society.

And who is this society? The mob, the crowd. The majority consists of stupid people, they control. The society means the lowest mob – they control everything. Yes, society will respect you if you follow it, but following it you will become stupid yourself. If you want to be respected then you will have to become stupid, if you want to be intelligent, forget about respectability. An intelligent person will live, live tremendously, live greatly, live joyously, but he should not hanker for respect.

Disrespect is more possible than respect; poison is more possible than prestige. You may be beheaded rather than being honored – that is more possible, because society has not yet come to the point of growth, it has not yet evolved so much that it can respect the real persons.

That has to be understood.... If Socrates came back he would be poisoned again. If Jesus came back he would be crucified again. Time has not made much difference – society remains the same. Society has not yet evolved to the point where it can respect a true person. To respect a true person will mean that society has become intelligent.

The goal seems to be far away. Will it happen or not? It seems it would be almost a utopia if a day came when Socrates would be worshipped. Do you remember the people who killed Socrates? Do you know anybody's name? They were the respectable people, they were the guardians of morality in society. Do you remember the name of the judge who sentenced Socrates, who ordered that he had to be poisoned? Do you know who these people were? From where they came? They were respectable people, they were the guardians of morality, they were the protectors of society, they were the leaders and the politicians and the priests. Nobody knows where they have gone, but Socrates remains.

The man who was the opponent, who had brought the case against Socrates in the court, said that he was corrupting the minds of the young people. That was the crime that he was doing. He was corrupting the minds of the young people – that's the crime they say I am doing. I corrupt the minds of the young people. I would like to corrupt the minds of the old people but they don't have any! So naturally I have to corrupt the minds of the young people – only they have them.

When the man had won the case – Socrates had been sentenced and the order was declared that he would be poisoned – he looked at Socrates and said, "What do you say?" Socrates laughed and he said, "Remember one thing: for thousands of years people will think about me, but they will remember your name only because you put the case against me – that's all. They will know your name only because you were the man who moved the court to kill Socrates. Nothing else will be remembered of you." And exactly that has happened. Nobody remembers anything about that man. Socrates will be remembered and remembered.

Who were the men who killed al-Hillaj Mansoor? Their names are forgotten. And they were the pinnacles of morality, they were the paragons of morality, they were the people who were afraid that al-Hillaj Mansoor was destroying morality, religion; that he was a dangerous man and society had to be protected from him. But who remembers their names? Their names are not even known. Mansoor will live. As long as humanity continues to aspire to go beyond, as long as humanity has goals of transcendence, as long as the arrow of human consciousness moves towards God, Mansoor will be remembered. One day, one can hope, somewhere in the future a time will come when the *real* man will be respected.

Confucius is not a real man. Mo Tzu is not a real man. They are conventional people, conformists, traditional people, dead. And says Hui Ang, *"You would be far greater than Confucius and Mo Tzu."*

This is the whole trick; this is how you have been distracted from your center. You have been told not to be yourself, otherwise you will not get any respect, any honor. If you want to be yourself nobody will give you any respect – so don't be yourself, be that which society wants you to be. This is how you have been distracted from your center and you have become pseudo-beings, phony, unreal. You are just a mask. You don't have any soul, you have lost your soul. The soul comes into being only when you declare, "I am going to be myself. Respect or disrespect, society or no society, honor or no honor, that is irrelevant – I have decided to be myself because this is my life and I have to live it in my own way. Whatsoever the cost I will live like a free man." Once you declare that you become centered.

That's what the whole effort is in sannyas, that's what sannyas is all about – to bring you back to your center. That's why I don't give you any outer discipline, just an inner consciousness, an awareness; no duty, only a responsibility; no outer pattern, no style from the outside, but an inner flow, an inner glow. To live in that glow, to move into that flow and allow your life to have freedom, to be in a let-go – that's what sannyas is. And that's what Tao is.

> Hui Ang hurried out. And the king said to his courtiers, "Clever, the way he talked me round with his argument!"

It is not clever, it is cunning. It looks clever because all cunningness looks clever. Remember, cleverness and cunningness are not going to help – only intelligence, awareness, alertness will.

This man has deceived the king but my feeling is that you can deceive somebody only if you yourself are deceived. This man is not a master otherwise how can he deceive somebody?

Let me tell you another story which is just exactly parallel. A great sage came to China, his name was Bodhidharma. The Emperor Wu of China came to receive him on the border. The emperor had been waiting for years because Bodhidharma had been coming and coming from India. He had to cross the whole Himalayas – it took years. Then he arrived. The emperor was a little bit puzzled seeing him because he looked a very strange man. The most strange thing was that he had one shoe on one of his feet and the other shoe he was carrying on his head. Was this man mad?

But the king was a very polite man, cultured of course. He tried not to see it because that would be too.... He simply tried not to see it and not to say anything about it. That would be too impolite and this was the first meeting with this great sage – and what type of man was he?

But how long can you avoid it? He was just standing there holding his shoe on his head. And the king said, "Sir, you can put it down. Why you are holding it on your head? And in the first place why do you have it on your head? It is meant for your foot." Bodhidharma said, "I want to make everything clear from the very beginning that I am this type of man. You can think me mad or you can think me enlightened, but I am strange. And be clear from the beginning that you are meeting a strange man. I am absurd, illogical. I am as absurd as this shoe on my head. There is no reason for it, it simply happened. I enjoyed it. And the poor shoe has always been carrying me so why can I not carry it?"

This was just a Zen gesture. He was trying to fathom this man, this Emperor Wu who had invited him from India. He was trying to see whether he would be able to understand the illogic of truth. Truth has no argument to prove it; it is a statement, remember. Bodhidharma was standing there – he was a statement, illogical, absurd. Thousands of people had gathered to receive him and all were feeling puzzled.

But he was saying, "I am not going to argue. If you are going to listen to me you have to forget all argumentation. I am not going to persuade. I am not here to convince you about anything. I am a simple statement, an absurd statement, about the truth. I will not give you reasons, there are none."

Then Bodhidharma looked at the king. The king was puzzled, he was perspiring. And Bodhidharma said, "Have you something to ask, Sir? You have called me from India and it took many years to get here. For what have you called me?" Wu said, "I had many questions but you have confused me. But I will try. The first question: I have made many temples for Buddha – thousands – I feed thousands of Buddhist monks, I have made many monasteries for Buddhist monks and Buddhist nuns, I have done much virtuous work. What will be my gain in the other world?" And Bodhidharma said, "Nothing! Nothing whatsoever! If you can escape hell that will be enough."

Bodhidharma said, "The very idea of doing something for

gain is irreligious, worldly. You have not done it because you love, you have done it because you are greedy. Greed will take you to hell. Listen, Wu, these monasteries and these thousands of monks that have gathered here are not going to help you. I know that they tell you again and again, 'Great King, great is your virtue. God will be ready to receive you in heaven' – but I tell you, you will go to hell because greed is the door to hell and you are greedy and you are ambitious. Look at your ugly greed. If you want to make a temple, make it, but make it out of love. If you want to feed somebody, feed him, but feed him out of love. Finished! You have had the benefit. There is no other benefit beyond it. You enjoy feeding a man – what more do you need? The value is intrinsic. Act out of love."

This is how a master, a real master, is.

Then Bodhidharma turned away, he didn't enter the kingdom. And Wu said, "Why are you turning away?" He said, "When you cannot understand me, what about the others? They will not understand me. I will stay outside the kingdom. Those who want me, they can seek and come." And he remained outside the kingdom. He would not enter. He said, "If even the king cannot understand me, then what about the masses? Your courtiers are standing here puzzled and they cannot understand me, so what about the masses? And these foolish monks that are gathered here – they cannot understand me. So I will not come into your kingdom. I will wait outside. Those who are really desirous, they should come to me."

Then he sat for nine years outside the kingdom looking at a wall. People would come and say, "Sir, why are you looking at the wall? Why don't you look at us?" He would say, "It is all the same. Whether I look at you or I look at the wall is the same. I will turn only to look at you when the real person who wants to know truth has come."

Then came Hui Nang, his first disciple. He stood at the back and he said, "Sir, I have come. Turn towards me." And Bodhidharma said, "Show the sign." And Hui Nang cut his hand off, gave it to Bodhidharma and said, "You turn around otherwise I will cut off my head – what else can I show as a sign?" And Bodhidharma turned immediately. He said, "So you have come!"

One has to pay for truth by life. What about respectability, prestige? All nonsense. One has to give all – only then does one become capable of knowing the truth.

Enough for today.

CHAPTER #2

A Thousand Pound Sledge Hammer

The first question:

> Osho,
> It seems to me that Gramya's question on Tuesday was practically the same as mine on Sunday, only worded differently. But you answered her very lovingly and gently and me with a thousand-pound sledge hammer. Osho, excuse me for asking this, but I too mean to ask lovingly. Why have you become so hard on old disciples? And, Osho, don't you love me any more? I am with you whatever is the case.

The question is from Ananda Prem.

The first thing, is that you cannot ask a question that Gramya asks. Nobody else can ask the question that you ask. Even if yon use exactly the same words, the question will be different and you will get a different answer from me.

I am not answering the question, I am answering the questioner – that must be understood. You can write a question in exactly the same way as Gramya and I will not answer in the same way. You are not Gramya, Gramya is not you. Everybody is unique, everybody is individual; never before has there been anybody like you, never again will there be anybody like you. You are simply you, there is only one you, there is nobody else like you.

So how can somebody else ask a question like you? How can you ask a question like somebody else? The wording, the language, the formulation of the question is not important at all; it arises out of your consciousness, out of your mind. And you have a different mind and a different consciousness, a different character, a different past. It arises out of your past.

So never compare others' questions. When I answer you, I answer you, that's why I insist that you should write your names on the question. Otherwise the question becomes general and then the answer is in the abstract, it is not addressed to anybody. And the answer, to be meaningful, has to be particular. It has to be addressed to a particular individual in a specific way – only then does it apply to you, otherwise not.

"It seemed to me that Gramya's question was practically the same as mine on Sunday..." – no, neither practically the same nor theoretically the same only worded differently. Don't deceive yourself. It was worded differently, true, but even if it had not been worded differently my answer would have been the same.

Even when we use the same words we don't mean the same thing. The meaning is not in the words, the meaning is in the mind that uses them.

Meditate on this anecdote.

The business executive was told by his doctor that he had a heart condition. On the same day he was advised by mail that if he didn't meet a heavy mortgage payment, his home would be seized. Driving nervously down the highway in a new car on which five payments were due, he rammed into the compact car of one of his best customers and made a sardine can out of it. Continuing to his office, he arrived at the factory just as the firemen were watering down the hot embers. There his bookkeeper handed him a note informing him that all his insurance policies had lapsed.

Disgusted, he took a cab home, walked slowly into the living room and was greeted cheerfully by his wife. "Darling," she said enthusiastically, "I hope you'll forgive me but I must run; tonight is my bridge night."

"Just give me a chance to change my shirt," answered the husband, "and I'll jump with you!"

Her bridge night. But how can it mean the same thing to the husband? In that state it cannot mean the same. You speak the same words but still you convey different meanings. The meaning is given by the mind. The word is an outside thing, the meaning is an inside thing.

Because of the fog, the plane was in serious trouble. All the passengers were numb with fear, except the minister aboard. He took complete control of the situation.

"Let us kneel and pray," he suggested to the passengers, and everyone kneeled except a small-time bookie.

"Why aren't you praying with us?" asked the minister.

"Because," confessed the bookie, "I don't know how."

"In that case," the minister advised, "just behave as though you were in a church."

So the bookie went down the aisle and took up a collection.

That is the only thing the bookie can understand, that is the only thing he would become interested in, in a church.

Remember always that it is you who comes through loud and clear in your questions. I am not much interested in how they are worded, in how they are formulated. I seek for you, I grope for you in your question and unless I have got hold of you I don't answer because then it is meaningless.

Don't feel jealous of Gramya. It seems that Ananda Prem has become jealous of Gramya. That again shows her mind. Rather than understanding what I have said to her she is more worried about why I have answered Gramya so lovingly and her not so lovingly. She was not so interested in the answer, she was more interested in love being shown to her. That again shows her mind.

The question was not asked for the answer, the question was just a trick so that I could show my love to her. Then why go so roundabout? Why not simply write: "Osho, say some beautiful things about me?" That would be easy, simple – why send such big questions? Then be direct: "I need to be appreciated, applauded." But the mind is tricky. You may ask something but you may not be at all interested in the question or in the answer. There may be some secret desire lurking behind it. Seeing that desire I had to use the thousand-pound sledge hammer.

But you missed. You ducked. You should have bowed down before that thousand-pound hammer, you should have received it, accepted it, welcomed it. It would have given you tremendous insight. But you missed. Rather than listening to what I said to you, you listened more to what I said to Gramya and now you feel jealous – why have I not said the same thing to you?

It was not your need. When you come to me I have to give you the medicine that you need. You cannot say, "Why have you given Gramya a very sweet medicine and me a very bitter thing?" You need it. The sweet medicine may kill you: it is not your need. I am a physician, I am trying to help you to come out of your diseases. You may not be too interested in coming out of your diseases, but that is my only interest. I am not interested in anything else. You may be simply hankering for sympathy. Sympathy is poison and has to be used only when poison is needed. Sometimes an ill person needs poison too – all of Allopathy depends on poison.

But you should not tell the doctor what medicine should be given to you, you should not prescribe for yourself. Not only have you come with a disease, you have come with a prescription also! You want me to sign it, then you will be very happy. If you can doctor yourself then the need for me is not there – then doctor yourself. If you cannot doctor yourself then listen to what I say, meditate over it – all the nuances of it, all the meanings, subtle and gross, in it. You should have meditated. That hammer would have helped you tremendously.

A thousand-pound sledge hammer had to be used because, Ananda Prem, you have a very thick head. It is almost a rock. In fact, when I use the hammer I am always worried whether the hammer is going to survive or not!

And you ask: "Why have you become so hard on old disciples?" That's what the old disciple is for. You have graduated, Ananda Prem. Gramya will also graduate – wait! The older you are, the harder I will be; because I hope that you will have become more capable. I hope that now you will be able to receive greater shocks.

Naturally, when a new disciple comes, I cannot hit him very hard. I have to be very cautious, I go slowly. The closer and closer the disciple comes to me, the more and more I can become certain when the moment is and the disciple can be hit hard. Because deep down the whole function of a master is to behead you. The master is a sword. Says Jesus. "I have not brought peace into the world, I have brought a sword."

Buddhists have given a special name for it, they have called it "Manjushree's sword." Manjushree was a great disciple of Buddha, he functioned as Buddha's sword. Whenever Buddha *saw* that somebody needed a real shock he would be sent to Manjushree. Manjushree was really terrible! He would simply smash you. He would not allow any illusions. He was so hard in his hitting that the moment Buddha prescribed, "Go to Manjushree," people would start trembling. Manjushree? That meant almost death. But Manjushree was really a great, compassionate Buddha and it became famous in Buddha's time that whenever a disciple had really grown, Buddha sent him to Manjushree the butcher.

When you are older I hope that you will be capable of much more understanding. The day you are really old and you have come very close to me, I am going to cut your head off. And that has to be done so suddenly, so fast, that not even a drop of blood comes out. It has to be done very fast. But for that you have to become by and by more and more prepared.

The work of the master is not to console you. If you have come here for consolation you have come into the wrong company. Go somewhere else. If you have come for transformation only, then be here – otherwise I am not the person for you. I know your secret desires are not for transformation, your secret desires are for improvement. And improvement and transformation are just diametrically opposite. Improvement means that you remain the same but you become more and more rich, your ego becomes more and more decorated. You remain the same – whatsoever happens becomes a new layer on you but you remain the same. The new is an addition to you but you remain continuous with the old. You ale for improvement. You want to become beautiful, you want to become more blissful, you want to become more knowledgeable, you want to become a buddha – this and that. The buddha disease....

I am not here to improve upon you; if the base remains wrong all improvement is going to lead you into more and more trouble. The base has to be transformed; from the roots you have to be cut. Naturally it is going to be hard, arduous.

Just the other day I was telling you about the Hebrew word *mariam,* Jesus' mother's name. It means rebellion. It has another meaning also – both meanings are beautiful. One is "rebellion," another is "arduous, hard." The path is a razor's edge. It is hard and arduous. Jesus comes through that arduous path, through Mariam – it is rebellious and arduous.

The greatest difficulty to be encountered is the ego. Ananda Prem asked the question and she must have been listening with the idea that I will decorate her ego a little bit here and there, will give her new enthusiasm. And I took away the very ground underneath her feet. That shocked her.

If you are one of the old around me, wait for many shocks. That's the only way I can show my love to you.

You ask: "And, Osho, don't you love me any more?" Now I have started loving you, Ananda Prem, hence the thousand-pound sledge hammer. And when I love you even more I will have to take even weightier hammers. Otherwise why should I bother to hit you at all? For what profit? By hitting you there are only two possibilities: either you receive it and you become more understanding, or you escape from me. What am I going to gain out of it? Either you are going to gain or I am going to miss you – there is no gain for me in it at all. The alternatives are two: either you escape from me become very much afraid – then I have lost a disciple; or you become enlightened – then too I have lost a disciple. So what is the gain? For me at least, there is no gain. I am going to be a loser either way.

And finally she says in a bracket: "I am with you whatever is the case." That I know – I know your stubbornness.

During a flood in a little town, a little girl was perched on the top of a house with a small boy.

As they sat watching, they noticed a derby hat float by. Presently the hat turned and came back. Then again it turned and went down stream and once more turned and came back again.

The little girl said, "What do you think of that derby? First it goes downstream, then it turns and comes back."

The boy replied, "Oh, that's my father. He said, 'Come hell or high water, I'm going to cut the grass today.'"

And I know Ananda Prem is that type. She is absolutely stubborn. I can trust her that much. She will not leave, so only one possibility is left. If she becomes capable of receiving the shocks that I am going to give – this is just the beginning – then there is a possibility of a new light dawning in her soul.

The second question:

> Osho,
> What do you mean when you say to "ponder" or "meditate on" a parable? What is the process? PS. I can hardly even remember the parable after the discourse.

That means the discourse has succeeded. I don't mean you to memorize it. If you have understood it the fragrance enters into your soul. It is not a question of memorizing. This is not a university. And nobody is going to examine your memory, nobody is going to ask you how much you remembered.

When I say ponder over it I don't mean repeat it, remember it, cram it – no. When I say ponder over it I mean: let the fragrance of it be released into your soul.

Buddha has said that there are three steps in how to listen to a buddha – three steps. First, hearing; second, pondering; third, living. Hearing means that when you are listening to me you should simply listen, not think about it. Do not go on commenting inside you: right, wrong, good, bad. No commentary on your part is needed, all commentary will be a distraction. And you will miss.

When I say "listen" I don't mean concentrate, because if you concentrate you will become very tense. In a tense mind meditation is not possible. So when I say "listen," the first step – it means: simply be relaxed, open, available. I am singing a song to you, let this song reach and vibrate in you. You should not be worried about whether you will be able to remember it or not – that is not the point at all. Once you have vibrated with it, something of it will have penetrated into your being, will become part of you. In fact, that which becomes part of you is real knowledge and you need not cram it. The unreal knowledge is that which you have crammed and has not become a part of you.

When a student goes to an examination he remembers a thousand and one things, but after three months, if you ask him, ninety-nine per cent of it has gone down the drain. Somehow it was just managed, with very great tension and strain. He was keeping it, holding it, for the examination, once the examination is finished he will lose that hold and things will disappear.

Can't you observe it in your own life? How much do you remember of that which you crammed in your university days, how much? If you are examined again you will all fail. You will not be able to remember. Even the professors who teach in the universities will all fail if they are examined again because the examination was just a momentary effort. But real knowledge is never forgotten because real knowledge is never remembered. That which is remembered will be forgotten: that which is not remembered cannot be forgotten, there is no way to forget it.

There are a few things you cannot forget for example, swimming. You cannot forget it. You may not have been to a river for fifty years but you cannot forget it because it has never been remembered, it has gone into your being, it has become part of you. This is real knowledge. All that is real becomes part of you, it remains available forever and ever. There is no way to forget it. That which I call know-ledge is that which cannot be forgotten. Even if you make an effort to forget it you will fail you cannot forget it.

Watch in life – and you will find two categories, different categories. One is that which you have to remember but you go on forgetting again and again. Another is that which you don't remember but is simply there – is there not as a memory but as part of your being. There is no need to hold it, it is simply there. Even if you want to throw it out you cannot. That is real knowledge.

So when I say "listen" I am not saying "be attentive" – because in attention there is tension. The very word is out of "tension" – "attention" means "at tension." Your mind is narrowed. When I say "listen," I mean be relaxed, open; become a sponge. Soak it up. Let it sink into you. Listen to me as you listen to the birds singing in the trees or to the sound of running water. There is no meaning in it. Or, listen to me as you listen to music. Music has no intellectual meaning. You listen to it – you simply drink it, you let it in, you allow it into your very innermost core. And you enjoy it. If somebody later on asks if you remember what music you have heard, you will not be able to say anything. You will say, "I enjoyed it, it was beautiful, it was something that thrilled me to the very core. I was refreshed through it. I became more alive through it, I felt a sudden joy bursting in my heart." But these are the impacts that happen to you: there is nothing to say about the music. Listen to me as you do to music.

So don't be worried. If you forget, good. I am not saying these things to be remembered. I am not here to make you knowledgeable, professional pundits, no. I am not here to give you a memory training. But an upsurge of understanding can happen. You can respond. To whatsoever I am saying you can respond, you can vibrate with it. And that will be real hearing. That is the first step.

The second step is pondering. The first step, hearing, is through the mind door, because you have to use the ears and you have to use the mechanical device of the mind. It goes through the mind. If you are not thinking, the mind allows it. If the mind is thinking, the mind obstructs, distorts, and does many things to it. If the mind is not thinking then mind becomes simply a pure passage, a receptivity.

Hearing is through mind, pondering is through heart. When the mind has allowed it, all that you listen to in silence, in love, in rapport with my being – falls into your heart and accumulates there. Remember the difference. If you want to remember it, it will be retained in the head. The memory exists in the head. If you don't want to retain it, if you are not interested in remembering it, then it goes into the heart; it falls, pours into the heart and accumulates there.

But then it has a totally different impact on your being. You will not remember it but it will surround you like a fragrance. When I say, "ponder," I mean: let it reach to your heart. Don't listen through thinking, listen through feeling – that is the meaning of pondering. To ponder over it means: let your feeling be aroused – not your thought, not your logic, but your love. Let your love respond. That's the difference.

When an outsider comes to listen to me just as an out-sider, he will at the most be able to accumulate something in the head. When you become a sannyasin it changes, it changes completely. Then you listen in a totally different way. Then you are not fighting me, you are not arguing with me – then you are simply enjoying the song. You dance with me, you sing with me, you be with me – then it reaches to the heart and you feel with me.

Whatsoever I say to you has nothing to do with my head. It comes from the heart. I say it because I feel for you, I say it because I love you, I say it because great compassion is there, I say it because I want to share my heart with you. It is not a lecture. I am not lecturing you, I am not your enemy. Why should I lecture you? I am simply opening my heart, I am allowing you to come into me, I am inviting you to become my guest, I am inviting you to partake of something of my being. That's what Jesus means when he says to his disciples, "Eat me. Drink me." This is a feast! When I say, "ponder," I also mean: eat me, drink me, feel me. Let your feeling be thrilled, stirred. Let your heart dance. Rejoice with me. It is a great tiding. I bring you a gospel.

And the third is living. First hear, with thought not interfering; then feel, fall in rapport with me, in tune with me; and then live it. It is not a question of cramming, remembering. Living, yes, living is the thing.

You hear me. If it goes into your heart it will be very easy to live it, because from the heart where else can it go? It will go into your being. These are the three layers. The first layer is thinking, the head. Deeper than the head is the heart, feeling. And deeper than the heart is being. So if it soaks through the head it reaches to the heart. If it soaks through the heart it reaches to your being. And from there comes living.

I am not saying practice it. Practice happens only when something has not reached your heart but has been retained by the head. And then you try to practice it. Practice means that you are avoiding the heart, keeping in the head, and now you are thinking about what to do, how to manage, how to practice, how to create a character on the base of it. If it reaches your heart then you can relax. By and by it will start affecting your living.

So what has to be done about the third point? You only have not to force it and not to obstruct it when it comes. Don't stand in the way. To many people it is happening every day. Something I said to you six months before, which you had completely forgotten, is suddenly there when a situation arises – it starts functioning and you behave accordingly.

Not that you try – if you try that is not the real thing, that is pseudo – but suddenly, one day, you feel you are not behaving in the usual pattern, the gestalt has changed. Somebody insults you and you don't feel hurt. You are surprised yourself. What has happened? If this happens allow it to happen, support it, cooperate with it; it is very new and fragile, it will need your support. Sometimes it happens but you obstruct it because you think, "This man is insulting me and this is not the time to ponder on great things. If I allow him to insult me he will insult me more. Today he will insult me but tomorrow he will start beating me."

Then your mind starts bringing in the old pattern. Your heart is saying, "Relax, this is the moment, smile." All those beautiful parables and all that fragrance you have been accumulating in your heart is ready to explode, but your mind says, "Wait, this is not the moment to meditate and this is not the moment to think about great things. This is dangerous." And you shrink. If you shrink then that which was happening naturally has been obstructed.

So all that you can do is negative. Don't obstruct. Hearing, don't think, that is negative. Let it be there. Pondering on the heart is positive, feel. Again, living is negative. Don't obstruct. Let it take its own form and shape. Let it flow wherever it goes. Don't be worried. Don't start manipulating the energy. Allow it. Be in a let-go. Hearing is negative, pondering is positive, living is again negative.

And then you will come to know the ultimate positive, the fourth step, what in India we have called *turiya*, the fourth. That is your selfless self, beingless being, being as non-being – what Buddha calls *anatta*, no-selfness. That is the most positive thing that will happen. Negative, hearing; positive, pondering; negative, living; and then happens the ultimate positive, the ultimate being.

But the most basic problem arises in the first step. The first step is always the most basic. The second follows easily, the third even more easily, the fourth without any problem – it comes on its own accord. But the first is the most difficult step.

Have you not watched a small child starting to walk? The first step is the most difficult step. The child hesitates. He has never walked. The child has no self-confidence. He cannot trust that he will be able to walk – how can you trust the unknown? That which you have never done before? Again and again the child starts crawling, afraid that he may fall, that he may hurt himself. The first step is the most difficult step. Once he has taken the first step then it is very difficult to prevent him from taking the second, from taking the third. It is impossible to prevent him. Whenever the mother is not looking he will try again. He may fall but now he has known the adventure, the beauty of it – that he can stand on his own.

So the first step is listening without thinking. When I am talking there is every possibility that you are continuously thinking about how to practice it. That is your greed. Beware of it. The greed will not allow you to hear.

Two millionaires were discussing their personal buying habits.

"I like to shop at Lord & Taylor's. They're very reliable," said the first. "I tore my coat on a nail in front of the store and they immediately gave me ten dollars."

"Really?" gasped the second. "Do you think the nail is still there?"

Now this man cannot listen. He has already moved into greed. "Do you think the nail is still there?" He only appears to listen but he has gone into the future. He has started planning what to do, how to get those ten dollars. He may even be a millionaire – that doesn't matter.

When you listen to me don't start trips in your mind. It happens every day. I can even feel when a person has gone on a trip. His face changes, he is no longer here. A certain lust can be seen on his face, a greed. He has started thinking about what to do, how to do it and how beautiful it will be if he can do it.

Listening, just listen; don't move from here. One way is to

move into the future – don't do that; another way is to move into the past, don't do that either. When you listen to me you start thinking, "Yes, I have heard this, I have read about this. That's what I also think." But you have stopped listening.

It was one of the greatest manhunts of all time and Detective O'Sherlock was hot on the trail of the killer. He trailed him into a department store, then he trailed him into a restaurant, then he trailed him into a trailer. But he lost him eventually.

"How in God's name did you lose him?" the chief roared angrily.

"I followed him into every hole in town," explained the great O'Sherlock, ace of the force. "Into everything from men's toiletries to men's toilets but I didn't follow him when he went into the movies. That's where I lost him."

"And why didn't you follow him into the movies?" the chief calmly queried, bursting a blood vessel.

"Because I had already seen the picture."

Remember, don't bring in the picture you have seen before. Don't bring in your memories. When I am taking you into something, just relax and go with me. Don't allow the future to interfere, don't allow the past to interfere. When the past and future are not interfering, you are hearing. When you are hearing, the second step is very easy – your heart will gather the fragrance of whatsoever is being poured into you, has been told to you. Your heart will start throbbing with a new rhythm that you had not known before, with new energy, with new vitality. The heart will start a new movement of energy.

Then enjoy it, don't be afraid of it – you are very afraid of the heart. You have been taught to control the heart. You have been taught to reduce the heart to being a slave and to make the head the master. You will have to do just the opposite if you really want to go with me into the unknown. The head has not to be the master any more. Instead of the head, the heart has to be crowned again, the heart has to become the emperor again. The heart is the master. Feeling should be the master, not thinking – because joy is a feeling, not a thought; because love is a feeling, not a thought; because happiness is a feeling, not a thought; because silence is a feeling, not a thought; because God is; feeling, not a thought. Let feeling be the supreme-most, the sovereign, and let the head serve it. This turn, this conversion, makes one religious.

And then the third is even more easy – just don't obstruct. When your heart starts functioning in your day-to-day life, allow it, go with it. Take the risk. That's what I mean when I say, "Meditate over this parable."

The third question:

Osho,
I am terribly scared to ask this question. Why do you mention Swami Yoga Chinmaya's name when he asks a question? And why does something in me have to ask this question?

This is from Deva Nirvesh. First, Swami Yoga Chinmaya's name makes you laugh – and it saves me a joke. That is economical. Second it makes you happy, it makes Swami Chinmaya happy, it makes me happy. You are happy, you laugh; Chinmaya is happy, his name has been mentioned; I am happy because you all are happy. So at no cost everybody is simply happy! That's why.

And it is a tacit understanding now that when Swami Yoga Chinmaya asks a question it is bound to be ridiculous. So just mentioning the name is enough! He is a great seeker and when you are a great seeker you stumble upon many ridiculous questions. He goes on thinking about everything and when you go on thinking about everything you are bound to find many ridiculous questions.

In fact, deep down, every question is ridiculous. Life simply is; it is not a question and there is no answer to it. It simply is. There is no question-mark to life. If you look deeply you will find there is an exclamation-mark but no question-mark. Life is a wonder, a mystery. But that happens only when you look at life as a poet.

Chinmaya looks at life as a thinker – then the exclamation mark appears to be a question mark. That is the mistake every thinker is bound to commit. And he is a very logical thinker. He thinks logically. But logic always leads into absurdities so what can he do? He goes to the very end and then the thing turns into a ridiculous question. He is courageous to ask.

So it is a tacit understanding – when I mention the name of Swami Yoga Chinmaya you can relax. You know that something beautiful is coming.

I have heard.

It happened that in a madhouse, a new superintendent had come to take charge. The old superintendent introduced him to the inmates. A great meeting was called of all the mad people, of which there were many.

The new superintendent was very surprised. He could not believe what was happening because, instead of a speech, the old superintendent merely said a few numbers. He said, "Forty-nine," and everybody started laughing. And they laughed so uproariously that they were bursting. They started rolling on the floor. And then he said, "Seventy-two," and they started going mad.

The new superintendent could not understand what was happening. So when the speech was finished, it was just numbers – he asked, "What is the matter? What are these numbers?" And the old superintendent said, "I have been here for many years and they have also been here for many years so we have a tacit understanding. I have numbered my jokes. What is the point of telling the same joke again and again and again? Forty-nine – and they know, so they laugh. It is an arrangement. Seventy-two is the most ridiculous, that's why they were jumping and rolling on the floor. Everybody knows!"

The new superintendent said, "This is beautiful. I will try tomorrow." So he listened to a few jokes, remembered the numbers and the next day he stood there and said, "Forty-nine." But nobody laughed. What had happened? So thinking that maybe they were not in such a jovial mood that day he said,

"Seventy-two." But they just sat there, nobody smiled. He looked at the old superintendent and said, "What is the matter?" The old man said, "You just don't know how to tell a joke."

So please remember, if you say "Swami Yoga Chinmaya," nobody will laugh. It is a number, a tacit understanding: one has to know how to say it.

The woman sought the hallowed advice of the marriage counselor.

'I just don't know what to do!' She was obviously distressed. 'The first year my husband spoke to me only once and we had a son. The second year he spoke twice and we had twins. The third year he spoke to me thrice and we had triplets. The fourth year, four times, and we had quadruplets. What shall I do?'

'Tell him just to point, you'll know what he means.'

It is a tacit understanding by now that if I say Swami Yoga Chinmaya it is enough. You can trust me.

You ask me: "I am terribly scared to ask this question." You should not be scared. Why you should be scared? This is such a beautiful question. If you go on asking such questions you can become a second name. I need a Ma too. Swami Yoga Chinmaya is one, Ma Deva Nirvesh can become a second. So go on, persist, persevere. You should not be scared. And I have heard the rumor that Nirvesh is moving with Swami Yoga Chinmaya. It is a rumor, I cannot vouch for it. Rumors go around here fast – so many women, you know. Women may not have a sense of humor but they have a sense of rumor.

And you ask: "And why does something in me have to ask this question?" Now, that you have to ask yourself. You must be feeling sympathetic to Swami Yoga Chinmaya. Beware. Only wrong people feel sympathetic to Yoga Chinmaya. Beware. Up to now he has had only one great follower – Ma Ananda Prem – now you may be the second.

The fourth question:

> Osho,
> Why don't I have any other question than this one? I am not enlightened so I feel my mind is becoming dull.

It is just the other way round. Your mind is dull that's why you are not getting enlightened! Now you are putting things in completely the wrong sequence. Don't wait for enlightenment to come and don't hope that when enlightenment comes then you will be intelligent.

It will never come. Intelligence is the first requirement for it to happen at all. Intelligence is the preparation for it. Be intelligent. Behave intelligently. Live intelligently. Otherwise enlightenment is not going to happen at all. If you are hoping that one day enlightenment will come and then you will be intelligent, a genius, you are wrong.

There are a few people who go on saying nonsense things like this. One of them is old Pundit Gopi Krishna. He thinks that when kundalini arises one becomes a genius, one becomes tremendously intelligent. This is not true. If you are tremendously intelligent only then does your kundalini arise, otherwise not. If Gopi Krishna is right, it means that a dull-head, a stupid person, can make his kundalini rise and can become intelligent. That is impossible.

To help your energy rise and soar high you will need tremendous intelligence, sharp intelligence. Otherwise you will not be able to bring your energy up so high. A stupid person cannot do that. Enlightenment, nirvana, *moksha*, liberation, the arousal of your kundalini, whatsoever the name – are just names, symbolic. But one thing is certain: intelligence has to precede them. You cannot afford to be stupid and hope that someday something will happen and you will become enlightened. Then you are hoping in vain. You will have to create intelligence.

How to create intelligence? First become more and more alert in small things. Walking along the road, become more alert, try to be more alert. For such a simple process walking along the road – you need not have any alertness. You can remain stupid and walk well. That's what everyone is doing. The stupidity does not hinder you at all. Start from small things. Taking your bath, be alert; standing under the shower, become very alert. That cold water falling on you, the body enjoying it...become alert, become conscious of what is happening, be relaxed yet conscious.

And this moment of consciousness has to be brought in again and again, in a thousand and one ways: eating, talking, meeting a friend, listening to me, meditating, making love. In all situations try to become more and more alert. It is hard, it is certainly difficult, but it is not impossible. Slowly, slowly, the dust will disappear and your mirror-like consciousness will reveal itself; you will become more intelligent.

Then live intelligently. You live in such a confused way, in such a stupid way, that if you see somebody else living that way you will immediately say that he is stupid. But you are doing the same, although somehow one manages not to look at one's own life.

A man came to me and he said, "What to do Osho? I have fallen in love with two women." Now one is enough, one will do enough harm but he has fallen in love with two women. So both are struggling and he is crushed. And he says, "I am in misery; both are fighting over me." And naturally from both the sides he is being hit. And if I say to him, "Choose one," he says that it is difficult. This means that one person is riding on two horses. He says it is difficult to choose one. Then let it be, have it your own way. You will destroy your life. Choosing two women or two men as your love-objects is bound to split you. You will become a schizophrenic and you will start falling apart.

This is stupid. It is so simple to look into the phenomenon. Maybe sometimes it is difficult, it *is* difficult – but then too one has to choose. You cannot go in all the directions simultaneously. If you have come to listen to me you have chosen. You have missed a few things. You could have been in a restaurant sitting with friends, sipping coffee, but you have chosen not to do that. You could have gone to a movie, but you have chosen not to go there. Or you could have chosen just to lie down on your bed and relax and be a Taoist – but that you have not chosen. You have come to listen to me and to sit on this hard marble floor, cold and hurting – but you have chosen.

What will you say about a man who just stands outside his house and says, "I am in difficulty. I cannot go to the lectures and I cannot go to bed because I want to do both together. So I am standing here." He will miss both.

If you look into your life you will find how unintelligently you have been behaving. You read a book and you accumulate knowledge and you start thinking that you know. You have learned the word *God* and you think you have known God. You are ready to argue – not only argue, you are ready to kill and be killed. How many Mohammedans, how many Hindus, how many Christians have been killed for something they have read only in book! Tremendously stupid people. One is fighting for the Koran, another is fighting for the Gita, another is fighting for the Bible – for books you are fighting and killing living people and sacrificing your tremendously valuable life! What are you doing?

But man has behaved in stupid ways. Just because everybody else is behaving in the same way does not make it intelligent. If all are fools it does not make you intelligent because you are following them.

I have heard.

A flock of birds was flying into the sky and one bird asked another, "Why do we always follow this stupid leader?"

And the other said, "I don't know. I have heard that only he has the map."

The map! Nobody has the map. But you go on following the Pope, and the Shankaracharya, and a *maulvi* and a pundit and you think that they have the map, that they know. Just look into their lives. What do they know? They may even be far more stupid than you are. Just look at the unintelligent way they are living. Watch their life. Are they happy? Is there a dance in their life? Is there fragrance in their life? Just looking at them do you feel a silence showering on you? Nothing of the sort. Just because they have a book and they have read it and studied it for years, it does not make any sense to follow them.

Become a man of knowing, not a man of knowledge. Then you live intelligently.

To me intelligence is the basic morality, the basic virtue. If you are intelligent you will not harm anybody because that is foolish. If you are intelligent you will not harm yourself because that is foolish. Life is so precious, it is not to be wasted; it has to be lived in deep celebration, in deep gratitude. And one has to be very careful and watchful because a moment gone is gone forever. It will never return. So if you waste it in stupidity you are wasting a great opportunity. Live each moment so totally, so fully aware, that you never repent later on that you didn't live, that you could have lived more, that you could have enjoyed more. That's what intelligence is: to live life so totally that there is no repentance, never. One is always contented. One knows that one has lived to one's uttermost.

Then, in the uttermost state of awareness, enlightenment happens. You say: "I am not enlightened so I feel my mind is becoming dull." No, sir, your mind is dull, that's why you have not become enlightened. So don't wait for enlightenment to come and do everything for you – do something so that your dullness is dropped.

And it can be dropped, because nobody is born dull, every child is born intelligent. Can't you see it in children? – how intelligent they are, how full of life, how full of love, how full of joy. Look into their eyes. How much shine there is in their eyes. They are the glories of God. Then the society jumps on them and the parents and the teachers and the education system and everybody starts making them dull because the society needs dull people. Only dull people can be dominated, oppressed. Only dull people can be ordered to go here and there, to do this and that. Only dull people are needed by the society because dull people are very efficient, they don't have any mind, they are not dangerous. Dull people are very convenient. Dull people drag their whole life.

Just think of people who are intelligent. Do you think anybody would be ready to waste his whole life as a clerk? Just think of it. Would anybody be ready to waste his whole life as a politician? Would anybody be ready to waste his whole life as a soldier? For what? One would like to live an intelligent life of love, art, creativity. Many things would disappear from the world if people were intelligent; almost ninety-nine per cent of things would disappear.

War would not be possible. On the earth, war is almost the major work of humanity – it has been for centuries. Seventy per cent of money is wasted on war – seventy per cent! What are you doing? Simply preparing for war? You don't know anything else. You know only how to kill. People have become efficient only in killing. This can be done only by dull people. Intelligent people will throw away the arms. They will dump all the atom bombs in the Pacific and they will say goodbye to all war.

For what? Life is so short and there is so much to enjoy – the stars and the moon and the flowers and the men and the women and the rivers and the mountains. And you are just fighting and living a very dull and stupid life.

Society needs dull people, remember it. So be aware that the society would not like you to become intelligent. It would like you to become a machine; efficient, certainly, but not intelligent. Do the work that is given to you and die. Drag your life from the office to the house, from the house to the office, your whole life is from the office to the house, from the house to the office. In the house you will have a wife to nag you and in the office you will have a boss to insult and humiliate you. And on the road there is the mad traffic. Go to the office, back home, to the office, again home – and then one day you die. That is the only hope – that one day you will die!

Mulla Nasruddin went for a world trip. He was on a ship for the first time. And, of course, he was suffering tremendously, terribly, from sea-sickness. He could not eat anything, he could not drink anything, he was continuously vomiting.

Then the Captain came and he said to Nasruddin, "Don't be worried. I have been in the force for twenty years and I have never seen or heard of a man dying of sea-sickness. Don't be worried."

And Mulla beat his head and he said, "That was my only hope! I was hoping to die, but now you say that nobody has ever died!"

Your only hope is that one day you will die. So just a little more, tolerate it a little more, a few more days of the office, a few more days of the house.... Tolerate. Death is coming to deliver you. That is your only hope.

What kind of life is this where man hopes that death will deliver him? What kind of life is this where people commit suicide? What kind of life is this where people go mad, insane, just because they cannot tolerate it any more, because it becomes too much, it breaks their nerves. No we are living very unintelligently. And in this unintelligence enlightenment is not possible.

But remember, basically you came with intelligence, unintelligence is forced on you by society. So there is hope. It can be dropped too. It is just dust that has been gathered on the mirror. The mirror is still clean and clear, the dust just has to be removed. Once the dust is removed the mirror will be as clear as ever. Everybody is a genius. God never creates anything else, God only creates geniuses. Everybody is intelligent, nobody is mediocre, cannot be. How can somebody come out of God and be a mediocre? God does not deal in mediocres, he only makes masterpieces. But the society has forced you to become dull. So much dust has gathered on your mirror that you don't look like a mirror at all.

What is enlightenment? It is to attain to your mirror-like quality again. It is a recovery. It is not something that you invent, it is already the case – deep down you are enlightened. Dust has just gathered on the surface, you need a good cleansing.

That's what we are doing here. You need a good cleansing. You need a good bath. Meditation is an inner bath. Sannyas is a total cleansing. It is trying to live intelligently, whatsoever the cost. It is trying to live courageously. It is trying to live your life in your own way, trying to do your own thing in your own way and not bothering what others say. With that declaration you become intelligent. With that declaration of individuality you become intelligent. And only through intelligence does the bird of enlightenment one day come. Open the window of intelligence and wait.

The last question:

Osho,
Why are you against marriage?

Why should I be against marriage? First, I have never been married so why should I be against marriage? You need experience for such things.

A youngster was thinking about getting married. So he wrote to his father for some personal advice. His father wrote back:

"I can't tell you how happy I am to hear about your impending marriage. You will find marriage the most beautiful state of bliss and happiness. As I look across the table at your dear mother, I realize with great pride how full and wonderful our years together have been. By all means, get married. You have our blessings. It will be the happiest day of your life. Sincerely, Dad. PS. Your mother just left the room. Stay single, you idiot!"

I have no experience, why should I be against marriage? And fortunately my parents were very simple people. They have also not created anything in me to be against marriage. They have loved each other tremendously, innocently. In my childhood I never saw them fighting, quarreling, nagging. They have lived as peacefully as possible. It is very rare to find such a peaceful couple.

She watched the young man have his soup with the wrong spoon, grasp the utensils with the wrong fingers, eat the main course with his hands and pour tea into the saucer and blow on it.

"Hasn't watching your mother and dad at the dinner table taught you anything?" she asked.

"Yeah," said the boy. "Never to get married."

I could not have deduced it from my parents so why should I be against marriage?

Those who know, they are against but then it is too late.

Once a friend told Alfred Adler about a certain Miss X who was going to be married soon. Usually in such situations people inquire "to whom?" but Adler asked "against whom?" He had suffered much. He knew that a marriage is not with somebody, but against somebody, so it was not right to ask "with whom?" but "against whom?"

What you call marriage is nothing but an arrangement, a social arrangement. What you call marriage is nothing but an institution. And it is not good to live in an institution. It is not love, it is a poor substitute for love. If marriage arises out of love it is beautiful – but then it is not really marriage, it is a totally different thing. But if marriage is just a legal binding and there is no love in it then you are entering into an imprisonment – and on your own accord.

Marriage as such is going to disappear from the world; it should disappear. Love should be enough cause to be together. I know that there is danger, because love is something like a breeze: when it comes it comes, when it goes it goes. It is not very dependable. It is not an electric fan whose button you switch on and the fan starts. Marriage is a electric fan, you can depend on it. Love is a natural breeze sometimes it is there, then it is beautiful, but then it can go too, any moment it can be gone.

Love is like a rose flower – it blooms and withers. Marriage is a plastic flower – it never blooms and it never withers. It is very permanent. Many people have chosen the plastic flower against the rose flower, the real flower, because they are afraid of its momentariness.

But life is momentary, life is a flux. To hope that one can create something permanent in life is to hope in vain. You are looking for frustration. The whole of life is a continuous movement: things change. Except change, everything changes. The only thing that is permanent is change.

So whatsoever is real is changing that's why fear arises in man's mind. Love cannot be depended on so you have to bring the court and the law in so that things become permanent. When love disappears the court will bind you but anything that binds is ugly. Unity is one thing, to be tied together is another.

One night, Mulla Nasruddin and his wife were sitting by the fireside. It was a cold night. Mulla was reading his newspaper and his wife was doing some knitting. And the dog and the cat of the family were also resting by the fireside, dreaming, enjoying.

The wife suddenly said, "Nasruddin look at the dog and the cat and how peacefully they live together. Why can't we do that?"

Nasruddin said, "Why can't we do that? Tie them together and see what happens."

Once two persons are tied together freedom is lost and anger arises. When freedom is lost everything becomes ugly. Love means that freedom remains intact: marriage means that freedom has been dropped. You have bargained for permanence, for security, and you have paid for it with freedom.

Marriage is going to disappear, should disappear. And now the point is coming in the history of humanity where it becomes possible that marriage can disappear. It is already an outmoded phenomenon, it has lived too long and it has created nothing but misery. Marriage should disappear and love should flower again. One should live with insecurity and freedom. That I call intelligence.

To seek for marriage is to be dull; to seek for love is to be intelligent. Anything that gives you a false sense of security makes you dull, makes you less alert; anything that keeps the insecurity as it is – and life is insecure, love is insecure, everything is insecure – makes you remain alert. Because then you have to be alert every moment, you cannot depend on anything, you cannot go to sleep, you have to keep aware. Then life will have a deeper significance and life will become more natural – that is the meaning of living the life of Tao. Living life in insecurity is to live the life of Tao.

I am not against marriage, I am against the ugly institution that has evolved in the name of marriage. If marriage allows freedom and love to exist together, it is good but then marriage is totally different. Always be aware: never lose your freedom and never dominate anybody so that he or she loses his or her freedom. Freedom is the goal and freedom should be the very foundation of life. Love is beautiful when it flowers in freedom; when it flowers in a hothouse, closed from everywhere, it is simply a phony thing. It is not true and it cannot satisfy you. To be real the flower needs the storm, the lightning, the thundering, the clouds, the sun, the wind – it needs all these challenges to be real. When you protect it too much, in that very protection it loses all reality, it becomes pale, it becomes anemic; it is already dead before its death.

I am not saying that through love your life will become more secure – no, I am not saying that. Through love your life will become more insecure. But I am all for insecurity because through insecurity is growth. When you are secure you are in your grave.

Enough for today.

CHAPTER #3

The Secret Taste of Honey on the Tongue

In the middle age Hua-tzu of Yang-li in Sung lost his memory. He would receive a present in the morning and forget it by the evening; give a present in the evening and forget it by the morning. In the street he would forget to walk; at home he would forget to sit down. Today he would not remember yesterday; tomorrow he would not remember today.
His family were troubled about it and invited a diviner to tell his fortune but without success. They invited a shaman to perform an auspicious rite but it made no difference. They invited a doctor to treat him but it did no good.

There was a Confucian of Lu who, acting as his own go-between, claimed that he could cure it. Hua-tzu's wife and children offered half of their property in return for his skill. The Confucian told them: "This is clearly not a disease which can be divined by hexagrams and omens, or charmed away by auspicious prayers, or treated by medicines and the needle. I shall try reforming his mind changing his thoughts there is a good chance that he will recover."
Then the Confucian tried stripping Hua-tzu and he looked for his clothes; tried starving him and he looked for food; tried shutting him up in the dark and he looked for light.

The Confucian was delighted and told the man's sons: the sickness is curable but my arts have been passed down secretly through the generations and are not disclosed to outsiders – so I shall shut out his attendants and stay alone with him in his room for seven days." They agreed and no one knew what methods the Confucian used but the sickness of many years was completely dispelled in a single morning.

When Hua-tzu woke up he was very angry. He dismissed his wife, punished his sons, and chased away the Confucian with a spear.
The authorities of Sung arrested him and wanted to know the reason. "Formerly when I forgot," said Hua-tzu, "I was boundless, I did not notice whether heaven and earth existed or not. Now suddenly I remember, and all the disasters and recoveries, gains and losses, joys and sorrows, loves and hates of twenty, thirty years past rise up in a thousand tangled threads. I fear that all the disasters and recoveries, gains and losses, joys and sorrows, loves and hates still to come will confound my heart just as much. Shall I never again find a moment of forgetfulness?'

This is one of the greatest parables of Lieh Tzu, pregnant with profound significance and insight. It is based on a great experience of the inner world of consciousness. It is paradoxical but it indicates something absolute.

Let us go into it very softly, delicately, carefully. It has much to give to you, it has much to show to you. It can give a great clarity to you on your path. But before we enter into it a few paradigms of Taoism will be helpful.

First, Taoism believes that the memory is the problem. Because of the memory we are not really alive. The memory holds us back in the past, it never allows us to be in the present. It is a dead weight. And it goes on growing every day. Every day the past becomes bigger and bigger and bigger. Every day more and more experiences, more and more memories, become accumulated. And they hold you back.

The child is free. He has no past. The old man is not free. He has a long past. The child has nothing to look back to, he has everything to look forward to – he has the future just opening up for him, a great adventure. The old man has nothing in the future. Everything has happened. And all that has happened goes on cluttering his mind. It is a weight that pulls him down backwards, it does not allow him to move with the times. He lags behind.

Memory is what roots you in the past. Unless you become so free of memory that you need not look back – memory no longer disturbs you, memory no longer clouds you – you will not be able to live in the present. And if you cannot live in the present the future is not yours – because the future is contacted only through living in the present, the future becomes a reality only through living in the present. The present is the door by which the future enters in and the past goes out. If you are looking at the past you will miss the future, because during the time you are looking at the past, the future is entering into the present and you cannot look both ways simultaneously. You have eyes to look forward, you don't have eyes at the back of your head. Nature never intended you to look back otherwise your eyes would have been at the back of your head. Nature has intended that you should be looking forwards, nature has not given you any instrument to look backwards.

So when you look back you have to turn back, and during the moment that you are looking back and your head is turned to the dead past, the future is turning into the present. You will miss that birth, you will always miss the future turning into the present – and that is the only reality there is.

Now, what happens? If you are interested too much in the past, attached too much to your memories, you start creating an unreal future too – in the imagination. A man who is too attached to the past projects a future also. He lives in the memory and through the memory he creates an imagined future. Both are unreal. The past is no more, you cannot live it again, there is no possibility. That which is gone is gone forever, it is impossible to bring it back. Because it is impossible to bring it back you start imagining a similar type of future, something similar –

a little more decorated, a little more sweet, a little better. You start imagining a future but that future is based on your past experience. On what else can it be based?

You loved a woman. Almost everything was good in the woman except for a few things. Now you project a dream: in the future you will find a woman who will be as good as the past woman but with those wrong habits deleted, with those wrong habits dropped. In the future you will have a house as beautiful as in the past, more beautiful – but you will manage to have a few things which were not there in the past.

Your imagination is nothing but a modified past. This is how people are living. The past is no more and the future is nothing but a desire to repeat the past – of course, in a better way, but it is the same past. You ate something yesterday, you would like to eat it again tomorrow. Yesterday you loved a man or a woman, tomorrow you would again like to love a man or a woman. You want to repeat.

The mind is a repetitive mechanism; the mind continuously hankers for the same. And every moment the reality is new; it is never the same. You cannot step in the same river twice. Life is constantly moving, changing. Only change is permanent, everything else is changing. Only change is not changing. That is reality.

But then you create a false, a pseudo-reality of your own invention – fabricated in the mind, manufactured by your desire – and you start living in it.

Taoism says that to be in reality a man has to get out of his mind, a man has to become a no-mind. To be in reality a man has to uproot himself from the past, he has to forget the past. To remember that which is, the eyes have to be completely unclouded from the past – only then can you see in the reality. Eyes that are clouded with the past are eyes that are blind. You are not really blind, you are just clouded by the past. You cannot see directly because of so many screens covering your eyes. Those screens have been created by the past.

A man insulted you yesterday and today you come across him

on the road. The past arises. A screen falls over your eyes. This is the same man who insulted you. You have to take revenge. You have to pay him back in the same coin – tit-for-tat. You start getting angry, you get into a rage. Now you are missing this man. It is possible that this man is no longer the same man; in fact, he cannot be the same man. He may have repented, he may have brooded the whole night, he may have decided to come to you and apologize, he may be coming to apologize now. But you cannot see. Your eyes are clouded with anger and your anger colors the reality. Even if he tries to apologize you will think that he must be trying to deceive you, or he has become afraid of your vengeance, or he is a cunning man – beware, he is trying to cheat you, to deceive you. Right now he is trying to befriend you but some day he will again bring trouble to you.

All these thoughts will be there and you will not be able to see what he is, you will miss the reality. And seeing all these clouds on your face, there is every possibility that, though he had come to apologize, he may now not apologize. Seeing that you are in a rage and you will not understand, he may change his own ideas. We affect each other. And then, if he changes his mind, your ideas are confirmed, they become even stronger. This is how things are happening.

A man who has clarity never carries the past. He simply looks into reality with no interference from the past. That is the meaning of this story. Dropping the memory means dropping the mind. Dropping the mind means dropping the whole world. Dropping the mind means dropping the ego – then you are no longer self-centered, then you don't have any mind whatsoever. Then you live a life with no mind of your own – that is the meaning of Tao. Then God's mind functions through you, you don't have your own mind. You function but now you don't function from your own center. Now the center of the whole becomes your center. You act but you are not the doer any more, God acts. Your surrender is total.

Just the other day I was reading a beautiful Hassidic parable.

A young man asked an old rabbi, "In the past, in the old, golden days, we have heard that people used to see God with their own eyes, people used to encounter God. God used to walk on earth, God used to call people by their name. God was very close. What has happened now? Why is God not so close? Why can we not see him directly? Why is he hiding? Where has he gone? Why has he forgotten the earth? Why does he not walk any more on the earth? Why does he not hold the hands of people stumbling in darkness? He used to do that before."

The old rabbi looked at the disciple and said, "My son, he is still there where he used to be, but man has forgotten how to stoop down low enough to see him."

To stoop down.... Man has forgotten how to stoop, man is standing very haughtily, man is standing very proudly, man is standing very erect, man is standing separate from God, man has become an island, man is no longer part of the universal, part of the whole. God is exactly where he used to be – he is still trying to hold your hand but you are not willing. He is still confronting you but you look sideways. He is still there, calling you by your own name, but you are full of your own noise, the inner talk, the continuous chattering – you have become a chatterbox.

Man has forgotten to stoop, to bow down.

In the East, bowing down has been always a very significant gesture. The disciple goes to the master, bows down, lies down flat on the earth. That is a gesture of surrender. He says, "I am no more." He says, "I will not exist any more as myself. Now I will be a vehicle, I will be passive. You pour and I will be a womb, you pour and I will be a receptacle. I will not fight. I surrender." In that surrender something of tremendous value happens.

With the master you start learning the ABC of surrender – then one day, when you have learned what surrender is, you try it with God. The master is just a kindergarten, just a beginning, the beginning of surrender. When you have learned the joy of it, the beauty of it, the benediction of it, then you want to go on to deeper seas. You have learned swimming near the banks, now you would like to go to the farthest point. Then God is available. But if you exist as you, if you exist as a self, then it is impossible. Then you exist as an ego.

This ego is what this parable means by memory. These Taoist parables are very subtle.

Now let us go into it.

In the middle age, Hua tzu of Yang-li in Sung lost his memory.

That is a way of saying that he became a meditator.

That is a Taoist expression – lost his memory. It means: became a non-individual. It means: became a non-ego. It means: became loose from the grip of the mind, dropped the weight of the past. It is not something condemning, remember, it is a great appreciation.

In Taoist circles, when somebody says "He has lost his memory" he is praising the man, remember. Taoists have their own way of saying things, very peculiar ways of saying things. But the meaning of their gestures is profound.

In the middle age, Hua tzu of Yang-li in Sung lost his memory.

He became a no-mind, he forgot all about his past, he forgot all that had happened – it was as if all the dust from the mirror dropped away. He came to exist in the present – that's what it means. He was no longer in the past, he did not exist through the past, he did not function through the past, he had started functioning in the immediate present. Moment to moment he now lived – not gathering, not accumulating, not hoarding any knowledge or any information. Whatsoever the totality brought in the moment was all. If he felt hungry he looked for food, but he had no idea about any food that he had eaten before. And the moment his appetite was fulfilled he forgot all about it. He did not carry the idea in the mind, he had no fantasy about food, either before or after. The moment was all, the now and the here was all, there was no then and there was no there.

This is the first satori – when a man becomes loosened from the grip of the past, the hold of the past, as if a snake has slipped from the old skin. He has become absolutely new, like a tree which, after dropping all her old leaves during the fall, has sprouted new leaves. The moment something becomes old, one moment old, it is dropped immediately. One goes on slipping again and again into the present. It is a totally new style of life – the way of Tao, the way of Zen, the way of sannyas.

Watch it in your own life. How do you live? Do you bring the past in again and again? So you always live through the past? Is your life too colored by memory? Then you are living the worldly life. To live in memory is to live in the world, *sansara*; to live without memory, is to live in God, to live without memory is to live in nirvana, enlightenment.

Remember, by saying that Hua Tzu lost his memory, you should not translate it to mean that he became absent-minded, no. That is not the meaning of it. To become absent-minded is a totally a different thing. It is a disease, Absent-mindedness means that memory persists but becomes distorted. You know but you don't know clearly. An absent-minded person is not a man of Tao. An absent-minded person is simply absent-minded. The man of Tao is very much present, he is not absent-minded. In fact, he is *so* much present that the memory cannot interfere. His presence is tremendous; his presence is so intense, the light of presence is so intense, that the memory cannot interfere. He functions out of the present, you function out of memory.

So when somebody becomes absent-minded he looks as if he is ill – naturally – because he goes on forgetting. But it is not that he has really forgotten, he remembers that he has forgotten – the difference has to be understood. He remembers that he has forgotten; he knows that he knows and yet he cannot remember it. That is the man who is absent-minded.

I have heard many stories about Thomas Alva Edison. He was a man who could be called perfectly absent-minded.

One day he went into a restaurant, ate his lunch, came out and met a friend at the door, just on the street. They talked for a few minutes and then the friend said, "Why don't you come with me and have your lunch?" So he said, "Right. You made me remember. I came for my lunch."

Then they went inside the same restaurant again. The food was served. The friend said to Edison, "You look a little puzzled." And Edison said, "Yes. What's the matter? I don't feel any appetite at all." And the waiter laughed and he said, "Sir, you ate your lunch here just five minutes ago."

This is absent-mindedness.

Once it happened that he forgot his own name. He was standing in a queue and when his turn came and his name was called he started looking here and there, looking for the man whose name had been called. And then somebody who was standing behind him said to him, "Sir, as far as I know, you are Edison. So for whom are you looking?" And Edison said, "Thank you. In fact, I had completely forgotten."

This is absent-mindedness. Edison is not a man of satori; he still lives in the memory but his memory is a chaos. He cannot figure out what is what. He is not a buddha, he is not a Hua Tzu. He does not live in the moment, he still lives in the past. Of course, his past is very clumsy. Absent-mindedness is a clumsy past, a clumsy memory, a lousy memory.

But a man who has lost his memory in the sense that Taoists use this term is a man who functions out of the presence of his mind – presence of mind.

Just a few days ago I was reading the memoirs of a very rare man. He was a saint who died a few years ago. He lived for a really long time – almost one hundred and forty years. His name was Shivapuri Baba, Shivapuri Baba of Nepal. In his memoirs he tells a story.

When he went to Jaipur a very rich man gave him a box full of notes, hundred-rupee notes. While in the train he looked into the box; it was full of notes and he wanted to know how many notes he had. So he started counting. In the compartment there were only two persons, Shivapuri Baba, a very old ancient man, at the time he must have been about one hundred and twenty years old – and an English lady, a young woman. She became interested. This old beggar was in the first class and was carrying a whole box of one-hundred-rupee notes?

An idea came in her mind. She jumped up and said, "You give me half the money otherwise I will pull the chain and I will tell them that you tried to rape me." Shivapuri Baba laughed and put his hands to his ears as if he were deaf. And he gave her some paper and said, "Write it down. I cannot hear." So she wrote it down. He took it and put it in his pocket and said, "Now pull the chain."

This is presence of mind! It is not functioning out of the past because this has never happened before and it may not happen again. But, in a flash, like lightning, a man who is really present will act out of his presence.

You would have been in trouble because you would have looked into your memory – what to do now? You would have started groping in your memory – is there something in the past from which you can have some idea of what to do now?

But in real life nothing is ever repeated. Everything is new. That's why your responses always fall short. You act out of the past and the thing is absolutely new, it has never happened before, you don't have any experience of it. Your experience may be of something similar but it cannot be about exactly the same thing. It is not a repetition, the situation never repeats. Maybe it was something similar – you were cheated by somebody, something similar. You were deceived by somebody, something similar. You were threatened by somebody, something similar. But it was not exactly the same. So when you start looking into your memory you are showing that you don't have presence of mind.

This is a paradox: a man of no-mind is a man with presence of mind; and a man of mind, a man with memory, is a man who is absent. He looks into the past. The situation is herenow, confronting you; it is an encounter. Respond right now, like a mirror. A mirror reflects whosoever comes in front of it. It does not look into the memory: this man has been here before, in front of me, so how to reflect him? It simply reflects. When there is no memory it is not absent-mindedness, the mirror is simply clear, the dust is not there, the dust is not a distraction. The reflection will be clear and out of that reflection will come the act. When you act out of the present moment your act is always total. You will never feel frustrated.

Two Englishmen were in London.

"I say, Derrick !" called Quincy. "How are you, old chap?"

"Fine. Just fine," said Derrick. "Lots doing. Business grand, children fine, weather pleasant and all that sort of balderdash."

"Jolly good. Anything else?"

"Let me see – oh yes – buried my wife."

"Really?"

"Had to. Dead, you know."

Now this man is an absent-minded man. It is not that he has lost his memory, he has a lousy memory. Remember the distinctions. Sometimes they may look the same, but they are not.

This story of Hua Tzu is about a man who lost his memory, who lost his mind, who lost his past, who became unburdened.

To say it in Christ's words – who became a child again, capable of entering into the kingdom of God.

But to his family, to his friends, he must have posed a great problem. Naturally. They must have wondered what had happened to this old man. A calamity. They must have thought he had fallen into a deep sleep, a sort of sleep. But exactly the contrary was the case – they were asleep and this man had awakened out of sleep. But they could understand only the language of sleep so they must have thought that this man had fallen asleep.

A big-city sharpie made a wrong turn and found himself helplessly lost in the sticks of Kentucky. After bouncing along a rocky country road for more than an hour, he reached a large intersection. There, standing on the side of the road, was an odd-looking hillbilly.

"Hey, fellow!" he shouted. "Could you tell me where the road on the right leads to?"

"I don't rightly know," the country boy answered slowly.

"Well, then, I wonder if you can tell me where the road on the left would take me?"

But again the boy shook his head. "I don't rightly know that either."

A little perturbed, the city fellow barked, "You're not too bright, are you?"

"Maybe not," drawled the hillbilly, "but I ain't lost."

The others must have thought that this old man, Hua Tzu, was lost. He had changed so diametrically, he had changed so tremendously, that the whole village – the relations, the friends, the family, the sons, the daughters, the wife – must have become very worried. What to do with this man?

> He would receive a present in the morning and forget it by the evening...

He had really become a child again. That is the quality of innocence.

> ...give a present in the evening and forget it by the morning. In the street he would forget to walk; at home he would forget to sit down. Today he would not remember yesterday; tomorrow he would not remember today.

This is not absent-mindedness. He is simply not gathering the past any more. It is not that he has a lousy memory, he is cut away from memory utterly. He is like a child.

You are angry with a child and the child is angry with you. Look at his face! He is so angry and so red that he would like to kill you. He says, "Never again will I talk to you. Finished!" And the next moment he is sitting in your lap again and talking beautifully. He has forgotten. Whatsoever he has said in a rage, he has not carried it. It has not become luggage in his mind. Yes, in the spur of the moment he was angry, he said something, but now the anger is gone and all that he had said that moment has gone. He has not become committed to it forever, it was a momentary flare-up, a ripple. But he is not frozen in it, he is a flowing phenomenon. The ripple was there, a wave had arisen, now it is no more. He is not going to carry it always and always. Even if you make him remember, he will laugh. He will say, "All nonsense!" He will say, "I don't remember. Is it so?" He will say, "Have I really said that? Impossible!" He will say, "How I can say that? You must have imagined it."

It was a flare-up. This has to be understood. A man who lives moment to moment is sometimes angry, sometimes happy, sometimes sad. But you can depend on it – he will not carry these things forever. A man who is very controlled and does not allow any emotion to arise in his being is very dangerous. If you insult him, he is not angry. He holds it. By and by he will accumulate so much anger that he is going to do something really nasty.

There is nothing wrong in a momentary flare of anger – it is beautiful in a way. It simply shows that the man is still alive. A momentary flare-up simply shows that the man is not dead, that he responds to situations – and responds authentically. When he feels that the situation is such that anger is needed, anger is there. When he feels that the situation is such that happiness is needed, happiness is there. He moves with the situation. He has no prejudice for or against. He has no ideology as such. He does not have a certain idea that you should not be angry, that whatsoever the situation you should remain non-angry.

If a man tries to be non-angry in that way, what will he do? He will repress his anger. And sometimes that anger will arise in situations where it will look almost mad, out of all proportion. He will be capable of murdering somebody or committing suicide or doing something really harmful – because when so much anger is released it is very poisonous, very destructive.

Ordinary anger has nothing wrong in it. In fact, a person who can become angry and forget all about it the next moment is really a very good person. You will always find him friendly, alive, loving, compassionate. A man who is always holding onto his emotions, controlling and controlling and controlling, a man of so-called discipline, is never a good person. He will always show that he is holier than you, but you can see his anger in his eyes, you can see it in his face, you can see it in his every gesture – the way he walks, the way he talks, the way he relates with people – you can see it always there, boiling. He is ready to burst every moment. These are the murderers, these are the criminals, these are the real evil-doers.

And if he goes on controlling, all his control will make his ego more and more strong. And the ego is far more dangerous than anger. Anger is human, nothing wrong about it. It is simple It is simply a situation in which you are provoked, and you are alive so you respond to it. It is saying that you will not yield; it is saying that this is not a situation you can accept; it is saying that this is a situation in which you want to say no. It is a protest, and nothing is wrong about it.

I am not against anger, I am against accumulated anger. I am not against sex, I am against accumulated sexuality. Anything that is in the moment is good, anything that is carried from the past is bad, is diseased, is illness.

This man became like a child.

> Today he would not remember yesterday, tomorrow he would not remember today.

Jesus says to his disciples, "Think not of the morrow. Look at the lilies in the field, how beautiful they are. They don't think of the past, they don't think of the future. They are not worried at all about what is going to happen and what has happened. They simply live here and now, that is their beauty." That is the beauty of the trees and the rocks and the stars and the rivers. The whole existence is beautiful because it has no past.

Man is ugly. The past makes him ugly. Apart from man nothing is ugly, because it is only man who goes on brooding about the past and the future and goes on missing the life that is available in the present. That is the only life there is, the only dance there is. Naturally you become ugly – because you have no opportunity to live, to live authentically.

I have heard a beautiful anecdote.

The man was talking with his friend, the tailor, about hunting trips.

"Once," said the tailor, "I was in Africa hunting lions. I discovered one standing ten feet away – and there I was without my gun. The lion came closer. Now he was only five feet away."

"What happened?" the man asked breathlessly.

"Well, to make a long story short, he leaped up and killed me."

"What do you mean he killed you?" the man asked. "You're sitting here, very much alive."

"Ha!" said the tailor. "You call this living?"

Even people who look alive are not really alive. They have been killed and not once, many times. Killed by the past, the lion of the past; killed by the future, the lion of the future. And they are being killed every day, they are being murdered every day by these two enemies.

There is a beautiful Buddhist parable of many meanings. All the meanings are beautiful, but today try to understand it in one certain meaning.

In a forest a man is running, trying to escape from a lion who is following him, chasing him. The man comes to a precipice. There is no other way to go so he stops. For a single moment he doesn't know what to do. He looks down. It is a very deep valley, a great abyss. If he jumps he is gone. But still there is a possibility for him – miracles happen. So he looks down more closely and there, deep in the valley, two more lions are standing, looking up. So that possibility is finished.

The lion is coming closer, roaring; the man can hear the roar. His only possibility is to hang from the roots of a tree sticking out over the valley. He cannot jump and he cannot stand on the precipice so he holds onto the roots of the tree. The roots are very fragile and he is afraid that at any moment they will break. Not only that, it is a very cold evening, night is gathering, and the sun is going down. And his hands are so cold that he is afraid he will not be able to hold on for long. Already the roots are slipping out of his hands. They are frozen. Death is certain. Each moment death is there.

Then he looks up. Two mice are chewing through the roots of the tree. One is white and one is black the symbol of day and night, the symbol of time. Time is running out fast and the two mice are chewing through the roots and they are really doing a great job. They are almost at the end, they are just going to finish – it is evening and they have also to go and rest so they are finishing in a hurry. Any moment the root will break away from the tree.

The man looks up again and there on the tree is a beehive out of which honey is dropping. He forgets all and tries to catch a drop on his tongue and he succeeds. And the taste is really sweet.

Now this parable has many meanings. I have talked about this parable in different ways. This time I would like to indicate a certain meaning: this moment. In the past a lion is coming, in the future two lions are waiting; time is running out fast, death is very close by as it is always; the two mice are cutting away the very roots of life but, if you can live in the present, the taste is tremendously sweet. It is really beautiful.

The man lived in the moment and forgot all. For the moment there was no death, no lions, no time, nothing existed – only the secret taste of honey on his tongue.

This is the way to live, this is the only way to live – otherwise you will not be living. Each moment…this is the situation. The parable is really very existential. You are the man clinging to the root of the tree, surrounded everywhere by death, with time running out. Any moment you will drop into death and disappear. Now what to do? Worry about the past? Worry about the future? Worry about death? Worry about time? Or enjoy this moment?

To think not of the morrow means to let this moment become a drop of sweet honey on your tongue. Even though death is, life is beautiful. Even though the past was not very good and who knows about the future – it may not be very good, as things are it is hopeless to hope but this moment is beautiful. Look at this moment. Let it become a drop of honey on your tongue. This moment is tremendously beautiful. What is missing? What is lacking?

Be in this moment – that is the meaning of the Taoist expression: Hua Tzu lost his memory.

> His family were troubled about it and invited a diviner to tell his fortune, but without success. They invited a shaman to perform an auspicious rite, but it made no difference. They invited a doctor to treat him, but it did no good.

Now that is beautiful – and meaningful. It was not a disease so no doctor could cure it. Had it been a disease then the doctor could have cured it. It was not anything physical. The man was perfectly healthy.

In fact, he could never have been as healthy as he must have been at that time. When you forget about your past you forget about all your ilinesses also. The past is a reservoir of all illnesses. When you forget the past you are neither young nor old, you simply are. And that is the moment of being healthy and whole.

The man must have been very healthy so what could doctors do? The family called the doctors but they could not treat him. It was not a disease. A disease could have been treated, but this was not a disease.

And the family asked a diviner to tell his fortune but without success because a man who has no memory has no imagination for the future. And a man who has no imagination for the future is unpredictable. You cannot predict anything about him. He is just open. Ordinarily men are predictable because they have a certain projection into the future some idea about the future, a seed for the future. That seed will one day sprout.

That's how the diviners, the palmists, the fortune-tellers live they live on your imagination. If you go to a fortune-teller he will look at your hand and he will say, "There is a great possibility that money will come – but it will not stay." It can be said about anybody except a man like me. You cannot say that about me! But it can be said about anybody – money will come. Everybody is hoping for it so who is going to deny that it will come? That's why he has come to the fortune-teller – for his ideas to be approved, to be confirmed. Money will come, but he will not be able to keep it. Who has ever been able to keep money? Money comes and goes.

In fact, money exists only in its coming and going. If you are able to keep it, it is no longer money. You can keep a thousand notes in your house, you can hoard it underground, but it is no longer money. You could have kept stones there, it would have been just the same. Money exists only in its coming and going. When somebody gives you a hundred-rupee note, when the note changes hands, then it is money. Just for a moment it is money – when it changes hands. Then that man is getting something out of it and you are getting something out of it. When you give it to somebody else, again it will be money. That's why notes are called currency. Currency means movement. They should move. The more they move, the more there is money.

That's why there is more money in America and less in India. There is so much movement. Everybody is just spending – spending what they have and spending even that which they hope they will have one day. People are purchasing cars and fridges and everything on the installment basis. Some day they hope they will have the money and then they will pay. But they are purchasing things right now. There is money in America because people have come to know that money exists in its movement. Let the money change hands. And the more it changes hands, the richer and richer and richer the country becomes.

Let a one hundred-rupee note circulate here. If we are five hundred people and a one hundred-rupee note changes hands, it becomes five hundred notes of one hundred-rupees. Each time it comes to one person he will have one hundred rupees. But let one person keep the note and then this group will be poor. Then only one person has a hundred-rupee note. If it had changed hands and moved, then everybody would have enjoyed a hundred rupees. Of course, there would have been much wealth.

Predictions are possible only about people who have an idea about the future.

There is a story about Buddha. When he became enlightened he was going along the bank of a river and an astrologer passed who was coming from Benares. He had become a great scholar of astrology and was coming home with all the degrees and diplomas that were available in those days. And suddenly he saw the footprints of Buddha on the sand. He could not believe his eyes because in his books it was said such a footprint belonged to a man who had conquered the whole world, a *chakravatin* one who is the emperor of the whole world, all the six continents. But why should an emperor of all the six continents come on a hot afternoon to walk by this poor river? And walk on the hot sand without shoes? Impossible!

He became very puzzled. He was just fresh from Benares and it seemed that this first encounter was undoing all his learning. Is his science wrong? What has happened? Why should the emperor come here?

So he followed the footprints. Buddha was sitting under a tree. Looking at the Buddha he became even more puzzled. A beggar! And the puzzlement became greater still because he looked like an emperor – his face, his grace, his peace. He had seen emperors; in fact, nobody had looked more emperor-like than this man. But his clothes, and the way he was sitting under the tree, and not even a servant around…?

He went to Buddha and he said, "Sir, this is a very decisive thing for me. Allow me to disturb you. Please tell me just one single thing because my whole life will depend on it. I am coming from Benares carrying all these books. I have spent twenty years studying astrology, and here you are sitting and disturbing all my knowledge. So either you tell me that astrology is useless then I can throw these books into the river and go back home and forget all about it or tell me what has happened. These footprints are the footprints of a *chakravatin*, an emperor who rules the whole world, the greatest emperor, one who is the ruler of all six continents. All the indications are there. But what are you doing here?"

Buddha laughed and said, "You need not throw away your books, you can take them home. You will not come across a man like me again very easily. Don't be disturbed. The people that you will meet, you will be able to predict. But it is true, about me you cannot predict anything – because I have gone beyond mind. All predictions are about the mind. People who live in the mind are predictable."

This is significant. People who live in the mind are predictable because they are mechanical. You can say what they will do tomorrow because they will repeat. Nothing new is going to happen. They will simply repeat their past. But a man who has gone beyond mind is unpredictable because he will never repeat anything. So you cannot use any clue from his past to predict.

The diviners failed. They could not say anything about this man. And the shaman was called but he also could not do anything. The shaman can only do one thing: he can pray. He can do certain rituals to help. But a man who has gone beyond mind needs no prayer; no prayer will be of any help to him. In fact, prayer means asking God to do something for you. A man who has gone beyond mind has become part of God – there is nobody to pray and nobody to be prayed to. Who is there to ask? Only God is.

No, these auspicious rites and rituals were of no help so nobody could help.

There was a Confucian of Lu who, acting as his own go-between, claimed that he could cure it. Hua tzu's wife and children offered half of their property in return for his skill.

Confucians are the first Behaviorists of the world. Pavlov and B. F. Skinner are their disciples. Confucius says that a man's behavior can be changed, manipulated, through punishment and reward. That is the technique that has been used down the ages by the moralists. You reward the child if he follows your idea, you punish the child if he goes against you. Through punishment and reward you by and by condition his mind.

All minds are conditioned – and what Maoists are doing in China today is very ancient in China. Confucius taught it very well. The idea has to be understood. The idea is that a man can be manipulated if you torture him or if you reward him. Through greed and fear a man can be manipulated. That's what you have been doing to your children, that's what has been done to you by your parents and by your society.

What are you doing to criminals in your prisons? Torturing them. Trying to condition their mind. Why does the priest go on talking about hell and heaven? What is the idea of hell and heaven? It is just the simple idea of punishment and reward. If you follow the priest you will be rewarded in heaven; if you don't follow the priest you will be punished in hell. And they have painted hell in such colors that every body will become afraid, everybody will start trembling. Then one starts holding on to oneself, repressing oneself.

The Confucian said he could cure him. Now, firstly, the man was not ill so to say that he could be cured is stupid. But the same stupidity continues, even now. There are many people in Western countries who are not mad but who are being cured by psychologists. They are not really mad; in fact, they have gone a little higher than ordinary man. They are what Sufis call *mastas* those who have become drunk with God. But they are being treated. And what is their treatment? Electro-shocks, beating, torturing, in a thousand and one ways. Electro-shock treatment is a torture. the latest invention to torture man. These people are put into asylums and forced to live a very routine life.

Many of them are farther ahead than ordinary humanity, many of them have achieved a better consciousness. But naturally they have become separated from the ordinary humanity.

And the normal seems to be the rule, the normal seems to be the healthy person. The normal is not the norm, remember, the normal simply means the crowd, the mob, the mass. The mass is not healthy and the mass is not in any way sane; in fact, no individual behavior is as insane as the behavior of a mass. Masses are more insane. No Hindu is as insane as the Hindu society. No Moslem is as insane as the Moslem society. The Moslem mob can go and burn a temple and kill Hindus, but ask each individual of that crowd and you will not find any individual who is so insane. Every individual will say that somehow it happened. He was just there and he somehow joined in with the crowd. Ask each individual and you will be told that it was not good. The crowd did it. The crowd has always been the insane. The wars, the conflicts between religions and nations – these are all just because of crowd minds.

The crowd mind is insane, but the psychologists and the psychiatrists and the psychoanalysts try to adjust the person if he goes a little beyond. If Freud had been available Hua Tzu would have been psychoanalyzed. If Skinner had been there he would have been reconditioned. That's what this Confucian said.

> The Confucian told them, "This is clearly not a disease which can be divined by hexagrams and omens, or charmed away by auspicious prayers, or treated by medicine and the needle. I shall try reforming his mind, changing his thoughts. There is a good chance that he will recover."

He said that he would recondition, reform, his mind. How do you recondition a mind? You start torturing the body. When the body is tortured, the consciousness that was flying beyond has to come down to look after the body, naturally. You exist in the body, the body is your vehicle. If your body is harmed you naturally cannot fly very high, you have to come back to protect the body. That's the way to recondition. And that's what he did.

> Then the Confucian tried stripping Hua tzu...

If it was winter and he stripped Hua Tzu naked, naturally, when he started shivering, the mind would suddenly come back: "You are shivering, Hua Tzu. Find your clothes." And he would start looking for his clothes.

> ...and he looked for his clothes, tried starving him, and he looked for food, tried shutting him up in the dark, and he looked for light.

His consciousness was flowing higher than the mind. If you torture the body, the consciousness has to come back to the body. Have you observed it? If a small thorn enters your foot your consciousness will go there. A small thorn, but the consciousness has to go there, it is a safety measure. Otherwise the thorn will become poisonous, will become septic. It is part of your life-survival mechanism that the consciousness has to go there and look after it and see that the thorn is taken out. When the thorn is there you forget everything else.

Have you not watched it? If your teeth hurt you forget everything else. Then your whole consciousness gathers around your teeth. That pain has to be tackled first. If you have a headache then everything else is forgotten. Somebody may be playing beautiful music but if you have a headache you cannot hear. Somebody may be dancing but you cannot look at it. There may be beauty all around but how can you look at the beauty? You are not free. Your headache is pulling you down into the body.

This is what the Confucian follower did. He starved the man, stripped him naked, put him in the dark – naturally he started looking for light, looking for warmth, for clothes, for food.

> The Confucian was delighted and told the man's sons: "The sickness is curable, but my arts have been passed down through

> generations and are not disclosed to outsiders – so I shall shut out his attendants and stay alone with him in his room for seven days." They agreed….

The art is not much of a secret. The art is simply to threaten the man with death – either to beat him or to jump on his chest with a spear. So the man is threatened with death. In that moment he has to come back to his body. And when one comes to one's body the mind starts functioning again because mind is part of the body. Mind is a subtle mechanism of the body.

This man, Hua Tzu, had lost his contact with his mind but the mind was there – the mind is always there. Even when a person goes beyond mind the mind remains there, dormant, sleepy, in the body. If you are pulled back into the body, the mind is stirred again and starts functioning.

> They agreed, and no one knew what methods the Confucian used, but the sickness of many years was completely dispelled in a single morning. When Hua tzu woke up he was very angry.

In fact, he was awake all this time, but now he has fallen asleep. But to the Confucian mind, or to the ordinary mind of humanity, it seems as if he has woken up.

> When Hua tzu woke up he was very angry.

Naturally what is sleep to us was not sleep to him.

It used to happen in Ramakrishna's case. Singing the song of Kali, dancing before Kali, many times he would fall and become unconscious. He would be unconscious to us, but to himself he would be superbly conscious. From the outside it looked like he was in a coma. If you had asked psychoanalysts they would say this was hysteria, a hysterical fit.

If you go to a psychiatrist and ask about Ramakrishna he will prove that he was neurotic. They have done the same to Jesus so they will not leave Ramakrishna alone. Jesus is neurotic, they say. Ramakrishna would have been even more neurotic to them. For six days sometimes he would remain unconscious – unconscious to us. Let me remind you again and again: to himself he was superbly conscious. In fact, he was so conscious within himself that his whole consciousness was involved there, all consciousness was taken from the outside to the inside, it came to the center. That's why on the outside he was unconscious.

You are conscious on the outside because in the inside you are unconscious. In the deepest core of your being you are fast asleep and snoring, that's why you look so awake on the outside. Things change. When a man like Ramakrishna moves into his core he falls asleep on the outside, and in the inside he becomes awake. To us it seems he has forgotten all, to him it seems he has remembered all.

> When Hua tzu woke up he was very angry.

The same used to happen to Ramakrishna. People would try to bring him back. Naturally the disciples would become very much afraid – would he come back or not? And they would massage his feet with ghee and camphor and they would massage his head and his whole body and they would try to bring him back somehow. Sometimes the disciples would even do something which looks ugly and cruel. They would suffocate him by closing his nose – because when the body is suffocated and a great need for air arises, the consciousness has to come back.

Or sometimes they would burn very bitter things around him and the smoke would get into his nose and he would suffer terribly. And he would start moving, moaning, and then he would come back. And these were disciples, not enemies. But sometimes you can do harm even while thinking you are doing good.

When he came back he would start crying and the disciples would ask, "Why are you crying?" He would say, "What have you done? Why have you brought me back? I was so tremendously happy inside. I was in a totally different world. I was in the world of God. God was very much present. I was showered by bliss. Why have you brought me back? Let me go again."

> When Hua tzu woke up he was very angry.

Naturally. Obviously.

> He dismissed his wife, punished his sons, and chased away the Confucian with a spear.

Maybe that was the same spear that the Confucian had used to threaten him to death.

> The authorities of Sung arrested him and wanted to know the reason. "Formerly, when I forgot," said Hua tzu, "I was boundless; I did not notice whether heaven and earth existed or not. Now suddenly I remember, and all the disasters and recoveries, gains and losses, joys and sorrows, loves and hates of twenty or thirty years past rise up in a thousand tangled threads. I fear that all the disasters and recoveries, gains and losses, joys and sorrows, loves and hates still to come will confound my heart just as much. Shall I never again find a moment of forgetfulness?"

What you think is remembering is forgetfulness for a man who has arrived home. What to you looks like forgetfulness is really remembering for a man who has awakened to his soul. Remember this paradox.

The languages are different. You are asleep but you think this is a waking state, you think this is a state of awareness. You are mistaken. Therefore, when a person becomes really aware, it seems to you as if he has fallen asleep. You are too self-conscious, so when a person loses his self and really becomes conscious you think he has gone mad. It appears as if he is ill. He has become whole, he has become healthy.

Hua Tzu said, "I was boundless formerly, when I forgot. There was no boundary to me, there was no definition to me. I was all, I was whole, I was one with the universe, nothing separated me. I was in a tremendous unity – *unio mystica* there was oneness. And it was beautiful, it was a benediction.

> "Now suddenly I remember, and all the disasters and recoveries, gains and losses, joys and sorrows, loves and hates of twenty or thirty years past rise up in a thousand tangled threads."

Now I am back to madness. The whole past is again opening its doors. It is a nightmare."

Now he has tasted a few moments of forgetfulness, or self-remembering. Now he is in a state to compare, that's why he is angry. You cannot compare because you have not experienced anything beyond the past, beyond memory, beyond mind. You have never tasted anything, not a single drop of no-mind. That's why you cannot compare.

This will happen one day if you continue meditating. One day suddenly you will see that you have taken off from the mind. The airport of the mind is left far behind and you are soaring high in the sky. Then for the first time you will say, "How beautiful life is. How beautiful existence is." You will feel tremendously grateful. Then to come down back to the mind will feel as if you are coming back into the madhouse. The memory is a madhouse.

> Everything is rising "in a thousand tangled threads. I fear that all the disasters and recoveries, gains and losses, joys and sorrows, loves and hates still to come will confound my heart just as much."

This is past and now the future is coming and he will be burdened more and more because the past will grow every day.

> "Shall I never again find a moment of forgetfulness?"

In that forgetfulness you come home. In that forgetfulness you remember. In that forgetfulness you become for the first time aware. In that forgetfulness you are in the present, herenow. You enter eternity. That forgetfulness is the door to eternity.

Kabir has said, "When I was, God was not. Now I am not and God is." Kabir has said, "When I used to think, I used to miss. Now I have forgotten how to think and all is available. First I used to seek and there was only frustration and frustration, now I am no longer there to seek and he is there seeking for me. I have forgotten all, and in that very forgetfulness I have remembered."

To forget means to forget the world, to forget means to

forget the non-essential, to forget means to forget the dust and remember the mirror, remember consciousness.

The mind is continuously fabricating, imagining. The mind is a liar, it goes on Lying to you. The lie is that it gives you something which is not real, something which looks as if it is real but is not real.

Are you still not fed up with it? A man becomes religious when he is fed up with the mind.

Listen to this small anecdote.

"Why should I buy that mutt for twenty bucks?" the TV producer asked the agent.

"Because he is a talking dog," said the agent.

"Listen, I'm sick and tired of that talking-dog routine," said the producer. "Take the mutt and get lost."

Suddenly the dog jumped onto the producer's desk. "Please, sir, I know I don't look like the most attractive dog in the world, but it's not my fault. My present master never feeds me. He's a cheap, conniving, dishonest agent. He has made a fortune booking me into the largest theaters and concert halls in the world. I have entertained kings and noblemen, presidents and premiers. I assure you that if you buy me I'll make you half a million the very first year."

The producer was amazed at the dog's fluency, his power of speech, his intense projection.

"This dog talks like a Harvard graduate," he said. "Why do you want to sell him to me for twenty dollars? Have you gone mad?"

"Because," said the agent, I'm fed up with his constant lying."

The mind is a lying mechanism. It never allows you to see the truth. Either it is lying about the past or it is lying about the future. And remember, whatsoever you memorize about the past, it is not true, it is touched-up, it has been created again and again by the mind. Much is dropped, much is added and the mind goes on touching it up every day. You can never be certain with the mind – it is a lying mechanism.

When a person is really fed up with this mechanism then the turn, the conversion, the quantum leap, becomes possible.

This parable is about the mind – and how, because of the mind, we have forgotten God, we have forgotten Tao. This parable says that unless you get out of the mind you will never be able to know the truth. If you want to know the truth there is no other way than to get out of the mind. That's what meditation is all about – how to get out of the mind, how not to allow the mind to constantly interfere with reality.

This is a great parable. Ordinarily the so-called religions are nothing but moralities. They condition your mind. Tao is a process of unconditioning. Ordinary religions hypnotize your mind, Tao is a process of de-hypnosis. One simply peels the mind away, just as you peel an onion and you find layer upon layer, layer upon layer. Go on peeling, go on peeling…and a moment comes when nothing is left in your hand. That nothing is what Tao is. That nothing is all, what Buddha calls *shunya*, nothingness, emptiness.

That emptiness is the source of all. When you have once touched, lived, been in that emptiness, only then will you know how much you were missing. For the first time you will become aware that you were asleep for centuries, for lives together. Right now you are asleep.

Gurdjieff used to say to his disciples that they were somnambulists – moving, walking, talking in their sleep. The first thing is not morality but how to shock you into awareness. Gurdjieff's greatest disciple was P.D. Ouspensky. P.D. Ouspensky has dedicated his book *In Search of the Miraculous* to his master with these words: To Gurdjieff, to my master, who has disturbed my sleep forever.

Yes, the master is there to disturb your sleep. The sleep is nothing but the mind; mind is another name for your sleep. This is the distinction between the Confucian thought and the Lao-Tzuan thought. Confucius is an ordinary moralist, a puritan, one who believes in conditioning people, in disciplining people. Lao Tzu is a rebellious man who believes in taking people beyond all conditionings – unconditioning people. Only in freedom is God possible, only in utter freedom is truth possible.

Seek this utter freedom. Destroy conditionings. Destroy by and by all the layers that hold you down. Take off. The whole sky is yours – in fact, even the sky is not the limit.

Enough for today.

CHAPTER #4

Tao Tantra

The first question:

Osho,
You have talked much on love, relationships, union, etc. Is there a merging between the Tao and Tantra?

Tantra means technique – and Tao can have no relationship with any technique whatsoever. Tao is non-methodological, non-technical. Tao means spontaneity. How can spontaneity have a technique? You cannot practice it; if you practice it you miss it. There is no way to cultivate it; a cultivated spontaneity could be anything else but it could not be spontaneity.

Tao means let go. Wherever your energy moves, allow it to move. Don't swim – float with the river. Swimming is a technique – if you are just flowing with the river what technique is needed? Technique means that you have a direction, you want to reach somewhere. Technique means that you want to impose your will on reality, you want to be someone. somewhere, in some state; you have a desire, you have a projection.

Tao says you are already there, you are already that. There is nowhere to go and nothing else to be, so just relax and let things happen. And whatsoever happens is good – because there is no denial in Tao, no rejection, no repression. It is the greatest rebellious attitude possible. Never has man's intelligence risen higher than in Tao. But there is no way to it. You cannot be guided to it.

Buddha has talked about five ways to reach truth. The first he calls the way of *sheela*, the way of morality, character, virtue. The second he calls the way of knowledge. The third he calls the way of *dhyana*, meditation; the fourth he calls the way of devotion; and the fifth he calls *ashiksheya* – that which cannot be taught.

That fifth is Tao. It cannot be taught. It can be learned but it cannot be taught. And when I say that it can be learned, I mean that if you relax, if you allow life to happen to you, if you don't create a barrier, if you are ready to go wherever it leads, you will learn it. It is the most dangerous path because you will not be in control. Your mind cannot manipulate; your mind cannot prepare in any way. You will have to live moment to moment – as the trees live, as the stars live, as the mountains live. You will have to live in the same way, the same natural way. Tao is nature.

So the Indian Tantra cannot have any merger with Tao. The Indian Tantra is very scientific. It is the science of how to transform sexual energy into spiritual energy; how to create the dynamo that changes, transforms, transmutes energy; how to move from the lower to the higher; how to go from the earth to heaven. It is a way from sex to super-consciousness. It is very technological.

Tao has no technique – this is the first thing to be understood. But there is another thing of great importance – that is, Tao has its own Tantra. But it is not technique.

There is no meeting possible between the Indian Tantra and the Chinese Tao, no meeting is possible. They are far away, poles apart, and it is impossible to mix them. If somebody tries to mix them Tao will be destroyed, Tantra will not be destroyed. Always remember whenever you mix a higher standpoint with a lower, the higher is destroyed not the lower. It is always the higher that loses because the higher is delicate, the higher is very, very vulnerable, fragile, like a flower. If you crush a flower with a rock, the rock is not going to be destroyed. The rock may not even come to know that there has been a clash. But the flower will be gone – crushed, destroyed. Tao is the highest possibility and Tantra can destroy it. So remember not to mix them.

But Tao has its own Tantra because Tao is a total world view. It has everything that is possible. It is the whole. So there must be something in it for love, for sex there is.

What is Taoist Tantra? I have to use the word *Tantra* remember, but I am not using it in the Indian sense. What is Taoist Tantra? It is spontaneity in sexuality; it is spontaneity in love.

For example, if you read a Tantra manual, an Indian Tantra manual, there is great ritual in it. Every step is very clearly indicated. It is not easy to practice Indian Tantra – you will have to become adept at it. Don't fool around. Don't think that while you are making love to a woman you are practicing Tantra. Tantra is difficult. It is a long process. And it takes years to get trained in it.

The greatest training that is involved and the most difficult problem that arises is that Tantra allows a man to make love to a woman only when the man has lost all sexual attraction towards the woman. There is no sexual attraction at all. That is the whole process. The woman becomes almost a mother to you or a sister to you a goddess. She has to be worshipped. In Tantra ritual the woman has to be worshipped like a goddess. And for months together one has to practice that worship.

The woman sits naked in front of you on a throne and you worship and you bow down and you pray to her and you create the idea in the deepest core of consciousness that she is just a representative of all womanhood, motherhood. She is a goddess.

Day by day, slowly, slowly, you lose all sexual interest in her. You become auto-hypnotized with your own idea. The day you lose all sexual interest in her body and you can look through and though her and her body is no longer a thrill, her body is not even seen at all, she becomes luminous, she is just a presence only then does the master allow you to make love to her. Now love will have a totally different quality. There is no sex involved in it, no attraction involved in it, no physicality involved in it. It is absolutely spiritual – a meeting of two souls.

But it is a long process. Many rituals, many prayers, many *yantras*, many meditations are needed. After years of training you come to the point where the woman is no longer a woman to you, she has almost become a mother – "motherhoodness" has arisen. You have projected that motherhoodness on her. You see her breasts but they no longer provoke any sexuality in you, only the idea of a mother. You see her body and you start feeling that you are part of her body just as you were part of your mother. It is recreating the mother. And it is a long process. Tantra is very procedural, ritualistic, and a great experiment in hypnosis, auto-hypnosis.

And it is a great experiment in getting rid of the idea of sex. It is not sexual at all, as is commonly misunderstood. It is a totally different attitude not sexual at all. It is very prayerful. And when you make love to a woman after you have become an adept in Tantra and the master has allowed you.... It has to depend on the master's agreement, it does not depend on you. When the master sees in your eyes that all sex has disappeared, that your body has become almost asexual, he sees that now you are standing before the woman as a small child, unaware of sexuality – you are naked, she is naked but you are not at all interested in sexuality – when the master confirms it, when he gives you a signal, then you are allowed. It depends on the master. He has to watch, watch carefully. It takes months, sometimes years, to prepare for it.

Tao has its own Tantra. The first thing: Tao never divides into the lower and the higher, that is the beauty of it. The moment you divide reality into the lower and the higher you are getting schizophrenic. The moment you say something is sacred and something is profane you have divided. The moment you say something is material and something is spiritual you have divided, you have split reality. Reality is one. There is neither matter nor spirit. Reality is one. It expresses itself in many forms: on one level as matter, on another level as spiritual. The spiritual is not higher and the material is not lower – they stand on the same level. That is the Taoist attitude. Life is one. Existence is one. It is a tremendous oneness and there is no evaluation.

The first thing in Tao is to drop duality. Sex is not lower and samadhi is not higher. Samadhi and sex are both expressions of the same energy. There is nothing laudable about samadhi and there is nothing condemnable about sex. The Tao acceptance is total, absolute. There is nothing wrong about the body and there is nothing beautiful about the spirit – they are both beautiful. Devil and God are one in Tao, heaven and hell are one in Tao, good and bad are one in Tao – it is the greatest non-dual understanding. There is no condemnation and no preparation. To prepare for what? One has simply to relax and be.

If you can love a woman spontaneously.... In fact, Tao will say that Tantra has a wrong attitude, because you have to prepare. Preparation means that you are preparing for the future. Tao knows only one time – which is now; and only one place – which is here. Now is the only time and here is the only place. Here is heaven and now is nirvana. So don't prepare.

If in some moment love flows, love takes possession of you, go with it. Don't push the river. Don't try to give it any shape. Don't try to fix it into any ritual. Just go with it. In deep trust, in deep gratitude, go with it. While making love to a woman don't try to prove anything – as they are trying to do in the West. Don't try to prove anything – because when you start trying to prove, your mind has come in. While you are making love to a woman forget all about the fact that you are a man and she is a woman. Let boundaries merge and mix. Don't remain a man otherwise you will miss – because again a dualism comes in: you are the man and she is the woman. Nobody knows why two persons really make love. Many times it happens that the man becomes the woman and the woman becomes the man. Who bothers who is who?

And if you are thinking about it then the mind is there and the mind is the barrier; it does not allow the unison to happen totally. So Tao simply says: go spontaneously, with no ritual, with no idea to prove. And remember, never use sexuality for anything. Tantra uses it as a step towards samadhi. Tao says: never use anything as a means. Everything is an end unto itself. The moment you start thinking of somewhere to go, something to reach, some result to attain out of it, you are not total, your mind is divided, you are already in the future. There are no means and no ends. Everything simply is an intrinsically beautiful end unto itself.

In Tao this is very basic. Love, eat, go for a morning walk, swim in the river, sit in the sun, watch the stars – but let everything be simple, not for anything else. Sing a song, but not for any result. Look at this tree, but not for any result. Go for a morning walk, but not for health! Don't be a naturopath! Just go for a walk, it is beautiful. Health is a by-product; you need not worry about it, it happens. Lie down in the sun, enjoy it, but not for anything else. Lie there for its own sake. That is what Tao is.

And in that relaxed attitude life starts pouring into you from everywhere. All doors open, all windows open. Existence flows into you, you flow into existence.

Tao is very simple; therefore, because we are very complex, it is very difficult. Simple things don't appeal to us. Tantra appeals to many people but Tao has not that much appeal. Tao appeals very rarely. If Tao appeals to you, consider yourself to be fortunate. The very possibility of your getting interested in Tao is a great blessing.

When you translate everything in terms of Tao it becomes spontaneity.

The second question:

Osho,
Can you summaries your teaching in short because I am here only for a day or two.

It is impossible. In the first place I have no teaching to summarize. I am not a teacher, I am a presence. I have no catechism. I cannot give you ten commandments – do this, don't do that.

And whatsoever I say today I may contradict tomorrow – because my commitment is to the moment. Whatsoever I said yesterday, I am no longer committed to it. The moment I said it I became free of it. Now I won't bother about it, I won't look at it again. Whatsoever I am saying to you right now is true this very moment tomorrow I will not be committed to it. Whatsoever tomorrow brings, I will say it. Whatsoever today has brought I am telling you now. And if they are contradictory who am I to make them consistent? I don't make any effort on my own.

My commitment is to the moment. I am never committed to the past. I am like a river: where I will be tomorrow nobody knows, not even I myself. You will be surprised, I will also be surprised.

The question must be from someone who comes from the continent I call "Acirema" – it is "America" read in the reverse order. America is topsy-turvy. Everything has become chaotic. People are in such a hurry that they have forgotten that there are a few things which you cannot get in a hurry, for which patience is a must.

You cannot get truth in such a hurry. Patience is a basic condition for it. It is not like instant coffee and it does not come packed in tins. It does not come ready-made. Truth is not a commodity that somebody can give to you. It grows in you.

That's what I mean when I say I am a presence, I am not a teacher. If you are here, something may grow in you. I say, "may" because it depends on you. I am here. If you are ready to receive me, something will start growing within you. It is like a child becoming a young man. Yes, truth is like that. The false personality drops and the true being arrives it is a child becoming a young man, a young man becoming an old one. There is no way to hurry the process. You cannot make a child grow up fast in one night, in a day or two. It will take time. And it is good that it takes time because only through time do things become seasoned.

But in America there is a hurry, a mad hurry.

I have heard.

An American bride and a French bride were discussing love. "A Frenchman is very subtle when it comes to love," the French girl explained. "He begins by kissing the fingertips, then he kisses the shoulder, then the back of the neck...."

"Boy!" the little American bride interrupted. "By that time an American husband is back from his honeymoon!"

In America things have gone crazy. Everything has to be done with speed, fast. Speed seems to be the only value. It has never been a value anywhere else before, it had to wait for America to be discovered to become a value. Speed has become a value. If you are doing something fast, it is good – nobody bothers what it is or for what you are doing it. If you are doing it fast, perfectly good. If you are driving fast nobody bothers where you are going. You may not be going anywhere in particular but if you are going fast, everybody is happy. You may be going directly into death but everybody is happy – going so fast! Beautiful!

No, I cannot do that, I cannot summarize. I have no teaching. And even if I had a teaching I would not summarize it, because the more you summarize something, the more it becomes less alive. Love is vast, life is vast; law is limited. Law can be summarized; love cannot be summarized. Law is defined but life is excessive. You cannot summaries life, there cannot be a synopsis of life; you can summarize law. I am life. There is no way to summarize me.

And I am still alive so whatsoever you summaries I will destroy tomorrow.

I have heard.

A Hollywood producer studied the large script submitted by a new writer and complained, "It's much too long. Just give me a synopsis."

The next day the writer returned with a five-page synopsis.

"It's still too long," insisted the producer. "I'm a busy man. Just give me a digest of this."

An hour later the writer returned with a sheet of paper on which was written: Hero is a lieutenant, heroine is married to his colonel. Madly in love with each other. Commit suicide.

"It's no good," said the producer. "It's *Anna Karenina* word for word!"

When you summarize, by and by things become absurd.

Never summarize anything that is alive. I am still alive. When I am dead and gone then people will summarize. And I am going to give them a hell of a lot of trouble. It will not be an easy thing. They will go nuts. It will be impossible to put me into a synopsis.

It has been always so. You cannot summarize Buddha. Because of summarizations many schools were born. Buddha died, then there was a question. People wanted to summarize. For forty years the man had been teaching – morning, afternoon, evening – for forty years. He had talked a lot, he had said many things, and now he had gone and it had to be summarized.

A great assembly was called. Five hundred of the oldest disciples gathered together and they started reciting whatsoever they had heard the master say. There were many contradictions. One said something and somebody contradicted him, saying, "I have heard him say exactly the opposite." Now there was great debate, discussion – and splits. Thirty-six schools were born out of summarization, and those thirty-six have now become three hundred and sixty.

When a man like Buddha is there he is talking to different people in a different way because everyone's need is different.

Truth is not like a commodity. When you come to me, if you really want to know what my truth is, you will have to be here. My truth can be expressed to you only when I have come to know your truth too. When I have come to know you and you have come to know me, in that meeting will be the glimpse. It cannot be given to you. You will have to receive it and you will have to prepare for it. You will have to become a very relaxed being. You will have to be able to soak me up and allow me to sink deep into your heart.

No, I cannot supply a catechism as Christians do. That is not possible. And it will not be of any use to you.

Recovering from a severe operation, the man believed that the doctors were withholding from him his proper share of food. All he got each mealtime was a teaspoon of custard.

"Is that all I get?" he asked the nurse.

"That's all for a while," she answered.

He swallowed it with a good deal of grumbling.

"Nurse," said the patient later, "bring me a postage stamp. I want to do a little reading."

Summarized, it will be a postage stamp. It will not help. It will not be enough to read. If you want to read, read me. Don't be bothered with summarizations. Time will be needed – because it is a love relationship between the master and the disciple. It needs time to grow, to become intimacy. Only in deep intimacy can something be revealed, transferred. It is a transfer of energy, not of words.

So please, if you are going away in a day or two, you can go, you are free. But don't carry any idea about what I am teaching you here because that will not be understanding; or, even worse, it will be misunderstanding. If you have heard me say something, forget it, because in a day or two you could not have heard anything significant. And whatsoever you feel you have heard will be very non-essential.

It happened.

In the Amsterdam National Museum an elderly couple came to see Rembrandt's masterpiece *The Nightwatch*. When, after a long walk through the many corridors, they finally reached the famous painting, the usher overheard the man say to his wife, "Look, what a beautiful frame!"

The frame may have been beautiful but can't you see that something is missing in the admiration? Something essential is lost. I am not saying that the frame was not beautiful, the frame may have been the most beautiful frame in the world, but to go to see Rembrandt's masterpiece "The Nightwatch" and then to talk about the frame is absurd. Even to see the frame is foolish, stupid. The painting is not the frame. The frame has nothing to do with the painting.

What I am saying is just a frame, what I am is the painting. Look at the masterpiece and don't be bothered with the frame.

The third question:

Osho,
Can the master really save the disciple?

Certainly, absolutely...if the disciple is really a disciple he is already saved. It is not that first you have to be a disciple and then you will be saved – in your very being a disciple you are saved, in your very surrender you are saved. It is not that the master will save you afterwards because you are a disciple – just by being a disciple you are saved. In that very surrender you have dropped the ego. That ego was the barrier, that ego was hindering the path. When the barrier disappears you are saved.

In fact, you have always been saved. You were carrying an unnecessary load and because of that load you could not fly into the sky. Now you can fly. The master is just an excuse. Without a master it is difficult for you to drop your ego because you need some excuse. Otherwise how to drop it? Where to drop it? At whose feet to drop it? The master is just an excuse.

You fall in love with a man – a man like Jesus, a man like Buddha, naturally attracts thousands of people, seekers, who fall in love – and the man is so tremendously beautiful that you would like to surrender all. That is just an excuse. Once you have surrendered you will know that you are not saved by anybody else, you are saved by your surrender. But it will be known only when you have surrendered, not before it. To become a disciple is to be saved.

You ask: "Can the master really save the disciple?" It is very simple. It is nothing much to fuss about. Sometimes it has even happened that a disciple has saved a master – because, in fact, it is love that saves. Sometimes it has happened that the master was not really a master, was not himself enlightened, but was a charismatic man, a man of great magnetism. And somebody surrendered to him and through surrender became enlightened. Many times it has happened that the disciple has become enlightened before the master – you will be surprised because you think that you can only become enlightened through an enlightened master. All rubbish! You become enlightened through surrender. Even if you have surrendered to somebody who is just a pseudo-master, who simply pretends that he is a master, if your surrender is total you are saved. And it has happened sometimes that the master was saved by the disciple when the disciple became enlightened.

Let me tell you one beautiful Hassidic parable.

Elisha Ben Abuya was a great religious scholar. But he was just a scholar. He attracted many people, many talented people. His name was known all over Israel. Many people came and surrendered to him. But he was just a scholar, a pundit, he was not a real master. He knew about God but he had never encountered God. *And* it happened that late in his life he turned a skeptic and became rebellious – became irreligious, turned against God. And he was a great logician and well versed in scriptures, so it was very difficult to defeat him. When he started talking against God he was as impressive as when he was talking for God. He was a real intellectual.

His chief disciple Rabbi Meir tried many times to bring him back to the fold. The disciple tried to bring him back to the fold. Rabbi Meir, who was Elisha Ben Abuya's disciple, had become enlightened.

And the disciple tried many times to bring him back to the fold but the old man was really a logician and it was impossible to argue with him. The disciple suffered very much because he loved the man. He knew that he was not enlightened and he knew that he was not a real man of knowing but he loved the man and he felt grateful because he had become enlightened through him. Whosoever he was, whatsoever he was, through surrendering into his feet Rabbi Meir had become enlightened. How could he be ungrateful? He persisted.

Rabbi Meir, however, persisted in his attempt when he heard that Elisha was dangerously ill he went to visit him.

He again asked him to repent and Elisha asked, "Will he receive me now? Will God receive me now? Will he forgive me?"

"Yes," replied Rabbi Meir Elisha wept and died.

And a few days after Rabbi Meir was told that a fire was issuing out of the grave of his master. He went there, covered it with a mantle and said, "Slumber tonight, for perchance the Lord will save you, and if not, I will save you. Sleep until morning."

This is of tremendous beauty. He says, "Sleep tonight, for perchance the Lord will save you. And if not, I will save you. Sleep until morning." That's why I say it is very simple for a master to save you because sometimes even the contrary has happened – that a disciple has saved a master.

But remember, it is love that saves; it is surrender that saves. Remember that love liberates – that is the mantra: love saves, love liberates. Fall in love with a master and you are saved.

The fourth question:

Osho,
Lieh tzu devastates Confucius with few words and subtly. You have been devastating his discourse after discourse with a cannonade of words and have virtually clubbed him to death. I doubt if anyone in the ashram would defend Confucianism. Please let Confucius and me rest.

Both together? It is impossible. If you want to rest, Confucius has to be killed utterly. With Confucius there is no possibility for rest.

Whatsoever I am saying or whatsoever Lieh Tzu is saying has

nothing to do with the historical Confucius remember it. I am not against that poor man, Confucius. Why should I be? He was a beautiful man in his own right.

Why am I trying to destroy Confucius so deeply? Because Confucius is part of your mind, everybody's mind. Confucius has ruled over humanity. You may not even have heard his name – that doesn't matter; you may not know who he is – but deep inside, Confucius is the ruler.

In India, Manu is the ruler. He is the Indian counterpart of Confucius. All over the world there are counterparts of Confucius. Confucius is symbolic. What does he represent? He represents the legal mind, he represents the formal mind, he represents the ritual mind, he represents the conventional mind, the "straight" mind. He represents tradition.

I am destroying tradition, convention, the legal mind, the structure of the conformist. Confucius is the conformist par excellence. And you all have him in your minds.

Lao Tzu rarely enters into your mind. He is rebellious. He is going beyond tradition. He is going beyond past. He is going beyond all structure. Confucius is a structure, Lao Tzu is no-structure. Confucius is character, Lao Tzu is characterlessness, freedom. Remember it. All character is imprisonment enforced on you by the society, enforced on you by the state, by the priest, by the politician. This character that you carry around you is a cage. Lao Tzu says there is a different character which is not imposed by the society; a different discipline which is not enforced from the outside but comes through inner awareness. Only that is true. Follow only that. Follow only your own inner, small, still voice.

Confucius says, "Listen to the scripture, listen to the ancient masters, listen to tradition." Lao Tzu says, "Listen only to your own inner voice and follow it, wherever it leads. It is God's voice. It is Tao."

You ask me: "I doubt if anyone in the ashram would defend Confucianism." In fact, everybody is defending it. Nobody will be able to say it, but deep down you are defending it; if you were not defending it you would all be enlightened. The moment you are not defending Confucius there is no barrier for you to become enlightened. You are enlightened! When Confucius is dropped you become enlightened; when Confucius goes out at one door, from another door enlightenment enters.

If you are not enlightened you must be defending Confucianism. It may not be very conscious, it may be just an unconscious habit – because you have been conditioned for it. That's why you ask me: "Please let Confucius and me rest."

I cannot help you to rest. I am here to help you to rebel. And only with rebellion will the real rest come. Whatsoever you now call rest is nothing but slumber, is nothing but a sort of sleep. All sleep is not rest, because in your sleep you are dreaming a thousand and one things and you are going through many nightmares.

I would like to give you the real rest – what Jesus means when he says to his disciples, "Come to me and I will give you rest. All those who are heavy-laden, come to me. I will give you rest." That rest is a totally different thing. It is not the rest that comes by living in a crowd with the herd, following the herd. Certainly you feel okay – but okay is just okay. No problem, no inconvenience – comfortably you live and comfortably you will die. That is not the rest I am leading you towards. The real rest means you have come to your own being; you are centered, grounded. You have been daring enough to assert that you are yourself and you are no longer trying to imitate anybody else; you are not trying to become a carbon copy; you have become an authentic person, an authentic being. Then comes the rest, the real rest.

With Confucius that is not possible. With Confucius you will always be in conflict – Confucius means conflict. He will always say, "This is bad and this is good. Choose the good against the bad." Then what will you do? You will have to repress the bad and enforce the good. You will become a hypocrite. Follow Confucius and you will become a hypocrite; follow Lao Tzu and you are not following anybody, you are following yourself. And you will become an authentic being.

To be authentic is the only rest there is.

The fifth question:

Osho,
I like to listen to your talks very much but I hate the meditations. Is it okay, Osho? Perhaps my path is that of prayer.

If you really enjoy my talks you will enjoy the meditations too because they are interconnected. In fact, my talks are nothing but appetizers – if you enjoy the appetizer and you don't enjoy the lunch you are going to die sooner or later. You will die, starved. The talks are just to prepare you for the meditations. If you hate the meditations then you have not heard me. Then you may think you have heard me but you have not.

Hearing me, what else is there to do? If you have heard me you will be ready to go deep into the meditations. And whatsoever I am saying will become a real experience only when you have gone into the meditations. Then it will become your experience. Listening to me it will remain borrowed, listening to me you will be thrilled by the possibility of it, listening to me it is as if I am talking about the beautiful Himalayas – and you listen to me and you enjoy it. But you have never been to the Himalayas and whatsoever I say is nothing compared to the beauty of the Himalayas. How can it be put into words? You will have to go.

If you are really listening to me, one day, suddenly, you will feel, "Now the time has come and I have to go on the adventure. I have to take the risk." Meditations are the real journey. Here I simply seduce you to meditate. It is not the end, it is the beginning.

I have heard.

A movie-house usher was astonished to see a big, brown bear sitting in the front row, munching peanuts.

"Say, you!" he shouted. "You're a bear! What are you doing in here?"

"Why, I enjoyed the book so much," replied the bear, "that I thought I'd like to see the picture."

If you are really listening to me and enjoying it, one day you will want to see the picture too.

If it is true that you enjoy whatsoever I am saying then how is it possible that you hate the meditations? I am not an entertainment. Maybe you are using me as an entertainment. Maybe sitting here for one and a half hours every day you forget your worries – for one and a half hours you are transported into another world, into my world. And you see beautiful things – at least you visualize, imagine them – and then you are gone. Then you become addicted to it. Every day you have to come and listen to me. Now it is just an intoxicant. It is not going to help.

I am talking about the food – just the talk about the food is not going to help. The menu is not the food. The talks are just the menu, and you will have to make an order.

It happened.

The American playboy checked into one of the most exclusive hotels in gay Paree. He told the room clerk he wanted the best room in the place.

When he reached the room he was impressed with its exquisite furniture and tasteful decor. However, he spied a number of colored buttons on the wall. "Tell me," he asked the bellhop, "what are those buttons for?"

"Well, monsieur," said the bellhop, "when you press the gold one, a beautiful blonde appears."

"Go on," said the playboy gleefully.

"When you push the red one, a redhead appears. And when you push the brown, a beautiful brunette appears."

"Let's forget about the room," said the playboy. "I'll take the buttons."

But the buttons come with the room; just taking the buttons

home won't help – because you can go on pushing the buttons but nobody will appear.

In the memoirs of Lawrence of Arabia he writes that once he took twelve Arabs to France with him. This was the first time they had gone out of their country. There was a great exhibition in France and Lawrence was taking them to see it.

But he was very puzzled. Once they entered their bath they would not get out. They would remain for hours in the bath! But he thought, "It is natural. They come from a desert country where water is very scarce so they are enjoying their tub and their shower." They would jump and dance in the bathroom and were not at all interested in the exhibition. The moment they came back – and they were always in a hurry to come back to the hotel they would say, "Let us go upstairs." And they would run into the bathroom and enjoy themselves.

The last day, when everything was packed and put into the cars and they were leaving for the airport, all the Arabs disappeared suddenly. Lawrence inquired where they had gone to because they would be late. Suddenly he remembered that maybe they are back in the bathroom. So he rushed upstairs and they were all there trying to take out the faucets.

He asked, "What are you doing?"

They said, "We thought we would take these faucets. We will enjoy them in Arabia."

They thought that the water came through them. It was a miracle! They were not aware that there was a pipeline and a great mechanism behind it and you couldn't just take the faucets – they would not be of any use.

What I am saying to you is just like a faucet. There is a great source behind it from where it all comes. Unless you go in there, just listening to me is not going to help. It may be a solace, a consolation, an addiction, but it is not going to bring any revolution in your life.

You say: "Is it okay, Osho?" It is not okay at all. You are wasting your time. If you stop listening to me and continue the meditations that is far better than stopping the meditations and listening to me.

Then you ask: "Perhaps my path is that of prayer." Don't try to deceive yourself. Have you done any praying? Have you been praying? You say "perhaps" – you have not tried even that. Maybe you are using the word *prayer* just to avoid meditation. Prayer itself is a meditation and to avoid meditation in the name of prayer will not help. These escapes are for weaklings. Don't be a coward.

People come to me. If I give them prayers and I tell them,

"Say this prayer," they come and they say, "Osho, maybe prayer is not my path." If prayer is given to them they say that prayer is not their path. So it is difficult to do the praying. If meditation is given they think that meditation is not their path. In fact, you don't want to do anything; you don't want to grow, you don't want to be transformed.

There is a story about two ministers who were crossing one of the Scottish lakes. This was in the days before roads and automobiles so a person got to his destination by getting into a boat and being ferried across the lake. These lakes were sometimes treacherous. Storms could come up suddenly and within five minutes a boat could capsize and the people in it drown.

The two ministers wanted to cross the lake. One was a tall, husky, six-foot countryman with muscles like a blacksmith, and the other was a small, weedy, studious townsman – the long and the short of it. They hired a boat, the old boatman got out the oars and they started off.

In about five minutes' time a terrible storm came up and churned up the lake. The boat was rocking and the boatman said, "Me lads, you'll have to help me. Grab hold of those other oars if you want to come out of this alive." So the two clergymen picked up the oars and began to bend their backs. It was pretty hard work, but for a few minutes they kept the boat straight into the eye of the wind.

Suddenly the storm got worse. The husky minister threw down his oars and said, "Let us pray."

But the boatman yelled, "No, no, the little 'un can pray, but you keep on rowing."

Don't be a coward. Let the little ones pray. You take up the challenge of meditation. It is a challenge. Prayer seems to be easy because you have nothing to do you just have to say, "God, do this, do that." In prayer you give God work to do – if he does not do it then he is responsible. You said it, so what more can you do?

Meditation is to do the work yourself. And my feeling is that if you do your work to your uttermost capacity only then does God start doing work on you – never before it. Unless you help yourself, no help ever comes from God.

Understand my approach: if your meditations succeed, only then can prayer start. Never before it. When you have done all that you can do, when you have not saved anything, when you have put yourself totally at the stake and you feel that nothing is happening, then you are entitled to ask the sky, "Now help me. What more can I do?" And help comes.

But not doing anything on your own, just saying a prayer every night, half asleep, when you are going to bed – "God do this, do that" – and then going to sleep...this will not help you at all. If you really want God to do something to you, first you have to try your uttermost; at the optimum help happens, never before it. When you are doing all that you can do, absolutely all that you can do, immediately help is available.

The sixth question:

Osho,
Recently you talked again about the adverse aspects of marriage. Would you please talk about what you mean by intimacy? Particularly, when is staying together through difficult times positive and when is it negative?

Marriage is a way to avoid intimacy. It is a trick to create a formal relationship. Intimacy is informal. If a marriage arises out of intimacy it is beautiful but if you are hoping that intimacy will arise out of marriage, you are hoping in vain. Of course, I know that many people, millions of people, have settled for marriage rather than for intimacy – because intimacy is growth and it is painful.

Marriage is very secure. It is safe. There is no growth in it. One is simply stuck. Marriage is a sexual arrangement; intimacy is a search for love. Marriage is a sort of prostitution, a permanent sort. One has got married to a woman or to a man – it is a permanent prostitution. The arrangement is economical, not psychological, not of the heart.

So remember, if marriage arises out of intimacy then it is beautiful. That means that everybody should have lived together before they get married. The honeymoon should not happen after marriage, it should happen before marriage. One should have lived the dark nights, the beautiful days, the sad moments, the happy moments, together. One should have looked into each other's eyes deeply, into each other's being.

How to decide? If your intimacy is helping you to grow and to become mature then it is positive and good and healthy, wholesome. If it is destructive and it is not allowing you to become mature rather, it is helping you to remain childish, immature then it is unhealthy. Any relationship that keeps you childish is evil. Get out of it. Any relationship that gives you challenges to grow, to go on an adventure, to go deeper and higher into life.... I am not saying that a positive marriage will not have problems, it will have *more* problems than the negative marriage. A positive relationship will have more problems because every day new challenges will be there. But each time a problem is solved you will have gone a little higher; each time a challenge is taken you will find something has become integrated in your being.

A negative relationship has no problems – or at the most pseudo-problems, so-called problems, not real problems. Have you not watched it? Wife and husband fighting over trivia. They are not problems. Even if you fight they don't give you anything, they don't help growth Watch wives and husbands, watch yourself. You may be a husband, a wife

Just watch. If you are fighting over trivia – small things which don't mean anything any way – then you will remain immature, childish. Real problems, authentic problems, which really have to be faced, create great turmoil in your being; they bring a cyclone. One has to face them. Never avoid them. The trivial questions are an escape from the real questions. A husband and wife will fight on very small things: which film to go to and which not to go to; what color car has to be purchased, what model, what make; to what restaurant they are going this evening. Such trivia! They do not make any difference. You are making too much fuss about such problems and your relationship is not going to help you, give you any integrity, any center. I will call it negative.

The positive relationship will face real problems. For example: if you are angry or if you are sad, you will be sad in front of your wife, you will not smile a false smile. And you will say, "I am sad." This has to be faced. If, walking on the road with your wife, you see a beautiful woman pass by and a great desire and longing arises in your heart, you will tell your wife that this woman created a great desire, stirred your heart. You will not avoid her. You will not take your eyes away. And you will not pretend that you have not seen the woman at all – whether you pretend or not your wife has already known it! It is impossible for her not to know because immediately your energy, your presence, changes. These are real problems.

Just getting married to a woman doesn't mean that you are no longer interested in any other woman. In fact, the day you are not interested in any other women, you will not be interested in your wife either. Why? For what? What has your wife got that is special? If you are no longer interested in women you will not be interested in your wife either. You are in love with her because you are in love with women still. She is just a woman. And sometimes you come across a woman who enchants you. You will say it to your wife. And you will face the turmoil that will arise. It is not trivia – because it will create jealousy, it will create a struggle, it will disturb all rest, you will not be able to sleep at night. The wife will be throwing pillows at you.

To be true creates real problems. To be authentic creates real problems. And say whatsoever is the case never demur, never look sideways. Look straight and be true. And help the wife to be true, help the husband to be true.

Yes, there are problems in real intimacy, more problems than in a negative state more problems. Because if you are really intimate with the woman how call you avoid the fact that you become interested in another woman? You have to say it. That's part of love, part of intimacy. You denude yourself, you expose yourself totally you don't hold anything back. Even if during the night you dream a dream about another woman, in the morning you can relate it to your wife.

I have heard about a film director. During the night he started talking to his girlfriend in his sleep and he was talking loudly. He was saying beautiful things and the wife started staring at him. When you are married, even in your dreams you remain afraid of your wife, so suddenly he became afraid. What was he saying? He felt his wife looking at him and with great presence of mind he said, "Cut! Now another scene."

.... as if he was directing a film!

If you really love the woman, in the morning you will tell her your dream – that you made love to a woman in the night in your dream. Everything has to be shared. The whole heart has to be shared.

Intimacy means that there is no privacy. You don't carry anything private now – at least with the person you are intimate with. You drop privacy. You are nude and naked. Good, bad, whatsoever you are, you open your heart. And whatsoever the cost you pay for it; whatsoever the trouble you go through with it. That brings growth.

And you help the other person also to drop all inhibitions, screens, masks. In an intimate relationship one comes to see the original face of the other and one comes to show his own original face. If a relationship helps you to find your original face then it is meditative, then it is religious. If your relationship simply helps you to create more and more masks and hypocrisies then it is irreligious.

Try to understand my definition. If my definition is understood then out of a hundred marriages, ninety-nine are irreligious because they are simply creating more and more falsity. From the very beginning the falsity starts.

I have heard.

The minister, casting an appraising eye over the bridal couple before him and the goodly crowd come to witness the ceremony, intoned, "If there is anyone here who knows why these two should not be joined together in wedlock. Let him speak now or forever hold his peace."

"I've got something to say," a voice rang out bold and clear.

"You shut up!" snapped the minister. "You're the groom."

From the very beginning! They are not even married yet. The minister said, "You shut up! You are the groom." And that's how the life of a married couple starts.

People keep quiet. They don't say anything. They don't say the truth at all. They pretend lies. They smile when they don't want to smile, they kiss when they don't want to kiss. Naturally, when you kiss and you don't want to kiss, the kiss is poisonous. Naturally, when you don't want to smile and you have to smile, your smile is ugly, it is political.

And then somehow one gets accustomed to these things, one settles to the falsity, to the inauthenticity of life. And one consoles oneself in a thousand and one ways.

"Oh, we're very happy," insisted the husband. "Of course, once in a while my wife throws dishes at me. But that doesn't change the situation one bit, because if she hits me she's happy, and if she misses me I'm happy!"

One by and by comes to such an arrangement – both are happy.

The car in which the elderly couple were riding went over the cliff. It was an awful wreck.

"Where am I?" moaned the man when he opened his eyes. "In heaven?"

"No," said his dazed wife. "I'm still with you."

These settlements are very hellish. What you know in the name of relationship is just a pseudo-game.

So remember it as a criterion: if you are growing more and becoming an individual, if life is happening more to you, if you are becoming more open, if more beauty is felt in existence, if more poetry is arising in your heart, if more love flows through you, more compassion, if you are becoming more aware, then the relationship is good. Carry on. Then it is not a marriage. Then it is intimacy.

But if the reverse is happening; if all poetry is disappearing and life is becoming prosaic; if all love is disappearing and life is becoming just a load, a dead load; if all song is dying and you are just living as a duty, then it is better to escape out of this prison. It is better for you and it is better for the partner with whom you are living.

The seventh question:

Osho,
Was the man in today's story (where a man had no memory) enlightened? Or had he a glimpse? Do we get it and forget it and get it and forget it and one day maybe not forget?

Yes, the man had a glimpse. If he had really become established then there was no way to bring him back – you cannot bring a buddha back. He had only a glimpse. He was just entering the door and he was pulled back. If he had entered the temple then he would have been gone, gone forever.

Many times a glimpse will come and will disappear. It is natural. If enlightenment suddenly came like lightning, like thunder, you would be crushed. You would not be able to receive it. It would be too much. You would go mad.

Glimpses come and prepare you. More and more glimpses will come and by and by you will become acclimatized for a totally different world, a totally different dimension of being. Otherwise you would go mad. Sometimes it has happened that a man who was working alone without a master and was not aware that one should not rush into it, rushed into it and became mad.

The master is needed for many things. He is needed mostly when you are coming very close to enlightenment. Then he is needed very, very deeply because he will allow you only so far. Slowly, slowly, in quantities, he will help you to absorb the vastness of the experience, the tremendousness of it. It is a "mysterium tremendum." You are just a drop and enlightenment is like an ocean dropping in you. One has not to be greedy. First the master pushes you into it and then he holds you and allows you to go into it very slowly.

The man must have had only a glimpse.

You ask me: "Do we get it and forget it and get it and forget it and maybe one day not forget?" No. One day one forgets both getting and forgetting. Then, then it is there. One day one forgets both getting and forgetting – one day one simply recognizes that it is your innermost nature that it is not something that you can get or you can forget.

You can get something from the outside, you can forget something from the outside, but this is your own flowering. It is you, it is your fragrance how can you get it and how can you forget? One day one forgets both getting and forgetting. Then one has come home.

The last question:

Osho,
Six hours of sleep every night. An hour and a half of "satsang" – playing the beautiful spiritual game with you. Then suddenly switching over from the cold marble floor to a swivel chair – playing the orange airline executive! Spectacular evening performances – changing daily. From absurd comedy to heavy melodrama. Many roles, many plots. Always extempore. Playing father, husband, friend, stranger, wiseman, fool!!
The one real factor in all this which isn't a game is a deep, deep love for you. This is what makes all the games exciting. Can this be what they call – "working with the Master"?

Yes, that is exactly what is meant by "working with the master" – to live suffused with the presence of the master, to live suffused with the love of the master and to play all the games that God wants you to play. Where God has placed you, go on playing. Everything becomes a game. Yes, that's exactly what it is. Only love remains a reality, everything else becomes a game.

And if you can play the many games of life without being serious, without being identified, remaining a witness and enjoying the fun of it, you have understood.

To be with the master is to learn that the whole of life is a game, a *maya*. Nothing is serious. Nothing has to be avoided. Nothing has to be chosen in particular – whatsoever happens is a game, a *maya*. Nothing is serious. Nothing has to be avoided. Nothing has to be chosen in particular – whatsoever happens, allow it to happen. Remain alert and allow it to happen and your alertness by and by will help you to slip into totality.

Remain aware and go on playing the games. Never escape, never run away. To run away from the world means that you have rejected God. To reject the world means that you have rejected the God who has made the world. Love the world, because that is the only way to love God. And enjoy. And whatsoever he wants you to do, wherever he has placed you – enjoy that place. Sometimes it is on a marble floor, sometimes on a swivel chair; sometimes it is as a wiseman, sometimes a fool; sometimes it is this, sometimes that – remain fluid. Move into one role, then to another; flow, don't get frozen.

Seriousness freezes. Remain non-serious. Take life as a joy and it becomes prayer.

Enough for today.

CHAPTER #5

The Fundamental Rule

Mr. P'ang of Ch'en had a son who was clever as a child but suffered from an abnormality when he grew up. When he heard singing he thought it was weeping; when he saw white he thought it was black; fragrant smells he thought noisome, sweet tastes he thought bitter, wrong actions he thought right. Whatever came into his mind – heaven and earth, the four cardinal points, water and fire, heat and cold – he always turned it upside down.
A certain Mr. Yang told his father: "The gentlemen of Lu have many arts and skills, perhaps they can cure him. Why not inquire among them?"

The father set out for Lu, but passing through Ch'en he came across Lao Tzu and took the opportunity to tell him about his son's symptoms.
"How do you know that your son is abnormal?" said Lao Tzu. "Nowadays everyone in the world is deluded about right and wrong and confused about benefit and harm. Because many people share this sickness no one perceives that it is a sickness. Besides, one man's abnormality is not enough to overturn his family; one family's to overturn the neighborhood: one neighborhood's to overturn the state; one state's to overturn the world. If the whole world were abnormal how could abnormality overturn it? Supposing the minds of everyone in the world were

> like your son's, then, on the contrary, it is you who would be abnormal. Joy and sorrow, music and beauty, smells and tastes, right and wrong – who can straighten them out? I am not even sure that these words of mine are not abnormal let alone those of the gentlemen of Lu, who are the most abnormal of all. Who are they to cure other people's abnormality? You had better go straight home instead of wasting your money."

Tao is a unique vision. It is a vision, mind you, a *darshan*, it is not a philosophy. It is a clarity, a transparency, but not an ideology. It does not propose any system of thought – it does not propose anything at all. It neither proposes anything, nor supposes anything. It is not a system of thought, it is just a way of looking directly into reality, into that which is.

It does not project anything from the mind, it does not allow mind to interfere, compare, interpret – it is *wu-wei*, non-interference with reality. Whatsoever is, is; it cannot be altered, it cannot be changed; whatever is, is, and whatever ain't, ain't. Things should be left untouched, as they are. The moment man enters and tries to change or improve, confusion arises.

Tao is a great acceptance, Tao is a tremendous acceptance, Tao is an unconditional *tathata*. Whatsoever is, is – nothing can be done about it.

And there is no need to do anything either. The moment you start doing, you create mischief – the doers are the mischievous people. The non-doers are the real people; through non-doing, one can know what is. When you start doing something you bring your mind in, and the moment mind comes in there is confusion – all clarity is lost. Try to understand this as the basic, fundamental Tao.

Then today's parable will be very easily understood. It is of tremendous beauty, this parable. It can open a new vista, it can open a door in your being, it can give you a vision of reality. But the fundamental rule is: do not interfere. That is real non-violence.

If you go to Lao Tzu and you say that somebody is a thief, he says, "So what! Somebody is a thief. Let it be so." Lao Tzu is unworried about reality. If somebody is mad. Lao Tzu will say, "So what! Let it be so. If that's how the whole wills it then that is how it has to be. Who are you? Who has given you the authority to change anything, to transform it? Leave reality to itself and everything goes beautifully, rhythmically. Interfere, and everything is disturbed."

You have heard about the non-violence of Mahavira, you have heard about the non-violence of Buddha, but they are nothing compared to Lao Tzu. In their non-violence there is a subtle violence still: the violence of interference. The good has to be brought in, the bad has to be destroyed; the immoral has to be changed into moral, the wrong has to be put right. They are still not in *wu-wei*, non-interference. The violent person is trying to change reality violently, the non-violent person is trying to change reality non-violently, but both are trying to change reality. And to change is to be violent. To accept things as they are, to accept with no mind at all – that is the Tao understanding.

If you have a mind you cannot accept. You will judge, you will compare; you will say that this should not be so, it has not to be so; you will say that this can be improved, this can be changed and made better.

The very idea that the world can be made better is the very root of all ego trips. The world is perfect; there is no way to make it better. If you try to make it better, you will make it worse. Things are in perfect rhythm nothing is bad, nothing is good. The good and the bad are man-created concepts. Nothing is right, nothing is wrong – those are our conceptions. Reality simply is neutral, neither good nor bad, neither beautiful nor ugly. It simply is. This "isness" is Tao.

Now, enter this parable. We will go into it very slowly. Taste it step by step – it can become a revelation.

Mr. P'ang of Ch'en had a son who was clever as a child....

Every child is born clever. No child is ever born idiotic. To become an idiot one needs to be educated. To convert people to idiocy, schools and colleges and universities are needed. It is a great achievement. Idiocy is not natural; it has to be learned, it has to be earned. Great effort has to be made before you can become stupid. A Buddha or a Lao Tzu or a Jesus are people who somehow escaped from society, who somehow managed it that society did not change them into stupid people. They look rare because the whole society has become stupid otherwise they would be the norm. It be natural to be clever, intelligent – as natural as breathing, as natural as health.

Watch a child, any child, black, white, Indian, Chinese, German – yes, even German! Watch any child. All children are intelligent and all children are beautiful. Have you ever seen an ugly child? The phenomenon does not exist at all. Have you ever seen a stupid child? Their intelligence is tremendous.

But society starts to cripple the child because society cannot allow that much intelligence. That much intelligence is dangerous. An intelligent child is a dangerous person. Society immediately jumps upon the child, from the very first day. The child is not even allowed the freedom to breathe on his own – the doctor slaps him on his bottom and society has started. The child is not even allowed to breath on his own. You should wait. There is no need to slap the child.

Go and watch in a maternity home. When the child is born, the doctor will take the child by his legs, hold him upside down and slap him on the bottom to help him breathe. It is as if nature is not enough so your help is needed. Nobody slaps the animals – yet they are breathing, breathing beautifully. No doctor is needed, no nurse is needed, no mid-wife is needed.

Wait! But society cannot wait. Within seconds society enters. Society has to slap the child. And now people who have been studying the phenomenon of slapping the child say that the first slap comes as a shock, because the child is very delicate. For nine months he has lived in a very protected environment – that slap is like a great shock. With a shock his life starts.

Then there are even more cruel people. Jews will do a circumcision – it is a great shock to cut the foreskin of the genital organs. You have started violence, you have started butchering the child. Society is on the way.

And immediately everything has to be forced on the child. Now the mother is told when to breast-feed the child and when not to breast-feed the child – after three hours

As if every child is a Ford car, just like every other Ford car. Each child is an individual. His needs are different. One child will find that he is hungry within two hours, another child will find that he is not hungry after five hours. This average of three hours is dangerous. One child will not be hungry but the mother will force him to feed because three hours are over and another child will be hungry and crying and weeping but the mother will wait and look at the clock and because three hours are not over yet how can she feed him?

These are subtle tricks to destroy the delicate intelligence, the delicate life of the child. Then he has to be trained about everything. From toilet training to God, he has to be trained about everything. He is not allowed any spontaneity. And intelligence thrives in spontaneity, intelligence dies in discipline. The more disciplined the child, the more stupid he will be; the more intelligent the child, the more rebellious he will be. Rebelliousness and intelligence are synonymous; stupidity and discipline are synonymous. If you have succeeded in ordering the child to obey you and in making him conform to your ideas, you have succeeded in killing his intelligence.

Your schools, your colleges, your universities, all teach nonsense because they are all against sense. Nowhere is sensitivity taught nowhere. In fact, sensitivity has to be destroyed. It is dangerous to allow the child to be sensitive and intelligent because, if the child remains sensitive, then society will not be able to force the child to do foolish things throughout his life.

For example: a person goes on being a clerk his whole life, just piling up files. To do such a thing you need to be very insensitive. If you have a certain sensitivity you will want to break out of this nonsense, you will want to go into the fields, into the forest. You may want to become a gardener, you may want to become a farmer, or a fisherman, or a carpenter, or a sculptor, or a poet – but you will not want to become a clerk in an office. For what should one want to be a clerk? The sun is so bright and the flowers have bloomed and the birds are singing and you are just doing a clerical job! It will not be possible. Society has to kill your intelligence, your sensitivity, so that you can be put into any job. When you are dull it is easy to force you into any direction. Then a person can keep on doing any nonsense job. And when you do a nonsense thing for your whole life, naturally, by and by, you lose all possibilities of being intelligent.

A person can be sent into the army. If people were intelligent who would go into the army? For what would they kill others and be killed? Life is to live, not to be killed and not to kill. Life is to enjoy; it is a divine gift. But millions of people are in the army, just getting ready to be butchered or to butcher. And their whole life – from morning to evening – is spent parading, polishing their rifles, following some foolish man's orders: left turn, right turn. Doing this their whole life! And not even for a single moment do they think about what they are doing – what they are doing with their life. Is life meant for this? Is this the destiny of life?

If you are singing and dancing maybe it is meaningful, but turning left and right, doing the same march every day, just preparing for death.... How can life be just a preparation for death?

Brutality, violence, insensitivity is taught only then can millions of people be turned into slaves. You think you are free people? Slavery has just become more sophisticated, that's all. Slavery still exists. No society up to now has ever been a free society. All societies have been slave societies.

Yes, one thing is certain: slavery changes its forms. First it was very gross, now it is very subtle. And remember, subtle slavery is far more dangerous than gross slavery – because you can rebel against gross slavery, it is so apparent, so obvious, but when the slavery is very subtle then you are not even aware of it. If you are a Mohammedan, if you are a Hindu, if you are a Christian, if you are a Jaina, you are a slave. Your mind has been conditioned to be a Hindu, to be a Mohammedan, to be a Christian, and you have become that.

And you have never thought about it. Why should you be a Christian? Why should you be a Mohammedan? You were not born as a Christian, as a Mohammedan, you were born as pure consciousness. Why these limitations? Who has forced these limitations on you? You were born as a pure human being – who has made you an Indian and who has made you Chinese? You are slaves. If you are Chinese or Indian or English, you are a slave. Slavery is very subtle.

And if you are doing things which others want you to do and you never do the thing that you always wanted to do, you are a slave. You go on loving a person you don't love, you go on sleeping with a person you don't love, you go on living in a relationship which is simply destructive, horrible, a hell, but you go on. You are a slave, you are not a free man.

A free man is one who claims back his intelligence, who claims back his sensitivity. To me, that is what sannyas is: to claim back your intelligence, to claim back your sensitivity, to become again sensuous, alive, to become again intelligent, to become again a child.

Mr. P'ang of Ch'en had a son who was clever as a child...

All children are clever. No child is ever born who is not clever. Even if you sometimes think that a child is not clever that is just your thinking.

I have heard about a boy who was sitting on the fence watching his father working in the field. A bull came running.

The child shouted, "Papa, a bull is coming!"

And the father jumped and saved himself.

But he was more surprised than the bull was because the child had not spoken for seven years – he was seven years of age. He had not spoken a single word.

So the father said, "Forget about the bull. You surprised me more! Why have you not spoken up to now? And you spoke so suddenly – 'Papa, the bull is coming!'"

The boy said, "There was nothing to say before, so there was no point in speaking."

Even when a child appears to be stupid to you, beware of making judgments. It may be only because of your stupidity. Because whatsoever you have become, you compare from that point. If a child is not clever in mathematics you think he is stupid. But there can be a society where mathematics is not valued – music may be valued and the child will have a tremendous capacity for music. Then in that society he will be valued as intelligent. In your society a boy who can do mathematics well is valued and nobody bothers about his musical qualities. He may be absolutely non-musical. It depends. What society values is not a natural value, it is a chosen value.

In some societies silence is valued – then to be silent is to be intelligent. In some societies talking is valued, so to talk is to be intelligent. It depends. In some societies dance is valued greatly and one who cannot dance seems to be stupid. In another society dancing is not thought about at all. Then nobody bothers whether you can dance or not. If you can be good at mathematics, at the 3 R's reading, writing, arithmetic then you are intelligent.

But for thousands of years man has lived without these 3 R's – yet people have been intelligent otherwise they could not have survived. In fact, to survive today is very simple, problems have almost disappeared. To survive in the jungle, when there was no house over your head, no food supply, no security, and you were constantly in danger…man must have been very, very intelligent, otherwise there would have been no possibility of his surviving. Man is not a very strong animal, all other animals are far stronger, but still man has survived because of his intelligence, his sensitivity. He can feel more, he can become more aware and more alert.

Remember this: you were also born clever, talented – a genius. God never creates less than that, God always creates geniuses. This beautiful whole always creates perfect people, how can imperfection be born out of perfection? Have you thought about it?

In the Upanishads they say, "Perfection comes out of perfection. Perfection is born out of perfection." God is born out of God – nothing else can be born out of God. You are gods and goddesses because you come from that source of divineness.

Each child brings heaven into the world again but we jump upon him and we destroy him and we destroy his heaven and his paradise. Again and again each child loses his paradise, that's why we go on seeking and searching for it. If we had not known it, how could we search and seek for it? We can only seek that which we have known before. Each child has known something which has become lost, so again we start seeking for it. We have lost our own inner capacities; we have lost our own inner kingdom.

.... but suffered from an abnormality when he grew up.

Everybody becomes abnormal. It is very difficult to find a grown-up person who is normal, because whatsoever you call the growing-up process is the process of turning people abnormal.

For example: a man is obsessed with money; he is abnormal. Why should one be obsessed with money? You cannot eat it, you cannot love it, you cannot be loved by it. It cannot give you life, it cannot give you beauty, it cannot give you joy. But there are millions of people who are madly in love with money – money is their God, their only God. Now these are abnormal people.

Once this abnormality settles then there arises another abnormality: a few people renounce money and become great mahatmas. First these mad people are obsessed with money, then a new obsession arises from that obsession – they become obsessed with the fear of money. If you take money to Vinoba Bhave he will not touch it. Now what is wrong in touching money? A poor currency note is just paper – why are you so afraid of touching it?

There is some deep fear. And fear is nothing but lust standing on its head; deep down there is still some desire. The fear is that, "If I touch the money I may again become interested in it."

A man who is free of money will use the money and he will not be obsessed either way, for or against. He will live in the world, he will not renounce the world there is no need.

You cannot drop out of one madness by creating another – you are simply changing your madness. Your so-called money-mad people are mad and your mahatmas are just at the other extreme of the same madness. They are not different. Somebody who is mad after prestige, power, pull, is abnormal. Sitting on a very high chair is not going to make you happy. You can become a president and you can become a prime minister but that is not going to make you happy. And life is to be happy, life is to celebrate.

The more power you have, the more and more unhappy you will become – because the more power you have, the more you will constantly have worries, constantly be in conflict. You cannot be at ease because others will be rushing towards you; they will be ready to overthrow you because they also want the same chair, the same power. Power is scarce and everybody wants power. So you will be in a mad-house.

If you really want to see a madhouse go to New Delhi. In India that is the greatest madhouse. And right now, because the elections are coming near, you can find out how many people are mad in this country.

To find a grown-up person who is still intelligent is very difficult, very rare. You can become intelligent only if you become very conscious about what has been done to you, about how your intelligence has been destroyed or covered up. You will have to rediscover it.

And when I am saying these things remember that I am not saying them only about others, I am talking about you. Watch your own being, watch how you behave, what you do with your life, and you will find many, many mad obsessions. Those mad obsessions have been given to you by society. You have been made ambitious, and ambition destroys intelligence. You have been put on a wrong track, you have been made competitive, you have been made jealous of others, you have been taught only one thing: to compete and to be first.

But life has nothing to do with being first. You can enjoy it wherever you are. You can enjoy it right this moment, there is no need to postpone it. To postpone life is to become unintelligent. You say, "Tomorrow I will live" so tomorrow you will be intelligent. Intelligence comes only when you live; intelligence is a function of living. When you live tremendously you become intensely intelligent; when you postpone life, dust gathers on the mirror of your being.

And you have been postponing. You say, "Tomorrow," always, "Tomorrow." People come to me and they say they want to take sannyas, but not today tomorrow. They say they will come again. But why? Why wait? For what are you waiting? And who knows? Tomorrow may come or may not come. This moment may be the last moment to breathe, you may not breathe again. So why not live this moment as totally as possible?

A person becomes intelligent when he starts living moment to moment totally – as if this is the last moment. Then there is a great passion, a great intensity. One becomes aflame with life. In that aflame state of consciousness one is intelligent, otherwise one is dull, dragging. Tomorrow, the day after tomorrow, one is going to live – so what is the need of being intelligent today? Today you can afford to become stupid: tomorrow, when you will try to live, you can become intelligent.

But if you are stupid today, you are creating a trend of stupidity, and there is every possibility that tomorrow will not be different from today because it will be a prolongation of today, a continuity of today.

> Mr. P'ang of Ch'en had a son who was clever as a child but suffered from an abnormality when he grew up. When he heard singing he thought it was weeping; when he saw white he thought it was black; fragrant smells he thought noisome, sweet tastes he thought bitter, wrong actions he thought right.

> Whatever came into his mind – heaven and earth, the four cardinal points, water and fire, heat and cold – he always turned it upside down.

That's what everybody is doing. Look into your life and you will find that you have turned everything upside down. That which is valuable has become valueless and that which is valueless has become valuable.

Look into your life and be very true and honest in looking – because if you deceive, you deceive only yourself and nobody else. Look straight into your own being and you will be surprised. What have you been doing with yourself? Everything has become upside down. You are living for the non-essential and you have forgotten the essential. You are living for things, and things will be taken away when death comes. Money, power, prestige – nothing is going to be with you when death comes.

Only that person lives who lives in such a way that death cannot destroy anything; who creates his inner being in such a way that death cannot take anything away from him; who lives in an eternity which death cannot touch; who lives in consciousness – that man only is intelligent. Otherwise everything has been turned upside down: white you see as black and black you see as white; fragrant smells you think as nauseous; sweet tastes bitter. You have settled on the artificial. Plastic flowers – yes. that's where you have settled.

Instead of moving into love you have settled with a marriage; instead of searching a real religion you have settled with Islam, Christianity, Jainism. Instead of searching for God you have settled for words about God. Instead of looking into existence you are carrying dead books. Instead of really living life you have only ideas about how to live life. Just ideas. Nothing else.

You have not lived at all, you only carry a few ideas. That's what I mean by saying that you have taken the menu instead of the dinner. You may call the menu the Vedas, or you may call it the Koran, or you may call it the Bible, but it is a menu, it is not food, it cannot nourish you.

So if you are feeling unnourished, if you are feeling weak, if you are feeling death-like, it is natural. Nobody else is to be blamed for it.

> .... he always turned it upside down.
> A certain Mr. Yang told his father, "The gentlemen of Lu have many arts and skills perhaps they can cure him. Why not inquire among them?"

Remember the last story? It was also concerned with the gentlemen from Lu. This town Lu was a Confucian town. It was almost like Varanasi. In India, if you come from Varanasi, if you can say that you come from Varanasi, you are already a great scholar. It has a prestige. It is the Hindu citadel. The town of Lu was exactly like Varanasi. It had Confucian scholars. It was a sort of Confucian university where Confucius lived with his disciples and created much scholarship, created many scholars and pundits. It had become very famous.

> A certain Mr. Yang told his father "The gentlemen of Lu have many arts and skills perhaps they can cure him. Why not inquire among them?" The father set out for Lu but passing through Ch'en he came across Lao Tzu and took the opportunity to tell him about his son's symptoms.

One thing to be remembered at this moment of this parable is that the mind always looks for the Confucian. It comes across the "Lao Tzu" only accidentally. Mind is basically Confucian. Mind looks for a structure, an ideology. Mind looks for a principle. Mind looks for some technology so that it can become more powerful in controlling. Mind looks for power. It is only accidental that you come across a Lao Tzu: you were not really looking for Lao Tzu, you were looking for Confucius.

For example: you have come here. You were not looking for me, you were looking for a mahatma. You have come across me only accidentally. You may have been in search of a guru, a *mahatma* but accidentally you came across me. You were not looking for me, the mind cannot look for me. For the mind to look for me is simply for it to commit suicide. The mind looks for something that helps it to become stronger.

The father set out for Lu.... He was in search of a Confucian man who would be able to help cure his son. One thing is certain to the father the son is ill. He has not taken any trouble to think about it, to ponder over it – whether he is really ill, whether he is really abnormal. He has simply accepted the idea that he is abnormal. He does not know anything – what normality is or what abnormality is.

Be a little more aware when you make such assumptions. You think that somebody is mad? Don't be in such a hurry. He may not be mad; on the contrary, you may be mad. Don't judge. You immediately assume that somebody is a criminal – he may not be. On the contrary, you may be the criminal. The criminal may not be the criminal the magistrate may be the criminal. The judged may not be the criminal, the judge may be the criminal. Things are very complicated; don't assume. Don't fall victim to easy assumptions.

The father had taken one thing for granted: his son was abnormal. Beware of taking things for granted. Never take anything for granted. The moment you take anything: for granted you are falling from intelligence. Intelligence never takes anything for granted. It looks into it and it remains open. It never creates a prejudice. Who knows?

You must have heard the story about a woman who was brought to Jesus because she had committed a sin. Those who were condemning her were ready to kill her because the old law said that if a woman committed a sin adultery – then she had to be killed by throwing stones at her; she had to be stoned to death.

They came to Jesus. It was also a good opportunity to judge Jesus whether this man followed the old law or was against the old law.

They asked, "What should we do?" And Jesus said, "Do one thing first. Those who have never committed any sin, those who have not even thought about committing adultery, they should take stones in their hands. They are allowed to stone this woman."

The people started disappearing. Nobody was left – there was not even a single man who had not committed adultery, even if only in the mind.

Within minutes the crowd had gone and Jesus was Left with the woman. The woman started crying. She felt tremendous respect for this man who had saved her. She said, "I am guilty. I have done wrong. You punish me." And Jesus said, "Who am I to punish you? Who am I to call you a sinner? That is something between you and your God. I am nobody to judge."

Jesus said, "Judge ye not, so that ye may not be judged." All judgment is stupid. Only stupid people judge fast. The more intelligent you are, the less judgment you carry. If you are *really* intelligent all judgments disappear. Then suddenly you see whatsoever is. But you don't carry any judgment, you don't say, "This man is bad and this man is good." You don't say, "This man is a sinner and this man is a saint." These are all judgments. Who are you to judge? Who has given you the authority to judge?

And when you don't judge anybody, when you drop all judgments, suddenly the whole of life looks so beautiful, so immensely beautiful, so divine. The devil disappears the moment your judgment disappears.

This man came across Lao Tzu by accident so he *took the opportunity to tell him about his son's symptoms*. He was not aware of whom he was talking to.

Lao Tzu is superb, unsurpassed. Unsurpassed before, unsurpassed after. There has never been such a clarity in any man ever, anywhere. Such total understanding, such absolute transparency! Even in a Buddha, even in a Mahavira, even in a Krishna, you will find a little judgment – but not in Lao Tzu.

"How do you know that your son is abnormal?" said Lao Tzu.

"How do you know that your son is abnormal?" He raises a very fundamental question. Who is normal? What is the norm? And how do you decide? The crowd – many people are like that so that is normal? But the whole crowd can be mad.

There is a Kahlil Gibran story.

A magician came to town and threw some medicine into the town well. He said that whosoever would drink from this well would go mad.

There were only two wells in the town: one for the ordinary people and one for the king.

By the evening the whole town had gone mad. They had to drink from the well, even though they knew they would go mad, because it was the only well available to them. And it was a summer day, hot, and they tried not to drink but how long can you try? By and by they yielded. By the evening the whole town had gone mad.

The king was very happy. Standing on his palace terrace he looked around and he said to his prime minister, "We are grateful to God that we have a separate well, otherwise we would also have gone mad. The whole town has become mad." People were dancing, singing, jumping, screaming, howling. The whole town was simply unbelievable. What has happened? It was a nightmare. People were doing sorts of things they had never done before.

But within hours the happiness of the king disappeared because the people came to the palace and they started shouting that the king had gone mad. The king's army was also in the town and they went mad, and his bodyguard and his cook, and his servants. Only the king and the queen and the prime minister, three persons, were left.

Now what can you do against the whole town when it is mad? The king became very afraid and said. "What to do now" The prime minister said, "There is only one thing to be done. I will try and prevent them for a few minutes. You run and drink from that well. There is no other way. You go fast."

The king went, drank from the well, and when he came back he was dancing. The crowd shouted in joy and they said, "Thanks be to God. We are grateful to God. Our king's mind has come back!"

If the whole crowd is mad, the sane person will look mad.

How do you know that all people are not mad? The exceptional looks mad; the common seems to be the norm.

Lao Tzu asked, "How do you know that your son is abnormal?"

I have heard.

A Britisher was having tea on his lawn when a spaceship appeared in the sky. He watched calmly as it circled and came to earth nearby. A weird-looking creature stepped from the craft and slowly approached. The thing had two heads with one eye in the center of each head. It had only one arm which protruded from the middle of its chest. It had no legs but walked on a pair of short flippers.

"Earthman," the apparition squeaked, "I wish to see your leader!"

The Englishman stirred his tea and gazed with distaste at his visitor.

"Nonsense, old man," he said calmly. "What you want to see is a good plastic surgeon."

The exceptional seems to be abnormal. He may be normal on another planet. If you go some day to some other planet you will be abnormal; they will send you to a plastic surgeon immediately.

Lao Tzu says, "How do you know that your son is abnormal?" What criterion is there? What standard do you follow? Norm means the standard. But how do you decide who is normal? Is Buddha normal? Is Jesus normal? Jesus was not normal to the people amongst whom he lived. They murdered him because he was abnormal, because he was talking about things which should not be talked about. Socrates – was he normal? Athens poisoned him because he was abnormal. If you look down the ages, all great people were abnormal. The ordinary seems to be the normal.

Lao Tzu wants to destroy the criterion. He wants to tell you that there is no criterion to judge. Each individual is unique – that is the Tao vision. Each individual is so unique, so incomparably unique, that there is no way to judge who is normal and who is abnormal Look at the freedom Tao gives – you can only say that people are different: nobody is normal, nobody is abnormal. People are simply different.

Once you understand that people are different you drop the idea of inferiority and superiority for the first time. I or the first time comparison disappears that somebody is this way, somebody else is that way.

Somebody asked Bokuju, "Why are you so good and I am not so good? Why are you so silent and I am not so silent?"

Bokuju said, "Come out with me into the garden." And he took him into the garden where there were two trees. One was very tall, almost touching the clouds, and another was very small. He said, "Look. This tree is small and that tree is tall, but I have never heard any discussion between them. The tall one has never said to the small one, "Look, I am superior." And the small one has never said to the tall one, "Because I am so small, I feel very inferior standing just by your side."

No, the small is small and the tall is tall, there is no comparison. The small is beautiful in its smallness, the tall is beautiful in its tallness. The tall is close to the clouds, the small is close to the earth. The tall enjoys tallness, the small enjoys smallness – what is wrong in it?

Nothing is wrong – that is the Taoist vision. Everything is good as it is.

Comparison comes from the human mind. The birds are birds; they are not worried about why they are not animals. The rose is a rose; the rose is not worried about why it is not the lotus. Hence they are not neurotic. Otherwise the rose will become neurotic because he is not a lotus, and the lotus will become neurotic because he is not the rose. And the small bush will lie down somewhere on some psychiatrist's couch because he is not the Cedar of Lebanon. "Why? Why am I not the Cedar of Lebanon? Why has God made me so small – just a bush? For what karmas am I suffering?" She will make some philosophy to console herself, "I have done bad karmas in my past life, that's why."

All rubbish! All theories are rubbish! They are needed because you ask rubbish questions. And then somebody has to supply rubbish answers. There is a law in economics: whenever there is a demand there is a supply. If you ask a foolish question some wise guy is going to give you a foolish answer.

It is very simple. Things are as they are. Things are different, certainly but they are not unequal. Let me repeat it: things are different but they are not unequal. Everything is unique. You cannot find a single leaf in the whole world which is like another leaf. You cannot find a single pebble on the whole earth which is like another pebble. No, nothing is similar, but nothing is unequal. Each thing exists in its own way. That is the meaning of the saying that each thing has its own soul. That uniqueness is what soul means; that uniqueness is the meaning of the saying: "A man has a soul." It simply shows that he is unique. The tree has a soul; it shows it is unique. The mountain has a soul; it simply shows it is unique. Nothing else is just like it.

> "How do you know that your son is abnormal?" said Lao Tzu. "Nowadays everyone in the world is deluded about right and wrong and confused about benefit and harm."

First: because of these comparisons people have started to become imitations. Because you don't recognize your uniqueness, you are not respectful towards your being. You are disrespectful.

Some woman came to me and she said, "What should I do? I am fat." And she is not very fat. Nothing. If she had not said so I would not have thought that she was fat. But she herself goes on saying it. You must know her. She is called Veena and now she has become known as Fat Veena. And she is not fat. She is nothing like it. She does not know what a fat woman can be.

I have heard about one. She came out of a hotel and said to the doorkeeper, "Please call me a taxi."

The doorkeeper looked at her and said, "Okay, if you say so. I will call you a taxi – but you look more like a truck to me!"

But even if a woman is that fat she has a unique soul.

There is no need to be worried. Comparisons should not be brought in. One should be respectful towards one's own being. Comparison comes through others. You see somebody who is lean and thin and a comparison arises. You have a nose which is a little too long and somebody has one with exactly the proportion that is needed. Now a problem arises.

You may not have heard – even Cleopatra was worried She had a nose which was a little too long. Cleopatra is thought to be one of the most beautiful women of the world, but she was always conscious of her nose. It was a little too long. So she was very worried. Her whole body was in proportion, just the nose was creating some trouble.

If you compare, you are going to be neurotic. Somebody has beautiful hair, somebody has a beautiful nose, somebody has beautiful eyes, somebody has beautiful legs and somebody has the right proportion and somebody has the right complexion and somebody is more intelligent and so on and so forth. All these people will create inferiority in you. Or, if your start thinking the other way round, you may start feeling superior. Both are illnesses. To feel inferior is ill and to feel superior is ill – just to feel one is oneself is healthy. Not to compare is healthy.

This constant comparison creates imitation; people start becoming like others. You dress the way others dress, you purchase the cars that others have, you decorate your drawing-room as others have decorated theirs – you go on imitating. And an imitator is never happy because an imitator becomes untrue.

Now what has happened to this man? He thinks that his son is abnormal – maybe his son is not like the son of his neighbor, that's all. The comparison is bringing trouble to his mind. Maybe his son is not like him – but why should the son be like the father?

I have heard.

Three girls were arrested for soliciting. And a peddler, newly arrived in this country, was arrested for peddling without a license. They were brought before the court.

"What do you do for a living?" the judge asked, pointing to the first girl.

"Your honor, I'm a model," she answered.

"Thirty days," was the sentence. Then he turned to the second. "What do you do for a living?" he asked belligerently.

"Your honor, I'm an actress."

"Thirty days." Then he turned to the third girl. "What do you do for a living?" he demanded.

"To tell you the truth," she answered, "I'm a prostitute."

"For telling the truth," he said, "I'm going to suspend sentence."

Then he turned to the little immigrant peddler. "And you," he said, "what do you do for a living?"

"To tell you the truth," the peddler said twisting his ancient cap in his hands, "I'm a prostitute also."

That's how people go on imitating and they think that by imitating one can be true.

By imitating, nobody can ever be true. Imitation is the basis of all falsehood.

> "How do you know that your son is abnormal?" said Lao Tzu. "Nowadays everyone in the world is deluded about right and wrong and confused about benefit and harm."

The mind is confusion. The moment you start thinking about what is right and what is wrong you will be confused. The moment you start thinking about what is harmful and what is beneficial you will be confused.

Have you not heard the story about the centipede?

A centipede has one hundred legs.

A rabbit saw him and could not believe it! It was almost impossible! A hundred legs. How does he manage? Which one has to be moved first and second and third and fourth A hundred legs. How does he manage?

The rabbit was very puzzled and said, "Uncle, I am very confused. I cannot imagine how you manage. If I had one hundred legs I would never be able to walk. I would get so confused."

The centipede had never thought about it, hence he was not confused. But now he said, "I have never thought about it, I will think over it." And he pondered over it. For the first time he became self-conscious. He looked at his legs and he *was* confused. He fell down!

And he said to the rabbit, "Never ask such a question! I have always walked, and there was never any problem. Now you have confused me. Now I will never be able to walk correctly. The problem will haunt me. Which one first? Which one second? And there are one hundred legs!"

Lao Tzu says that mind is confusion. The moment you think, you are confused. Thinking is confusion, hence nobody can go out of confusion by thinking. Thinking will make you even more muddled. One comes out of confusion by non-thinking, by dropping all thought, by dropping all distinctions between right and wrong, between harm and benefit. And how can you know how can the part know what is beneficial and what is harmful? The universe is so vast that one never knows what will finally be the result of your act.

You go and save a man who was drowning in a well; you make all efforts and you get him out. And then the next day he commits a murder. Now, was your saving the man right or wrong? If you had not saved him there would have been no murder. Now the murder has happened. You are also part of the crime. Without you it would not have been possible. But you never thought that way. You were just saving the person. Your whole idea was to help the person who was dying. So what is harmful and what is beneficial?

Sometimes poison becomes beneficial and sometimes nectar can prove poisonous. Sometimes the person who wants to do good to you may do harm and sometimes the person who wanted to do harm to you may do good. Things are very complex; in fact, almost incomprehensible by the human mind. Life is so deep and so complex and we are so small, so tiny. There is no way to figure it out.

So what does Lao Tzu say? Lao Tzu says,

> "Nowadays everyone in the world is deluded about right and wrong and confused about benefit and harm."

How do you decide what is right? What is the criterion? Was Mohammed right when he took up a sword? He was not right according to the Jainas. To take up a sword is wrong. But according to the Mohammedans he was right because he took the sword in his hand to save religion. According to the Mohammedans, Mahavira is an escapist. When people were suffering he was standing there and meditating. When people were being exploited he was just selfish. He escaped to the forest.

When Arjuna sad to Krishna in the Gita, "I don't want to kill so many people, this seems to be the greatest sin that can be committed. I want to renounce the world and go to the forest and become a forest dweller," was he right or wrong ? If you ask the Jainas he was right. But Krishna says, "No, this is wrong. Don't go. This is your duty. Do it. God wills it this way so let it be this way. Escaping from your duty will be going against God. You have not arranged this war. It is happening. You just be instrumental in it. Go into it, but not as a doer, go into it just as an instrument. There is no need to escape anywhere.

"And, Arjuna, even if you do escape you cannot escape because your whole training, your whole discipline of life, is that of a warrior. You cannot escape so easily. Where will you go? You are not a Brahmin, you are not a meditator, you are a warrior. You have to attain your reality only through yourself. *Svadharme nidhanam shreyah* it is good to die into one's own nature; *paradharmo bhayavaha* it is very dangerous to follow somebody else's religion. To be a warrior is your religion. That is what you have trained for your whole life. Each cell of your being is that of a warrior. You cannot meditate, Arjuna. Even if you go into the forest and you sit under a tree, if you see a lion passing by, you will immediately search for your bow. And you will kill it. You will become a hunter, you will not become a meditator. That is not right."

Now what is right and what is wrong? And who decides? If Arjuna had asked Mahavira, Mahavira would have blessed him. He would have said, "Right. For the first time reality has dawned upon you." But Krishna says, "You are an escapist, a coward. This is cowardice." Now who is right and who is wrong?

Ask Lao Tzu. Lao Tzu says that even the distinction between right and wrong is not possible. You simply live, whatsoever. As naturally as possible for you.

I have heard.

A man hired a taxi to the station. From the hotel to the station it was a fixed rate – one rupee. When the man got out of the taxi he gave one rupee to the taximan but the taximan looked unhappy. So the man asked, "Is it not right? Is it not correct ?"

The taximan said, "Sir, it is correct but not right."

You see the distinction? It is correct but not right.

"You have paid me. Legally it is correct. But it is not right. You have not tipped me. That is not part of the formal law but it is a convention."

So what is right? What is correct? Law is limited and life is excessive. If you live according to the law you may be correct but you may not be right. If you live according to life you may be right but you may not be correct.

Lao Tzu's standpoint is that to make the distinction, to bring the distinction in, creates confusion. One should live spontaneously, naturally, and one should not try to follow any right and any wrong. One should remain surrendered. One should live out of a let-go.

> "Because so many people share his sickness no one perceives that it is a sickness."

Because this confusion has become so common, nobody now thinks it is a sickness. All are ill with the same sickness, the same confusion. Not only those who follow but those who lead as well – they are also in the same boat.

Hungry, exhausted and frightened, the hunter dropped his rifle, stumbled forward, and threw his arms about the man who had just emerged from a patch of timber.

"Am I glad to see you," he cried. "I've been lost for two days!"

"What are you so glad about?" mumbled the other hunter. "I've been lost for a week!"

The leaders and the followers, the teachers and the taught, are all in the same boat. Whom to ask? All are ill. The confusion is so common that people have completely forgotten that it is an illness.

> "Besides one man's abnormality is not enough to overturn his family...."

And then he says, "Why be so worried? Even if you think one man is abnormal, what is wrong?"

> "Besides, one man's abnormality is not enough to overturn his family; one family's to overturn the neighborhood; one neighborhood's to overturn the state; one state's to overturn the world."

So why be worried? A single individual, even if you think he is abnormal, even if it is agreed that he is abnormal, why be worried? He cannot overturn the whole world. He can be accepted the way he is. Why try to change him?

> "If the whole world were abnormal how could abnormality overturn it?"

And then, as far as Lao Tzu's own vision is concerned, he says the whole world is abnormal. People may be abnormal in different ways but the whole world is abnormal. But nobody looks at one's own abnormality. It is very easy to think about the other as being abnormal, it is very difficult to think about yourself as being abnormal. It is very easy to have a condemnatory attitude about somebody. Have you ever seen a madman who thinks that he is mad? Never. You can go to the madhouse, you can ask, and they will laugh. They will say, "Are you mad?" A madman never thinks that he is mad. He cannot. If a madman can think that he is mad, then it is certain he is not mad. Such a man, a man who can think that he is mad, cannot be mad.

A few anecdotes....

In a crowded restaurant the psychiatrist was approached by a woman. "See that man over there?" she whispered. "He's my husband and he needs your help. He thinks he's a traffic light. All night long he keeps opening one eye, then closing it, then opening it...."

The headshrinker nodded and said, "I'll go over and have a talk with him."

"No, wait," shouted the woman. "The light's against you!"

It is very difficult to see that oneself is mad and it is very easy to think that the other is mad. It is part of the mad mind to think about the other as mad.

The woman pleaded for help from the psychiatrist. "My husband thinks he's a washing machine. He rolls his head around and around and back and forth and soap and hot water come out of his ears."

The psychiatrist said, "I know it's distressing, but I can't see that this hallucination is doing any harm."

"You don't understand, Doctor," the woman said. "He isn't getting the sheets clean!"

Whenever you think about somebody as mad, wait a minute. There is a greater possibility that you are mad. A really sane man like Lao Tzu says that nobody is mad.

People are simply different. Many people are suffering unnecessarily in hospitals, in madhouses, in mad asylums – suffering unnecessarily. They are not mad, they are different. Certainly they are different. They look at things in a different way, but there is nothing wrong in it.

Van Gogh painted trees so high that they touched the stars. He painted the sun and the moon so small and the trees so big… they go higher and higher and touch the stars. Somebody asked, "Are you mad? Where have you seen such trees? – and suns and moons so small and trees so big?" Van Gogh said, "Whenever I look at a tree, I see the desire of the earth to touch the sky. The tree is the desire of the earth to touch the sky. It is the ambition of the earth. So why be a miser? What the earth cannot do, I can do in my paintings. That's the way I see it: desires of the earth to touch the sky." That is a way of seeing things: nothing is wrong in it. It is very poetic. A man of real understanding will be neutral. He will be like the sun. The sun shines beautifully and poetically as beautifully and as poetically on the dunghill as on the diamond. No distinction is made. That's how real understanding is.

Nobody is sane; nobody is insane. If someday the Tao vision becomes the universal vision many people will be saved from suffering unnecessary suffering. Who decides who is insane? As yet there are no criteria. If you go to a psychiatrist he cannot decide who is mad. All that psychiatrists decide is that this person is too different from others – that's all. But why should he be mad?

And the psychiatrist cannot help much. Even when he tries to bring an insane person to sanity, what can he do? At the most he forces the person to adjust to the view of the crowd. He makes him less individual. He destroys his individuality. Nothing much changes.

A man met a friend who had been under psychiatric care. "How are you progressing?" asked the man.

"Fine," said the friend. "For months I thought I was a fox terrier, but analysis has helped me."

"Are you cured?" asked the man.

"Not exactly," his friend replied, "but I have stopped chasing cars."

At the most this much can be done. Certainly you will think that a person who thinks he is a fox terrier is mad, but what about Adolf Hitler? What about Josef Stalin? What about Chairman Mao Zedong? They don't think they are fox terriers but they are more dangerous. The man who thinks he is a fox terrier, what can he do? Even if he chases cars it is very innocent. He is not doing any harm to anybody. It is an innocent idea. Nothing is wrong in it. But this man will be put into a madhouse and Josef Stalin will become the dictator of Russia and will kill millions of people. And nobody will think that he needs psychiatric help.

This is a very strange world. Innocent people are thought to be mad but nobody thinks the real culprits are mad. Adolf Hitler killed many people – but nobody thought that he was mad while he ruled Germany. Politicians, power-addicted people, money-mad people – nobody thinks that they are mad. But if somebody sitting under a tree starts laughing for no reason at all you think he is mad. He is not doing any harm to anybody. And he may have some reason to laugh which may not be apparent to you.

And, finally, what is *wrong* if somebody laughs without any reason? Why is a reason needed to laugh? A reason is needed to be miserable; to be happy no reason is needed. Happiness should be natural – for no reason. It should be bubbling up. One should be radiant, in tremendous joy, for no reason at all.

> "If the whole world was abnormal, how could abnormality overturn it? Supposing the minds of everyone in the world were like your son's, then, on the contrary, it is you who would be abnormal."

He is raising a beautiful point. He is saying, "Just think! If everybody was like your son then you would be abnormal. Now everybody is like you, so your son is abnormal." The question seems to be only of numbers. Who is in the majority? Whosoever is in the majority is normal and whosoever is in the minority is abnormal.

But is this a criterion for judging? Then all buddhas are abnormal – that's what psychoanalysts really say. They say that Buddha is abnormal because he is so rare. He must be abnormal. Mahavira is abnormal. Jesus is abnormal. You don't find so many Jesus', no crowd of Jesus' exists. Then he must be abnormal. If the majority means normality then Jesus and Buddha and Mahavira and Krishna are abnormal.

But what do you want to be? Would you like to be a buddha or would you like to be just a part of a mob? Even if Buddha is abnormal one would like to be a buddha because he is so happy, so serene, so calm, so tranquil.

Lao Tzu is saying to drop these ideas; they are meaningless. Those distinctions and judgments are foolish.

> "Joy and sorrow, music and beauty, smells and tastes, right and wrong – who can straighten them out?"

He says that joy and sorrow are indefinable, so are music and beauty. Who can figure out what is what? Nobody has yet been able to define what beauty is. And nobody has yet been able to define what good is. Good remains indefinable – so does beauty and so does music. And what music is to one is just a maddening noise to another. If you are trained for classical Indian music then modern Western music will look insane. If you are trained to listen to modern Western music – George Harrison and others – then Indian music will look very boring, dull. It depends on your training. What is music? Nobody has yet been able to define it. All that is significant remains indefinable. *"Who can straighten them out?"*

> "I am not even sure...."

Look at the beauty of it. Says Lao Tzu:

> "I am not even sure that these words of mine are not abnormal...."

What can I say? This is Lao Tzu's absolute health. Only such a healthy person can say, "I am not certain that my words are abnormal or not. There is no way to say." Only a really sane person can say, "Maybe I am mad."

Recently a girl we know found an old love letter which her father had written to her mother when they were courting. The daughter copied the letter, signed a masculine name to it, and mailed it to herself. Then she showed it to her father. There was an explosion like that of an erupting volcano. The father could scarcely express himself. He snorted, "That fellow is the biggest fool I have ever heard of. You better not let him come poking around here or I'll make mince-meat out of him. We don't want such a simp in our family. Any ding-busted, fat-headed idiot who would write such a mess of sickly, silly hogwash to any girl deserves to be ducked in a mud hole – and I'd like to do it!"

Now, he himself has written that letter. Have you not done foolish things when you are in love? Have you not written foolish letters when you are in love? Have you not observed that lovers always look mad to other people? But the same will happen to them – when they are in love others will think that they are mad.

Religious people have always looked mad to the non-religious; worshipping and praying in a temple you look mad to an atheist. You look like a fool, foolish. What are you doing? To whom are you praying? There is no God. A happy person looks mad to unhappy, miserable people.

Those miserable people sometimes accidentally come here too, and when they come here they see a great crowd of mad people around me laughing, dancing, enjoying, singing. They cannot believe it! They are so miserable, how can they believe it? You only believe that which you are. More than that looks impossible, cannot be, should not be. You think that you are the limit of existence, or, you are the definition of existence.

Lao Tzu says:

> "I am not even sure that these words of mine are not abnormal, let alone those of the gentlemen of Lu who are the most abnormal of all."

About Confucius and his followers he is absolutely certain – they are the most abnormal people. They are. The moralists, the puritans they are the most abnormal people in the world. In fact, they have driven the whole of humanity to abnormality. They have not allowed spontaneity, they have not allowed people to be natural. They have condemned everything, they have condemned so much that people are simply at a loss as to how to be, what to be. They have condemned reality so much that all humanity has become fake, pseudo. Everybody is wearing a mask. And all people have lost their original faces.

Two women met on the street for the first time in several months. One of them asked, "How's your son?"

"Haven't you heard?" the other asked. "It's all over town. My son's a schizophrenic."

"Really?" her friend said. "Where's his office?"

All schizophrenic people have now become psychoanalysts. The question "Where is his office?" is relevant. All mad people have turned into moralists, moralizers. They are trying to change the whole world. Whenever you come across a person who is trying to change the whole world, escape from him. He is dangerous.

Nobody is needed to change the whole world. Missionaries are the most mischievous people in the whole world.

Live your life, enjoy your life. If, through your enjoyment and delight, somebody else's life becomes a little more beautiful, good. If not, that too is good.

> ".... let alone those of the gentlemen of Lu who are the most abnormal of all. Who are they to cure other people's abnormality?"

Who are they to cure, to help, to manipulate? Who are they to change others? Don't become self-appointed dictators.

Moralists are self-appointed dictators. They are ready to change everybody. They are ready to sacrifice their life to change your life. And they do sacrifice their life! In sacrifice they are insane. And then they cling around your neck, they suffocate you. The do-gooders are very suffocating. They try to kill you. And you cannot even defend yourself because they say, "We are doing good to you. We are servants of the people. We serve."

These servants are the enemies. They have poisoned the whole of nature. Not only is the atmosphere poisoned, humanity is also poisoned. Scientists have poisoned the outside nature and the so-called religious people have poisoned inner humanity. The whole ecology is disturbed outer and inner, both.

> "Who are they to cure other people's abnormality? You had better go straight home instead of wasting your money."

Look at this advice. You may not be able to understand immediately, but the message is very simple. The message is: don't interfere. The message is: don't judge. The message is: you are nobody to change somebody else. That is not your responsibility. You are not meant to do that. You live your life and allow others to live their life. Let everybody have the freedom to do his thing.

All judgment is immoral and all effort to change somebody is destructive and violent. And that's what your mahatmas and your saints have been doing up to now. That's why I say that Lao Tzu is incomparable, unique, unsurpassed before and after. His vision is the ultimate vision of spontaneity, suchness, nature. If you understand him your life will start moving in a totally different rhythm. You will become a non-interference, *wu-wei*. And only when you don't interfere in another's life do you respect life that's what reverence of life is all about.

My teaching is exactly the same. I cannot say that about anybody else but about Lao Tzu I can say that my teaching is exactly the same. With Buddha I have differences – although I may not tell them. With Mahavira I have many, many differences – although I may not talk about them. But with Lao Tzu I am absolutely in agreement. The agreement is unconditional and absolute because he seems to be the only one who has looked at life without any mind, who has looked at life straight, who has no idea, no ideology.

You can also have exactly the same clarity and transparency that will be the day of benediction, that will be the day of enlightenment. That's what enlightenment is.

Enough for today.

CHAPTER #6

The Cyclone Is the Center

The first question:

Osho,
You have helped me to be in touch with my spontaneity, yet it is the most dangerous quality of life I have ever encountered – especially in relationship. I lose myself. And what hassles you have created through it! Now I feel totally helpless, too vulnerable, possessed by you and this spontaneous union. Where is the center of this cyclone?

There is no center to this cyclone, the cyclone is the center. We have a chronic habit of dividing things into two, we have a chronic habit of duality: God and the world, body and soul, the lower and the higher the good and bad. The habit persists. Now it is the center and the cyclone.

Let me insist on it: the cyclone is the center and there is no other center to it Once you understand this oneness of life then all tension, anxiety, anguish, disappears. The anxiety is created because you are always dividing. Through division you become split; through division you become schizophrenic. Now you think that you are on the circumference – the cyclone – and the center has been lost, so now the center has to be found.

It is the old habit of duality. The "center and the cyclone" is a new language, but this habit is very old, the gestalt is very old. It is always that wherever you are you are not right, you should be somewhere else.

My whole emphasis is that whatsoever is, is right. There is no other right. There is nowhere to go. This is the only life there is, the only dance there is. Only then you can be spontaneous, really spontaneous.

Why have we lost spontaneity? By what trick? The trick is to divide. You cannot be spontaneous about today because you have to think about tomorrow. You cannot be spontaneous this moment because you have to think of the coming moment. You cannot be spontaneous in this life because you have to think about the after-life. You cannot be spontaneous in your act because you have to think about the consequences. It is always a division of now and then, of here and there. Hence spontaneity is lost.

Who is spontaneous? One who lives in this moment as if this is all, is spontaneous. And this *is* all. In the beginning it will be "as if," but slowly, slowly, as you get into tune with it, you will come to know that it is not "as if," it is the only reality there is.

The second thing: spontaneity is dangerous. It will be better if we say "spontaneity is danger." To say "dangerous" means that dangerousness is a quality, accidental. So I say that it is better to say, "spontaneity is danger" – then it is not a quality, it's very intrinsic nature is spontaneity. There can never be spontaneity without danger: danger is spontaneity.

What do I mean? The first thing: when you are spontaneous you are not in control, you cannot be in control. If you are in control then the act is not spontaneous, then you are thinking of the consequences, the results, this and that – a thousand and one things. You are managing. A spontaneous act is one in which you are not the manager; in which God manages, the whole manages – call it Tao; in which you are no longer in control, you have dropped your control, you have surrendered your control. Now you don't know what is happening, you don't know where you are going, you don t know what will be the outcome – and you are not worried about it at all, not even a bit. You are simply herenow, totally. The act is so total that you are absorbed in it, you are not standing outside of it. To control something you have to be outside of it. A controller can never be inside an act a controller is always on the outside – hence the controller can never enjoy. To enjoy, you have to disappear in the act. That disappearance is danger. Now you will be vulnerable – naturally so, obviously so. Now you don't know. Anything is possible. And you are not in control so you cannot direct – this is the danger. There is no direction any more. You are completely drunk with the moment, drowned in it relaxed in it so much that you cannot even feel who you are.

Remember, the feeling that "I am" is the feeling of a tense mind. When the tenseness disappears the "I" also disappears. The ego is nothing but accumulated tension of the past, of the future. Have you not observed some moments in your life when you were not? Those were moments of benediction – those were moments of great blessing, beautitude. In those moments heaven opened for you.

But heaven opens only when you open – and when you open there is danger. The danger simply means that now the future is not in your hands, the future becomes unpredictable. You are at the mercy of the whole – this is what danger is.

So right, Sahajo, your feeling is absolutely right. "You have helped me to be in touch with my own spontaneity, yet it is the most dangerous quality of life I have ever encountered." In fact, this is the first time you have encountered life, because life is spontaneity and life is danger.

Have you ever heard of any man who has lived without danger? To live means to be in danger, to die means to be out of danger. Those who are in their graves are out of danger, out of all danger. Now nothing can happen to them: nobody can insult them, nobody can kill them, nobody can rob them. Not even death is possible. They are absolutely beyond all danger.

So people who are too afraid of danger start living in a sort of grave; they create a grave of security around themselves and they start living in that grave, a subtle grave, a mind grave. They feel protected. But against whom are you protected? Against life. The moment you protect yourself you are creating barriers against life – then less and less life will be coming. A person who is secure is a person who is dead.

To live means to live dangerously; to live means to remain available to all possibilities. And infinite are the possibilities. You are not limited to any possibility, you have an unlimited being, unbounded. You can be anything; the next moment can bring anything. Deep down each individual is a whole humanity – not only a whole humanity, a whole existence. The tree exists in you, the dog exists in you, the tiger exists in you; the whole past exists in you and also the whole future. In a very atomic way all that has happened in the world and all that is going to happen exists in you potentially. You can be in millions of ways hence to live means to live dangerously, to live means to live through change, movement. One remains a river.

If you are secure you become a pool of water; there will be no movement, no dynamism. Static, stagnant, the pool of water becomes dirty and by and by it dies. A river is alive and nobody knows what will happen. It may get lost in a desert. What is going to happen is unpredictable. A predictable life is a mechanical life; unpredictable and you are throbbing with life, pulsating, vibrating. Then God, or Tao, or the whole, lives through you.

You have come across life for the first time, Sahajo don't lose this contact whatsoever the cost. I know it is costly to be alive and it is very cheap to be dead. It costs nothing to be dead, it costs much to be alive. One has to pay for it.

"...yet it is the most dangerous quality in life I have ever encountered – especially in relationship." Yes, it will become more clear in relationship because when you are alone you don't have any mirror. Just as you need a mirror to see your face so you need the mirror of relationship to see your being. Love functions as a mirror, it shows you where you are, what you are, who you are. Hence many people become afraid of relationship. They are cowards. They escape to the Himalayas or to Tibet or to the monasteries or to the caves. Why are they escaping and from what? They are escaping from mirrors.

I have heard about an ugly woman who would never look in a mirror because she used to think that mirrors were against her. While she thought she was one of the most beautiful women in the world, they showed her ugliness. If somebody presented her with a mirror she would simply throw it away or break it immediately. She would never go into a room where there was a mirror because she felt that mirrors had always been against her.

These are your mahatmas. They escape from relationship because relationship shows their ugliness, relationship shows where they are, who they are. Sitting in their caves in the Himalayas they feel perfectly beautiful because there is no mirror.

Never escape from relationship. That's why I have introduced sannyas with relationship, not without it. There is great meaning in it. Never on the earth has sannyas existed with relationship, that's why I say that sannyas has not really existed, or, the sannyas that has previously existed was anemic, bloodless. People thought they were beautiful, without the mirror they thought they were beautiful. It is very easy to befool yourself when the mirror is not there.

When you are in relationship with people, in a thousand and one ways you are provoked, challenged, seduced. Again and again you come to know your pitfalls, your limitations, your anger, your lust, your possessiveness, your jealousy, your sadness, your happiness all moods come and go, you are constantly in a turmoil. But this is the only way to know who you are.

Self-knowledge is not the knowledge of a dead self, self-knowledge is the knowledge of the process of the self. It is an alive phenomenon. The self is not a thing, it is an event, it is a process. Never think in terms of things, the self is not there inside you just like a thing waiting in your room. The self is a process: changing, moving, arriving at new altitudes, moving into new planes, going deeper into new depths. Each moment much work is going on and the only way to encounter this self is to encounter it in relationship.

Love is the mirror. Let your meditation be mirrored in love. If you find that something is missing, meditate more – but never escape from love; let it be mirrored in love again and again, because that will be the only criterion of whether you are growing or not. If you are really growing in love soon you will see that love has remained and jealousy has disappeared; love has remained and possessiveness has disappeared: love has remained and hatred has disappeared. A great purity arises, a great innocence. A fragrance is released into your soul. Go on meditating and go on loving. Let love and meditation be two wings. Let them help each other.

I am showing you a path which is arduous, which is really arduous. Love alone is good because there is nothing to reflect, meditation alone is simple because there is no mirror to reflect, but meditation and love together.... I am throwing you into the very eye of the storm. But that is the only way one comes home.

And when things become silent after the storm, the silence is alive, it is not the dead silence of a cemetery.

".... especially in relationship. I lose myself. And what hassles you have created through it!" That's my whole work here – to create hassles for you, to send you on hazardous journeys, to push you into new ways of being, into new styles, into the unknown, the unfamiliar, the strange. You would like to remain with the familiar because there you have become very efficient. My whole effort here is to push you again and again out of the familiar into the unfamiliar because wherever you have become efficient you have become mechanical. Machines are efficient. So when you become efficient, know well that now you have to move. Now this is no longer of any value, you have to move. You have learned it, now move and learn something else.

If a person remains a learner each moment of his life, from birth to death, only then enlightenment comes, otherwise not.

So never stop anywhere. Somebody asked Buddha 'What is enlightenment?' And he said, *"Charaiveti, charaiveti"* – go on walking, go on walking, never stop, become an eternal journey.

Yes, you can stop for an overnight stay, you call rest under a tree, but don't make your house there. Let the eternal growth be your only house. There is no end to it – that is the meaning of saying that God is infinite. There is no end to it. You go on arriving and arriving and arriving but you never really arrive. You go on coming closer and closer and closer but you can never say that you have arrived…reality is so infinite, how can you claim it in your fist?

"Now I feel totally helpless…" Good. Blessed are you, Sahajo. To be totally helpless is to be in the hands of God. If you still feel that a little help is possible through your own effort, then God will not be available.

There is a beautiful story.

Krishna was just going to take his lunch, he had started, he had taken a bite, he was chewing but suddenly he jumped up and ran towards the door.

Rukmani, his wife, said, "What are you doing my Lord? Where are you going? What is the hurry? This is so sudden!"

Then Krishna stopped at the door, waited for a moment, came back, looked very sad, sat down again and started eating.

Rukmani was even more puzzled. She said, "Now you have puzzled me even more. Why did you jump up so suddenly to go to the door and why did you come back? You jumped up as if the house was on fire. I don't see anything happening anywhere. And why have you come back if there was something happening?"

Krishna said, "There was something. One of my devotees is walking on the earth in a certain city. And he is singing my song, playing on his veena, dancing in the street, but people are throwing stones at him and blood is flowing from his forehead. He had not reacted at all, he was absolutely silent, absolutely centered, absolutely helpless. I was needed, I was needed to help him immediately."

And Rukmini said, "Then why did you come back from the door if you were needed so urgently?"

Krishna said, "There was no need then. The moment I reached the door he had taken a stone in his hand. Now he is helping himself. My help is not needed."

This is a beautiful parable. God helps you only when you are really totally helpless, absolutely helpless. In your absolute helplessness ego is completely gone. What is helplessness? Egolessness. Egolessness is helplessness. You cannot do anything. How can you be when you cannot do anything? The ego functions through the doer. If you can do a little bit still then the helplessness is not total. And God only comes to you when you are totally lost. When you are really helpless, help comes.

Become totally helpless. I don't think, Sahajo, that you are totally helpless. You are feeling helpless but not totally. Go a little deeper into it. And a moment will come, the moment of transformation will come, where you disappear and the whole takes everything in his hands.

"I am feeling too vulnerable, possessed by you and this spontaneous union. Where is the center of this cyclone?" Nowhere. The cyclone is the center. Lose yourself in this cyclone. Losing yourself in this cyclone you find the center. But the center is not separate from the cyclone. God is not separate from the world, the soul is not separate from the body, mind is not separate from matter, the outer is not separate from the inner, the lower is not separate from the higher, it is one reality, one solid reality. Lose yourself in it and you will find that the cyclone is the center. The moment you have found that the cyclone is the center you have found a great truth, you have arrived at the door from where you can enter the innermost shrine of life, love, meditation, existence.

The second question:

Osho,
What is in my womb – a ghost, or a goat, or God?

A difficult question because I am not a womb-reader. Wait a little. Time will show who is in your womb.

An old man had a set of monkey glands installed in his system and shortly thereafter was married. In due time his wife was in the maternity room while he waited outside the door. When the doctor opened the door the husband besieged him.

"What is it," he begged, "a boy or a girl?"

"Don't be so impatient," said the doctor. "Wait till it comes down off the chandelier and I'll tell you."

If you have monkey glands installed in you then a monkey is born. So the doctor said, "Don't be so impatient. Wait till it comes down off the chandelier and I will tell you."

Wait a little, I don't know how you have managed, what kind of soul you have called into your womb. But a few inferences can be made. They are just inferences, guesswork.

You must have heard the proverb: Hope for the best and expect the worst. So I hope it is a God and I expect it is a ghost. But these are extremes and extremes generally don't happen; what happens usually is the middle, so the greater possibility is that it is a goat. A goat is just midway between a God and a ghost, a cross between a God and a ghost. But, in a way, a goat is better than either because if a God is born I will not find a new sannyasin because God need not be a sannyasin, and if a ghost is born it will be difficult to persuade him, he is already in the service of the devil.

But if a goat is born it will be a beautiful sannyasin, Swami Goatananda Paramahansa.

Wait!

The third question:

Osho,
If Krishnamurti is enlightened he must see what you are saying himself, right? So why doesn't he just come here and find himself a chair and a case of cold sodas and lean back and forget all that?

He sees what I am saying and I see what he is saying, but neither will he come here nor will I go there. I am doing my thing, he is doing his thing.

Remember, even after enlightenment the uniqueness of the individual remains intact. That uniqueness is so deep that it never leaves you. When a man becomes enlightened his uniqueness blooms rather than disappears. It comes to bloom. A buddha becomes enlightened in his own way. The enlightenment is the same, the experience of the light is the same, the experience of truth is the same, but the experiencer has an individuality, a unique individuality.

For example, during the night, on a full-moon night, the moon is one – but it will be reflected by the sea in a different way, it will be reflected by the river in a different way, it will be reflected by a cool, placid pool in a different way. The moon is one but the sea will reflect it in its way – great waves will be arising. The river will reflect it in its own way – small ripples, small waves will arise. A placid pool, a silent pool, will reflect it in its own way – there are ripples. The moon is still the same, the reflections are also not different, but the medium of reflection is different.

So what I am saying Krishnamurti sees, what he is saying I see – but I will go on doing my work and he will go on doing his work. There is no other possibility. When Buddha becomes enlightened he functions in his own way. When Meera becomes enlightened she functions in her own way. Buddha cannot dance and Meera dances so beautifully. Buddha sits silently under the Bodhi tree, there is not even a slight movement, he is almost like a statue.

The first statues were created of Buddha and it cannot be just accidental, he looked so statue-like. In fact, in Arabic – Urdu – the word for statue is "budh" and the word itself comes from Buddha. Those were the first statues ever created of any man. It is difficult to create a statue of Meera – she is such a movement, a dance. Buddha's statue is very simple and the marble reflects him perfectly well. Even when he was alive, sitting under the Bodhi tree, he was almost a marble statue; there was no movement, no wavering. That is beautiful, it has its own beauty, it has its own variety. And Meera is also beautiful.

Mahavira became naked when he became enlightened, Buddha continued to use his clothes. Mahavira's nakedness is beautiful – such innocence. Krishna is totally different, Christ is totally different. And then there is this man, Lao Tzu. No two enlightened persons have ever been the same, cannot be. Even unenlightened people are not the same, how can enlightened people be the same? Even unenlightened people, imitating each other, cannot destroy their individuality completely, utterly. They react in their own ways even though they try to efface them.

Society wants you to efface your individuality completely; society does not like individuals. It likes you to become a member of the society, not an individual. It does not want you to become independent, it wants you to be a dependent link and it wants you to live the way others are living. The moment you assert your individuality, society comes in and puts you back into your place, it forces you to be just like others. There is danger when you assert your individuality, because you are becoming chaotic, you are becoming anarchic. No, you have to follow the order.

But even unenlightened people, forced by society and the state and the church, still retain their individuality. There is really no way to drop your individuality utterly. Something unique is there – what can you do? You can hide behind the same clothes, you can hide behind the same masks, you can hide behind the same words, same philosophies, same slogans, same flags, but still, all this is just skin deep. Scratch a person and you will find an individual soul, unique. Never has there been such a person before, never will there be again.

Two hipsters were visiting a small Alaska town when they heard some rumbling in the distance.

"Hey, cat," one hipster said to a native. "What's that crazy noise?"

"That noise means an avalanche is starting," said one of the locals. "In the past we've had to leave here for safety's sake."

"Man," said the second hipster, "I don't dig this. Let's beat it."

"You can go if you want to," screamed hipster number one, "but I'm staying. I've got a feeling this town is really going to move tonight!"

If you look into people you will find that in situations absolutely alike – or even in one situation – they react differently, they respond differently.

So what to say about enlightened persons? They are like peaks, peaks of the Himalayas, absolutely alone, unique. Never compare two enlightened persons. If you understand well, never compare any two persons – but at least about two enlightened persons never be comparative, because whatsoever you think will be wrong.

It is very natural. If you are close to me you fall in love with me and naturally you start thinking that this is the only way to be enlightened. Then other enlightened people start looking wrong somehow, because you have a fixed idea of enlightenment. How can they be enlightened? If you are with Krishnamurti the same will happen there – you will fall in love with him and you will start thinking that this is the only way a person can be enlightened.

Beware of this stupidity. There are as many possibilities of enlightened people as there are unenlightened people. Every person will be unique when he becomes enlightened. He will be a flower, new, incomparable. And always remember, God loves variety. That's why there is so much variety – there are millions of forms and never any repetition.

Krishnamurti is beautiful, so is Buddha, so is George Gurdjieff, so is Raman, so is Ramakrishna. They are all beautiful. If you fall in love with one enlightened person don't let love make you blind. It you are alert you will go on loving me but that will not make you blind. You will be able to understand that there are other possibilities too. All the possibilities are not exhausted by me, cannot be exhausted by me. Nobody can exhaust all the possibilities.

And it is beautiful that nobody can exhaust all the possibilities otherwise Buddha or Lao Tzu or Mahavira or Buddha would have exhausted all the possibilities. Then what would we have been doing here?

The fourth question:

Osho,
What is the difference between being special and being unique?

Being unique is everybody's nature, being special is relative. When you start feeling that you are special you are comparing yourself with somebody. Special: in comparison to somebody; unique: there is no comparison. Unique means you are alone as you are – how can you be compared? You cannot compare a car with an elephant. They are so different, how can you compare? Each individual is so different from any other individual that there is no possibility of comparing.

Uniqueness is everybody's nature, but specialness is comparative. Uniqueness is religious, specialness is political. When you claim that you are special you are claiming that you are higher, superior to others; that others are lower, inferior to you. You bring the other in when you use the word "special" and this is violent. To compare yourself with somebody in any way is violent because he is he and you are you and you are both so different. The very idea of comparing is stupid.

And through comparison misery arises: either you feel you are inferior, then there is misery, or you start feeling you are superior, then too there is misery. If you feel superior, ego arises – and ego hurts. If you feel inferior, ego is wounded – and those wounds hurt. And you may feel superior to one person but what about others? You may one day or other come across somebody to whom you feel inferior. With one person you may feel intelligent, with another you may look like a pygmy. With one you may feel beautiful, with another you may start feeling ugly.

To carry the idea of comparison you are carrying seeds of illness which will create misery and nothing else. Comparison creates hell. Heaven is an inner space where you live a life uncompared. You simply live yourself, it is your life, you are you just think of the beauty of it, the tremendous purity of it. You are simply you. Then are you beautiful? Are you ugly? Are you intelligent, or unintelligent? If you are simply you and there is no comparison, how can you say you are this or that? Then both disappear. There arises neti-neti, neither this nor that. Then you are simply there.

Just think...the whole world disappears and you alone are left. God takes away the whole world and only you are left, nobody else. Then what will you be – strong, weak, intelligent, unintelligent, beautiful, ugly? Then who will you be? All comparisons will disappear, you will simply be yourself. That is the way to be.

Right now, be that! Don't create unnecessary misery for yourself and for others. Start living a unique life.

Uniqueness is everybody's nature. With the feeling of being special ambition enters, comparison enters, jealousy enters, conflict enters. You become political. Then you start pulling others down because you have to be superior. Then you start fighting, struggling, and then you start using all sorts of means. You have to prove and perform and your whole life is wasted in this nonsense.

Three ambitious politicians were walking along the beach, planning a strategic move to defeat a powerful rival, when they came upon Mulla Nasruddin looking for crabs. As each crab was caught, the Mulla put it into a wicker basket.

Looking into the container, one of the politicians warned Nasruddin, "Mulla, you should cover your basket. If you are not careful the crabs will climb out and run away."

"Oh, I don't need any cover," explained Nasruddin. "These crabs are born politicians and if one crab tries to climb up, the others will pull him down."

This is what is happening continuously in life. You are pulling others down, others are pulling you down, and the whole life is wasted in this unnecessary struggle. Just be yourself and you are unique, and that uniqueness is non-violent.

Never try to be special. In the very idea of being special you are feeling inferior. In the very idea of being superior to somebody or inferior to somebody you have lost contact with yourself, with your uniqueness. In that very idea you have become your own enemy. Now you will be in trouble, you will create more and more misery for yourself and for others, you will create ripples of misery all around you.

A man who simply relaxes in his uniqueness is a man who creates ripples of bliss around him. He lives in bliss and he creates pulsations of bliss for others also. If you are around such a person you will suddenly be showered with great peace and love and silence and happiness – because he is happy. The moment you accept your uniqueness, your individuality, how can you be unhappy?

Just think of it in this way: God has never created anybody else like you and he will never create anybody else like you. God has created only one you – only *one* you, mind – and he is never going to repeat you again. This is your uniqueness. Feel grateful, feel thankful, once you start comparing you feel ungrateful. Why has he created somebody more beautiful than you, or somebody more intelligent than you? You are bringing misery upon yourself. He has created only you, he has conferred uniqueness on you. It is a gift. Uniqueness is a gift of God, specialty is your own effort. Your effort is not going to be of much use, your doing always proves your undoing.

Ambitious persons become cruel and hard; ambitious persons become rock-like, they lose their softness, they become closed. Their heart is no longer like a flower. How can you be like a flower when you have to fight and struggle? And it is a very difficult world then – cut-throat competition everywhere. Everybody is at your neck and you are at everybody's neck; everybody is trying to destroy you and you are trying to destroy everybody. Where will you find a creative break? Where will you find a break-through? Where will you enjoy and how?

No, all your moments of so-called joy will only be when you are able to crush somebody, when you are able to destroy somebody. But how can destruction bring joy? It is not the law of life.

A grocer was delivering some groceries in his wagon one morning when he ran down and badly injured an old lady. The old lady sued him and collected big damages. A few weeks later he ran down an old gentleman. The old gentleman also sued and collected big damages, which almost ruined him.

One Sunday the grocer was sitting at home when his son came running through the door. "Father! Father!" the little boy cried. "Mother's been run over by a hundred-and-eighty-horsepower touring car."

The grocer's eyes filled with tears and, in a voice trembling with genuine emotion, he cried, "Thank the Lord, the luck's changed at last."

His wife is dying on the road but he says, "Thank the Lord, the luck's changed at last." Now he call sue somebody and get all the money back.

An ambitious mind, a greedy mind, a jealous mind, becomes hard, stone-like. And remember, if you are stone-like you will hurt others – but that is only secondary, you ill he hurting yourself continuously. Only sometimes will your stone hurt others but your stoniness will hurt you continuously, twenty-four hours, day in, day out, year in, year out. The stone will be there in your heart pinching, hurting, wounding.

One is happy only when one is flower-like – delicate soft, a lotus: To remain a lotus one has to drop all comparisons, all jealousies – and they are stupid anyway, meaningless.

The fifth question:

Osho,
I have been here two years doing nothing to improve myself, just reading, eating, sleeping, drifting. Now I feel as empty and lost as the day I came. Is there any point in staying longer?

This is from Sambuddha.

The first thing, you have not been just reading, just eating, just sleeping, just drifting. If you had been doing that you would have been enlightened by now. That is the ultimate relaxed state – just eating, just reading.... No, you must have done a thousand and one other things too. While reading you must have been thinking many, many things; while eating you must have been thinking; even while sleeping you must have been dreaming....

One thing: if you can really do this, then nothing else is needed – that is all. The very ultimate in *sadhana* is just to do the thing that you are doing in that moment with no other thought interfering. Eating, you are simply eating.

Not a single thought moves in your mind. Eating, you are just an eater; walking, you are just a walker; listening, you are just listening.

But no, when you are listening you are not just listening, you are interpreting, criticizing, appreciating, saying yes, saying no, agreeing, disagreeing. You are not listening, you are doing something else. You are hearing, certainly, but you are not listening.

A small boy was brought to a psychoanalyst. The mother who had brought the boy talked for a long time and the psychoanalyst was getting bored. Then, when he got the chance, he talked about many things. The boy was getting very bored, and the psychoanalyst, seeing that the boy was not listening to what he was saying, was somewhere else, said, "Have you some difficulty in hearing me?"

The kid said, "No, I have no difficulty in hearing but I have much difficulty in listening."

The hearing is perfect. If your ears are healthy you hear perfectly well – but hearing is not listening. Listening has a depth to it; listening means that the mind is quiet, still, no thought wavers in it. Otherwise you go on interpreting and you will certainly interpret in your own way.

An old lady, who was walking her dog, decided to go into the local supermarket which didn't allow dogs. She tied the animal to a fire hydrant. No sooner was the dog tied up when every dog in the neighborhood that was loose started sniffing the defenseless animal. The cop on the corner, observing what was happening, called to the old woman and told her that she couldn't leave her dog there alone.

She asked him why and he replied, "Lady, your dog is in heat."

She answered, "Eat, she'll eat anything."

He countered, "The dog should be bred."

The old lady replied, "She'll eat bread, cake; anything you give her, she'll eat."

In complete frustration he said, "That dog should be laid!"

The old woman stared directly into his eyes and answered. "So lay her. I always wanted a police dog."

How you listen depends on you. Your mind is continuously creating its own interpretations.

No, it is not possible that you have been just reading, eating, sleeping, drifting. If you could do that then nothing else is needed.

Second thing: "I have been here two years doing nothing to improve myself." That's what I told Sambuddha – not to do anything to improve. But he must have been watching out of the corner of his eye again and again to see whether any improvement is happening or not. When I say to you "don't do anything to improve yourself," you agree, just to improve. You agree and yet you don't agree. You say, "Okay, if that is the way to improve, I am ready."

But you miss the point! You miss absolutely. You say. "Okay, if that is the only possibility to improve...." Deep in the unconscious that's how the logic goes. "Osho says drop all ideas of improvement, so I will" and then you continuously watch what is happening. Then one month has passed, two months have passed, one year has passed, now two years have passed... and improvement has not happened.

It cannot happen because you are still looking for it. It can happen only when the whole idea has become simply foolish, when you have dropped it. If the idea of improvement continues, no transformation is possible – because the very idea comes from the ego. The ego wants to improve.

Remember the difference between improvement and transformation. I am here to help you to be transformed, transmuted, you are here to improve yourself – that's where our languages are different. You are here to add some more experiences to your life to become a little more loving, a little more meditative. You are here to decorate yourself a little more, to succeed in life, to have more pleasures. You are here to improve, you are not here to die and be reborn.

My whole effort here is to destroy you utterly so that you can be created in a totally new way. I would like to create a discontinuity in your life – you want the same continuity. Sambuddha wants Sambuddha to improve, he wants some more decorations, some more gold medals – but the original center remains the same. That's the problem and that's why transformation cannot happen.

Even if you improve, nothing will happen.

I have heard about an old woman who went to a theater. Suddenly her ears started buzzing. She was an old woman and something went wrong with her ears so she stopped hearing anything. But she thought that it must be because she was sitting so far away from the stage that she could not hear.

So she changed her seat and went to the front, but there also she could not hear anything.

Naturally she thought, "What is the matter? The acoustics

of this hall are not good. Maybe the people in the balcony are hearing." She looked up and the people were looking very interested so she changed her ticket and went to the balcony. Again she could not hear.

The manager, seeing that she had changed her ticket again and again, came to her and asked her what the matter was. She said, "Something is wrong. The acoustics of this theater are not good, because wherever I go I cannot hear." And the manager said, "Lady, maybe something is wrong with your ears."

Now if something is wrong with the ears you can change your place but nothing will happen, no improvement will happen. You will have to change something inside you. If the ego is there you can improve – if you are poor, you can become rich; if you are immoral, you can become moral: if you are a sinner, you can become a saint. You call change seats, you can move from the ground floor to the balcony, but nothing will happen because the ego is there. You will remain in the same suffering. The labels may change, names may change, but the suffering remains the same.

My effort here is to help you to drop the ego. And the greatest difficulty in dropping the ego is to drop this plan to improve. The ego exists by planning: how to improve, how to become more and more, how to become great, how to become a hero, how to become a buddha. That's how the ego exists – by projecting.

I told Sambuddha to drop all projecting – just to be. Now, after two years, he says: "I have been here two years doing nothing to improve myself...." No, you were doing nothing only to improve yourself. That's what you were doing and that's why you have failed and you will fail continuously.

Look into the whole phenomenon, go deep into your own mind and see what you have been doing. On the surface you were not doing anything, but you were waiting for the transformation to happen. What I am saying is: forget about the future and live the now. Now is the only time and here the only space. Live now and here.

Forget about improvement, forget about transformation,

then one day it happens – but only when you have completely forgotten it, only then. If you remember it, *you* function as a barrier.

"I have been here two years doing nothing..." Doing nothing is not so easy. Doing nothing means allowing the whole to do thing, allowing Tao to happen. Doing nothing is the greatest thing in the world. If a man can do nothing then everything happens, then all is possible, because to do nothing means one becomes nothing, nobody, emptiness. And out of that emptiness arises all that is, all that is possible, all that is potential. Out of emptiness opens the lotus of being.

"Now I feel as empty and lost as the day I came." You have been changing seats but, because you are deaf, you can go to the balcony, you can go to the front seat, you can go to the back and nothing will change. Yes, in two years or two hundred years or two hundred lives, nothing will change. Change comes only when you are no longer interested in change, when you are no longer interested in any improvement, when you are in total acceptance, when "suchness" happens.

But one thing has happened. When you came two years ago I knew well that you were not aware of your emptiness. Now you are aware. That is something that has happened. Now you are more aware of your emptiness, more aware of your misery, more aware that you are not going anywhere, that nothing is happening. This is good. This awareness will become more and more penetrating, will become more and more crystal-clear, and one day this awareness will come to a point, to a conclusion, where you will see that nothing ever happens.

Right now you think nothing is happening to you this is the beginning. One day you will come to understand that nothing ever happens. Nothing has ever happened – not only not to you, to nobody. Nothing has ever happened. How can anything happen? All that is, is. What else can be? And in that moment all happens.

Buddha searched for enlightenment for six years. Remember, you have been here only two years. For six years he searched hard and he did all sorts of things; whatsoever was said to him he did he fasted, meditated, did yoga, did everything that was told to him, did everything that he had heard, did everything that was traditionally available. He tried all. He went to many masters and he was such a great seeker that each master to whom he went became interested in him. And his search was so honest, he was so earnest, his thirst was so authentic, that even though he had not arrived at the goal, the masters wanted him to succeed them, to be their successor.

Wherever he went every master told him, "Be here. Don't leave me. You will be my successor." But he said, "What am I going to do as your successor? I have not attained yet. I don't know exactly what life is. I am not interested in being a successor or becoming a great master, I am interested in knowing. I am not even a disciple yet so how can I be a master?" And he left.

After six years of hard struggle, of strenuous, arduous struggle, one day he came to understand that nothing is possible, nothing ever happens, nothing has ever happened to anybody, that he had been searching in vain, the whole search was futile. This was not a frustration, remember, this was not a hopelessness, it was a great understanding. A great light came to him – that nothing ever happens, whatsoever is, is. What is, is, and what ain't, ain't.

So he sat under the Bodhi tree and forgot all about his struggles – and that very night he became enlightened. The moment he dropped all struggle and became non-tense, anxiety disappeared. There was nowhere to go so he was there in that moment, total, no desire left, no nirvana, no moksha, no enlightenment. Nothing ever happens; whatsoever is, is.

He rested. After six years he slept without a dream because dreams come only because you desire. Dreams are reflections of your desires. No dreams. The whole night he slept. He slept for the first time – it was almost samadhi. In the morning when he opened his eyes there was no effort even to open his eyes. Listen to it well: there was no effort, the sleep was complete so the eyes opened. That's how the Buddhist scriptures say it he did not open his eyes, because he was no longer there. With sleep complete, the eyes opened. The doer was gone, utterly gone. There was no one to open the eyes, it was a natural phenomenon – just as a bud opens in the morning because it is ready to open, the energy is ready to open. The tree does not try to open it. Buddha found his eyes opening and he looked at the sky and the last star was disappearing. And with that last star disappearing he disappeared utterly, forever.

And he laughed. It was so simple. He was making it difficult by his doing, by his effort.

If you really leave your efforts, nobody is barring the path you can become enlightened this very moment. As far as I am concerned you are already enlightened, it is only your delusion that you are not enlightened. The day I became enlightened the whole existence became enlightened for me; from that day since, I have never come across a person who is not enlightened. You may think you are not but that is your thinking, it is not true, it is not the truth. I know you are enlightened, that's why I give you such beautiful names – Sambuddha. It means one who is enlightened. For me you are enlightened, Sambuddha; for you you are not enlightened. So drop your idea of your being and your ego, it is already the case.

And you say: " I feel as empty and lost as the day I came." No, you are more aware of your hopelessness. The day you came you were full of desire, the day you came you were full of hope. I remember very well, you may have forgotten. You came to me only because of hope, otherwise why should you come to me? For what? You came to me in the hope that you would attain. You were full of hope. And you were doing many things – meditations, groups – and you were enjoying the trip. And then I said, "Don't do anything." And you were very happy thinking that now you must have attained a very high state – that's why I was saying, "Don't do anything." But then you became depressed, then you became desperate – that I have been watching for two years. Now you are feeling very, very hopeless.

But things have changed. This hopelessness is good. That hope was illusory, this hopelessness is on the right track. If you really understand that nothing ever happens, that nothing can ever happen in the nature of things, that all is already there, then no improvement is possible. How can you improve upon God? How can you improve upon the whole? The perfect is perfect, how can you make it more perfect? There is no way.

When this understanding goes a little deeper.... The moment is coming. If you don't escape, the moment is coming. But remember, don't start hoping because I say that the moment is coming, otherwise again you will settle and you will start looking out of the corner of the eye to see if the moment is coming. The moment can come only when you stop all this nonsense of having to become something, to do something, to be something.

The situation is different. You are less hopeful. That's why you are saying: "Is there any point in staying longer?" There was never any point. In the very beginning there was no point in staying here. But there is no point in going anywhere else either; in fact, there is no point! So if you want to go, you can go but there is no point, remember. If you want to stay, stay, but remember, there is no point. And you will have to be somewhere so why not here?!

But relax because there is no point. You can relax.

Mind is very cunning, very clever, and because of its cunningness it misses much.

In a discussion between Mulla Nasruddin and his friend Sheik Abdulla, the Sheik maintained that no one could pray without having his mind wander. However, the Mulla positively stated that his mind never wandered while he was praying.

"If you come to me next Saturday and tell me honestly that your mind did not wander once from your prayers on Friday," said the Sheik, "I will give you one of the best horses from my stables."

On the following Saturday the Mulla presented himself to get the horse.

"Are you sure, Nasruddin, that your mind didn't wander once during the prayers?" asked the Sheik.

"Well, maybe it did, once, at the end of the last prayer," was Mulla Nasruddin's reply, "when I wondered whether you would give me a saddle too!"

Now when you are hoping for the horse the idea may come into the mind, "I wondered whether you would give me a saddle as well."

When you are waiting for something, ideas cannot stop. If you are not waiting for anything ideas can stop. I repeat it again: there is no point, life is pointless, purposeless. Existence is not going anywhere, it has no destiny, no purpose. It is. Simply, purely, it is. There is no why. It is because it cannot be, because it cannot not be.

Relax, and start enjoying. Rather than planning and thinking, start enjoying. Read, enjoy: eat, enjoy; listen enjoy: love, enjoy. These are small things but out of these small things arises the great understanding. The ego always says these are small things, seek the big, seek the huge, seek the great, seek God, seek buddhahood and I say to you, there are no great things, only small things. You love well, you love deeply; you sing well, you sing deeply: you dance well, you dance deeply. Sleep well, go for a morning walk, do small things – cleaning, taking a bath, working in the ashram. Enjoy small things. There is no other point and there is nowhere to go.

Drop hopes, drop desires, and be. And suddenly you will find you have always been a buddha. It has never been otherwise. Buddhahood is our intrinsic nature.

But listening to me, even listening to me, you listen with ideas, with a mind standing just around the corner. You have a fixed desire, you never leave that.

A young suitor was being led through the voluminous pages of the old family album by his girl's proud father. After seeing scores of members of the clan, the young man was finally shown the picture of a solid-looking old gentleman. "This," said the father proudly, "is the founder of the family."

"What did he do?" asked the young man.

"He founded the family," the older man said again.

"I mean, sir," the suitor floundered, "what did he do to distinguish himself?"

"He was the founder of the family," the father rasped in exasperation.

"I understand that, sir," the suitor sighed. "I just wondered what the old gent did in the daytime."

If you have a certain fixed idea, it has to come sooner or later.

Sambuddha has a fixed idea, a curiosity, a desire – a desire to become enlightened. So, I understand, it must have been hard for him to wait and wait and wait for two years with nothing happening. Nothing is going to happen ever.

Drop waiting, start being. Waiting is a thought process, being is existential. Live, live as much as you can, as intensely as you can, as passionately as you can. And through that passionate love for life, through that flame of passion of authentic living something burns down in you – the ego. And when the ego is burnt down, something happens. That happening has nothing to do with your effort. It comes. It is a happening.

The sixth question:

Osho,
I am attached and addicted to sitting before you at the discourse. Should anyone sit in what I call "my seat," I have to use every ounce of restraint not to freak. You are my everything, everything else can go but it seems this possessiveness remains. I am, it seems without love or mercy when it comes to giving up "my seat."

The question is from Divya.

I have been missing her for many days. She is not in her seat. And it has nothing to do with possessiveness. She should not be worried about it. In fact, she has found the right spot for her, hence it is difficult for her to leave that spot. It has nothing to do with "my seat," it has nothing to do with "my." When she sits in a particular place she is flowing. From that angle she receives me best.

And everybody has to find his particular seat by and by. Those who are permanently here, they have to find their seats by and by. They will have a certain angle from where they will be more capable of receiving me, a certain place where they will feel more relaxed.

Divya has found her place, so she need not be worried about it. And nobody should disturb her, let Shiva note it. For a few days she has not been in her seat, other people have been in her seat, and nobody has been flowing there. One day Sagar was sitting there and he was sitting like a thief. Guilty! Ill at ease! When Divya sits there she sits like a queen. She creates a certain space around her.

And I also enjoy her sitting there. So, Divya, no need to worry. Not seeing you there I have been missing you.

And the last question:

Osho,
I have never heard religion talked about in such a delightful way. What are you doing, Osho?

To me religion is not religion but life; to me religion is not religion but love; to me religion is not a serious thing, it is fun. To me religion is more like laughter, like dancing, like singing. It is not a serious church thing.

I am not interested in the after-life, I am not interested in heaven and hell, I am not interested in virtue and vice – I am interested only in how to impart to you an understanding of living intensely, delightfully, because God is delight.

A talkative individual in a coffee house was demonstrating his ability to catalogue people as to their occupations. He had gone around the group with considerable success: a lawyer here, a salesman on the left, a banker in the corner, an editor by the window.

Finally, the self-announced expert's eyes fell upon the interesting face of Mulla Nasruddin, a little pale, slightly drawn, with a certain glassiness in the eyes. "Here," he said, "is a religious man, a preacher."

A moment's hush and then Mulla Nasruddin said softly, "You got me wrong, sir. I am no preacher. I just have stomach ulcers."

The preachers that you have known are really pathological people, ill people. They have lost their taste of life.

I teach you the taste. I don't teach you to be against life, because to me life is the very shrine of God. I don't teach you to go against the joys of life but to go into them as deeply as possible. I am affirmative, I am a "yea" sayer. I am not negative. I don't want to deny anything to anybody. Whatsoever God has given has to be accepted in deep gratitude and lived. To me God and life are synonymous. That's why whatsoever I am saying to you has a different quality to it the taste of Tao, the taste of life and love, the taste of delight.

"When I am sick," Mulla Nasruddin was saying to me, expounding his views on the subject of illness, "I go to see the doctor. For, after all, doctors have to live. He writes me out a prescription, which I take to the pharmacists. I pay the druggist willingly, for, after all, a pharmacist too must live. Then I go home and pour the medicine down the drain. For, after all, I have to live."

So even if you go to a preacher, or to a church, remember that you have to live. Don't forget it. Even if you accept their medicine out of politeness, pour it down the drain. They have to live so they have to preach. You have to live – so never listen to their preaching.

Enough for today.

CHAPTER # 7

A Tree Grows

Tzu-hsia asked the Master:
"What sort of man is Yen Hui?"
"For kindness he is a better man than I am."
"What about Tzu-kung?"
"For eloquence he is a better man than I am."
"Tzu-lu?"
"For courage he is a better man than I am."
"Tzu-chang?"
"For dignity he is a better man than I am."
Tzu-hsia rose from his mat and asked:
"Then why do these four serve you?"
"Sit down, I will tell you. Yen hui can be kind but cannot check the impulse when it will do no good. Tzu-kung can be eloquent but cannot hold his tongue. Tzu-lu can be brave but cannot be cautious. Tzu-chang can be dignified but cannot unbend in company. Even if I could have the virtues of the four men all together I should be unwilling to exchange them for my own. That is why they serve me without misgiving."

The greatest enemy of religion is not materialism but morality. Why? Because morality tries to impose spirituality, it is a conditioning and religion can flower only from the within, it cannot be imposed from the without. Hence morality creates an illusion of false religion.

Morality is a pretender, morality is a pseudo-religion. It gives you respectability but it does not give you understanding. It gives you a great ego trip but it cannot give you humility. It makes you feel superior but it doesn't help inner growth. And the man who feels superior cannot grow. He is stuck with the ego.

Morality is a sort of decoration of the ego. Yes, through morality you can cultivate great virtues, but you will never be virtuous. Through morality you can become very talented in certain directions but those talents will remain unconscious. Morality cannot bring awareness because morality is not based on enlightenment.

The essential has to come from the inner, the essential has to grow like a tree, the essential is alive. The non-essential is imposed from the outside.

Before we enter this beautiful parable four things have to be very clearly understood. First, there are two kinds of unity in life. One unity is mechanical – for example, a car. A car has a certain unity, a functional unity, but it is assembled, it comes out of an assembly line. You cannot assemble a tree, you cannot assemble a baby. They also have a sort of unity – but it is totally different. Their unity is organic. A car is mechanical, a baby is organic. A machine is mechanical, a tree is organic. You cannot put a tree together, it grows. It grows out of its own inner center. At the most you can help – or hinder – but you cannot put a tree together.

You can put a car together, you can assemble a car – hence a car has no soul, no self, no center. It is a superficial unity. And the car cannot grow, it cannot give birth to new baby cars.

The tree grows and can give birth to millions of trees. And the tree has a center, it is run by its innermost center. When fall comes and the old leaves drop, who brings the new leaves? From where do they come? They evolve from the innermost core of the tree.

If a mechanical part of the car is missing you will have to replace it. The car cannot evolve it itself. It depends on you; it has no soul, it has no inner discipline of its own. If you cut off a branch of a tree another branch is supplied by the center, but if you destroy a machine nothing will come from the center...there is none, there is no center.

Morality is mechanical, religion is organic. This is the first basic thing to be understood. Morality is put together from the outside, religion grows from the innermost core of your being. Morality comes out of conditioning, religion comes out of meditation. Morality is enforced by others, religion you have to seek and search for yourself. Morality is a social device, religion is an adventure. Morality is dominated by the politician and the priest, religion is a rebellion. Very rarely is a person religious – and whenever there is a religious person there is a great revolution around him.

Moral people are ordinary people, as ordinary as the immoral – sometimes even more ordinary than the immoral. The immoral may sometimes have courage but the moral has no courage. The immoral may sometimes have intelligence but the moral has no intelligence. The immoral may sometimes be original but the moral is always repetitive.

Morality is the greatest enemy of religion because it is a pseudo-coin. It pretends and it can deceive people. It has deceived down the ages; millions and millions of people are and have been deceived by morality. And they think that when they have morality they have religion.

The second thing: morality is always relative. You can have more intelligence than somebody else or somebody else can have more virtue than you. Somebody can be more courageous than you or more cowardly than you. Somebody can be more sharing, more loving, or you can be more loving than somebody else. Morality is comparative.

Nobody can be more religious than you or less religious than you – religion is non-comparative, when religion is there it is simply there. Can you say Buddha was more religious than Jesus? Can you say Mahavira was more religious than Mohammed? Can you say Lao Tzu was more religious than Krishna? It would be absurd, the very statement would be absurd – because religion is not quantity, it is quality of being. You cannot have more or less. There are no degrees. You can be more honest than somebody else, you can be more of a thief than somebody else – there are possibilities – but how can you be more religious or less religious than somebody else? Religion means awakening. Religion means you have come home. How can you be less at home or more at home than somebody else?

When a man has become aware, his awareness is always total and complete, utterly complete. It does not come in parts, it comes as a whole – hence it is holy. Religion comes as a whole, morality comes in all shapes and sizes. You can have a family size or a medium size morality – like toothpaste. Morality comes in all shapes and sizes, religion is just complete. Either it is or it is not.

Sometimes people come to me and they ask, "Who is more enlightened – Buddha or Mahavira?" The question is absurd. Who is more enlightened? Enlightenment means that you have gone beyond relativity; more and less cannot exist now. Who is more enlightened? Enlightenment means that you have disappeared – and so have all relative concepts. You are simply there a pure isness. Whenever anybody becomes a pure isness, a pure existence, a primordial innocence, there is no comparison. To go beyond comparison is to become enlightened – so you cannot ask the question, "Who is more enlightened?" The very question is meaningless.

Religion either is or is not. This is the second thing to be remembered.

The third thing: when religion comes you are naturally moral but the vice versa is not the case – you may be moral but you may not be religious. When you are religious you are naturally moral; morality comes like a shadow.

A disciple came to Lieh Tzu and asked Lieh Tzu, "What should I do, master, to become enlightened?" And Lieh Tzu said, "You stand in the sun, walk, and watch your shadow."

The man went out, stood in the sun, walked and watched his shadow, came back, bowed down, thanked the master and said, "You have shown me the way."

The other disciples were very much puzzled. What had transpired between the master and this new man? They asked Lieh Tzu and he laughed. He said, "It is so simple. I told him to go into the sun and walk and watch his shadow. And he understood the point. If the body walks the shadow follows. The shadow cannot walk on its own. And even if you can arrange for the shadow to walk on its own, the body will not follow, there is no necessity."

Morality is like the shadow, religion is the real figure. When religion is there, morality comes on its own – it has to come, there is no other possibility. But if morality is there, there is no necessity for religion to be there. You can become a moral person without becoming religious at all. You can have good qualities. You can be honest, sincere, true, non-violent, but that doesn't make you religious. If you are religious all moral qualities simply follow you.

When you are moral you have to manage those good qualities continuously they have to be maintained otherwise they will disappear. A moral man has to manage his honesty continuously because every moment there is a fear that he may function dishonestly. The dishonesty has not disappeared, it has been repressed. It is there, it is waiting in the basement of his being for its opportunity, and once the opportunity is there it will assert itself with vengeance. It is there and the moral person knows it well. He may be trying to be loving but he knows that the hatred is there boiling within him. He may be smiling but he knows that his eyes are full of tears. He may not be showing his anger but he knows that his heart is burning, and he wants to kill. He may be praying but really he wants to curse. He knows it. There is no way not to know.

You can deceive others but how can you deceive yourself? Even if you try to deceive yourself, reality will assert itself again and again and you will have to encounter it again and again. And you know that although you can pretend that you are a very good man, deep down you know how bad you are. That hangs like a stone around your neck, like a rock and keeps you pulled down.

The moral person is dual: he is one thing on the outside and just the contrary on the inside. There is a continuous struggle in his being. He is split. The moral person is a schizophrenic. The whole earth has become schizophrenic because of moral teachings. Teach a person to be moral and sooner or later you will send him to the psychiatrist's couch. You have created madness in him. The person is feeling angry and you say, "Don't be angry, anger is bad – because Moses says so, or Mohammed says so, or Mahavira says so. Anger is bad. Don't be angry." Anger is coming up naturally but you teach against it – because great is the stake. If he becomes angry he will lose his respect. He can be respected only if he is not angry, so he has to pretend in order to get respectability.

Look at people. They have lost their original faces. They are carrying masks, they are hiding behind masks. You can never be certain who is hiding behind the masks. You love a person but by and by you will find it is not the same person you fell in love with. Have you not observed it again and again? When you fall in love with a person, after a few months – or even after a few days if you are a great observer you will find that the person is something else. The woman is not the same woman, the man is not the same man that you fell in love with. You fell in love with the mask and now, by and by, the reality becomes clear. When you live with a person he cannot wear the mask for twenty-four hours. It is heavy and he wants to rest. And sometimes he is on a holiday even saints have their holidays.

I have heard.

In a circus there was a man whom the circus manager used to claim was the tallest man in the world – he was somewhere near nine feet tall.

A press reporter went to interview him because he was the tallest man in the world. He naturally chose Sunday because Sunday morning was free for him. He went to the circus and found the man Lying down in front of his tent, sunbathing. He was very much surprised to find that although the face was the same the body wasn't nine feet tall at all.

He asked, "What is the matter? You don't look more than five-foot-five to me. But your face seems to be the right one."

The man laughed. He said, "Yes, you are right. I am the right person – I am the tallest man in the world."

"But," replied the reporter, "what is the matter? You don't look more than five-foot-five."

And the man said, "This is my Sunday. This is my holiday. If you want to see me nine feet tall then you have to see me on duty."

It is a managed thing.

When you see a leader delivering a lecture to the masses it is a different face. When you see a priest in the temple worshipping it is a different face. When you fall in love with a woman it is a different face. She is trying to be as good as possible – but that is not the reality, that is a managed reality. She cannot manage it forever – that's why wives are not very beautiful, that's why husbands are ugly. You know them. You have seen them on their holidays.

Morality creates a division – the inner, the real, becomes hidden and the outer, the false, becomes manifested. This is one of the greatest calamities that has happened to humanity. Religion makes you one. It spreads the inner to the outer.

Religion makes you healthy – then you taste the same always and you are never on a holiday because you are always on a holiday. It is your natural quality.

The fourth thing: a tree is alive, a machine only exists, it is not alive. A man of morality only exists, he is not really alive. You will not find vitality, you will not find radiance, you will not find a surging energy, you will not find a flood of life coming from him. He has to curb his being and cut his energies continuously. He has to live at the minimum, he is never aflame. He is always afraid. If he becomes too much alive then that which is repressed will start asserting itself. So he is always afraid. He keeps himself pulled down. He goes on holding onto himself. He never allows himself a total let-go because a total let-go will naturally mean that that which is repressed will suddenly erupt on the surface. It will be like a volcano erupting. So he has to keep himself at the minimum, he has to allow only minimum energy – only then can he control himself. With the maximum energy flowing he will be out of control, he will be off-balance.

A man of morality just appears to be living, it is an appearance. Only a man of religion is alive. A man of religion lives at the optimum and the man of morality lives at the minimum. Naturally, at the minimum you live like an impotent person. You cannot be angry so you cannot love either because there is always the fear that if you love too much sometimes anger may come. When one energy is allowed total expression, other energies also get freedom. When you open your door for one thing, other things will also escape. You cannot open your door, you have to be always on guard. Just think of the misery of a man who is always on guard, who cannot relax. A man who is always on guard is a tense man.

A moral man is never happy. He may not be sad – at the most but he is never happy, he is never ecstatic. For millions of years man has existed on the earth but a single exception has never been seen. Never has a moral man been found who is ecstatic. He cannot dance, he cannot sing, he cannot rejoice. Joy is freedom – and he does not know what freedom is. Ecstasy is going beyond oneself and that is possible only when you move through your optimum, when you are aflame with a great passion to live, when you love totally, when you are flooded with God. Only then is ecstasy possible.

Ecstasy is not yours; ecstasy is God dancing in you. You cannot allow God to dance in you because you cannot allow nature to dance in you. You have not even been natural, how can you be spiritual? Remember, spirituality is a higher stage of being natural; spirituality is the ultimate flowering of being spontaneous.

A moral person is never spontaneous. A moral person lives

through the past. He has a character and he has to follow the character. He has a blue-print, he has a map, and he always looks at the map and functions through it. He never functions in the present, he is a dead man, he carries his character around with him. His response is never a real response, it is only a reaction. A man of religion is responsive not reactive.

And because he has a character, a man of morality is predictable. You can depend on him, you know that he will be honest tomorrow because he has been always honest. He will be honest even in circumstances where honesty is going to harm the other person. Where honesty is going to be destructive, even then he is going to be honest – you can depend on that. He has no freedom, he has no eyes to look into things, he does not respond to reality. He responds to principles. When you respond to principles you are simply reacting, you have a program in your mind, you are like a computer. You go according to the program – right or wrong is not the question.

And the circumstances of life change every moment – but your principles are rigid, your principles remain the same. Naturally a man of morality never fits anywhere; he is a misfit. It is very difficult to live with a moral man because he is always a misfit. He does not look at the reality, at what reality is. He simply lives through his principles; principles are more important than the reality.

A religious man has no principles. Let it sink deep into your heart. A religious man has no principles whatsoever, he has only an awareness. He looks into reality and whatsoever is required he responds accordingly. His response is spontaneous, not dominated by the past – hence a religious person is not predictable. You don't know what he will do. Not even he can say what he will do because it will depend on the circumstances. If there is a slight difference in the circumstances the response will be different.

A religious man has no character – it will be difficult for you to get that. A religious man has no character, because character comes from the past. A religious man has consciousness instead. Or, to say the same thing in other words, a religious man has no conscience. He has consciousness and the moral man has a conscience – no consciousness. He functions through dead codes. He carries the commandments, and he always looks into his commandments to try to find a way to behave. He is always a misfit, he is never true anywhere. A moral man cannot be true because he has a character. How can you be true when you have a character? If the circumstances are different what will you do? You cannot change so easily.

A moral man is very rigid; he has no dynamism, he is not flowing and fluid. He has a fixed identity: things should be done only this way. He cannot do things in any other way, whatsoever the situation. The situation may have completely changed but the things have to be done in only one way.

Zen Master Bokuju, asked a disciple, "What is the sound of one hand clapping?"

And the disciple remained silent. He closed his eyes and fell into deep silence. Bokuju was happy and said, "Good, good, I agree."

But another master was sitting there while this happened. When the disciple had gone the other master said, "You agreed too early. I don't see it. Call the disciple back."

The disciple was called back and the other master asked, "Tell me, what is the sound of one hand clapping?" And he again closed his eyes and remained silent. And the master laughed and he said, "Wrong, absolutely wrong." And Bokuju said, "Yes, I agree with this other master."

The disciple was puzzled. He said, "But why? Just a moment before, I answered the same way – through my silence – and you said, 'Right.'" Bokuju said, "That was true in that moment but now you are repeating. It cannot be true in this moment because everything has changed. That was a response, this is a reaction. Now you have become fixed. When you responded for the first time there was no idea in what you were doing. It came naturally. It came just simply, innocently. Your mind was not manipulating. Now it is not a response of a meditative consciousness, it is of a mind manipulating. Now the mind knows the answer. Now the mind says, 'Good. The same question again, so again the same answer.'"

The master says that although the question may be the same the answer cannot be the same the next moment. It will depend on a thousand and one things.

It used to happen to Buddha every day. Somebody would ask, "Is there a God?" and he would say, "No." Somebody else would ask, "Is there a God?" and he would say, "Yes." And somebody else would ask, "Is there a God?" and he would keep silent. And again somebody else would ask, "Is there a God?" and he would say, "Don't ask nonsense questions." In one day he gave a thousand and one answers to one question.

His chief disciple, Ananda, became very worried. He said, "Master, the question is the same but you answer so differently, you answer so contradictorily, that we have become puzzled, confused."

Buddha said, "I was not answering you, so you need not listen. Somebody asked a question and the answer was given to him, not to you. And the questioners were different, the time was different, the situation was different – how can the question be the same? One man who had asked, 'Is there a God?' was an atheist. He didn't believe in God. I had to say yes to him, I had to shake him, shock him. I had to bring him out of his ideology, so I had to say yes. But it is not that God exists – it was a response to that man's reality. Then somebody said, 'Is there a God?' and because he was a believer and believed in God I had to say no. I had to shake him and shock him too and bring him out of his sleep. If I had said yes to him he would have gone home thinking that I agreed with him, that I also believed in the same way that he believed. Then his ideology would have been strengthened and any strengthened ideology is a danger. All ideologies have to be shattered, utterly shattered, so the mind becomes completely free from ideologies.

"I had to remain silent to another person because he was neither a theist nor an atheist. His question was very simple and innocent. He had no ideology so I did not need to shock him. He was a really silent man so I kept silent. And he understood me. He understood the idea that about questions about God one should be silent. They are meaningless questions, there is nothing to be said about them."

Whether you believe in God or not makes no difference, you don't change. Go and look.... Look into the lives of the person who believes in God and the person who does not believe in God. Their lives are the same. There is no difference at all. Somebody goes to the church, somebody else goes to the temple, somebody else goes to the mosque, but look into their lives – there is no difference at all. So what is the point of believing?

You will find a different quality of being in a person who believes in nothing, who has dropped all beliefs, whose consciousness is freed, freed from all ideology. Every ideology becomes a fixation.

A moralist is a man of fixation, a religious man is flowing and fluid. The moralist has an idea about how to live his life; the religious person has no idea about how to live his life. He leaves it to Tao, to God, to the whole. He surrenders to the whole and the whole lives through him. He has no ideas about how to live his life.

Remember, if you have an idea about how to live your life, you will live wrongly. When somebody asks me, "What is the right way to live my life?" I say, "The right way to live your life is not to have any ideas about how to live your life." Live without ideas and you live rightly. Live without mind and you live rightly. Live moment to moment and you live rightly. Don't live out of the past and don't live out of the future – just live herenow and you will live rightly.

Tzu-hsia asked the Master,
"What sort of a man is Yen hui?"
"For kindness he is a better man than I am."

Tzu-hsia is asking the master about four persons who are the master's disciples. They all serve him. But they must have been very famous people, sometimes outshining the master himself. And these problems must have been in many people's minds.

Tzu-hsia asked, "What sort of a man is Yen Hui?" Yen Hui was a disciple, a famous disciple. And the master said, *"For kindness he is a better man than I am."*

"What about Tzu-kung?"
"For eloquence he is a better man than I am."
"Tzu-lu?"
"For courage he is a better man than I am."
"Tzu-chang?"
"For dignity he is a better man than I am."

The master is saying that if you take different qualities and you compare them, then these people are in some way or other better than him. If you take individual characteristics these people are better than him. Somebody is better as far as courage is concerned, somebody is better as far as kindness is concerned, somebody is better as far as eloquence is concerned, somebody is better as far as dignity is concerned. Relatively, morally, these people are better than him.

Tzu-hsia rose from his mat and asked...

He must have become very much puzzled.

"Then why do these four serve you?"

Why? If these four people are better in some way than you, you should be serving them. Why do they serve you?

And the master said,

"Sit down, I will tell you."

This saying from the master – *"Sit down"* – is very metaphorical. When Tzu-hsia stood up it means that he became excited, he became feverish, his mind was confused. A thousand and one thoughts started rumbling in him. He could not believe it. Yes, this was true. What the master was saying was true. Everybody felt that these four people had great qualities, that they outshone the master in some way or other. Tzu-hsia must have become very curious. He forgot that you are not supposed to stand in front of the master, that you are not supposed to ask a question while standing in front of the master.

These are just symbols – symbolical, metaphorical things. When you ask a question of a master you have to ask in a certain posture, bowing down, in a deep receptivity. The question should come from a very humble attitude. And the question should come out of deep silence, not out of a perturbed mind, not out of disturbance, not out of excitement. It should come out of a quiet, silent mind, out of tranquillity.

The master said, *"Sit down."* The disciple must have forgotten. With the answer the master gave he must have become really very much excited. He forgot what he was doing. He must have acted in an unconscious way.

The master says, "Sit down, first sit down." And it is not only that the body should sit down, the deep indication is towards the mind. Let the mind settle down. Only then will one be able to understand what the master is going to say...that's what he means when he says, *"Sit down, I will tell you."*

Remember, only when the mind is in a deeply settled state will you be receptive. Otherwise, if the mind is stirred and there are clouds and dust arising all over, you are in a sort of storm. Then how are you going to receive the master's answer?

These are not philosophical discussions, these are penetrations into reality, into your own nature. And the answers to the questions that are being asked are not meant to satisfy curious people.

One day it happened that a great philosopher came to Buddha. Buddha was sitting under a tree.

This man, Buddha, must have loved trees tremendously. He was always sitting under a tree. He became enlightened under a tree – although it is not such a big thing to become enlightened under a tree; many people have. But you will be surprised to know that Buddha was also born under a tree. And he died under a tree as well.

Although Buddha was a king's son he was not born in a palace. His mother was traveling and they came to a garden and suddenly she felt the pain arising. There was no other place so she got down, stood under a tree and Buddha was born. Later he became enlightened under a tree and then, when he was dying, he again lay down under a tree and died under it.

He must have loved trees very much. For five hundred years after him the tree remained his symbol. For five hundred years no statue of him was made – just trees were painted. Trees were placed in temples and people worshipped the trees. In a way it was very beautiful.

I would like to remind you again – the tree is symbolic of religion because it grows. And it grows out of the innermost core.

Buddha was sitting under a tree and this great philosopher said, "Have you said everything that you know?" Buddha had become very old – almost eighty years old – and within a few months he would be gone. The great philosopher had come from a long way to inquire if he had said all that he knew.

And Buddha took a few dry leaves in his hand and asked the philosopher, "What do you think, sir? How many leaves have I got in my hand? Are they more than the number of dry leaves in this forest?" The paths, the whole forest, was full of dry leaves; the wind was blowing here and there and the dry leaves were making much noise and much music. The philosopher looked and he said, "What type of question are you asking? How can you have more leaves in your hand? You have only a few, a dozen at the most, and there are millions of leaves in this forest." And Buddha said, "So remember. That which I have said is only like the few leaves in my hand. And that which I have not said is like the dry leaves in this forest."

The philosopher said, "Then one question more. Why have you not said that?" said, "Because it will not help you to attain nirvana, it will not help you to meditate – that's why I have not said it. And moreover, it cannot be said. Even if I wanted to say it, it cannot be said. You will have to experience and know it. It is experiential, it is existential."

The master will say something only when he feels it is going to help your enlightenment. The master will say something only when he feels you are ready to receive. The master will say something only when he sees that clarity is there and the mind is open; that transparency is there and you are ready, with great humbleness and gratitude, to receive it. You are not quarrelsome, you are not ready to discuss and debate. Only in great sympathy, in great love, when the disciple is in rapport with the master, can these things be transferred. These are delicate things.

The master says, *"Sit down"*: Not only physically – settle down inside and don't get excited.

> "I will tell you. Yen Hui can be kind but cannot check the impulse when it will do no good."

This is the difference between religion and morality. Listen well. Sit down and listen well. Many of you are standing up. Sit down and I will tell you.

> "Yen Hui can be kind but cannot check the impulse when it will do no good."

This kindness is not of awareness. One has to be capable sometimes of not being kind. Great kindness is capable of being kind and of not being kind, both. Great kindness is capable of being hard too. If your kindness is such that you cannot be otherwise then it is not strength, it is weakness. If you cannot act otherwise that simply means that you are fixed, you are not fluid. Sometimes it is necessary to be hard.

I have heard about a Zen master who was driving a carriage with a woman and her child in it. Much snow was falling and the morning was very cold and there was no sun in the sky, it was cloudy. The master started freezing and the woman in the carriage did too. By and by he saw that she was becoming blue and was losing consciousness. So he took away the child, pushed the woman out of the carriage and drove away.

The woman was shocked. She was left standing there in the falling snow, her child had been taken away – what type of man was this? And he had taken the carriage. She started running and shouting and screaming and cursing – and within half a mile, because of all the running and cursing and shouting and screaming, she was perfectly okay!

Then the master stopped the carriage, took her in and said, "Now it is okay. I had to do that otherwise you would have died."

Sometimes to be really kind implies that you can be unkind too. If you cannot be unkind then your kindness is not of much worth. It is cultivated. It is not out of awareness.

Now think. If you had been that driver you could not have done that. It looks immoral. But it is not.

In the Zen tradition there are thousands of cases which look very immoral. Sometimes the master jumps on the disciple, beats the disciple, throws him out of the window. And the story says he becomes enlightened – when he falls out of the window he becomes enlightened. To people who are not acquainted with the Zen methods it looks absurd. How can a person become enlightened like this?

But you must be made alert that the disciple may have been working for twenty years – meditating, working, meditating, working. And then one day the master finds that only a thin layer of unawareness is left, a very thin layer. He watches the disciple but he cannot get through that thin layer. Remember, when the unconsciousness is very thick you can fight with it but when it is very thin it is very difficult to fight with it. In fact, there comes a moment when it is so thin that you think it is not there. It is almost like transparent glass; it is so transparent you don't see it. Then how can you fight it? Only the master can see that you are still behind a glass. You are seeing very clearly, almost as if there is no glass, but still you are behind glass. In those moments the master will be very hard. He will do something very shocking. In that shock that thin layer will be broken. And only when it is broken, not before, will you be able to know that something was there in front of your eyes. When it is gone you will understand that a thin layer was there – a thin film which was so thin and so transparent that there was no way for you to know. Then you will feel thankful to the master.

> "Sit down. I will tell you. Yen Hui can be kind, but cannot check the impulse when it will do no good."

This kindness is impulsive. You are almost a victim of it – you are not the master of it. If you cannot help but be kind it is an impotency.

In Japan there exists a statue of Buddha, a very rare statue, of tremendous significance. One of my friends went to Japan where somebody gave him a replica, a plastic replica, of the statue. My friend is a Jaina, and he could not understand it because it looked a little illogical and unhistorical.

In this statue Buddha has a sword in one hand. A sword? Buddha has never been known to carry a sword. He was not a Mohammed, neither was he a Krishna. A sword? But in this statue he has a sword in one hand.

And the one side of his face is tremendously illuminated by the sword – and it does not look like the face of a buddha, it looks like that of an Arjuna, a great warrior, a great soldier. The expression of the face has a sharpness to it.

In the other hand he is carrying a lamp, a small earthen lamp, and on that side of the face the expression is very quiet, very silent, very buddha-like.

Now this is very absurd. When my friend came back from

Japan and showed me the statue he said, "I cannot understand it. What does it mean?" I said, "It is very meaningful. It is a Zen expression. It shows that your silence should be capable and strong also."

The lamp of peace should be capable of becoming a sword any moment it is needed to be that way. And the sword should be capable of becoming a lamp of peace any moment it is needed to be that way. One should be fluid and all the polarities should meet in one.

A man is rich when all the polarities meet in him. When all the contradictions have lost their contradictions and have become friends, when you can befriend the contradictions, then you are really rich. This is the state of a religious man. The moral man chooses, the religious man lives in choicelessness.

> "Yen Hui can be kind but cannot check the impulse when it will do no good."

Even when it will not do any good, in fact, it may even be doing harm – then too he cannot check the impulse. He is incapable of checking it. He is incapable of being responsive to the reality. He functions according to a principle. So the master says, "For kindness he is a better man than I but still there is something missing in his kindness. He has moved too much to the extreme. He has lost balance. And a balanced man is the goal – not the bad nor the good but the one who is exactly in the middle; not the bad nor the good but the one who has transcended both."

And he is capable of being both – whatsoever the situation may demand. Listen to this point: the capacity to be all is the capacity of a religious person.

> "Tzu-kung can be eloquent but cannot hold his tongue."

If you can be eloquent but cannot be silent your eloquence is meaningless. Unless words come out of silence they are dead. Unless words come out of your inner emptiness they are not full. When words come out of your inner emptiness they carry a fullness; when they come out of your silence, soaked with your silence, they have a music around them, they have a poetry and a life totally of their own.

When you cannot be silent, when you have to speak and you cannot do otherwise, then your words are meaningless, gibberish. Then there is no poetry, then they are very ordinary. Have you not watched it? Jesus speaks the same words that you speak, Buddha uses the same words that you use – then what is the difference? When you speak certain words they carry no meaning, not at all. When Jesus speaks the same words they are tremendously significant – so burningly alive, so aflame with his vitality. From where do they come? They come from his silence.

Jesus used to go into silence again and again. Whenever he came to the masses, for a few days he would talk to people, meet people, convert them, and then one day suddenly he would say, "Now I will go to the mountains or to the desert. I would like to be silent." He would leave even his disciples and go alone into the wilderness, just to be silent. He had exhausted his silence by speaking, the silence was spent in words – now he had to go back to become full again, to be full of silence. Then he would be full of poetry, then he would be full of song, then his words would not be ordinary words, they would be full of luminosity. Then they would hit you and go directly into the heart.

Remember, the words go to exactly the same depth from which they come. If my words come from my heart they will touch your heart. If they come only from my head they will touch only your head. It depends.

Have you seen an archer pulling his bow backwards? The farther back he pulls his bow, the farther ahead will go the arrow. If the bow is not pulled back the arrow will fall short.

The deeper the words come out of the silence of your innermost core, the further they will go – like an arrow – into the hearts of the people.

The master said:

> "Tzu-kung can be eloquent but cannot hold his tongue."

Eloquence is of no importance as far as religion is concerned. Eloquence is important in politics, but in religion eloquence is secondary. The basic, the fundamental importance is silence. Words are secondary, stillness is primary. If words come out of stillness then they have some significance. If they don't come out of stillness they are just rubbish.

The master said:

"For eloquence he is a better man than I am."

But he makes the difference. Tzu-kung may have practiced eloquence but he does not know what silence is. He cannot hold his tongue.

"Tzu-lu can be brave but cannot be cautious."

When you are brave but cannot be cautious you turn into a fool – you become foolhardy, you become stupid. Bravery in itself is of no value. It can be suicidal, it can be murderous. Bravery in itself is of no value unless there is a light inside it of awareness, alertness. That's what cautiousness is.

"Tzu-lu can be brave but cannot be cautious."

His bravery is not of much use. Either he will create trouble for others or he will create trouble for himself. His bravery is not going to become a beneficial thing to anybody. Bravery is beneficial not because of bravery but because of cautiousness.

Just look into these things. This is a simple parable but the master is showing what morality and religion are. If you practice eloquence you will forget about silence. If you practice bravery you will forget about cautiousness. If you practice kindness you will forget that sometimes it is kindness not to be kind. You will become fixed. You will have one pole but the other pole will be missing. You will be half, you will not be whole.

To be positive and negative together is what a religious man is. The immoral man has chosen one pole, the negative pole;

the moral man has chosen another pole, the positive pole – and the religious person lives in choicelessness. He has not chosen anything but he uses all, whatsoever the need. Sometimes he is as negative as the immoral and sometimes he is as positive as the moral. But nothing holds him. He is not confined either to positivity or to negativity. He is a free man. He has freedom. He uses all and he is not used by anything.

"Tzu-chang can be dignified but cannot unbend in company."

You can be dignified but if your dignity becomes an ego trip then you cannot bend. And with an ego how can you really be dignified? How can ego be a dignified thing? How can ego give you grace? It will be just a superficial posture, an empty, impotent posture, nothing inside, just a container without any content.

"Tzu-chang can be dignified but cannot unbend in company."

A man should be able to be undignified sometimes too. If you are always dignified you cannot laugh, if you are always dignified you cannot joke, if you are always dignified you will become inhuman, you will lose all humanity.

Have you not watched it? People who can become undignified sometimes have more grace. Someone who can laugh, laugh like a fool sometimes, has more wisdom than a person who is obsessed with wisdom and cannot laugh. He has to protect his wisdom, he has to be continuously on guard. He cannot laugh, he cannot allow himself to laugh, because people will think that he is a fool. He is a fool. A wise man is capable of being foolish sometimes too.

You must have heard that in the old days great kings used to have a fool in the court – the court fool. And you will be surprised to know that they were not ordinary fools, they were some of the wisest men in the country. The king used to have wise men and a fool too – to keep a balance. Otherwise the wise people would make things very sober, dry, dull, sad. All joy would be lost. Sometimes you can become too serious, and the very seriousness can become a barrier in looking into things. The fool was needed. When things would be getting too serious he would do something or say something and bring the atmosphere back to human altitudes.

For example, a king was seriously thinking of turning the whole country moral. Nobody should be allowed to say anything untrue. Untruths should be banned. The wise men were all agreed; in fact, because these wise people were his servants they were even going further than him, exaggerating. One wise man suggested that of course this was the right thing to be done – untruths should be banned – and one who was found to be saying some untruth should be immediately sentenced to death. He should be hanged in the marketplace so that everybody would know what the cost of saying anything untrue would be.

The fool was listening. He said, "Okay. Then tomorrow morning I will see you all at the gate." They said, "What do you mean?" He said, "At the gate." And he said to the king, "Keep the gallows ready because I am going to say an untruth." The king said, "Have you gone mad?" And he replied, "I have always been mad: But I will see you all, the whole court, at the gate – and keep the gallows ready. I will be the first person to be hanged."

It was a challenge. The gallows were made ready and the next morning, when they opened the gate of the town, the fool entered on his donkey. The king asked, "Where are you going, you fool?" He was very angry because they had had to get up early in the morning to get there. And the fool said, "I am going to the gallows."

Now he created a problem. If you killed him he had said a truth, if you didn't kill him he had told a lie. He said, "I am going to the gallows. Prepare them. I am going to die on the gallows." All these wise men and the king were puzzled. What to do with this man? He was telling a lie. If you kill him the lie becomes a truth. If you don't kill him the lie goes unpunished.

And the fool laughed. He said, "You are all fools. Who can ban untruth and who can ban immorality? Everything is needed in proportion."

Each great king used to have a fool because wise people tend to go to the extreme. And to go to the extreme is a sort of foolishness. To keep a balance one should sometimes forget all about dignity, one should sometimes bend in company, laugh like a fool, be like a child – be human.

You go and look at your mahatmas – they are never human. They will not laugh, they will not joke, they will not do anything that would prove that they are human. They keep above humanity. Hence, if they look sad it is nothing unexpected; if their eyes look dull and sad, if they look dead, it is natural.

> "Tzu-chang can be dignified but cannot unbend in company. Even if I could have the virtues of the four men all together I should be unwilling to exchange them for my own."

Now listen to this tremendously important sentence.

> "Even if I could have the virtues of the four men all together I should be unwilling to exchange them for my own."

That which is yours is true and that which you take from others is untrue. The borrowed is never true. The borrowed, the imitated, is always false. Morality is imitation, religion is always your own. On a rosebush flowers a rose flower; somewhere in a pond flowers a lotus. The lotus comes out of the lotus seed, the rose comes out of the rosebush. The rose cannot borrow the lotus, the lotus cannot borrow the rose. When religion flowers it is yours; when you try to be moral you borrow, you imitate, you try to become a carbon copy of someone.

A Christian is one who is trying to become a carbon copy of Christ; hence a Christian is ugly and Christ is beautiful. Christ is a rose flower, out of his own bush he flowered – that was his crime.

The Jews did not like it, they wanted him to become a Moses, they wanted him to become a lotus flower. And he asserted his own self. He said, "I will be my own being. I will be myself." That was his crime and the Jews could not forgive him. But Moses was a flower out of his own being, he was not imitating anybody. No religious person has been an imitator. And all so-called religious people who are imitators are not religious at all.

Never borrow. Even if your flower is small, it is good, it is yours. Even if somebody else's flower is very big, has much fragrance, has much color, don't borrow it. Yours is good. It is your destiny. God wants you to flower from your own being.

A great Hassid mystic was dying. His name was Josia. Somebody around him said, "Josia, have you made your peace with Moses?" Josia opened his eyes and said, "Forget everything about this Moses. He is not important. I am dying, and you are talking nonsense." The man became afraid – what is he saying? A pious Jew at the time of death is saying, "Forget all about Moses." And Josia said, "Listen, now I am going to die and I will be facing God. He will not ask me, 'Josia, why were you not Moses?' He will not ask me that. He will ask, 'Josia, why were you not Josia?' So forget all about Moses. At least in these last moments leave me alone. Let me gather together my being so that I can stand before him on my own feet. I have wasted my whole life and now in the end again you have come to ask, 'Have you made your peace with Moses?' What do I have to do with Moses? If Moses has nothing to do with me what have I to do with Moses?"

Sometimes people come to me and they say, "Do you agree with Buddha?" I say, "Nonsense! He never agreed with me so why should I bother to agree with him? He did his thing, I am doing mine. Where arises the question of agreeing?"

Why should you agree with anybody? If you can agree with yourself you have agreed with God. Enough, more than enough. If you have agreed with yourself, if you have accepted your being – finished. Your journey has come to an end. Now you can flower.

The master said:

> "Even if I could have the virtues of the four men all together I should be unwilling to exchange them for my own."

It would be a mechanical thing to borrow one thing from one, another thing from another. To borrow from so many people…it would be an assemblage, it would be a mechanical thing.

A car is to be assembled, a tree grows. The tree is the symbol of religion and the car is the symbol of morality. You can assemble a car. You can go to the market and purchase different parts from different places and assemble it. You can make your own hotchpotch car. But you cannot assemble a tree. You cannot go into one garden, take a branch, into another garden, take another branch, take flowers from somewhere, leaves from somewhere, roots from somewhere else – a tree cannot be put together.

You cannot assemble religion. Religion is not born out of an assembly line.

> "…I should be unwilling to exchange them for my own.
> This is why they serve me without misgivings."

"They know that I have an organic unity, and they know that they have only a mechanical unity. They know that they have talents but their talents are fixations, and they know that I have something coming from the inner to the outer, from the center flowing towards my periphery. They know it, hence they serve me without any misgivings. They are great in one way or other but their greatness is dimensional."

This is the last thing to be understood. A man of morality is dimensional, one-dimensional. He moves in one dimension. A man of religion is non-dimensional, he has no dimension. All dimensions are available to him.

A sportsman entered his horse in the Kentucky Derby. The horse won by twenty lengths. After the victory the horse was entered in more than a dozen races at different tracks and came in last in every one.

Puzzled, the sportsman took the horse to see a vet psychiatrist. After a thorough examination, the vet turned to the sportsman and said, "This is a very simple case – the trouble with this horse is that he has a one-track mind!"

Morality is a one-track thing, one-dimensional. And the moral man becomes lopsided because when he moves in one direction all other dimensions suffer. If you want to be very kind where are you going to get the energy from? From other dimensions? It is as if somebody's head becomes too big and the whole body shrinks and becomes small. Or somebody's legs become big and the whole body shrinks and becomes small. That is the shape of a moral man.

A religious man is an organic unity, in balance. His head, his hands, his feet, his body, his mind, his soul, all are in a deep harmony, in a deep rhythm. He is an orchestra.

This parable has to be deeply meditated upon. Remember always never to borrow; remember always never to imitate; remember always that you have to grow, not condition yourself. You have to become a tree, you have to bloom like a tree. You are not to become an efficient mechanism, you have to become a tree so that your fragrance can be released to the winds. That will be your offering to the feet of God.

And remember, he will ask, "Josia, why are you not Josia?" He will ask you, "Why did you miss your being? Why have you not arrived here with your being? Why did you miss your life following other people? I was always within your heart waiting for you but you never came there. You followed Moses, Mohammed, Mahavira, Krishna. You followed everybody. You looked in every nook and comer but you never came into your own being. And I was sitting there waiting for you."

When you come into your own being you have come home, you have come to God. God is nothing but a name of your innermost core.

Enough for today.

CHAPTER #8

For the Sake of Harmony

The first question:

Osho,
It is all jolly fine for everyone to do their thing but what should be an attitude when our "things" conflict? I am always giving in for the sake of harmony and to do one's thing under constant threat takes the joy out of it. But harmony is not in itself my thing.

First, if conflict is your thing then let it be so. Then don't try to impose any false harmony on top of it because false harmony will never be true, it will never be satisfying. It is ugly. A true conflict is beautiful – more beautiful, far more beautiful than an imposed harmony, because deep down the conflict continues. You are deceiving nobody, you only think you are deceiving. The reality cannot be deceived and you have to suffer the consequences.

If conflict is your thing then let it be so. That is the message of Tao. It has nothing to do with harmony, it has to do with let-go. If conflict is your thing and you allow it, then that is harmony for you – because you will be in harmony with your nature.

It is difficult because you immediately make ideals. You think Tao is harmony. It is, but not as an ideal. When you relax and you do your thing – whatsoever it is, mind you, *whatsoever*, I say – then you are in harmony.

So the first thing is that you are not to impose anything upon yourself otherwise you miss the path of Tao.

"It is all jolly fine for everyone to do their thing but what should be an attitude when our 'things' conflict?" Let there be conflict. Whatsoever happens, happens. What can you do? The conflict has to be accepted with great respect. You would like to have no conflict but this liking is your ego. If God wills the conflict to be there then it has to be that way. Relax and let the conflict be there.

To move on the path of Tao is to move relaxedly. Whatsoever happens, there should be a total acceptance of it – both of the act and of the consequence. If the conflict brings misery then that has to be accepted. You have to flow with the river wherever it leads. If it goes south, good; if it goes north, good; if it does not go anywhere, good; if it drowns you, good. This is total trust.

"I am always giving in...." Then you are not in a let-go. If you give in; you are giving in against yourself. Never give in. There is no need. It is better to be defeated, it is better to be cursed than to give in. To "give in" means that you are reluctant but still you are doing it – for harmony's sake. But harmony is missing from the very beginning. So if you give in to your wife she will never forgive you, if you give in to your husband he will never forgive you, because your whole being will vibrate with antagonism. You will say something in words, it will be on the lips, but your being will deny it, contradict it. And that is what is being broadcast continuously – from your eyes, from your face, from your gestures, from everything. Your words cannot hide it.

So nothing is attained by it. You give in, you lose your inner harmony, but no outer harmony is created out of it. Outer harmony comes only when there is an inner harmony. If you are angry then be angry, be totally angry. Risk all. Then you will be in harmony. And this will be difficult to understand but let me say it: if you are really angry with your wife she will be happy, more happy than when you give in, because you are authentic. Who does not love an authentic person? Now she can trust you – when you are angry you are angry, you are not false, you are not pseudo. And when you are loving you are loving, you are not false, you are not pseudo. Now you are reliable.

Otherwise even while you are making love she will feel you are not reliable. Perhaps you are thinking of making love to some other women, or at least thinking of some other woman. This woman may not be there at all in your mind. Making love to this woman you may think of other women and you will not be there, and it will be felt and it will hurt – because all the time the woman knows that you are false. When you are smiling you are not smiling, when you say, "I love you" you are not really saying it. You are always giving in for harmony's sake. You are not true. But if you are not in harmony within yourself how can you be in harmony with your wife, with your friend, with your husband, with anybody? First be in harmony with yourself – that means allow whatsoever is to be the case.

This is the new revolution that is happening all over the world, the new psychology of man. Gone are those days of repression, gone are those repressed people. They never lived, they only pretended. They were empty gestures. There was no substance in their life.

This is your life, live it – and live it in all the climates, don't try to fix a climate. Year round you can see that sometimes it is raining, sometimes it is hot, sometimes it is winter, sometimes the sun is there and sometimes it is very clouded. That's why the earth is so beautiful. It is not monotonous, it is rich. A man's life should be one of many climates, of many colors. A man's life should be a rainbow, an orchestra. It should not be a single note. A man who has a single note in his life is a monotonous man, he is a poor man, a dull man. He will not enjoy his life – and he will not allow anybody else to enjoy their life either. Wherever he is he will be a dead weight, he will make people serious, somber, unloving, unliving. Don't become that, that is to be a sinner – at least, in my definition. That's what I call sin.

A virtuous man is a man of many climates. A virtuous man is a man of tremendous richness. He has a whole orchestra, all possible notes, in his being. And you can only love a man who has all notes possible, all the potentialities flowering. He's always new, never old.

While angry, be angry. Don't give in. While loving, love; while hating, hate. Just be true, in harmony with yourself – that's what Tao is. And then a miracle happens: when you are in harmony with yourself you start being in harmony with other people and they start respecting you. You are authentic, you are a solid man. You are not hollow, you are substantial, you have a backbone.

How can a wife respect a man who always gives in? Impossible. No wife can respect such a husband. How can you respect a man who has no backbone, is always ready to crawl on the floor, always saying yes? It is impossible. This is not a true man.

Never give in. Don't give in, live your life, whatsoever it brings.... If sometimes it brings conflict then that is needed. Then storm is also needed. The storm is needed as much as silence. Anger is needed as much as compassion. Life needs all the polarities.

And then the miracle happens. When the other person starts feeling that you are true, then by and by, through that respect, through that love, conflict drops. When you love a person, when you respect a person, when you see the person is true and authentic, there is less and less conflict. Between two false persons there is always conflict. Conflict is a consequence of two false persons being together. When two true person live together, conflict by and by disappears because they start understanding each other and there is never confusion, there is no possibility of any confusion. Everything is clear, transparent. Then conflict by and by disappears. Without risking any of your inner harmony the conflict disappears. And then you and the other are also in harmony.

But the first step is to be in inner harmony with yourself. Only then can you be in harmony with others, otherwise not. If you have not attained an inner harmony how can you attain the outer? The basic thing is missing.

The question is from Anando. He can become a very authentic person, hence the question. He knows where he is missing, his question is not just intellectual. I understand. I have looked into his being deeply. This is his problem. Anando, you have to drop it, you have to be true. And whatsoever the cost is you have to pay it. Life has to be paid for. Each single moment of beauty, of joy, has to be paid for enormously. It is not free, it has to be earned.

"To do one's thing under constant threat takes the joy out of it." Certainly, it creates misery. That's why so many people are miserable in the world. It is very rare to come across a person who is happy because it is very rare to come across a person who has lived authentically, who has lived rebelliously, who has lived his own life and who has not bothered to make any compromise. To compromise is to poison your being. Never compromise. It is better to die than to compromise. Die if need be but die uncompromised – then you are unpolluted, unpoisoned. Then you are a beauty. Then you have dignity.

You will have the same dignity as Jesus had when he was crucified. What was he doing, this man? Why were people so angry about him? He was trying to live his life, that was his crime. That has always been the crime. What was Socrates doing? Why were people so angry about him? He was trying to live his life.

These miserable people cannot tolerate any happy person. These miserable people are so deep in misery that any happy person creates great jealousy, creates great restlessness in their being – they cannot tolerate it. The very presence of a happy and a rebellious person shows them how unreal they are. The happy, the true person becomes a comparison.

I am not saying that by relaxing, by accepting your being, by being in a Taoist attitude, you will not have any misery – I am not saying that. You will be happy. You will have much pain, you may have to suffer many sufferings, but still you will be happy. And all those sufferings will add to your taste, they will give salt to your life.

I am not saying that the path is full of roses – there are thorns, they always come with the roses. Wherever you find one rose you will find a hundred thorns. But still I say, go for the roses. The thorns have to be suffered but it is worth it. Those roses are so valuable that the suffering is nothing. If you want to avoid the thorns you will never have roses – that's what you have been doing, Anando, up to now. You have been avoiding the thorns so you are missing the roses. They always come together. You will be miserable – and only miserable. Your misery will be empty misery.

Jesus also goes through pain but his pain is full of joy – that is the difference. Three persons were crucified on that same day – two thieves were also crucified. On either side of Jesus was a thief. They were both crying and weeping but Jesus was silent. And people were throwing stones and saying ugly things and insulting Jesus as much as they could, but Jesus was silent, as silent as if nothing was happening.

One of the thieves became interested. This was rare. He was crying and weeping and he was not being insulted. Nobody cared about him. The whole insult was directed towards Jesus. And then he heard Jesus saying to God, "Father, forgive these people because they don't know what they are doing." When the thief heard this he could not believe his ears. He said, "So it seems you really are a son of God. Bless me before you go." And Jesus said, "Don't be worried. You will be with me in the company of God, in the kingdom of God, today." In that moment of illumination, in that moment of understanding, the thief became transformed. He died silently, and a peace surrounded him. He was happy to die with Jesus. He became part of Jesus. Then he did not cry, then death didn't matter, then he was moving into a deeper and higher life.

The other thief was crying and weeping – and also dying. Both the thieves were dying but in a different way. One was simply dying, another had a vision of a higher life. One's misery was empty, another's misery became full of joy.

This is the difference between people. There are miserable people, painful people, whose misery is empty, for nothing. And there are tremendously happy people who are very rare, they also suffer. Sometimes they suffer more than other people because they never avoid anything, they go headlong into things.

Anando, do your thing and do it truly. Never compromise. Never compromise with anybody, not even with God. No compromise. You be yourself. That is the only prayer there is.

The second question:

> Osho,
> When will I be ready to cut off my hand and give it to you as a sign?

The question comes from the parable I told you – the parable about Bodhidharma and Hui Koju Bodhidharma sat for nine years facing a wall. People would come to him and ask questions but he would not answer. And people would say to him, "Why do you go on looking at the wall?" And he would say, "I am waiting for the right man to come. When he comes I will turn and look at him." Then came Hui Koju. It was a very cold morning and snow was falling. He stood there in the falling snow and the snow gathered all around his body and he was freezing.

One day passed and then he said to Bodhidharma that now he would make his offering. He cut off one of his hands with his sword, gave it to Bodhidharma and said, "Now turn towards me otherwise I will cut off my head." Bodhidharma turned immediately and said, "Wait! There is no need to go that far. So you have come. I was waiting for you for nine years. I have a message to deliver to you. Once the message is delivered I will disappear."

Hui Koju became the second Zen master in China. The message was delivered.

After four years, when Bodhidharma was departing from his disciples, he asked four disciples the question, "What is truth?" The first disciple answered that truth is not in the scriptures, not in the tradition, not in the words. And Bodhidharma said, "You have my skin."

And he asked the second and the second said, "Truth has to be experienced, it is not a concept, it cannot be thought about. It is not philosophy. It is existential." And Bodhidharma said, "You have my flesh."

And he asked the third and the third said, "Truth is when you are not, when the ego disappears. Truth is when the mind is no more. Truth is a state of no-mind." And Bodhidharma said, "You have my bones."

Then he asked the fourth disciple – this disciple was the same Hui Koju who had given his hand to him. When he asked Hui Koju, he looked at the master, fell down at his feet and remained silent. Bodhidharma took him up, hugged him and said, "You have my marrow. And now I am ready to depart. You have all that I have. To a question about truth, only silence can be the answer."

The others were sad but still they were saying something. Without saying anything the fourth disciple said it. This was Hui Koju.

The question comes from this same parable. "When will I be ready to cut off my hand and give it to you as a sign?"

The first thing: I am not as gross as Bodhidharma, he was a barbarian. In fact, in China he was known as the Hindu barbarian from the south. I am not a barbarian like that. And this is the twentieth century, sir, these things are not needed. You will have to bring more subtle gifts to me. A hand? What will I do with your hand? I will get into trouble with the police! So please never do it.

And a thing that has been done once is meaningless now.

You will be repeating it, it will not be original. It will not be original at all, it will be imitative. You are doing it because you know the parable. It is not coming out of your being, it is not your response.

And you are even asking me: "When will I be ready to cut off my hand?" Hui Koju never asked. He did it. You ask me, "When?" You are certainly after me. You will get me into trouble. You ask me, "When?" Even if I say that the time has come you will not be ready, because this question is a question out of greed not out of understanding.

A parable is always a symbolic thing. Always remember that when I tell you parables don't be too literal. They are metaphoric. Cutting off the hand is symbolic. What is the symbol? The hand is the symbol of action. When Hui Koju cuts off his hand he says, "Sir, I am ready to drop all my activity, all my action. I am ready to drop my 'doer-hood'." That's what he is saying. The hand is symbolic.

So if you can drop your "doer-hood" that will be the real thing. Immediately, the moment you are no longer a doer, you will become a being, you will become a God. You are lost in your actions – doing this, doing that; you are thinking about having done this and not having done that; you sometimes feel successful and very egoistic, sometimes a failure and very inferior. And there is misery and happiness – and you just go on. You move in a wheel.

To become a meditator means to drop out of the wheel of activities. I am not saying don't do anything, I am saying let God do it, you just be a vehicle. That is the meaning of cutting off your hand.

One further thing which I have never told you about this parable is that Bodhidharma gave the hand back and again Hui Koju was whole. Now, if you cut off your hand, it cannot be given back and you cannot be whole again. Hands don't grow like trees. If you cut a branch it grows again. No, even to a person like Bodhidharma, nature will not change its laws; it never changes its laws. Nature is very neutral, that's why miracles never happen. Nature never gives way to exceptions. It is absolute.

This simply means that Hui Koju gave up his activity, surrendered his activity, and Bodhidharma gave it back again because Hui Koju was now no longer a doer so he could be allowed to do. Now God or the total, or the whole, or Tao, would be the doer through him.

These parables have to be meditated upon. They are not just to be literally understood, otherwise you will miss the meaning.

They are great metaphors, they are poetic. They are not logical things, they are symbolic. They indicate something. In Zen they have a saying coined by a very great Zen Master Lin Chi, which is, "Don't bite my finger. Look where I am pointing."

This is biting my finger.

The third question:

> Osho,
> Have you yet been able to say to one of your disciples, "So, it has happened!"?

If it has not happened it will not be true to say so, and if it has happened it will be futile. What is the point of saying it when it has happened? Either way it is meaningless.

If it has not happened I will not say it and if it has happened why should I say it? You know, I know – it will be a tacit understanding. I am not going to say to anybody that it has happened, remember. I will never say to anybody that it has happened. It is happening to many, it will happen to many; in fact, it has never happened to so many people as it is going to happen this time.

But I am not going to say anything to anybody. You would like me to say something because then you can create great politics around it. If I say to Maneesha "Maneesha, it has happened to you," then everybody else will be jealous. Then you will start finding fault with Maneesha. Then you will start trying to prove that it has not happened to her. How can it happen to Maneesha before you? Impossible!

Do you know that when Bodhidharma gave his robe to Hui Koju he told him a second thing? "Escape now. Take this robe and escape as far away as possible otherwise the other disciples will kill you." There were five hundred disciples. So four hundred and ninety-nine would be against this Hui Koju, who was just a simple poor man. They would kill him, certainly they would kill him. They followed him. The moment they became aware that it had happened to Hui Koju and the robe had been given to him, they followed him. Where had he gone? He had moved past a mountain retreat, running as far away as possible – as the master had told him to.

They got hold of him. The greatest scholar, who had been expecting that it would happen to him, got hold of him first. He was a very dangerous man. He said, "Give me the robe." Hui Koju said, "You can take the robe, because the robe is not the thing. You can take it." He dropped the robe on the ground and said, "You can take it. But remember, if you are not yet capable of taking it, it will be a crime against the master."

And the scholar started trembling and shaking and perspiring, because he was certainly not ready. He had an ego. He tried to get the robe but he could not pick it up, it was so heavy. It was not that the robe became heavy, he must have become too shaky, nervous.

Remember, I say again: miracles never happen. If you ask the Buddhists they will say that this was a miracle. The robe became so heavy that the man could not pick it up. That is not right. The man became very shaky, naturally. Hui Koju was standing there as a witness – in pure silence, in great meditation, in great ecstasy watching. And he said, "Remember one thing: you will be committing a crime against the master if you are not ready for it. You can take it if you are ready."

How can you deceive a man like Hui Koju who has become a mirror? He must have seen all this scholar's ignorance hidden behind the so-called knowledge. He must have trembled. He must have tried to take the robe but could not pick it up from the ground. He fell down at the feet of Hui Koju and he said, "I am sorry. I am not after the robe. Tell me what he has transferred to you."

For years Hui Koju was pursued and efforts were made to kill him.

This has been so always. I am not going to say to anybody that it has happened to them, because I am not interested in creating any politics. When it has happened, it has happened. You will know, I will know, and there is no need for anybody else to know about it. You will know that I have said it to you in deep silence. Not a single word will be uttered but the message will reach you. You will know my recognition – that I have recognized, that I have blessed, that I have patted you on your back and said, "Yes, it has happened." But it will not be in so many words; not a word will be uttered. It will be a gesture and you will understand and nobody else will understand.

This is going to be the way.

The fourth question:

Osho,
Should I throw away all my self-confidence?

Don't think you can do it, because you don't have any.

What you call self-confidence is just a lack of it, hence you need it. A man of real self-confidence never carries so much luggage. Why should he carry it? Why should he be concerned about self-confidence? He has it. Nobody can rob him of it, nobody can steal it. There is no way of losing it, you will not need to carry it. When you carry it you show only one thing – you don't have it.

People who don't have any self-confidence create a false self-confidence as a substitute. They are trembling inside, they are afraid inside. Deep down is cowardice but on the surface they pretend that they are brave people, very courageous. Deep down is ignorance but on the surface they are very knowledgeable. Deep down they don't know anything and on the surface they are ready with all the answers possible to every possible question.

What do you need self-confidence for? If you are, self-confidence will be like a shadow to you. It will follow you. You don't carry your shadow, you don't look back again and again to see whether it is coming or not, you don't get an insurance for it. You don't care. It follows. Self-confidence is always there when you have become a self.

You are not yet a self, you are just an ego. Remember this difference between the ego and the self. The self is divine, the ego is human. The ego is manufactured by education, society, ambition, politics, morality, and all that; the self is not manufactured, it is discovered. The ego is an invention, the self is a discovery.

You have to manage the ego, because if you don't manage it, it will be gone within hours. If you don't manage it continuously, if you are not on guard continuously, it will be lost. So you have to be on guard. Of course, it creates great tension, great heaviness in the head. You become a heavy person and you become very up-tight. Your flow stops. You become frozen.

It is very foolish but it is what you have. That is why you are afraid, that's why you ask: "Should I throw away all my self-confidence?" That which can be thrown away is not. How can you throw away your shadow? Or can you? What are the ways to throw away a shadow? There are no ways. Nobody has ever been able to throw away a shadow. When your self has been discovered, when you have become an integrated soul and you have come to know your center, self-confidence follows like a shadow. You cannot throw it away.

A Buddha has it, a Mahavira has it, a Lao Tzu has it – you don't have it. Hence you are always afraid it may be taken away. And sometimes you even start thinking about dropping it. It cannot be taken away if it is there; it cannot be dropped if it is there. It can be taken away only if it is not there, it can be dropped only if it is not there. This will look paradoxical but this is one of the fundamental laws of life. You think only of that which is not; that which is needs no thought to hold it, that which is, simply is, on its own accord.

So, if you want to drop it, you don't have it. And please drop it. Please drop it because it is meaningless, it is useless, it is not, it is bogus, it is a false coin.

Now I would like to make the paradox even deeper. First I say you don't have it, so how can you drop it? Then I say you don't have it, so please drop it. It is a wastage of energy to carry it. You are just carrying an idea; it is not there. And the moment you drop your so-called self-confidence, you will be able to discover yourself. The false has to be understood as false, only then does the real reveal itself. The false understood as false is the first step towards reality. Let the false cease to be and the real will enter in. Carry the false and you will not allow the real to penetrate your being.

The fifth question:

Osho,
This master-disciple game is Osho-roulette but I know the bullet is a blank, isn't it?

Yes, it is, but it kills all the same.

Just the other day I was reading somebody's memoirs. And he writes that once, in Sannen, J. Krishnamurti was conducting a small discussion. A few people had gathered to ask questions, which he was answering. Suddenly a man arose and he said, "Stop all this. It is almost as if we are blind, in a dark night, searching for a black cat which is not there." And Krishnamurti stood up and said, "Sir, but it is there."

Let me repeat it. Krishnamurti said, "Sir, but it is there."

I would like to tell you, yes, the bullet is a blank but it kills. It cures, it kills, it destroys, it recreates. In fact, because it is a blank it kills, because it is empty it kills. It comes out of my emptiness, it is part of my emptiness. If you allow my emptiness to enter you it will kill you and revive you on a totally different plane, in a new dimension. Yes, it will be a cross, a crucifixion – and a resurrection too.

It kills only because it is a blank. It is like a blank check – the value depends on you. If you accept it totally it has tremendous value; if you reject it, it is just a piece of paper.

You will have to write the amount on it. I simply give you a blank check. It will depend on your courage as to what amount you can write on it.

And don't be miser when you are writing out a blank check.

The sixth question:

Osho,
Sometimes I feel really that the other is hell. What about love then and being with somebody?

The other is hell only to the extent that you feel the other as the other. There is a way to feel the other not as the other but as your extension – that is true too, that is what reality really is.

The other is not the other. When you love, what do you mean by love? Love means only this experience: that the other is not the other. What else is love? What is love all about? Love is an experience in which you feel that the other is no longer the other, the other is me, the other is my being. Maybe on the bodily plane you remain separate, on the mental plane you remain separate, but further down the centers start overlapping, merging, losing definition. That's what love is.

The other is hell if you are only pretending love – then the other is really hell. If you are only playing a game and just trying to exploit the other as a means then he will also try to exploit you as a means. Nobody wants to be reduced to a means, everybody is an end unto himself. Hence so much misery in the name of love arises. It does not come out of love, it comes out of false love, pretended love.

Love, and then you will know the other is not the other. If you can love deeply, infinitely, you will by and by become aware that even the trees are not the other, even the stars are not the other.

This is what I call becoming a sannyasin – to fall in love with the total. That's what Lao Tzu calls Tao – to fall in love with the total, to make love to God. That is the ultimate Tantra – to make love to God, to be in love with the whole.

Naturally, when you make love to a woman or a man it is bound to be momentary because when two small tiny individuals make love you cannot expect more than that. Even that that much happens is a miracle. If you really want eternal orgasm, a continuous orgasm, then you have to love the whole and you have to fall in love with the whole. Make love to God, then God is not the other. Wherever love comes in, the other disappears. That is the sign of love – that the other is no longer there. And when the other is not there as the other, there is heaven – paradise regained. When the other is as the other, there is hell – paradise lost.

The seventh question:

Osho,
You said that the real morality is the shadow of enlightenment. But then how is one to live before becoming enlightened?

The moment you ask "how" you are asking again for a discipline. The moment you ask "how" you ask for methods, techniques. Why can't you simply live? Are not animals living? Are not trees living and birds living without asking any "how"? Why do you carry on continuously about everything with this "how"? How to love? How to pray? How to be friendly? How to be compassionate? How to be silent? How to live?

Drop the "how" and let life take its own course. It will. It is not waiting for any "how." That's what Tao calls spontaneity, *tathata*, suchness. Let life take its own course. Who are you to interfere continuously? Can't you simply eat? Why do you ask how to eat and how to taste? Can't you simply taste? Just eat, chew well, and enjoy.

Let life move, don't try to manage it. By trying to manage, you have mismanaged enough. By trying to improve you have destroyed all its beauty. With all your goals and ideologies you have poisoned your being. Be natural.

But that is very difficult for the ego. The difficulty comes from the ego, not from life. Life can be lived without any "how" but the difficulty comes from the ego. The ego says that then you will be like an animal. So what! Be an animal. What is wrong in that? Man is an animal. There's nothing wrong in being an animal. No animal is as ugly as man. No animal has done so much violence on earth as man. No animal has destroyed nature as man has. What is wrong with animals? Have you ever heard of any animal becoming Adolf Hitler or Joseph Stalin or Mao Zedong? They have not killed. They have not murdered and butchered. They have not created wars. It is man who brings ugliness into the world.

But the ego says you have to be higher than the animals. In trying to be higher than the animals you fall lower than the animals. Be natural, don't try to improve, and you will find a great transformation happening. Through nature God comes – not through improvement, not through any effort of the ego, but through effortlessness, through deep trust and surrender.

Can't you trust God, who has given you birth? You did not ask the same question when you were in a womb – "How to live for nine months?" You lived well, you did well, perfectly well – otherwise you would not have been here. And there was no yoga teacher to teach you to be in a certain posture, to teach you how to breathe, how to do *pranayama* and *pratyahar*, and which *asana* will be the best. You didn't ask anybody. There was nobody to ask. You lived in the womb naturally and you grew. God was taking care, the whole was taking care, everything was provided.

Then you were born and then you became a child – you did not ask how to breathe, how to walk, how to talk. Everything came by and by. Can't you trust life? One day you became a young man, youth came, and love started arising in your being. One day you will become old, life will start disappearing, and then one day death will come and the circle will be complete.

Why are you always trying to interfere? Tao says you should be in *wu-wei*, non-interference. Let the whole do things. This is a very radical attitude, this is the greatest revolutionary attitude ever. "How?" is very childish. Yoga is for children, Tao is for grown-ups.

So don't ask: "But then how is one to live before becoming enlightened?" Just live. And just living, I tell you, is fantastic. It is far out!

The eighth question:

Osho,
How to be a Taoist psychotherapist within a very Confucius-oriented mental institution? In other words, how to be a nut-healer instead of a nut-cracker?

You can be a Taoist anywhere; nobody can hinder you, no obstacles can prevent you – because to be a Taoist means taking the ultimate risk. I am not saying that you will not be in trouble, I have never said that. You will be in trouble, certainly you will be in trouble, but that trouble is good, beneficial. It is a birth pain.

Yes, when you become natural you will be continuously in trouble – the trouble will come from everywhere. Nobody is natural, so everywhere you will be an odd person. Nobody will feel at ease with you in the beginning. Because you are at ease with yourself, nobody will feel at ease with you – because they are not at ease with themselves. They are very tense people. They fit with a tense person, but with a non-tense person they are simply at a loss. What to do?

Once I was traveling in a train and there was only one other passenger in the compartment. Naturally he wanted to talk to me and he wanted to somehow get into conversation with me. Seeing his restlessness I remained very cool. When he tried to ask something I simply answered yes or no. And I didn't take any interest. When he offered me a *pan* I said, "I don't take it." When he offered me a cigarette I said, "I don't smoke." When he prepared a drink – he was a doctor – I said, "I don't drink." Then he went crazy. He said, "Then how can I be friendly with you? How? We are going to be here in this compartment for forty-eight hours together and there seems to be no bridge." I said, "There is none."

And I watched him. He started becoming more and more crazy. He would open his suitcase and close it again and arrange his clothes and then arrange them again and open the window, close the window, read the same newspaper again, and in-between he would look at me as if to say, "What is the matter?" And I sat there cool and silent, and I enjoyed it.

After two hours he called the conductor and said, "I want to go into another compartment." The conductor asked if there was something wrong. He said, "Nothing is wrong but this man is too silent. It hurts. It drives me crazy. He is just sitting there and I have to see him because I am here alone. And there seems to be no possibility of communicating with him."

Now, I was not doing any harm, I had not said even a single word to him – but he had become very much disturbed.

When you are silent you will find that people become very uneasy with you. Your silence brings a totally different world, a world that they are not attuned with. You bring a totally new music, a music they don't know at all. You introduce them to a new way of being for which they are not ready.

You ask me: "How to be a Taoist psychotherapist within a very Confucius-oriented mental institution?" The whole world is a Confucius-oriented mental institution. Confucius is the master of millions, of the whole world really. And the whole world has become a mental institution. It is very difficult to find a man who is sane. Insanity is normal.

So if you are in a mental institution don't be worried very much, because whether you are in the institution or in the world it is the same. There is not much difference – just a little difference of degree.

You can be Taoist anywhere because Taoism has no conditions to be fulfilled. The first thing you will have to understand is: don't think of the mad people as nuts, don't think of them as mad. That is disrespectful. Their family thought them mad, hence they were hospitalized or institutionalized. The politicians thought them mad, the priest thought them mad, everybody thought them mad. But I tell you they are only different, not necessarily mad. Certainly they are different but who knows who is mad? Jesus was thought to be a madman, Mansoor was thought to be a madman, Francis was thought to be a madman, Ramakrishna was thought to be a madman. But who is mad?

These people are different, that much is certain. Be respectful. Maybe by being respectful you will help them to come back, to become more alert.

Now this has to be understood: when a person goes mad it simply shows that he was the weakest link in the group in which he used to live – for example, in a family. If the family is neurotic – as families are – then the person who is the weakest in the family will become neurotic. And through that person the whole neurosis of the family will start flowing. He will become the scapegoat. He may be weaker, he may be more fragile, he may be more sensitive than the others. He may be of a softer heart and a softer build. So the whole neurosis of the family will start flowing through him and the whole family will start calling him mad. And they will start thinking about taking him to the psychiatrist, to the institution.

And he was helpful, he was a safety valve for the neurotic family. The family's neurosis created the neurosis of the person because he was the most vulnerable in the family. Maybe he was the most intelligent, the most sensitive, the softest of them, so he became affected first. The others were more hard, more insensitive, more stone-like – he was more like a rose so he was crushed.

Then he comes to the psychiatrist and the psychiatrist is ready to label him: he is a schizophrenic, or a manic-depressive, or this or that. He is labeled. The family is happy – they were right. And he cannot say anything because the family says he is mad and the people where he works say he is mad and now, finally, the psychiatrist confirms that he is mad.

The psychiatrist is in the service of the society. The psychiatrist is part of the politics. Just as in the old days the priest was in the service of the society, now the psychiatrist is in the service of the society. Now the psychiatrist is doing the same function as the priest. The old conspiracy continues. The priests and the politicians were together – they conspired against man – but now the priest has lost his prestige so he is being replaced by the psychoanalyst and psychiatrist. Now he is in service and the politician is using him.

You force the person into a mental hospital. The moment you force a man into a mental hospital you fix the idea that he is mad in his mind absolutely. The idea that he is mad, which you have given him, is irreversible. Now everything will prove that he is mad – the treatment, the medicine, the doctors, the nurses, the whole atmosphere. You are hypnotizing him into madness.

The first thing to do – if you really want to be a Taoist in a mental institute – the first thing to do is to help the person to feel that he is not mad, only different. Do you see the difference it will bring? Just the word "different." Nothing is basically wrong with him, he is just not like others. Then you are not destroying his self-respect, then you are not destroying his dignity, you are helping his dignity. Then you are not giving him a hypnotic idea that he is mad, you are helping him to be dehypnotized. Help him as a person but not as a patient. Nobody is a patient. Help him with respect, not with any derogation on your part.

Don't label him, because persons cannot be labeled. People are so infinite people are so glorious – how can you label them "manic-depressive or schizophrenic"? These labels are dangerous, very dangerous. And nobody knows exactly what schizophrenia is, nobody knows exactly. There is no exact definition of who is abnormal, who is mad. So don't play with words.

Help the person to understand that he is different. Help the person to understand that he will be existing in a crowd which is totally different from him so he has to be a little careful – that's all. If you can bring a little more awareness into him, you will be a great blessing to him. That's all that is needed.

In the East we have done it for centuries. In the East, in the old days, if a person was going mad they would not take him to a doctor, to a physician, they would take him to a certain sacred place, to a temple. Why? Because madness was thought to be something divine. It is beautiful to think of madness as divine. It has something in it of the divine of the divine spontaneity, of the divine chaos. It has something that transcends ordinary intellect. They would take him to the temple and in the temple he was not thought to be a mad person, he was thought only to be in a higher stage.

People would pray for him and he would be left surrendered to God. And in almost all cases people were helped. They would again become normal – whatever that means. They would come back home, they would be able to fit with people more easily.

In Japan, in Zen temples, they still do that. They don't consider a person to be mad, they simply accept him as a person in trouble, a person who is different. They help him to be in the monastery but nobody does anything else for him. He is left alone. His needs are fulfilled. And by and by, within three or four weeks, he settles. The stirring that was inside him settles. In fact, to take a person out of his family reference and context is to help him.

But mad-institutions should not be called mad-institutions. They should be houses to help different kinds of people, with respect.

Don't think of yourself as a doctor, think of yourself as a friend. Don't think of yourself as higher than the patient. You are nobody to prescribe; you have just to understand the person and help him come to more awareness.

Many things can be helpful. Music will be more helpful than medicine. Meditation will be more tremendously helpful than anything else and dynamic meditation particularly will be helpful. Just help him to cathart. He has gathered much rubbish in his heart which he has not been allowed to throw off anywhere. Help him to throw it off. Don't repress him any more. His family was repressive, his society was repressive, now at least you can help.

What I call the dynamic methods of meditation can be of tremendous value to future psychiatry. Just help him to bring his madness out, whatsoever he feels like. If he wants to scream, let him. And don't let him feel guilty that he is doing something wrong. It is perfectly okay. In screaming nothing is wrong. He must have been waiting from his very childhood. He wanted to scream and scream and scream and nobody allowed it. Now the scream has become too much of a burden. It needs release. Let him scream. Let him cry and weep. Let him roll on the ground. And by and by you will see all violence disappearing By and by he will cool down, he will settle down. Then give him silent methods of meditation – zazen, Vipassana, and other methods. First give cathartic methods, then silent methods. These two things.

And be respectful. Serve him, don't treat him – and you will be able to treat him.

The ninth question:

Osho,
In your discourses on Patanjali, you spoke of the need to develop a third psychology – a psychology of the awakened mind which would supplement already-existing psychologies of the abnormal and the normal mind. You also said that Gurdjieff had tried to develop such a psychology, but had failed to do so after Ouspensky left him.
Osho, could you say a little more about the general form and content of your third psychology? For example, could it be taught in the way that the first and second psychologies are taught? And what benefits might be expected from teaching such a subject?

The first thing: it has a content but it has no form; it is not formal. That is the first basic difference.

The second thing: it cannot be taught, therefore, as a subject. It is not a subject. You cannot make a curriculum out of it. It cannot become a textbook.

Then what can be done? In universities, in colleges, in schools, facilities can be made available where people can meditate. It has no form, so you cannot teach it – but it has a content, it can be learned. And you cannot impose it. Meditation cannot be imposed. You can only make facilities available: a temple on the university campus, a meditation hall, underground cells where people can go and sit silently and be with themselves. You can provide dynamic meditation to allow people to cathart and then you can give them facilities where they can sit silently and be alone, centered, grounded in their being.

This cannot be a subject to be taught, it cannot be made compulsory. Only those who are interested, who have a desire, a longing, only they will be able to come there. You can have a guide who can give indications of how to cathart and how to be silent and sit silently – general guidance. That too has to be very vague. If you try to be very, very concrete it becomes a pattern, and no meditation is possible in a pattern. Meditation is a fluid phenomenon, you cannot give it a pattern. So just fluid patterns can be given.

And each one has to develop his own pattern because each individual is so different from everybody else that one's meditation cannot be another's meditation. Buddha's meditation cannot be Jesus' meditation. Of course, the meditation is the same, but each one will have his own way.

It is like when you go to a tailor. He may cut out of the same material but he will have to make different clothes for different people. The material is the same but the dresses will be different.

The meditation, the quality of meditative consciousness, is the same.

These are things to be remembered. Firstly, people have to be helped so that they can throw off their repressions unconditionally. Nobody must condemn them. If they want to shriek and shout and scream, they have to be allowed. If they want to jump and run, they have to be allowed. If they want to dance, they have to be allowed. If they want to go almost crazy, they have to be allowed. And this is the beauty of it: when a person goes crazy on his own he is not crazy, deep down he always remains in control. Tremendous control arises and he becomes unburdened.

When a person has become unburdened then he can start the second step – Vipassana, zazen-type silent methods. Just tell them to sit silently. If thoughts come, watch. Don't fight with thoughts. They will come less if the person has really been cathartic. Not so many thoughts will come, the traffic will be very, very slow. Ordinarily your mind is always in a rush hour but now a thought will pass sometimes and then there will be a gap. You will be more silent. Thoughts will come and go but you need not be worried. Just watch. You have nothing to be worried about – good or bad, no judgment is needed. Just be a watcher.

These small instructions and a guide who will give the instructions is all that is needed. If people bring problems the guide can solve them. This guide has, of course, to be a meditator himself otherwise he will not be able to help. It is not that he knows about meditation and can be of help, no. It is not that he has read about meditation and can be of help, no. He will have to be a meditator.

That's what I am trying to do here. I am not interested in the universities, in the education system, because I know that unless I have thousands of meditators that is futile, that is not possible, that cannot be done. So the first thing is to create thousands of meditators. Once I have those thousands of meditators then my interest will be moving towards universities. Then those meditators can go to the universities, to the colleges, to the schools, and they can create facilities there. Their presence will help and their own experience on the path will be a help to others.

But the basic thing about meditation is freedom. It cannot be imposed. You cannot force everybody in the school to come and meditate at a particular time. That will destroy meditation forever.

That is being done with poetry. Poetry is destroyed by the universities and colleges and schools because people are forced to read it. Once they are forced to read it they lose all interest. Then never in their life again will they read poetry. Poetry is so beautiful it cannot be forced. You should make possibilities available. Poets can be called to be there to read their poetry. People can ask them questions and they can explain. Or you can ask poets to be there and create poetry before school children or before college and university students so they can see how poetry arises in a being, how poetry descends, how a person pours out poetry:

They can sing with the poet, they can dance with the poet, they can enjoy the poetry, but there can be no examinations.

Poetry is such a big thing that examinations cannot be given on it. You can examine mathematics. It is such an ugly thing that if you destroy it, nothing is destroyed. But poetry no, please, no. Never touch poetry. Examinations are destructive.

Just make possibilities available. Poets should be moving from one university to another university. Poets should be called from one university to another university. They should be there and people who are interested in poetry should sit by their side and wait, should sip tea with the poet and wait. If the poetry arises they should be able to see the birth of it. Then they can sing with the poet and they can ask questions of the poet.

Meditation will also be like that because meditation is still higher than poetry. Poetry at least has words, meditation has no words. Meditation is a wordless poetry; poetry is meditation in words. Music is meditation with instruments, poetry is meditation with words but meditation has no words, no instruments – only sound, only silence. It is the highest peak of human consciousness. You cannot teach it, but people can learn it.

The question is from Brian Lewis. He is a professor in England. A beautiful person. He can be of much help in creating a possibility in his own university.

But remember, textbooks are not possible and this is not a subject matter, you cannot make a curriculum out of it, it has no form. It has content. It's content is God. That's what God is all about – the content of meditation.

And the last question. Because of Divya's question at least half-a-dozen questions have come. Now everybody wants to have a special spot for himself. And I am not going to allow anything to anybody because these are imitative questions, they have not come out of your own experience. You are simply jealous of Divya. Jealousy has to be dropped. Listen to the questions and you will understand.

Dear Osho,
You are the most blatantly outrageous son-of-a-bitch I have

ever met. First you say no one is special – then you give Divya a permanent spot in the front of fronts, and bestow on her a queenship. I want a front row seat too – and I'll settle for empress!!

It is from Amida.

Now Divya's question was totally different. She was not interested in any row – neither first nor the second. And she was not demanding. Her question was that she was feeling guilty about clinging to her seat. She wanted to be freed from that possessiveness. Her question was totally different.

You have completely forgotten her question. Her question was: "Osho, why do I cling to this spot? Why can I not drop it? I have dropped everything, why not this spot? Why am I so possessive about it? Why can I not let it go?" That was really a totally different question. She was not asking for this spot, remember. She was not asking for permission to sit here forever and always, she was asking for help to drop it. Hence I have given the spot to her.

To Amida, no. Your whole idea is of jealousy. Your whole idea is of competitiveness. This is ugly.

The second question:

How the hell am I supposed to find my right seat when by the time I reach the auditorium there are already three hundred and twenty-five people sitting there?

This is from Vidya. So your seat is three hundred and twenty-sixth. That is your spot.

And the third question:

Could I have the seat next to Divya?

It is from Devesh. No, never. You will have to surrender to Shiva and wherever he gives you a seat that is your seat. And I would like him to change your seat every day.

Never be imitative. Then you miss the whole beauty of it. Never ask a question because others have asked. Can't you even create a question which is originally yours? Even the question has to be borrowed. At least be that much creative. At least ask your own questions.

And never refer to anybody else, because whatsoever I have said to one I am not going to say to anybody else. Whatsoever is right for one may be wrong for the other. The thing that is medicine to you may be poison to somebody else. My answer is always going to be different.

Keep it always in mind – let your own question come. Be authentic. And never become a victim. These are all victims. The spot is not important to these questions, something else is – the ego. Hence the very formulation of the question.

Devesh asked for the next seat to Divya. Do you know that Divya is going to hell? Are you ready to have the next seat there too? How long will you follow Divya and how are you concerned with Divya? Next seat? Do you want to be a carbon copy? Be an original. God loves originals. Carbon copies are never loved, carbon copies are ugly. Find your spot. Why next to Divya? How does Divya come in? Never think in terms of anybody. You are here directly related to me, not through Divya or somebody else.

My sannyasins are not an organization. Each sannyasin is related to me. You are related to other sannyasins only because you are related to me and they are related to me. But you are not directly related to me, naturally you are related together – but that is secondary. Your eyes should be directly on me, nobody should come in-between. You have to face me, you have to encounter me, and the encounter has to be absolutely immediate and direct.

Enough for today.

CHAPTER #9

There Is No Help Possible

Lung Shu said to the physician Wen Chih:
"Your craft is subtle. I have an illness, can you cure it?"
"You have only to command. Tell me the symptoms of your illness."
"I do not think it an honor if the whole district praises me nor a disgrace if the whole state reviles me; I have no joy when I win, no anxiety when I lose; I look in the same way at life and death, riches and poverty, other men and pigs, myself and other men; I dwell in my own house as though lodging in an inn, and look at my own neighborhood as though it were a foreign and barbarous country.

"Having all these ailments, titles and rewards cannot induce me, punishments and fines cannot awe me, prosperity and decline, benefit and harm cannot change me, joy and sorrow cannot influence me. Consequently it is impossible for me to serve my prince, have dealings with my kindred and friends, manage my wife and children, control my servants. What illness is this? What art can cure it?"

Wen Chih ordered Lung Shu to stand with his back to the light. He himself stepped back and examined Lung Shu from a distance facing the light. Then he said: "Hmmm. I see your heart. The place an inch square is empty – you are almost a sage. Six of the holes in your heart run into each other but one is stopped up. Can this be the reason why you now think the wisdom of a sage is an illness? My shallow craft can do nothing to cure it."

A parable...

Once in the garden of a master there lived a monkey. And, as monkeys are curious people, he became very curious about the master. He saw the master sitting silently, doing nothing, and by and by he started coming close to him – what is this man doing? It was a mystery. Certainly, to a monkey, the most mysterious thing is somebody sitting silently, doing nothing.

Restlessness is just natural to a monkey, so resting in silence...? Has this man gone mad? By and by he started coming closer to watch him. The closer he came, the more he was surprised. Not only was the man silent but the space around him was tremendously quiet. Even the monkey could feel the vibe as he came closer.

Then he started loving the man, and just to be close to him became one of his hobbies. Whenever he could find the time and whenever the master was sitting in the garden, he would come close and sit by his side.

One day he said to the master, "What do you do? Please tell me also. I surrender to you. Accept me as a disciple."

The master looked at the monkey, felt great compassion for him, and said, "I don't do anything. You can also do it. It is non-doing. Sitting silently, the spring comes and the grass grows by itself. You simply sit silently. When the right moment comes, suddenly you are full of tremendous joy and peace and God. You are not supposed to do anything. Anything done on your part is a disturbance, creates ripples, creates waves. And when your mind is wavy God cannot enter. When the mind is a quiet surface, when everything is silent and calm, God enters. He enters through the door of silence – but that is possible only when you are not a doer. So you can do it, you can try it."

The monkey shook his head. He said, "It is impossible. I thought that if there was something I could do I would do it, but this is impossible. If you told me to fetch the moon I could bring it; if you told me to remove the Himalayas I could do it; if you told me to force the Ganges to run up-current I could do it – because in the old ancient days other monkeys like Hanuman have been known to do it. I am a monkey, I have the potentiality, I can also do it – but sitting silently, doing nothing? Sir, that is impossible. It is against my nature, it would drive me crazy. If God comes through silence then God is not for me and I am not for God."

Human mind is nothing but a monkey. Man has not changed much. Charles Darwin says that man has evolved only on the surface – deep down man is as restless as other monkeys. Man has not evolved much. The real man is born only when your inner monkey completely disappears, utterly disappears.

To be a man means to be a no-mind. The constant chattering of the mind inside, the inner talk, the monologue, continues day and night, year in, year out, from birth to death. Whatsoever you are doing is irrelevant, it continues deep inside you. That chattering is the only thing that is irreligious, the only sin, the original sin. Once that chattering stops, miracles start happening to you. Such great mysteries become revealed that you cannot contain them. Such a vast sky starts pouring into you that you cannot believe it. It is incredible. You start expanding. Then the whole universe is something within you. Then you are not within the universe but the universe is within you. Then stars and moons and suns circle within your heart.

But if this happens without a master you will go mad. It is mind that is holding you together. Whatsoever you are – even if you are a monkey – it is mind that is holding you together. The mind is your illness and also your normality. Because of the mind you are tethered to the earth. Without the mind you would not be tied anywhere. You would be so loose and so free you might disperse. Who would hold you? What would be your definition then? Mind gone, ego goes. The ego is the center of the mind, the very heart of the monkey. Mind gone, greed is gone. Mind gone, ambition is gone. Mind gone, competition is gone. Mind gone, future and past are gone. Mind gone, Islam, Christianity, Hinduism, are gone. Mind gone, Indian, German, Chinese – nationalities are gone. Mind gone, the body is no more you. Your own mother is not your mother, your own father is not your father, your own son is no longer your son. All relationship disappears because the relationship exists in the mind.

Just think of a moment with the mind suddenly gone – where will you be? What will you be? You will lose all identity. You will simply melt and disappear, evaporate. It will be maddening… hence without the master the path is very risky. And when the glimpse of the beyond comes to you for the first time it will shatter you and you will not be able to see the positivity of it – you will see just the negativity of it. You will see what it has taken away from *you, you* will not be able to see what it is giving you. Naturally you are acquainted with your past and the past is going away, fast You will simply see yourself as disappearing.

And for the new that is being born you don't as yet have any language; for the new that is being born you don't as yet have any concept. The new that is being born is invisible, cannot be touched, cannot be heard, cannot be smelled cannot be tasted. It is beyond senses. You have never before known the new that is happening so how will you recognize it? The new will not be recognized and the old will be disappearing so you will feel yourself going mad, falling apart, dying. Death will be your experience or madness will be your experience. You will think that this is a curse that has happened to you. The blessing will look like a curse because you cannot yet see it as a blessing, your eyes are not trained or it. You can only see the curse, you can only see the negative part of it. This is what Christian mystics call "the dark night of the soul" – the light is so blinding it almost looks like darkness.

Have you not looked directly into the sun sometimes? Within seconds you will go blind, you will not be able to see. It will be so dazzling. It is not dark but the light is too much for you and your eyes are not able to take it in, they cannot absorb it. And, after looking at the sun for a few seconds, if you look around everywhere, you will find a tremendous darkness. If you look long enough at the sun you will go blind.

Why is light blinding? Why? Because we have certain capacities. Only in tiny capacities can we allow the light to enter in – and we can recognize only that much. Beyond that we lose recognition. That's how it happens that when you first enter into the world of no-mind it looks like madness – the dark night of the soul, the mad night of the soul.

All the religions have noted the fact, hence all the religions insist on finding a master before you start entering into the world of the no-mind – because he will be there to help you, to support you. You will be falling apart but he will be there to encourage you, to give you hope. He will be there to interpret the new to you. That is the meaning of a master: to interpret that which cannot be interpreted, to indicate that which cannot be said, to show that which is inexpressible. He will be there, he will devise methods and ways for you to continue on the path – otherwise you might start escaping from it.

And remember, there is no escape. If you start escaping you will simply go berserk. Sufis call such people the *mastas*. In India they are known as mad *paramahansas*. You cannot go back because it is no longer there, and you cannot go ahead because it is all dark. You are stuck. That's why Buddha says, "Fortunate is the man who has found a master."

I myself was not as fortunate as you are; I was working without a master. I searched and I could not find one. It was not that I had not searched, I had searched long enough, but I could not find one. It is very rare to find a master, rare to find a being who has become a non-being, rare to find a presence who is almost an absence, rare to find a man who is simply a door to the divine, an open door to the divine which will not hinder you, through which you can pass. It is very difficult.

The Sikhs call their temple the *gurudwara*, the door of the master. That is exactly what the master is – the door. Jesus says again and again, "I am the gate, I am the way, I am the truth.

Come follow me, pass through me. And unless you pass through me you will not be able to reach."

Yes, sometimes it happens that a person has to work without a master. If the master is not available then one has to work without a master, but then the journey is very hazardous.

For one year I was also in the same state that this parable talks about. For one year it was almost impossible to know what was happening. For one year continuously it was even difficult to keep myself alive. Just to keep myself alive was a very difficult thing – because all appetite disappeared. Days would pass and I would not feel any hunger, days would pass and I would not feel any thirst. I had to force myself to eat, force myself to drink. The body was so non-existential that I had to hurt myself to feel that I was still in the body. I had to knock my head against the wall to feel whether my head was still there or not. Only when it hurt would I be a little in the body.

Every morning and every evening I would run for five to eight miles. People used to think that I was mad. Why was I running so much? Sixteen miles a day! It was just to feel myself, to feel that I still was, not to lose contact with myself – just to wait until my eyes became attuned to the new that was happening.

And I had to keep myself close to myself. I would not talk to anybody because everything had become so inconsistent that even to formulate one sentence was difficult. In the middle of the sentence I would forget what I was saying, in the middle of the way I would forget where I was going. Then I would have to come back. I would read a book – I would read fifty pages – and then suddenly I would remember, "What am I reading? I don't remember at all." My situation was such.

The door of the psychiatrist's office burst open and a man rushed in.

"Doctor!" he cried. "You've got to help me. I'm sure I'm losing my mind. I can't remember anything – what happened a year ago, or even what happened yesterday. I must be going crazy!"

"Hmmmmmmm," pondered the headshrinker. "Just when did you first become aware of this problem?"

The man looked puzzled, "What problem?"

This was my situation! Even to complete a full sentence was difficult. I had to keep myself shut in my room. I made it a point not to talk, not to say anything, because to say anything was to say that I was mad.

For one year it persisted. I would simply lie on the floor and look at the ceiling and count from one to a hundred then back from a hundred to one. Just to remain capable of counting was at least something. Again and again I would forget. It took one year for me to gain a focus again, to have a perspective.

It happened. It was a miracle. But it was difficult. There was nobody to support me, there was nobody to say where I was going and what was happening. In fact, everybody was against it, my teachers, my friends, my well-wishers. All were against it. But they could not do anything, they could only condemn, they could only ask what I was doing.

I was not doing anything! Now it was beyond me; it was happening. I had done something, unknowingly I had knocked at the door, now the door had opened. I had been meditating for many years, just sitting silently doing nothing, and by and by I started getting into that space, that heart-space, where you are and you are not doing anything, you are simply there, a presence, a watcher.

You are not even a watcher because you are not watching – you are just a presence. Words are not adequate because whatsoever word is used it seems as if it is being done. No, I was not doing it. I was simply lying, sitting, walking – deep down there was no doer. I had lost all ambition; there was no desire to be anybody, no desire to reach anywhere – not even God, not even nirvana. The buddha-disease had completely disappeared. I was simply thrown to myself.

It was an emptiness and emptiness drives one crazy. But emptiness is the only door to God. That means that only those who are ready to go mad ever attain, nobody else.

But if you have a master things are simple. He can hold your hand when you are losing all track of your being. He can become your support. If you love your master that love will be the last link. Every link disappears but that link remains. It disappears only when you have attained your own perspective, your own clarity. It is just like an umbilical cord. The child lives through the mother in the womb for nine months and if you cut the umbilical cord he will die. He lives through it. That is the only link.

In exactly the same way, if you love the master, a subtle silver cord arises between you and the master – a very invisible phenomenon to others but very visible to the disciple. He can almost touch it. You become joined together with your master from your navel. The master is your mother, the master is your womb. And this umbilical cord, this invisible silver cord, remains nursing you until you are ready and the pregnancy is ripe, until you are ready to be reborn and you can breathe on your own.

The master is a must. If you can find one you are fortunate. Then he will interpret to you and the darkness will look like light, the illness will look like a new well-being; the curse he will transform into a blessing. In fact, it is a blessing but you interpret it as a curse. He is not doing anything, he is simply showing you what the case is.

With this background, listen to this story.

> Lung Shu said to the physician Wen Chih, "Your craft is subtle. I have an illness. Can you cure it?"

This man must have been like me, unfortunate. He must have been working without a master. Now he thinks that he has an illness. It is natural, that's how it appears – it looks like an illness. All the old has gone; your old intelligence functions no more, your old memory functions no more, your old identity is there no more. You cannot say, Who am I?' Your name, your address, all have become irrelevant. You don't belong to anybody, you don't belong to anywhere. For the first time you are an outsider in this world, you are a stranger. Unrelated, uprooted you are – like a tree which is uprooted from the ground and has started dying.

It happens that when you enter the inner emptiness, the state of no-mind, for the first time, you are uprooted from the earth. Before you grow your roots into the sky there is going to be a time-gap, an interval, in which there will be much suffering if there is nobody to make you alert about the blessing that is going to happen to you. If there is nobody to give you hope then the dark night of the soul can become your grave.

> Lung Shu said to the physician Wen Chih, '"Your craft is subtle. I have an illness. Can you cure it?"
> "You have only to command. Tell me the symptoms of your illness."
> "I do not think it an honor if the whole district praises me nor a disgrace if the whole state reviles me; I have no joy when I win, no anxiety when I lose; I look in the same way at life and death, riches and poverty, other men and pigs, myself and other men; I dwell in my own house as though lodging in an inn, and look at my own neighborhood as though it were a foreign and barbarous country."

Certainly the man must have been in terrific trouble, in great anxiety. He could not relate to people any more. He had lost the language to relate.

And what is happening? First he says, "I do not think it an honor if the whole district praises me nor a disgrace if the whole state reviles me." He is losing his ego. It is the ego that feels good when somebody praises you and that feels bad when somebody disgraces you, insults you. You live through it, you judge your life through it, it is the way you relate to people. You say that you love somebody, because somehow he buttresses your ego. You say that you hate somebody, because somehow he displeases you, he disgraces you, his presence is humiliating. The way he talks, the things he says, are hurting to the ego. They don't nourish you, they starve you. You hate the person. Sometimes it happens that you have not even known the person, you have met him for the first time – but immediately you feel that you hate the person because somehow his vibe is against your ego. The way he walks, the way he looks at you, the way he talks – he is trying to have the upper hand. Maybe it is not conscious, but you feel that he is trying to prove that he is superior to you. Somehow he makes you feel inferior. You hate him. Whenever a person makes you feel superior you like him, you love him; you say that he is beautiful.

Your ego is your criterion. Once you drop the ego, who is your friend and who is your enemy? Once you drop the ego, what is right and what is wrong? Once you drop the ego, what to do and what not to do? Then how will you be a sinner and how will you be a saint? Once you drop the ego you drop all duality, you become one. That oneness drives you crazy.

There is a beautiful parable in the life of a saint in Maharashtra, Tukaram. One day he comes home – he was a poor man, a very poor man he is coming home. Somebody has given him ten sugar-cane sticks. While coming home he meets many beggars and children on the road and he distributes these sugar-cane sticks. He keeps only one for himself, nine he gives away. He is very happy; happy because he could give something, happy because he had something to give, happy because when he gave those sugar-cane sticks to the beggars they thanked him, happy because the children were very happy – they laughed and enjoyed and they ran to their homes with their sugar-cane sticks.

He comes home very happy, very, very happy. He tells the wife the whole thing, "Somebody has presented me with ten sugar-cane sticks. Nine I have distributed, one I have brought for me and you."

Of course, as wives do, she became very angry. They were poor and these ten sugar-cane sticks would have been nourishment for them. For days they had been hungry and here was this fool he had distributed them. She became so angry that she took the one sugar-cane stick and started beating Tukaram. She hit him hard on his head. The stick broke in two and Tukaram laughed. He said, "So you are a dualist. I believe in the one, you believe in two. Good. So now the sticks are two – you can have one and I can have one. But I thought that we were one so I thought one stick would be enough."

Your understanding is different. The mind of man converts everything into two. The energy that you call light and darkness is one but you call it by two names: darkness and light. The energy that you call life and death is one but you call it by two names: life and death. The energy that you call hate and love is one but you call it by two names: hate and love. You are Tukaram's wife.

This whole human world exists in duality. Language depends on duality, expression depends on duality. When a person starts feeling one – when the ego disappears and the very phenomenon of duality disappears – then one feels one with the trees, one with the birds, one with the rocks, one with the river, one with the moon, one with the sun. Certainly the person will start feeling that something has gone wrong. Who is he?

If in this state a lion jumps on you, you will not be worried at all. It is possible that you may even enjoy the whole thing – the lion eating you – because you are not separate from the lion. You will adjust perfectly well. You will enjoy the fact that the lion is hungry and he is eating you. You will become the lion. There is no duality.

But in this state, in the beginning, one will naturally think, "Have I gone mad?" No enemy, no friend, praise means nothing, disgrace means nothing....

Just the other night a young man asked me, "Osho, can I displease you?" I said, "If you please you can do it but you will not be able to displease me because you are not able to please me either. To please me or to displease me is impossible. What can you do to displease me and what can you do to please me? To me both are the same."

> "I do not think it an honor if the whole district praises me nor a disgrace if the whole state reviles me."

The man is disturbed, very much disturbed, uprooted. What is happening? People used to insult him before and he used to get into a rage. Now nothing happens. Has he become impotent?

Has he lost all energy? People used to praise him and he used to feel happy, but now nothing happened. Now, even if people brought him garlands, nothing happened.

Or, if sometimes they insulted him and threw shoes at him, still nothing happened.

Once it happened in a public meeting in Baroda that somebody threw a shoe at me. He may have thought to displease me. I asked him to give me the other shoe too because what was I going to do with one? He became very embarrassed. He was very puzzled. Later on he wrote a letter to me: "What manner of man you are? I insulted you and you asked me for another shoe!" He was not expecting that.

But when it happens the first time you become disoriented. You don't know now what is what.

Second:

"I have no joy when I win, no anxiety when I lose."

Comparison is disappearing, competition is disappearing, jealousy is going – they are all shadows of the ego. When ego goes they cannot linger long. They have to follow suit. They go with the ego, they come with the ego. They are companions of the ego.

"I have no joy when I win, no anxiety when I lose."

What is there to lose in life? And what is there to win? All that you need cannot be lost. Your essential-most core can never be lost. And the essential-most core cannot be achieved – once you start looking into your being it is already there. You are that which you were always thinking to gain and attain and it is something that cannot be lost, cannot be robbed. Nobody can take it away. It cannot be destroyed because it is your very nature. When you start moving into the dimension of ultimate reality there is nothing to win and nothing to lose. Comparison, jealousy and competition go with the ego, as shadows of the ego.

Third:

"I look in the same way at life and death, riches and poverty."

Equanimity is born. When ego is gone and ego shadows are gone, *samyaktva* equanimity, is left. You start looking at things but you don't think this is bad and this is good, this should be and this should not be. All is good or all is bad. All is alike. That is the equal eye, equanimity, what in India we call *samyak drishti* – the eye which sees everything as equal, the eye which sees the small as the big and the big as the small, the worthless as valuable and the valuable as worthless, the eye which sees gold and the mud as the same.

Life and death, riches and poverty, all look the same to this man – and he is very much disturbed. What is happening to him? Has he lost interest in life or has he become dead somewhere in his being?

Fourth:

"I dwell in my own house as though lodging in an inn and look at my own neighborhood as though it were a foreign and barbarous country."

When you lose your mind, certainly you become a stranger. Now you don't have any common language with anybody else. Now your language is silence, and people cannot under stand silence. And you cannot understand their words. It takes time to get tuned to your inner silence and then to come back to your mind and start using it again. It takes time sometimes years, sometimes a whole life. One has to learn from ABC.

Once your mind is gone you have to start using it again if you want to relate. That's why Buddha says there are many people who become realized but there are only very rare people who become masters. A master is one who has become realized and has again entered into the world of mind, has again become proficient with language, has again become capable of using the mind.

The realized person is one who has gone beyond the mind but who cannot relate again to the people who are lagging behind. The master is one who has gone beyond the mind and has become again capable of using the mind. Now the mind is not using him, he uses the mind, he is the master.

But to come back, great effort is needed, great compassion is needed. Unless you love people tremendously, when you attain your buddhahood who cares? Why bother? Why not remain silent? Why not enjoy the beautitude that has happened to you, the blessing that has come to you? Why bother with foolish people? And anyway they are not going to understand, they are going to misunderstand. At the most they will not understand, at the worst they will misunderstand. And they are going to create unnecessary problems for you – they crucified Jesus, they poisoned Socrates, they killed Mansoor.

Mansoor could have remained silent, he could have avoided it all. That's what others were saying to him. In those days, in that part of the world where Mansoor lived, there were many enlightened people. Enlightenment comes like a wave – when it comes, then many people ride the wave. There were many enlightened people, Junnaid was one. Junnaid said to Mansoor al-Hillaj, "You stop talking, you keep quiet, otherwise they will kill you." And there were other enlightened people, they all came to Mansoor and told him, "You keep quiet! These Mohammedans around are dangerous!"

But al-Hillaj wouldn't listen. He started shouting from the house-tops, "I am God!! *Ana'l Haq*. I am the truth. I have attained. Come and have a taste." He started offering his cup of tea to everybody. People were enraged. Who is this saying that he is a God? To people it looked like the ultimate in egoism. Somebody calling himself a God? This seemed to be the last straw – this man had become a megalomaniac, he thinks he is a God. They were very much offended. They killed him, but even while they were killing him Mansoor was laughing, and the last thing that he said was again

"Ana'l haq! I am God!"

He was a master. He was trying to help people. A master is one who has gone beyond mind and come back. A master is one who has gone to the peak and traveled back to the valley to take others to the peak. Every enlightened person is not a master. In one thousand enlightened persons only one becomes a master – because to go to the peak is very arduous but to come back from the peak, back to the valley, is far more arduous. And it is a thankless job! You take so much trouble and nobody is even going to thank you. They Will curse you. They will say, "Why did you come back? Why won't you allow us to rest? Why do you bring such great challenges to us? Why don't you keep your peak to yourself? Why are you shouting and disturbing our sleep? We are happy wherever we are. Don't bring these dreams about the peak to us." They become angry.

One can understand their anger. You disturb their life. They are settled in the valley, enjoying a thousand and one trips. Of course, all are dreams, meaningless, but at the moment they look meaningful, at the moment even the dream looks real and they are absorbed in it. Then there comes a man from the peak back to the valley and he starts shaking everybody up and he becomes an alarm and it disturbs everybody's sleep. Somebody was having a beautiful, sweet dream – he becomes angry because you disturbed his dream. He has to take vengeance. "Why don't you go to your peak? If you have attained, you go. You forget us. We don't bother you so why should you bother us?"

But those few people who have come back to the valley are the rarest. Their compassion is infinite. To attain to God is just selfish, to bring it to people is service. Buddha has insisted again and again that while you are meditating, always remember compassion. Don't forget compassion. It is very easy to forget compassion while you are meditating, so continuously remember. And when you have come to the fulfillment of your meditation, don't forget compassion. Bring it back to people. Grow in compassion and meditation so simultaneously that when meditation brings you home, compassion takes you back to the valley, back to the foreign lands where barbarous people dwell, where they will not understand your language, where there is more possibility that you will be crucified. But that is nothing – for an enlightened person to be crucified is nothing. It makes no difference. If crucifixion can help people he will love to be crucified. Whatsoever will help people he will love to do it.

There is every possibility that Jesus helped those people who were going to crucify him. There is every possibility that Judas was not against Jesus but was an agent from Jesus. There is every possibility that Jesus planned the whole thing – because those people were so fast asleep that unless something very sensational happened they would not wake up.

The crucifixion was something really sensational. For two thousand years it has not allowed many people to go back to sleep again. It has been the most sensational thing in the whole history of humanity. Jesus has left the deepest mark. Buddha has not left such a deep mark, neither has Mahavira, nor Patanjali, nor Lao Tzu. Jesus has left the deepest mark – it is as if with the crucifixion history was split in two: before and after. All that was before Jesus became irrelevant and all that was after Jesus took on a new significance.

The Christian calendar is the most important calendar. There are other calendars but no calendar is as important. Jainas have their calendar – their calendar starts with Mahavira – but it is not important. Hindus have their calendar – their calendar starts with a great emperor, Vikramaditya – but a king is just a king, nothing compared with the Christian calendar.

With Jesus history simply split into two parts. With Jesus something of tremendous value enters into human consciousness. And that happened because of the crucifixion. His blood is still alive, his blood still shouts, his blood still calls people. If he had not been crucified he might have been forgotten. Many people have been forgotten, completely forgotten. There is every possibility that he conspired with the conspirators, that he helped them.

But when for the first time the glimpse enters into your being you will feel:

> "I dwell in my own house as though lodging in an inn and look at my own neighborhood as though it were a foreign and barbarous country."

That is because you lose your old language and the new one has to be learned. And it is arduous to learn the new language, it needs real effort to learn the new language – because when you have attained to the inner silence, if you make a word the word melts and disappears. You try hard to create a word but you do not create it and it disappears. For a man who has attained to the innermost silence all language is as if one is writing on water, you have not even written it and it has gone.

"Having all these ailments" – naturally the man thinks he has become very ill, these are ailments – *"titles and rewards cannot induce me."*

The fifth symptom:

> "...titles and rewards cannot induce me, punishments and fines cannot awe me; prosperity and decline, benefit and harm cannot change me...."

When equanimity happens, when you have become *samyak drishti* when you have attained to the equal eye.... Jesus says, "Attain to one eye, and if you can attain to one eye your whole body will become full of light." When you start looking at things as if they are the same – nothing Is inferior, nothing is superior, the dunghill and the diamond have the same value, or same non-value, no actual difference exists – then comes this fifth state, transcendence.

> "... titles and rewards cannot induce me, punishments and fines cannot awe me, prosperity and decline, benefit and harm cannot change me...."

Things happen but one remains transcendent, one remains aloof, nothing touches one. One has become a lotus flower. The lotus flower is in the water but the water does not touch it, the lotus flower comes out of the mud but is beyond mud, beyond all mud. Can you find anything like the lotus flower? It is difficult – that's why in the East the lotus flower has become the symbol of enlightenment itself. Buddha is depicted sitting on a lotus flower. Vishnu is standing on a lotus flower. And the ultimate state of consciousness, *sahasrar* means a one-thousand-petalled lotus flower.

The lotus flower is a symbol, a metaphor, for transcendence. You move but nothing touches you – that is what Zen people mean when they say, "When a master walks in a river the water does not touch his feet." He is transcendental. He lives in the world and yet he lives not in the world. This is not an illness, it is a great *siddhi* a great achievement. But when it happens for the first time it looks like an ailment.

Sixth:

"...joy and sorrow cannot influence me."

When joy and sorrow cannot influence you, you suddenly feel you have become a desert. Your whole life consists of joy and sorrow – sorrow you don't want, joy you hanker for. Your whole life exists on the two wings of joy and sorrow. When joy and sorrow both disappear, or both become meaningless, or you have attained the equal eye, equanimity, you have attained transcendence, joy and sorrow look alike, whatsoever comes is okay – then you will feel that you have become a desert. This is the state which in India they call *veetraga*. This is one who has gone beyond attachment, detachment, like, dislike; one who does not know at all what is beneficial, what is harmful, one who has become a child again.

Seventh:

> "Consequently it is impossible for me to serve my prince, have dealings with my kindred and friends, manage my wife and children, control my servants. What illness is this?"

The seventh means freedom. When you are completely free of the ego and all the shadows that the ego brings in; when you are free of all duality; when you are free of all distinctions and you start living in a world which is one energy, nothing lower, nothing higher; when Devil and God lose their definition, embrace each other, fall in love, make love to each other; when life and death meet and become one; when the whole world is one – in that state you are free. But first the freedom will look as if you have gone utterly mad.

> "…it is impossible for me to serve my prince…."

It is impossible to serve anybody now.

> "…have dealings with my kindred and friends…."
> It is impossible now. They will think you are a madman, and to you they look like phantoms, ghosts, not real.

> "…manage my wife and children, control my servants…."

In this state you cannot serve and you cannot control. You are not – how can you serve and how can you control? Freedom means you are not; freedom means to be free from oneself. Freedom does not mean that you have become free, freedom means that you are no more, freedom means that you have become free of you. Now there is nobody; just a deep emptiness exists.

This emptiness will look empty to a person who has no master. It looked empty to me also. But there is no way to go back, so one is simply helpless. One cannot go back but one does not know where to go ahead because there *is* no longer any ahead – all paths have disappeared. This is the moment when Tao arises. That's why I say "the pathless path." Tao is the pathless path. This is the moment when all paths disappear; you look back and there is nothing.

There is a beautiful Buddhist story in China.

In a certain town a very beautiful young lady suddenly arrived out of the blue. Nobody knew from where she came; her whereabouts were completely unknown. But she was so beautiful, so enchantingly beautiful, that nobody even thought about where she had come from. People gathered together, the whole town gathered – and all the young men almost three hundred young men, wanted to get married to the woman.

The woman said, "Look, I am one and you are three hundred. I can be married only to one, so you do one thing. I will come again tomorrow; I give you twenty-four hours. If one of you can repeat Buddha's *Lotus Sutra*, I will marry him.

All the young men rushed to their homes; they didn't eat, they didn't sleep, they recited the sutra the whole night, they tried to cram it in. Ten succeeded. The next morning the woman came and those ten people offered to recite. The woman listened. They had succeeded.

She said, "Right, but I am one. How can I marry ten? I will give you twenty-four hours again. The one who can also explain the meaning of the *Lotus Sutra* I will marry. So you try to understand – because reciting is a simple thing, you are mechanically repeating something and you don't understand its meaning."

There was no time at all – only one night – and the *Lotus Sutra* is a long sutra. But when you are infatuated you can do anything. They rushed back, they tried hard. The next day three persons appeared. They had understood the meaning.

And the woman said, "Again the trouble remains. The number is reduced, but the trouble remains. From three hundred to three is a great improvement, but again I cannot marry three persons, I can marry only one. So, twenty-four hours more. The one who has not only understood it but tasted it too, that person I will marry. So in twenty-four hours try to taste the meaning of it. You are explaining, but this explanation is intellectual. Good, better than yesterday's, you have some comprehension, but the comprehension is intellectual. I would like to see some meditative taste, some fragrance. I would like to see that the lotus has entered into your presence, that you have become something of the lotus. I would like to smell the fragrance of it. So tomorrow I come again."

Only one person came, and certainly he had achieved. The woman took him to her house outside the town. The man had never seen the house; it was very beautiful, almost a dreamland. And the parents of the woman were standing at the gate. They received the young man and said, "We are very happy."

The woman went in and he chitchatted a little with the parents. Then the parents said, "You go. She must be waiting for you. This is her room." They showed him. He went, he opened the door, but there was nobody there. It was an empty room. But there was a door entering into the garden. So he looked – maybe she has gone into the garden. Yes, she must have gone because on the path there were footprints. So he followed the footprints. He walked almost a mile. The garden ended and now he was standing on the bank of a beautiful river – but the woman was not there. The footprints also disappeared. There were only two shoes, golden shoes, belonging to the woman.

Now he was puzzled. What has happened? He looked back – there was no garden, no house, no parents, nothing. All had disappeared. He looked again. The shoes were gone, the river was gone. All that there was emptiness – and a great laughter.

And he laughed too. He got married.

This is a beautiful Buddhist story. He got married to emptiness, got married to nothingness. This is the marriage for which all the great saints have been searching. This is the moment when you become a bride of Christ or a gopi of Krishna.

But everything disappears – the path, the garden, the house, the woman, even the footprints. Everything disappears. There is just a laughter, a laughter that arises from the very belly of the universe.

But when it happens for the first time, if you have not been led slowly, slowly, you will go mad.

This Buddhist story says that he was led slowly, slowly. The woman was the master. The woman is symbolic of the master. She led him slowly, slowly. First, recite the sutra; second, understand intellectually; third, give a sign that you have lived it. These are the three stages. Then she led him into nothingness.

The master leads you slowly, slowly; makes you by and by ready.

This man was not fortunate enough to have a master. He has come to the emptiness, to the ultimate emptiness but he thinks it is an illness.

> "...what art can cure it?"

> Wen Chi ordered Lung Shu to stand with his back to the light.
> He himself stepped back and examined Lung Shu from a distance facing the light.
> Then he said "Hmm. I see your heart. The place an inch square is empty. You are almost a sage. Six of the holes in your heart run into each other but one is stopped up. Can this be the reason why you now think the wisdom of a sage is an illness? My shallow craft can do nothing to cure it."

This is the difference between modern and ancient medicine. The ancient Chinese medicine, acupuncture, is not as gross as modern medicine; neither is the ancient Indian medicine, ayurveda, as gross as modern medicine. Modern medicine is concerned only with the physical, it knows nothing of the beyond. Ancient Eastern medicine is more concerned with the metaphysical, with the paraphysical. Now a few insights in the West are gaining strength slowly; radionics, Kirlian photography, acupuncture and ayurveda are entering the Western consciousness.

But ancient Eastern medicine was not just medicine, not just a cure for the body, but a cure for the soul. The East says that the body only shows the symptoms, the symptoms are not the real illness. And the symptoms should not be treated directly. The illness should be treated directly then the symptoms will disappear. The allopathic approach is to treat the symptom and to think that the illness will disappear. That is not possible; that is going from the outer to the inner, which is not possible. What happens? It becomes a sort of repression.

Maybe the whole Christian tradition of repression is the cause. The whole Western mind is repressive. So wherever a symptom is found, repress it. The symptom is repressed and the illness is not treated at all. The illness remains within so it finds another way to come out. So you treat one illness and another illness is born; you treat that, and a third one is born.

In the East we have never been very interested in the symptoms. The symptoms are not to be treated, the person is to be treated. And, one thing more, the East knows that illnesses are not always illnesses – there are a few illnesses which are blessings. When a person moves beyond the body, the body will never be healthy in the same way it was before, it cannot be – because a distance arises between the innermost being and the body. The bridges are broken. That's why an enlightened person will never be born again – he cannot enter into the body again because the bridges are broken. So the enlightened person, once enlightened, can never come back. Then he is gone forever – *gate gate para gate*; gone, gone, gone forever – gone to the beyond from where there is no coming back, gone to the point of no return.

But the thing starts happening in this life. If you become enlightened you loosen your connection with your body. The body can never be as healthy as it was before, cannot be healthy in the same way that it was before. But those illnesses are not really illnesses, they are simply symptoms that your inner being is being transformed. Something of tremendous revolution is happening within you, a radical change is happening within you. So the body will have many changes.

This man, this physician, Wen Chih, must not only have been a physician, he must have been a man of great insight. What does he say? He says, *"I see your heart. The place an inch square is empty."* This is the beginning of enlightenment. The man is one step below. He is just one step below. One step more and his whole heart will become an empty space; for the first time he will have what is called "heart-space." Ordinarily your heart is cluttered, cluttered with a thousand and one thing: useless; useful, essential non-essential, discarded rubbish. Your heart is cluttered it has no space.

And unless the heart has a space, God cannot enter you. He comes only when the space is ready, when you have the room ready for him – your heart is the room.

According to the Taoist mapping of inner consciousness there are seven holes. That is exactly the same as seven chakras. Each Taoist hole is concerned with one chakra of yoga. There are seven chakras: *muladhar, svadhisthan, manipura, anahat, vishuddhi, agna, sahasrar*. These seven chakras of yoga are concerned with each hole in the heart. When you pass through one chakra then one hole opens in the heart; when you pass through the second chakra, the second hole opens in the heart; when you pass through the third chakra, the third hole opens in the heart. In yoga they have not talked about those seven holes because that will make it very confusing and complex. There is no need. One map is enough.

The Taoists have not talked about the chakras because there is no need – their map is also enough. When one hole opens you have passed through one chakra, when another hole opens you have passed through another chakra.

This man has six holes, only one is still blocked. That means in yoga mapping he has reached to the agna chakra, the third eye – that's why he has become one-eyed. He has passed beyond duality, he has transcended. He is just below the seventh. If he passes to the seventh his seventh hole will be opened. When all seven holes are open in the heart you disappear, because you are nothing but the furniture which is cluttering the heart. Once all blocks disappear then those seven holes are not seven because there is nothing to divide them. They become one hole. The heart space is created.

This is what Buddha calls emptiness, *anatta* non-being. This is what Buddha calls *shunya*, zero experience. And when your heart has become a zero then nothing is missing, your seventh chakra has opened, you have become a lotus flower. All one thousand petals have opened, your fragrance is released. You have become a buddha.

The physician was really a rare man and has a rare insight into Tao. In fact, in the ancient days, a Hindu physician, an ayurvedic physician, had to go through yoga. You will be surprised, you will not see what the relevance is. Not only did he have to go through yoga, he had to go through much poetry. In the old days the Hindu physician was called *kaviraj* the poet. This is nonsense! Why should a *vaidya* a physician, be called *kaviraj* a great poet? What has poetry got to do with illness? What has poetry got to do with treatment?

It has something to do with it. Man is not just physical, man is not just prose. He has poetry inside. Man is not just that which appears to the eyes, man has an invisible realm of poetry, song, dance, celebration. The Hindu ayurvedic doctor had to understand the subtle layers of the poetry of life, the song of life, the rhythmic flow of the inner being. And he had to be a great knower of yoga too

The same was the case with Taoist physicians. They had to go through deep meditation, because in those old days many people were searching. The world was not as poor spiritually as it is now. It is materially very rich today, it has never been so rich – but it is spiritually very poor, it has never been so poor. The world was spiritually very rich and millions of people were searching and millions of people were coming close to the innermost reality. And naturally they had to go to the physician when things like this happened.

It was an everyday thing, it was not rare. The physician had to come again and again to such people who were not really ill but who had moved within themselves so much that their body was suffering, their mind was suffering – or at least it looked like suffering. So the physician had to tell them that this was not a physical illness.

> "I see your heart. The place an inch square is empty. You are almost a sage."

Remember, he says "almost a sage" – just on the brink of it, almost a sage, not very far, the goal is just around the comer, very close by, within reach, one step more and the journey will become complete.

> "You are almost a sage. Six of the holes in your heart run into each other but one is stopped up."

Just one. He is still holding on to something of his individuality, still holding onto something of the ego – the last remnant, the last shadow, the last mark of the ego.

"Maybe that's why you think that the wisdom of a sage is an illness. You have come upon a treasure, the greatest there is, you are blessed, but you think that you have an illness. That may be the cause," the physician said. "One hole is still closed – because of that you may be holding this wrong notion that you are ill."

This man needed a master. For this man a master was the only physician there could be. Buddha says again and again, "I am not a philosopher, I am a physician." So says Nanak, "I am not a philosopher, I am a physician." The great sages have been physicians – better to call them metaphysicians because they treat not the physic but the metaphysic, the beyond. Or call them paraphysicians – they treat not the body, they treat the soul; they treat not the form but the innermost emptiness that is covered by the form. Your body and mind are just forms. You are empty.

But if you are close to a master you will never feel it as emptiness. The moment it happens the master will help you to understand it and it will start looking like fullness. It is fullness, it is not emptiness, but it is so new that you feel it as emptiness

– because all that you have known is no longer there. So you feel as if all that you have known has gone and everything is empty.

Just think…in your room you have much furniture. Once I stayed in a very rich man's house. As it always happens, rich people don't have much taste. It is very difficult to have both taste and money; it is a rare combination to be cultured and to be rich, to have a higher flight of the soul and to hoard money. It is very difficult to manage both. Very rarely does it happen, only by accident.

This man was very rich. He was a *bidi* king, one of the biggest *bidi* manufacturers in India. And, naturally, when you manufacture *bidis* you cannot have much taste. I stayed in his house. He had given me the best of his rooms but it was very cluttered with furniture. He had all sorts of furniture there; in fact, there was no room and to come in and go out was difficult.

He asked me, "How do you like the room?"

I said, "There is no room at all. There is no question of liking and disliking. Somehow I managed to enter and somehow I managed to come out. There is no room at all."

He said, "What do you mean?"

He had gathered all designs of furniture, antique and modern; all sorts of things – radios, TV – everything was there, but there was no room. And his concept of the room was this, these things.

He said, "But what is missing here? The TV is here, the phone is here, the radio is here, the radiogram is here – what is missing? You just tell me and we will order it."

I said, "You don't understand me. Your concept of the room is nothing but a list of the furniture that is there and my concept of the room is of the emptiness that is within those four walls."

The word *room* means emptiness. So if the furniture is removed completely, when this man comes into the room he will say it is empty – because his room is the furniture: the radiogram, the TV set, the radio, and this and that. That is his concept of the room. If everything is taken out he will say, "What has happened to this room? Everything is empty. This is just empty." This is no longer a room for him.

To Lao Tzu this will be room, to me this will be room. Now one can expand in this room, one can be in this room, there is space, there is spaciousness.

So when for the first time your mind goes off you suddenly feel empty because all that noise was what you used to feel you were; that was your concept of your being. When the mind goes off suddenly you will feel empty.

I have heard about a man who used to take care of a watch-tower. It is an old story, maybe a hundred years old. In those days each watch-tower had a gun and the gun used to go off every five minutes continually, twenty-four hours a day. That was the only way to give signals to the ships passing by.

This man used to live there, he used to sleep there, and although the gun would go off each five minutes he was never disturbed. For thirty years he lived there.

Then one day something went wrong and the gun didn't go off. He was fast asleep, it was the middle of the night. He jumped up and said, "What happened? What went wrong?" He felt very uneasy.

His mind had become accustomed to the gun going off each five minutes. It was no longer noise, it was his atmosphere, it was his mind, it was part of his mind. Now suddenly the gun was not going off and because of that his sleep was broken But the noise of the gun had never broken his sleep.

This is how it happens – when whatsoever you know about yourself suddenly goes off, you feel empty. It is not empty. It is full of silence. It is a new fullness, it is a totally new well-being. God is descending on you but you cannot feel God. You go on groping for your old furniture and it is not there and you become very much afraid – "What has happened to me? Have I gone mad?"

> "I see your heart " said the physician. "The place an inch square is empty. You are almost a sage. Six of the holes of your heart

run into each other but one is stopped up. Can this be the reason why you now think the wisdom of the sage is an illness? My shallow craft can do nothing to cure it."

This parable is very relevant to my whole life. I was also taken to a *vaidya* to a physician. In fact, I was taken to many doctors and to many physicians but only one ayurvedic *vaidya* told my father, "He is not ill. Don't waste your time." Of course, they were dragging me from one place to another. And many people would give me medicines and I would tell my father, "Why are you worried? I am perfectly okay." But nobody would believe what I was saying. They would say, "You keep quiet. You just take the medicine. What is wrong in it?" So I used to take all sorts of medicines.

There was only one *vaidya* who was a man of insight – his name was Pundit Bhagirath Prasad. His daughter lives here in Pune, is married to a physician. That old man has gone but he was a rare man of insight. He looked at me and he said, "He is not ill." And he started crying and said, "I have been searching for this state myself. He is fortunate. In this life I have missed this state. Don't take him to anybody. He is reaching home." And he cried tears of happiness.

He was a seeker. He had been searching all over the country from this end to that. His whole life was a search and inquiry. He had some idea of what it was about. He became my protector – my protector against the doctors and other physicians. He said to my father, "You leave it to me. I will take care." He never gave me any medicine. When my father insisted, he just gave me sugar pills and told me, "These are sugar pills. Just to console them you can take them. They will not harm, they will not help. In fact, there is no help possible."

This man, Wen Chih, must have been a man like that. He said: *"My shallow craft can do nothing to cure it."*

You have to go through it. Although you will be in search of somebody who can help, remember that the help will not be a cure – nobody can cure it – the help will only be able to help you to understand what is happening, to help you accept it, and fall in rapport with it so that the process becomes speedy. Then the one who is almost a sage becomes a perfect sage.

Enough for today.

CHAPTER #10

The Song of All Songs

The first question:

Osho,
Jesus, Buddha and T.D. Suzuki have been my masters for five years now. Whenever I had a problem I would call on Jesus' name for help. Now you are my master. What can I do with the rest of them? Jesus says a man can only serve one master. He will either love one and hate the other, or hate the one and love the other. Please comment.

The first thing: to be a disciple does not mean to be monogamous. To be a disciple simply means to be ready to learn. A real disciple becomes connected through one master to every other master possible. Your master becomes a link to all the masters of the past, present and future.

But human mind is very narrow. We turn everything into jealousy and possessiveness. At least don't do that with the master. It is difficult for you to conceive of how you can love two masters but the problem arises because you consider two masters as two. If you have really loved me you have loved Jesus through me, you have loved Buddha through me, you have loved Zarathustra through me. If you have really loved me and you have seen me, you have seen all the masters. If you have not loved and not seen me then the problem will arise. Then there will be a choice – whether to choose Jesus or Buddha or me.

And if the question arises it means that you are not yet a disciple, you are not related to me at all. If you are related to me then there is no problem. Then suddenly you will feel for the first time that you are related to all known and unknown masters. They will all become alive through me. That is the meaning of a master. If a master closes your mind and makes you narrow, he is not a master at all.

Remember it. You can still call on Jesus, you can still call on Krishna. There is no competition between me and them. In fact, my whole effort here is to make you able to call them more intensely. When you call Jesus, really you have called me; when you call me, really you have called Jesus. These are just names. Jesus is an emptiness, the emptiness we were talking about just the other day. His whole heart – all the seven holes of the heart – are open. He is a door. So is Buddha, so is Krishna. How can you make a distinction between two emptinesses? Can you?

I have heard. A small boy was playing in the garden when his father came home from the office, tired. The boy was very jubilant and he asked his father, "What do you do in the office the whole day?"

The father was so tired that he was not interested in the kid's question so he said, "Nothing." The boy stood there, puzzled for a moment, and then said, "But how do you know when you are finished doing it?"

If you do nothing how do you know when it is over? If you do something you know when it is over because there is a definition. But "nothing" has no definition.

If Jesus is nothing and Buddha is nothing and I am nothing, where do you make a definition? How do you demark where your master ends and Jesus begins? There is no fence between me and Jesus so if you enter into me you have entered Jesus, Buddha,

Krishna, Lao Tzu – you have entered all. If you enter Jesus, you have entered me. So drop these foolish ideas.

But it will certainly be easier for you to be related to me. I am here alive, present, Jesus has not been here for two thousand years. Whatsoever you know about Jesus is not about Jesus but about the people who have said things about Jesus. Whatsoever you know about Jesus is not direct, is not immediate. Two thousand years of corruption, two thousand years of distraction, two thousand years of interpretation, have changed a lot. The meaning of choosing a living master is that you can know the dead masters too. Jesus cannot be know directly – two thousand years are standing between you and him, millions of screens, much smoke. Whatsoever you know about Jesus is doubtful, is not certain. It cannot be certain. Even while you are facing me whatsoever you know about me is doubtful, so what to say about Jesus and what to say about Krishna – after five thousand years?

And Krishna has been corrupted more than Jesus – because Hindus are great scholars. Jesus' followers were very simple people – a fisherman, a farmer, a woodcutter. Even if they had wanted to corrupt Jesus they couldn't have. They were not efficient enough. They were not knowledgeable people. But with Hindus there are the Brahmins and the pundits. Krishna's lot is far worse because of all these Brahmins and commentators and interpreters – and two thousand years of commentaries.

The Bible has not a single commentary, the Gita has one thousand commentaries. Now if you want to know what Krishna said, it is almost impossible. You will go mad if you go through all the one thousand commentaries. And those are the famous ones, I am not talking about ALL the commentaries. If all the commentaries were counted there would be thousands and thousands. If you go through all these commentaries you will simply go crazy because they are saying such diverse things – things which are diametrically opposite to each other. How can you connect with Krishna?

The only way to make a connection is to find a living master to whom you can surrender – a living master who is still in the body, whose emptiness is still shrouded and enshrined in a body and a mind, whose inner space exists still within flesh. Through him you will have a taste of emptiness and through that taste you will know all the people who have ever existed on the earth – because the taste of emptiness is the same.

Just think of it in this way. When you go into a palace the walls are of marble, but when you go into a poor man's cottage, a hut, the walls are different. They may consist only of bricks, or maybe just of leaves and bamboos. But the inner space of the palace and the hut are the same. The walls differ – the palace has marble walls, very costly, and the poor man's hut has bamboo walls – but the emptiness that is surrounded by the palace walls and the hut walls is the same.

The space is the same. Krishna speaks one language, Buddha another, Jesus another still, but the meditation, the inner experience, is the same.

If you have chosen me – let me say it to you – if you have chosen me you have chosen all. Through me you will be able to understand all those who have lived before and all who are going to live after. I can promise about the future even, because the taste of emptiness is never going to be different. Many more enlightened people will walk on the earth – tomorrow, the day after tomorrow, centuries after centuries. We don't know their names but that doesn't matter because whenever there is an enlightened man on the earth the taste will be the same. You try to taste me. The taste is so clear – it is the taste of hot chilies – you cannot miss it!

"Jesus, Buddha and T.D. Suzuki have been my masters for five years now." Good, they prepared you to come to me, otherwise you would not have been here. Feel grateful, feel thankful. And always remain thankful to them because without them you would not have been here. They have prepared the path. Sometimes it happens that if you had come to me five years before, you may not have understood a word. Suzuki must have prepared you, Krishnamurti must have helped you. They have given you a direction, now you can understand me better.

Let me tell you one very beautiful story.

Master Tennen Tanka, a great Zen master, once visited a temple and stayed there for the night. The abbot of the temple was very happy because Tennen Tanka was a very famous master and it was a great blessing to the temple that he had come. But during the night Tennen did something which was unbelievable to the abbot. It was a cold night and Tennen burned a wooden Buddha to create a fire. The abbot of the temple was shocked. When he saw the fire in the temple he rushed in and found that one great Buddha statue was missing and the head was there just half burnt. He cried, "What have you done? Are you mad? You have burned my Buddha!"

Tennen laughed and poked the ashes with his staff. The abbot asked, "What are you doing now, you mad man?" Tennen said, "I'm trying to find the relics of the Buddha" – the bones, what the Hindus call flowers.

It was the turn of the abbot to laugh. He said, "You are certainly mad. A wooden Buddha has no relics." Tennen asked. "Are you certain?" The abbot said, "Yes, I am certain. How can a wooden Buddha have relics?" Then Tennen said. "Bring other Buddhas too. Your temple has many, you need not have so many. And the night is cold and I am shivering. See the living Buddha is shivering and the wooden Buddhas are sitting on their pedestals. Bring them."

The abbot could not do it but Tennen brought another two Buddhas and threw them in the fire. At that moment the abbot became a little doubtful about his own saying that a wooden Buddha has no relics. Now he started feeling guilty. If he had not said that, at least two Buddhas would have been saved. Now he was guilty. This man was mad but what was he doing here and why didn't he stop him? But he couldn't. He himself had said that a wooden Buddha had no relics so how could he stop Tennen?

A great doubt arose in him and therefore, the story says, the abbot tell into hell.

But not Tennen. He had burned the Buddha but he never fell into any hell – he reached nirvana.

A strange story, very illogical. If Tennen had gone to the seventh hell we would have understood. It serves him right. But Tennen is in nirvana, sitting with Buddha himself, maybe taking a cup of tea, gossiping. And the abbot is suffering in the seventh hell. These Zen people are strange. What type of stories do they make?

But there is logic in it, great logic in it. The logic is that when Tennen burned the Buddha there was no doubt in his mind, not a single doubt. In fact, it was not a Buddha at all, it was just wood. What nonsense to call wood Buddha. Just because you have carved a form on it does not make it a buddha. Because he was so certain he could bring two more statues and enjoy the fire – and the night was certainly cold.

I am all in favor of what Tennen did. He did well. And Buddha must have enjoyed it in nirvana! Sitting there in his moksha he must have enjoyed it. This man was doing well, perfectly well. That's what he had been teaching his whole life: don't look for the formless in the form, don't look for the message in the word. Go deeper. Enter into the formless. Don't look for the soul in the body. Go deeper. Reach the inner emptiness.

And that's what Tennen had done. When he poked his staff in the ashes what was he saying? He was saying that this was simply a wooden body, there were not even bones in it. So what to say about the soul? This is just wood, dead wood. He was absolutely certain; his certainty was utterly absolute.

But the abbot doubted. He became a little doubtful. "What have I said? Have I committed a crime?" He must have shivered deep in his backbone. He must have trembled. That fear, that doubt, that trembling, threw him into hell.

If you have really come to me, the problem of what to do with Jesus and what to do with Krishnamurti and what to do with Suzuki will never arise. If the doubt arises it simply shows that you are still on the way – you have not yet arrived. You are just in the middle, hanging in limbo, between the past and the present.

If you come to me you will see all the faces that you have ever loved. Sometimes my face will be that of Krishnamurti. Those who are close, they know. Sometimes my face will be that of Krishna. Those who love me, they know. Sometimes my face is that of a buddha. Those who have really surrendered, they have seen it.

You are still a little far away, you are still wavering. The past pulls you back. You cannot go head-long. If you come really close the question will dissolve on its own and you will not need to do anything with Jesus or Buddha or Suzuki or Krishnamurti. And remember, they have prepared you.

In this story of Tennen there is another part. I would like to tell that too.

It is said that when Tennen himself was a seeker he went to a great master whose name was Matesi. Matesi looked into his eyes, shook his head and said, "No, no, I am not your master – at least, not now. Go to Sekito." Sekito was a master who was an opponent of Matesi. His monastery was on a nearby hill. Matesi said, "No, no, I am not your master – not yet. You go to Sekito. He is your master." He didn't say, "He will be," he said, "He is."

So Tennen went to Sekito.

Now have the delicate and subtle taste of it. Because Tennen had accepted Matesi as his master, he had to follow his advice. He couldn't say, "I will not go. You are my master." That would have been foolish, that would have been disobedient. He said, "Okay, master, if you say so, I can go anywhere. Sekito is my master."

The others who were present thought, "Poor chap, where is he going? He should have insisted on staying. He should have forced himself. He should have waited at the door and fasted and insisted that Matesi was his master and that he would stay with him. Poor chap. Where is he going?" But Tennen was really innocent. He said, "Okay, if you say so, I can go anywhere. If you send me to hell I will go there."

He went to Sekito. For three years he served the master

meditated, served, meditated, served. After three years the master said, "Now you are ready. I am going to initiate you into sannyas." Tennen came, bowed down to his feet, and said, "Yes, master, you initiate me." Not a single doubt arose in his mind, "What is happening now? If he initiates me what about my master, Matesi? In fact, I am his disciple. He has sent me here and now I am getting into trouble. This man says he will initiate me." Sekito shaved his head as Buddhist *bhikkhus* have to be shaved and told him to repeat the vow of a Buddhist *bhikkhu*. He said, "Whatsoever I say, you repeat it." But when Tennen heard the first sentence he closed both his ears and ran away laughing.

The Buddhist monk has to take a vow, a traditional vow: "I will never commit any crime, I will never commit anything illegal, I will not steal, I will not murder, I will not do this and that" – a thousand and one things, it is a long list. The moment Sekito told him "You take this vow" Tennen put his hands over his ears so he wouldn't hear, laughed, and escaped. And Sekito's disciples said, "We had always thought that he was a little mad."

Somebody followed him, caught hold of him outside the ashram and asked, "What is the matter?" He said, "I have never committed any sin. How can a man commit a sin? The whole teaching of the Buddha is that all doing is false, illusory. I have never committed anything wrong and how can I commit it in the future? What type of nonsense is this vow? I am going to my master and I am going to hit him hard. Why did he send me to such a fool?"

He rushed to his old master's monastery but the master was not there. When he went into the temple only the Buddha statue was sitting there. He jumped onto Buddha's shoulders and he sat there mounted on them. And he was so mad that a few disciples of Matesi came and looked from the outside and said, "He looks mad. Sitting on Buddha!" They rushed to the master and they said to him, "A queer monk has come and has mounted upon the shoulders of the wooden Buddha. What shall we do?"

Matesi himself came to see. He recognized the young seeker and he recognized his awakening too. He said, "You are so innocent. You are nature itself, Tao itself. Tennen means nature, Tao, innocence. And now I am your master and you are my disciple."

Tennen came down from the wooden statue, fell at the master Matesi's feet and said, "I am grateful to you for giving me my monk's name."

And the master said, "Now I am your master and you are my disciple. Those three years were needed with Sekito. Those three years were a must."

So, being with me should make you feel grateful to whomsoever you have been with before. And I am not saying that only about Krishnamurti, Jesus, Suzuki and people like that, I am saying it about even the ordinary people you have lived with the parents you were born to and the friends and enemies that you had and the teachers under which you studied in the school, college, university. They were all part of your growth. If a single one had been missing you would not have been here.

So feel grateful to your parents, to your friends, to your enemies, to your masters, to your teachers; feel grateful to all your relationships that have existed in the past – because this is the culmination of them all.

And don't ask such a question: "Now you are my master. What do I do with the rest of them?" No, it is bad taste. Worship them. Continue to worship them, continue to be grateful to them.

"Jesus says a man can only serve one master." You have misunderstood Jesus. When he says that, he is not saying that you cannot serve two enlightened masters. He is not comparing two enlightened masters; he is not saying you can serve only Jesus or Buddha or Krishna – he is not saying that. Christians have interpreted it in that way – that you can serve only one master, and if you believe in Jesus you have to believe in Jesus absolutely, you have to believe that Jesus is the only door, the only begotten son. Others may be good, saintly people but not real enlightened masters.

This is absolutely a misinterpretation of Jesus' saying. When

Jesus says you can serve only one master, look at the context. He was talking about either serving money or serving God. That was the context. Either you can serve the world the worldly desires – greed, ambition, politics – or you can serve God – meditation, desirelessness, peace, silence. You cannot serve two masters. That was his reference. You cannot serve mammon and God both together.

A person cannot be religious and political together, not even a person like Mahatma Gandhi. Nobody can be religious and political together. If you are really political, religion will be a pretension; if you are really religious you will not bother about politics. Who bothers? Or at the most, politics will be a pretension. But a person cannot be both together because politics needs ambition, desire, competition, jealousy. All the poisons are needed. Religion says drop all the poisons, purification is needed.

When Jesus says you cannot serve two masters he means you cannot serve the outer and inner together. He is not comparing Buddha and Krishna and himself.

Beware of interpretation.

Whenever you are reading words of Jesus, Buddha, Lao Tzu, be very careful. Your mind can play tricks with you. Your mind can color them with your own prejudice.

I understand why this problem arises. This problem arises because our minds are very narrow, monogamous. You can love only one woman, you can love only one man. Even mothers think that they cannot love all their children in the same way. If you insist, they will say that one is a favorite. This is because of the narrowness of the mind, because you think love has to be directed. Love need not have any direction, love need not be a relationship, love can be just a state of your being. In fact, a man is satisfied only when he becomes love, not loving – when he becomes love.

The greatest, the deepest longing inside your heart is not to become more loving, the deepest desire is to become love. What is the difference? When you are loving, you will be loving to somebody – and when you are loving to somebody, others will be in the shadow. When you focus your mind on one thing, everything else goes out of focus. When you are looking exclusively at one thing, everything else is excluded, bracketed out. Love can be a concentration, then it is monogamous; love can be meditative, then it is not monogamous. And when love is not monogamous, then it is religious, spiritual.

You are listening to me. You can listen with concentration – as it is being taught in the universities. Concentrate! Out of fear and greed you concentrate, otherwise you will fail in the examination, you will not come first, you Will not get the merit, you will lose the possibilities of a good job and money and a car and a good house – this and that. So you concentrate because of fear. That's why the closer the examination comes, the more the students are able to concentrate – because the fear and the greed are becoming more actual, they are becoming solid realities. Concentration is out of fear and greed.

Meditation is totally different. When you concentrate you close your mind to everything else. Meditation means just an openness, a relaxed openness. It is not concentration. While listening to me you are listening to the birds singing in the trees too. The wind passing through the trees singing its song – you are open to it too. The airplane passing by, or the train – you are open to it too. This is meditation – you are simply open, available, conscious, available, all doors are open.

It would be very poor if you are only listening to me because these birds singing in the trees are a background music to what I am saying. They enrich it, they are not distractions. They don't distract the mind. They distract the mind only if you are concentrating – remember it. Distraction is only a by-product of concentration. If you are concentrating the bird is disturbing you because it distracts. The bird will not distract you if you are not concentrating. Be simply available here, whatsoever happens be available, open, with all the doors open. If it starts raining, be open; if it starts a storm, be open; if the clouds thunder, be open – whatsoever happens be open. Then your openness is total.

And you are open to me too because I am also happening here. And I would like to tell you that if you are open in such a way, your understanding will grow – but if you are concentrating on me your knowledge will grow. If you are concentrating on me, on what I am saying, then you will cling to the words. That's why one concentrates – so that not a single word is missed. You go on holding. You don't want to miss a single word. But you are missing the whole life.

If you are simply open here, meditatively open, you will listen to what I am saying in just the same way as you listen to the birds as they sing: Then both will enter into you together and you will have no choice – you are choicelessly silent.

Then your understanding will grow. Then you may not remember what I have said but you will understand what I have said. Then you may not be able to go and reproduce what I have said – you may say that you have completely forgotten – but you have absorbed it, you have digested it. It will show in your life although it may not show in your knowledge. It may not be possible for you to give a discourse on me, but it will transform your life in a subtle way. The next time you are angry suddenly you will find the quality is different. The next time you are making love to your woman or your man you will find the quality is more meditative, is less sexual. The next time somebody insults you, suddenly you will find that nothing is disturbed, you are not hit by it, it has not touched any wound. The next time you will be standing before the mirror you will start laughing at yourself.

You have laughed at others but that is violent. When one starts laughing at oneself one is being a little wiser. Then one knows the whole ridiculousness, one's own stupidities. And when a man starts laughing at himself he is becoming less ridiculous, he is becoming more and more aware, alert – that's why he can laugh. He can see his own foolishness. And when you can see your own foolishness you can become wise. Only fools are not aware that they are fools; wise people are always aware that there are a thousand and one stupidities. The more wise you become, the more aware you are – aware about everything.

Listen to me in a meditative way and love me in a meditative way, then my love will not distract you from Jesus, Krishna,

Buddha. Then my love will enrich all your loves, my love will enrich your life. I am here to enrich you, not to impoverish you. Without Jesus you will be a little poor, certainly a little poor. Such a beautiful person as Jesus has not to be forgotten, has not to be thrown into oblivion. And such a beautiful man as Buddha....

Humanity has suffered very much because of this monogamous mind. The Buddhists will not think of Jesus at all and the Christians will not think of Buddha. What a calamity! What a curse! If a Christian can love Buddha also, his Christianity will go very deep and if a Buddhist can understand Jesus also he will understand Buddha far more, far better. And if you can understand Mahavira and Mohammed and Zarathustra and Lao Tzu all together, and you can love them all together as a different expression of the same divine certainly your life will be the life of an emperor. Right now it is just the life of a beggar. A Christian is a beggar, a Hindu is a beggar, a Mohammedan is a beggar – I want you to become kings, kings of kings.

All these people have sung the same song, the song of all songs. Languages differ, expressions differ, gestures differ, but the content is the same.

The second question:

Osho,
Is there a possibility, sir, that people will misunderstand you?

You say a possibility? Every possibility, sir! At the best they will not understand me, at the worst they will misunderstand me. It is happening every day.

Just the other day I talked about being natural and authentic in your relationship. So one sannyasin outside the camp jumped on another sannyasin and they beat each other up. They thought that I had said it – I said be natural. They must have been feeling angry, they must have been feeling antagonistic to each other – they must have been carrying it.

Now I have said be natural, and I have said don't worry about the consequences – so they were fighting about a woman and they were at each other's necks. And the woman was sitting and looking at the whole affair. She seems to have understood better.

There is every possibility that I will be misunderstood. These words are dangerous. Whatsoever I am saying is like a sharp sword. If you are not very alert, aware, you will cut your own head or somebody else's. It has been always so. Jesus and Lin Chi and Bodhidharma have all been misunderstood.

In fact, Zen has become so appealing in the West not because people understand it but because it has the greatest possibility of being misunderstood. No other religion has that much possibility. It has the most potential. You can misunderstand Zen so easily that much intelligence is not needed to misunderstand it. To misunderstand Hinduism a little intelligence will be needed; to misunderstand Buddha a little more understanding will be needed; to misunderstand Jainism you will have to be really very intelligent. But to misunderstand Zen, no, nothing is needed. Anybody is capable of misunderstanding it.

Says Lin Chi, the founder of Rinzai Zen in Japan: "No effort is necessary, do nothing special. Just move your bowels, urinate, put your clothes on, eat your meals, and when you are tired go and lie down. The stupid may laugh at you but a wise man will understand. He who exerts himself is surely a fool." Now the beat generation has understood it perfectly well – the hippies and the yuppies and all. They say that they are doing their thing, and Lin Chi says that this is the way.

But you have not heard another saying of Lin Chi and it is fortunate that hippies don't know about it otherwise there would be great danger. The other saying is: "On the way, kill anything you meet, kill the buddha, kill your master, kill your parents and relatives. Only then can you be liberated." Now this is certainly an open license to murder! It is very fortunate hippies have not heard about it because it is very easy to misunderstand such a great statement.

"Kill everything that you meet on the way." The way is the way of meditation. When you go in and you are meditating whatsoever comes in on the way, kill it. Don't shirk it. Because whatsoever you allow on the way will become a hindrance. You are seeking emptiness, you are seeking a no-mind – then anything that is allowed will be part of the mind. When a Buddhist sits, the Buddha is there – Lin Chi was a Buddhist so he knows about Buddha. When you are a Buddhist and you sit in meditation then everything disappears except Buddha. All is gone. He remains in tremendous glory, in great luminosity – but he has to be thrown out also, out of the way. Otherwise that will hinder the path.

A Hindu knows. When everything else has gone then Krishna is still standing there with his flute, playing.

Ramakrishna knew it well. When everything went and his mind was becoming almost – I say almost – empty, Kali would be standing there. He had loved the idea of Kali so much that it was difficult for him to push Kali aside, impossible. Even to think of it seemed sacrilegious. Push Kali aside? No. But that was the barrier. When he was learning the last meditative step from Totapuri, Totapuri said, "You have to kill this Kali. This won't do. This woman is too much of hindrance. Gather courage."

And Ramakrishna closed his eyes. He wanted to kill her because now he knew well that only one barrier remained. But when he closed his eyes he forgot. The woman was so beautiful – the mother of the whole universe – she was so enchanting. He completely forgot about Totapuri and all the nonsense he had been talking about. And Totapuri was sitting in front of him and Totapuri knew that he had forgotten because his eyes started swelling with tears and tears and he started swaying and dancing. And Totapuri said, "Stop! Again, again you are doing the same thing!" And Ramakrishna opened his eyes and he said, "It is difficult, master. It is very difficult, it is impossible. I can kill my mother, I can kill my father, I can kill my wife, I can kill myself, I can kill you – but Mother Kali? The very idea simply disappears when I close my eyes and she is there, luminous, in all her glory. The very idea is not there. I forget again and again, I am sorry."

Then Totapuri said, "This is the last time, because I cannot stay any longer. Enough of your stupidity and your Kali." He rushed out. In the street he found a piece of glass which he brought in.

And he said, "Now close your eyes. The moment I feel that your tears are coming and the Kali has come I will cut your forehead with this piece of glass, hard. Blood will start coming. When I cut your forehead, remember that you have to cut the Kali in two." Ramakrishna said, "But how will I cut and with what?" Totapuri said, "How will you cut and with what? How did you create the Kali? By imagination. If you can create Kali by your imagination, create a sword by your imagination. Or take the sword that Kali carries in her hand. Borrow it and kill her!"

The master was hard and he threatened that he would leave immediately if he was not followed. So Ramakrishna closed his eyes and started swaying. Totapuri cut his forehead so hard that the mark remained for the rest of his life. When his forehead was cut he remembered. In a single moment of courage he took the sword from Kali's hand and cut the Kali in two. She fell, one part on one side, another on the other side, and opened the emptiness between the two.

For six days Ramakrishna was in samadhi. When he opened his eyes after six days, the first words that he uttered were, "The last barrier has fallen."

Now this is what Lin Chi is talking about – the last barrier. So he says, "On the way kill anything you meet. Kill the buddha, kill your master, kill your parents and relatives only then can you be liberated."

But you can become murderers. Please don't kill anybody at the gate. You may be carrying the idea for many days.

What I am saying here has to be understood very, very delicately, safely. You are not to bring your foolishness into it. Otherwise, rather than being helped by it, you will be destroyed by it. Truth is dangerous. If you can't take help from it, it will destroy you. Truth is dangerous because it is potential, it is powerful, it is fire. You are playing with fire when you come close to truth. If you are not alert you will be burned. A little mistake and you will be burned.

When Moses saw God on Mount Sinai he committed a little

mistake. When he saw God he naturally rushed towards him. But God shouted, "Wait! Throw your shoes away. This is holy ground." Moses had forgotten to throw his shoes away.

Now this is simply symbolic. The Jews have never been able to understand the meaning of this. Shoes protect the feet. Your mind is the shoe of your soul. As shoes protect the body, the mind protects the soul. The Jews have been thinking that God was worried about the shoes. What nonsense! The whole earth is a holy ground because everything is full of God. No, he was not talking about the shoes; in fact, he is even in the shoes. That's why we cannot show where God is – because where to show? He is everywhere. Even if I point with my finger – that there is God – he is in the finger too.

You cannot point out where God is, no. The shoes are a symbol. Just as shoes protect the body, so the soul is protected by the mind. "Throw your shoes away," means "Throw your mind away, Moses. Don't rush at me through the mind otherwise you will be burnt." If you rush to God through the mind it means that you will interpret, you will bring in your prejudices, your ideas, your thoughts. Naturally you will miss.

Then God said, "Go back and tell your people that nobody is to come on the mountain while I am here. And say it particularly to the priests because they may try to come." Moses said, "But why?" God replied, "If they come they will be burnt, they will be burnt utterly. Go down and tell your people that nobody is to come. And tell the priests particularly that they are not to be allowed because they are the most irreligious people. They are pretenders. They may think that because they are priests they are needed, that when God is there they should go, but they cannot see me."

In old Tibet there is a saying that if you see God and you are not prepared, you will die. Truth is dangerous. And what I am giving to you here is truth, bare truth, naked truth. I am not even dressing it up in any way. So you have to be very, very careful. Your responsibility is great. If you cannot understand what I am saying then please know that you don't understand;

don't interpret it in your own way. Keep your shoes off, otherwise there is every possibility that you will misunderstand, you will misinterpret. Then your whole life will go in a wrong direction.

Walk very carefully and cautiously. You are on holy ground.

The third question:

Osho,
I would like you to answer me, to tell me something, but I don't know the question.

Even if you know the question, the answer cannot be told. And when you don't even know the question then it becomes even more impossible.

What question can be answered? If answers were enough to answer questions, all questions would have disappeared long ago. But not a single question has disappeared. In fact, each answer creates more questions. No answer has been able to dissipate questions; each answer has created ten more questions. Humanity has more questions now than ever; five thousand years of thinking have created millions of questions, and not a single problem is solved. That's the whole story of philosophy.

Bertrand Russell has written in his memoirs: "When I was young and I went to university, I went to study philosophy with the idea that it would answer my questions. But when I came out of university I started laughing at the whole ridiculousness of it – because my old questions remained the same. They became more sophisticated, that is true, but they remained the same. And from university I got a million more questions. Not a single question was answered and millions more were created."

No answer is possible because really the question is not a question. When a question is there you may be able to feel it correctly or not correctly; when a question is there it simply shows that there is some block in your consciousness. The question is not the thing, it is the block. The block shows that you are not flowing as you should flow, that something is going wrong. It is not only a question, it is a question of an energy going wrong. Something is missing in your life, something that is needed, very much needed, and you are groping for it but you cannot name it or say what it is.

That's the situation. You say: "I would like you to answer me, to tell me something, but I don't know the question." In fact, even those who ask so many questions don't know what they are asking. That's why you go on asking again and again and again but still you feel you have not asked the right question yet.

A great, sensitive soul, Gertrude Stein, was on her death-bed. Suddenly she opened her eyes and said to the friends who were around, "What is the answer?" They were puzzled because she had not asked any question. Somebody said, "But what is the question? You have not asked the question." She opened her eyes again and she said, "So, okay. What is the question?" And then she died.

And we don't know what was in her heart.

Yes, that is the situation of man: you don't know the question, you don't know the answer, you don't know exactly what you want to ask. You go on asking many things and many answers are given to you, but no answer fits because, in fact, the question has not yet been asked.

Unless you ask the real question how can any answer help? But that real question is not an intellectual thing, let me tell you, that real question is, "Who am I?" All other questions are just formulations of this basic question.

Somebody asks "What is God?" but that is not a real question. If you don't know yourself, how you are supposed to know God? Somebody asks "Who created the world?" but that is meaningless. You don't even know how you came into existence, what to say about the world? First try to solve your own mystery. Encounter it.

So the basic question of all questions is, "Who am I?" How to answer it? Can somebody else answer it for you? That is not possible. How can I say who you are? If you cannot say it yourself, how can I say who you are? Whatsoever I say will again become information in the head.

I can say that you are God and you will carry this idea that you are God, but again and again you will feel that this is not right – because somebody insults you and the God becomes very angry. And then you feel, "What type of God am I?" And somebody takes your woman and you want to murder him and then you think, "What type of God am I?" And you see a beautiful woman going by and lust arises in you and you say, "What type of God am I?" And then you see a car and you want to have that car and you think, "What type of God am I? Hankering for a car?" There are so many small things, very small things, so small that you feel embarrassed if you have to talk about them. They are very small things – there is not enough salt in your dahl and the God is furious; the tea is cold and the God throws the tea and the kettle and everything on the floor and becomes mad.

Now trouble arises because Buddha, Jesus, Krishna, me, we all go on saying, "You are God." The answer is right but you are not at the point where you can catch it. You are not ready for it.

The more you look into yourself, the more you feel yourself to be like a dog rather than like a God. You simply become puzzled about all the great things that have been said about you. They have been said about you? These Upanishadic seers, they are saying that you are Brahma. You? Were these people just mad, saying things and not knowing what they were talking about? You, and Brahma? Not possible. You have not accepted it, you cannot, it is impossible. Hence you have created God in your own image. The Bible says God created man in his own image but the truth is just the reverse. You cannot trust this idea that God has created you in his image because that will create many difficulties in your life. So you have created a God in your own image.

If you go and look at your Gods...look at the Jewish God. The Jewish God said, "I am very jealous." How beautiful. This seems to be a man-created God. The Jewish God said, "I am a very jealous God. If you don't follow me, I will destroy you, I will throw you into hell. And don't worship any other God. I am the only God." And the Mohammedan God and the Christian God are very jealous. "Destroy all other Gods. I am the only God." This seems to be very human, it doesn't look very godly. God seems to be very political, he doesn't seem to be very religious. He cannot tolerate other Gods? God should be more non-serious, more playful.

Hindus have playful Gods but when you see the Hindu Gods play you will find human faces. Brahma created the world and created the first woman and fell in love with her – his own daughter – and started chasing her. A very Hindu God! More like Hindus than like God. Chasing his own daughter! And the daughter became very much afraid – naturally. She started rushing about, hiding herself in different forms. She became a cow, and the God became a bull – definitely a Hindu God! When the woman becomes the cow the God becomes the bull. And she tried all forms that is how all the animals were created. She became a bitch so the God became a dog. This seems to be a more human idea. Rather than thinking that you are God you would like to think that God is human.

And if you look at Hindu Gods you will see that they are very much afraid. Sitting in heaven Indira is always afraid. If some poor rishi starts meditating deeply, his throne starts trembling. He becomes very much afraid. He sends beautiful girls to corrupt the rishi. Now the rishi has not done anything, he was just meditating, but Indira sends beautiful girls to corrupt him. He is afraid for his status. If this rishi attains to the ultimate he may become the next Indira, or he may claim Indirahood. These Gods are very jealous, very ordinary.

If you look into Hindu *Puranas* you will be surprised. The stories seem to be about man, not about God at all.

Brahma and Vishnu once went to see Shiva. There was some trouble. In the first place, trouble should not exist in the world of God...but there there was some trouble.

Some political party must have been creating some trouble and they could not figure out what to do. The *asuras*, the devils, the opposite political party, have always been creating trouble for Gods.

So Brahma and Vishnu went to Shiva because he may be able to help. He is a dangerous fellow. This is just as politicians go to hooligans when they cannot manage! This Shiva is the God of death. He is dangerous. And he has very dangerous company – ghosts and all sorts of Beelzebubs and devils and satyrs. They are all his disciples. So he may be needed. Whenever there is some real problem he is needed.

They went to see him. The guard tried to stop them but nobody feels good about the guards. You don't, nobody does. They pushed the guard aside. They said, "Krishna, you keep away. It is urgent, it is an emergency." They pushed aside the guard and entered, rushed in. Shiva was making love to Parvati. It was not very polite of them to rush in but the problem was such that they didn't bother about courtesies. They stood there but Shiva is Shiva, he didn't bother at all. They were standing and he said, "Okay, stand." Hours passed and he went on making love and making love and they got fed up and they said, "Stop!" But Shiva wouldn't listen. Parvati was very embarrassed. She closed her eyes...since then all women have made love with closed eyes. Shiva was so involved that he was not even aware that somebody was standing there.

Vishnu and Brahma felt very much offended. This was a great insult. So they cursed Shiva: that forever and ever he would be remembered by his sexuality – hence the linga and yoni, the symbol of Shiva. The linga and yoni are male and female sexual organs. That became symbolic of Shiva.

These are very human stories. Can you improve upon them? It is impossible. They are very human stories. Too human. All too human. Rather than thinking that you are a God, you create Gods in your own image. No, if I say that you are God, this answer won't help – you will have to find your own answer.

The question is existential; you will need an existential answer. The question is out of your being; only out of your being can the real answer come. You will have to go deep inside yourself. First ask, "Who am I?" Ask, "Who am I? Who am I? Who am I?" Let this question penetrate into every fiber and cell of your body and your mind. Let your whole bodymind vibrate with the question, "Who am I?" It will take months, sometimes years, but it pays. Let your whole being vibrate with one question, "Who am I?" Let this question sink so deep that whatsoever you are doing the question remains vibrating deep down, "Who am I?" Walking, eating, talking, listening, the question goes on pulsating deep, deep down, "Who am I? Who am I?" By and by the question will not be verbal, it will be just a feeling – "Who am I?" not verbal, not these words, "Who am I?" It will be just a question mark in your being, just a questioning, a quest.

And then one day, when your total being is so full of the question that your whole being has become a question-mark, the answer comes. It will not be verbal, it will not be somebody saying, "Listen, Tushita" – the question is from Tushita – "Listen, Tushita." Nobody will say that. Suddenly something will explode, as a seed explodes, as a bud opens. And you will be full of the fragrance. When you open your eyes all questioning has disappeared, all problems have disappeared. Then you live the life of no problems. And only then will you live, only then will you be. Then everything is a benediction. Each breath is a blessing – and all, all is nirvana, all is God.

That is what is needed deep down in you, Tushita. You ask: "I would like you to answer me, to tell me something, but I don't know the question." It is good that you don't know, because if you know the question it is bound to be the wrong thing. This is the question. But don't use it as a question because the answer is not going to come from the outside the answer is hidden in the question itself. The question is a seed, the outermost core of the answer, and the answer is the hidden tree in the seed. Take the question as a seed and become the soil for it. A "skullful" soil will do, your head becomes the soil – that is what I call "skullful" soil. Only one question, only one question, only one question – you become pregnant with the question. And the pregnancy becomes so deep that you cannot forget it in any moment. Even while you are sleeping it will be there. Even in your sleep, in your dream, the question will continue – "Who am I?" Not so much in words, remember – again I repeat, not so much in words – but the question will be there, "Who am I?" pulsating, streaming, moving, moving deeper and deeper and deeper. And one day it reaches to the very core, it hits your heart, the inner space, the heart space. And then something opens.

If you can ask rightly within your own being, you will come to the right answer. And that is the only answer – the one you come to yourself.

The fourth question:

Osho,
Having been touched, can I pass through the whirlpool of you very fast? Since nothing pleases or displeases will I cease to be in contact with you and your love by no longer wearing orange and the mala?

First, you ask: having been touched can I pass through the whirlpool of you very fast? That shows you have not been touched. I have touched you but you have not been touched because those who have been touched don't want to pass through it at all. You ask Taru. She will say she does not want any nirvana.

If it is a question of choosing between enlightenment and me, those who have been touched will choose me. And because of this choice they will become enlightened. If you are still choosing enlightenment against me you will not achieve it, at least not through me. You will not achieve it.

You are in such a hurry you have not been touched. You are simply greedy.

This person has taken sannyas only one week ago. You are in too much of a hurry. You don't understand what you are saying. You don't understand what you are seeking. You don't understand where you are. You don't understand to whom you are talking.

You say: "Having been touched can I pass through the whirlpool of you very fast?" If you have been touched you will want to reside in this very whirlpool forever and forever. You will not want to get out of it. If you have been touched you have fallen in love. Who wants to get out of love? If you want to get out of it, it simply means you are not in love at all. You just want to go through it so that you can maybe gain something. You are not a sannyasin. You have taken sannyas but you are not a sannyasin. You only have orange clothes and the mala and nothing else. Your heart has remained uncolored. And when the heart is uncolored, whether you keep the mala and the orange or you don't, it doesn't matter. Even if you keep them you are not in contact with me. So dropping them doesn't matter. You can drop them.

I will not say this so easily to others if I see that their heart is getting colored, dyed in my color. I will not say to them "Drop your mala and clothes" easily, I will not say it at all. But to you I can say it because you only have the mala and the clothes and nothing else. The "plus" is missing – hence the question.

And you ask: "Since nothing pleases or displeases will I cease to be in contact with your love...." You are already out of the contact. Just by being here do you think you are in contact? Just by listening to me for four or five days do you think you are in contact? Just by breathing in the meditation and jumping a little do you think you are in contact? Then you don't understand at all. Contact takes time. Contact takes your commitment, needs your commitment. If you are not committed to me how is the contact possible?

And when I say "Nothing pleases or displeases me" I am saying it about me. It will not displease me at all if you all drop orange – it will not displease me at all. It has not pleased me that you have taken orange.

That is not a problem. If nobody comes here I will be as happy as I am now. If the whole world comes here I will be as happy as I am now. My happiness is my inner quality. It does not depend on you, I am not dependent on you. My happiness is mine. That sometimes hurts you too. You would like me to be dependent on you. You would like me to go after you and say, "Don't do it. It will hurt me very much." You would like me to persuade you because it will help your ego to feel more inflated. But my happiness is an independent phenomenon. I am simply happy – not for any reason at all. You or no you doesn't make any difference.

But it will make much difference to you. You can drop the clothes – it will not make much difference to me at all, but it will make a difference to you.

You say: "Will I cease to be in contact with your love by no longer wearing orange and the mala?" As far as my love is concerned it will go on showering on you – because it is unconcerned with you. Please try to understand it. When I am showering my love on you it is not a concern of mine. It is not that I don't shower my love on you, or I do shower my love on you – as if it is a choice. It is not a choice. I am not showering love on you, I am love. When you are not there then too it is showering, when I look at the trees then too it is showering, when I look at the rock then too it is showering.

You are not special. I am not doing anything special to you. It is just the way I am. It is very ordinary. It is simple. It is just as if I am alive in front of you, not because of you. If you go away I will not die. You are not the cause of my breathing. You will go away, I will breathe – breathe with the trees, breathe with the stars. But even if stars go away and trees go away that will not change anything because I am not causally related that way. In the same way is my love. I am not showering it on you. Yes, it is being showered but nobody is showering. There is nobody to shower it. I am love.

But it will make much difference to you. If you drop the mala and the orange, you will become closed. You will not be able to receive. It can be raining but if you put the pot upside down the clouds will go on raining. They don't depend on the pot to be right side up, they don't wait for it, they will go on raining. It is irrelevant whether the pot is right side up or right side down. Whether it is upside down or not doesn't matter, the rains will go on falling. But if the pot is upside down it will not collect any rainwater. Or, even if it is right side up and closed, then too it will not gather water. Or, even if it is not closed and gathers water but has leakages, then too it will miss. And the clouds will go on showering. They are not particularly addressing their water to a particular pot.

I am not addressing my love particularly to you. But it depends on you. If you want it to get into your heart you will have to remain open.

These clothes and the mala are just gestures, symbols that you are open towards me, that you show from your side that you are related. From my side there is no relationship possible. All relationship is from your side. There is no master here, there are only disciples. The master is dead. A master is a master only when he is not. The day I came to know, that same day I disappeared. It is an absence, it is an emptiness, a nothingness.

If you want to receive this nothingness you will have to be causally related to me, you will have to be open towards me. These orange clothes and mala are nothing. They are just gestures. But very significant as far as you are concerned.

How does it matter to me whether you wear orange or not? How is it concerned? But to you it matters much because you live in these small things. You are still your clothes because you are still your body. The mala and the locket mean much to you because you still think of yourself as the picture. When you look in the mirror you think that this is you. To me it makes no difference. It is not my picture because there is no possibility of getting a photograph of me. All that you will get will be only of the form and I am not the form. That is the whole message.

So, if it pleases you, drop wearing orange and the mala – but think before you do that, meditate over it. The first foolish thing you did was that you became a sannyasin – you must have become a sannyasin without thinking about it. Now this will be a second foolish thing – to get out of it without thinking. So please, at least, when you are going to do the second foolishness be a little more alert.

I have heard about Mulla Nasruddin. He took his pay one

month and there was a ten-rupee note extra. The accountant must have counted wrongly. But he was happy.

Next month there was a ten-rupee note missing so he immediately complained. The accountant said, "Mulla, and what about the other time when I had given you a ten-rupee note more? Then you didn't complain."

Mulla said, "Listen. When a mistake is committed once, it is okay. But when it is committed twice, I complain."

So remember it. You have committed a mistake once, now don't be so foolish again.

The last question:

Osho,
When I feel compassionate it is my holier-than-thou attitude;
when loving, too sad and serious; when playful, it irritates.
Should I kill myself and lessen other people's misery?

Good idea! Really good! But again with a wrong basis. You ask: "Should I kill myself and lessen other people's misery?" Again you will feel holier-than-thou. Even after you have killed yourself you will roam like a ghost and haunt people and you will say, "Listen, I killed myself for you."

Live for yourself, and if you want to kill yourself, kill for yourself. A man can be allowed to kill himself for himself if he has lived for himself – never before it. Because if you cannot live, if you cannot even live for yourself, how can you kill yourself for yourself? It will be impossible.

Life is the first step, death is the second. Death is a higher phenomenon. Those who are not able to live rightly cannot die rightly. How can you die rightly when you were not even able to live rightly? You missed the primary school and you are trying to enter the university. You will not pass there. Life is simple, death is very complex. First live.

But your life seems to be wrong. You say: "When I feel compassionate it is my holier-than-thou attitude." Compassion has not to be directed towards others. A real compassion always feels happy when somebody accepts your compassion, your love. He has made you grateful. You have to thank him. When somebody accepts your love, you have to thank him. He could have rejected it – then what? He could have said "No, I don't need your compassion" – then what? He gave you a chance to show your love. He helped you to flower. You have to be grateful.

But ordinarily we think he has to be grateful that we showed him so much love. Nonsense. By showing your love to him he may not have flowered, he may even have been crushed. But you have flowered. The real gain is yours. The real gain is of the one who loves: It may be the other's, it may not be the other's, it depends – but the real gain is always of the one who loves. The loved one may not gain anything, may even be harmed. Love can become a suffocation. Love can kill the other. So many children are killed by the mother's and the father's love and so many husbands are killed by the wife's love and so many wives are killed by the husband's love. People suffocate each other and they say, "We love you." And the more they love, the more they suffocate you, they don't allow you any freedom.

Love is not necessarily a blessing to the other but to the one who loves it is always a blessing. So the lover should feel grateful. Drop this attitude of being holier-than-thou. You are not obliging anybody else. When the flower flowers and the perfume is released to the winds, the flower does not feel that he has obliged anybody. When the sun rises and millions of flowers open and millions of birds sing and the whole earth becomes awake, the sun does not feel that he has obliged anybody. It is his nature. He is happy in being himself.

Your compassion seems to be wrong-rooted. You are thinking in terms of serving people. You are a dangerous person, you are a do-gooder. And these are the most mischievous people on the earth. You can become a mahatma. Avoid it. Enjoy that you love, that you have compassion, that you serve somebody – enjoy it. It is an opportunity to flower, to bloom.

And then you say: "When loving I feel too sad and serious."

Yes, because when you are loving and somebody loves you, being compassionate is simple. You are compassionate, you don't take anything from the other. In love you have to take something from the other. That hurts you. You? How can you take anything from the other? It is difficult to give, it is far more difficult to take – because in giving, the ego is fulfilled, but in taking, the ego is hurt.

Hence Patanjali says in his Yoga Sutras: Neither give nor take. He does not mean don't give and don't take – because then life would not be possible. Even he has given the Yoga Sutras No, he doesn't mean that. He means this: in giving, don't think that "I am giving" and in taking, don't think that "I am taking."

You will be surprised that in Hindi we don't have any equivalent word to "thank you." *Dhanyavad* is there but it is artificial, it has been created. It has been created to translate "thank you." Otherwise in Hindi we don't have any word for thank you. This is something. The society which has existed for thousands of years – the oldest society in the world – has no word for "thank you." Why? Because it is always God who gives and God who takes, so who are we to take a "thank you" or give a "thank you"? That is the meaning of it. Who are we? We are just instrumental. In Hindi, if you say thank you to somebody – *dhanyavad* – it looks a little awkward, it looks a little out of place.

Can you think of thanking your mother? I have never said *dhanyavad* to my mother. And I have everything to thank her for but I have never said thank you and I cannot say it. That word simply seems meaningless. She has not thanked me, she cannot. The word seems meaningless.

When you say "thank you" to somebody it means he has done something to you, he is the doer. And then, when you do something to somebody, you wait for the "thank you." Then you are waiting silently – "Give the thank you." Otherwise you will get angry.

In the Western society "thank you" is very common. People are very false. Even a son can say "thank you" to the father and to the mother. In the West it seems cultured, in the East it seems uncultured. Just to think of saying "thank you" to your mother is impossible. It cannot even be thought of.

It is always God who takes, who gives. Sometimes he takes from my side, sometimes he gives from my side. Sometimes he becomes a giver and sometimes he becomes a taker but it is always he. So who is there to thank and to be thanked? Nobody. It is one reality. That is the meaning of Patanjali when he says: Don't take, don't give. He is saying: Let God be the giver, let God to be taker – you don't come in.

It is difficult to give because of the holding mind – but not as difficult as to take. Because when you take, it hurts. It hurts very much. You have to take something from somebody. It makes you sad. You are on an ego trip.

"When loving I feel sad and serious, when playful, it irritates." Yes, an egoistic person cannot play. How can you fall so low as to be playful? Playfulness is for children, ungrownups. Playfulness is for foolish people. A serious person like you – how can you be playful?

It happened in one camp. Two sannyasins were found playing cards. A great political leader, one of the oldest M.P.s in India, was also in the camp and those two sannyasins were staying just by his side. He could not believe it. Sannyasins playing cards? He rushed to me. He was a very old man, seventy-five, renowned all over the country. It was late in the night, eleven o'clock, when he knocked on my door and he said, "What is happening? What type of sannyasins have you created?"

I said, "What has gone wrong that you have to come in the middle of the night?" He said, "Two sannyasins are playing cards." Now what is wrong in it? Who else can play cards if sannyasins cannot play? But he said, "I thought the whole idea was they should be serious seekers."

They are seekers, but why should they be serious? Have you ever heard of any person who has been serious and has attained to God? God is very playful. Can't you see the whole existence is so playful, so celebrating? If your mahatmas go to God they will not like it very much. They will say, "What do you go on doing? Why do you go on creating butterflies? Why in the first place are there so many flowers? Why so many trees? Why so many stars? Why?" God is excess. You exceed all limits only when you are playful. God is extravagant. God is very luxurious. That's why in India we call him Ishwar. Ishwar means: the ultimate in luxury. It comes from the word *aishvarya*, which means the ultimate in luxury. Play is ultimate luxury. Poor people work, rich people play.

And when a person becomes such a total player that he plays at whatsoever he is doing – his whole life is play – then he is the richest man in the world. He may not have a single *pai*, that is not the point.

Just look at me. What I am saying to you is not a serious phenomenon. I enjoy. It is play. I play with these words. I play with you. And I would like you also to be playful here. It is not a serious place. This ashram is not a serious ashram – in fact, the very word *ashram* means where you rest and play. The very word *ashram* means rest, relaxation.

I can understand. You are on a big ego trip. So the playfulness irritates you.

"Should I kill myself and lessen other people's misery?" Please don't do that otherwise you will haunt other people. Right now you are in the body so you cannot do much harm. If you become a ghost.... You will become a ghost – because such people have never been heard to go to heaven and recently I have heard that even the devil has started rejecting them. Hell is too full of these people.

Just a few days ago a politician died. Naturally he knocked first at heaven's door. He was thinking that he would be received there. But the doorkeeper said, "Sir, this is not the place for you." He said, "I am a great politician, a great leader." He said, "That I know, but leaders and politicians are never allowed in this place. You go to the other place."

This was not VIP treatment but what to do? Now he was alone and a nobody. Very reluctantly he went to the other place. The devil looked at him and said, "No, enough! We have enough of them, these politicians." So he said, "What do you mean? Have I to go back to New Delhi? No place in heaven, no place in hell, so have I to go back to New Delhi again?"

A ghost is not allowed anywhere nowadays. You will haunt these people. If you live, live for yourself; if you die, die for yourself. Let your life never be a life of a martyr. Let your life be always a life of a lover, not a martyr. Let your life be always a celebration, not a sacrifice.

Enough for today.

CHAPTER # 11

The Stage of the Sage

Lieh Tzu was studying archery, and hit the target. He sought advice from Kuan-yin who asked him:
"Do you know why you hit the target?"
"No."
"It won't do yet."
He went away to practice and after three years again reported to Kuan-yin.
"Do you know why you hit the target?"
" I know."
"It will do. Hold onto this awareness and do not lose it."
This applies not only to archery but to ruling oneself. Therefore the sage scrutinizes not the fact of survival or ruin, but its reasons.

One of the most fundamental questions that has always faced humanity and that will always be there encountering every human being that is ever going to be born, is the nature of knowledge. What is real knowing? Only through knowing does one attain liberation, only through knowing does one come to know oneself, only through knowing is the truth revealed.

Man is born in ignorance. The darkness is tremendous. Naturally, the first question that any intelligent being will ask is how to find light. What is light? We are born in darkness not knowing who we are. What more darkness can there be? We are not even aware of who we are, from where we come, to where we are going. We are just groping somehow, drifting somehow. We are accidental. We don't yet have a destiny. We are unconscious. We have not yet attained to the light of inner being which can enlighten our path. In this darkness, if failure happens, it is natural. In this darkness, if frustration happens, what more can you expect? In this darkness, if you only die and never live, it seems logical.

So the fundamental question is: What is the nature of knowledge? What is real knowledge? Man knows many things and yet remains ignorant. Man knows many things but the fundamental is missing. It is as if he has made a big building and the foundation is missing. Man knows much the knowledge has grown every day, and yet deep down man remains as ignorant as ever. We must have misunderstood the very nature of knowledge.

Before we enter this very symbolic and very significant parable, a few things have to be understood.

First, unless you know yourself, all knowing is useless unless you know yourself, all knowing is only pseudo-knowing – you appear to know but you don't really know. It is deception. You know science, you know things, you know the world – but you don't know yourself. If the knower himself is in deep darkness all his knowledge is just superficial, it cannot even be skin deep. Scratch the man of knowledge and soon you will find ignorance coming out of him. Just scratch a little and his knowledge will not be of any help. You will find as ordinary and ignorant a person as any other.

If you insult an Albert Einstein he becomes as angry as anybody else. If Albert Einstein fails he feels as frustrated as anybody else. If Bertrand Russell succeeds he is as happy as anybody else. There is no basic difference because the innermost core remains the same. Bertrand Russell of course knows more than you but the knowledge is quantitative. He is not more of a knower than you, the knowledge is not yet qualitative. As far as your being is concerned he is the same as you. He has more information but not more knowing. More information is not more knowing – and more knowing does not necessarily mean more information.

A buddha may not know as much as Bertrand Russell knows – he certainly never knew as much as Bertrand Russell knows – but Buddha is a knower and Bertrand Russell is not. Buddha's knowledge is not about things, his knowledge is about his own being. His knowledge is not an accumulation of information, his knowledge is an explosion, an inner explosion of light. That's why we call it enlightenment. He has become more aware – that is his knowing.

He no longer walks unalert and unattentive. If you hit him he will not react the way an unconscious man will react. He will respond, he will not react at all. And his response will not be because you have insulted him, his response will be out of his awareness. His response will not be mechanical – that's why I say it will not be reaction.

A reaction is a mechanical thing; anybody can push your buttons and you react mechanically. You don't have any control over your own mechanism. If somebody insults you, you are insulted. He is the master. He pushed a button and you are under his control. If somebody appreciates you, you are flowing and happy – he pushed another button. You are under his control.

You can praise Buddha or you can condemn Buddha hut it will not make any difference. You can go on trying to push the buttons but Buddha will not react. He is not a machine any more.

Once he was insulted. He was passing through a village and many people gathered and insulted and condemned him very much. Their anger was almost righteous because Buddha was destroying the very foundation of their rotten culture. He was destroying the very laws that Manu had prescribed for the Hindus. He was destroying the very foundation of this class-divided society – a society divided into castes, *varna*. And he was destroying the very foundation of the ancient sannyas, because in the ancient days a sannyasin meant a very old man. After seventy-five years of age one had to become a sannyasin – when life had already ebbed one was supposed to be a sannyasin. But Buddha was initiating young people, even young children.

He was destroying two basic fundamentals of Hindu society; *ashram*, four stages of life – sannyas is the fourth stage, the last – and the four-caste system, *varna*. In this system the *brahmin is* the highest caste and the *shudra is* the lowest and then in-between is the *vaishya* and the *kshatriya*.

Buddha was destroying this system because he said that one who knows Brahma is a *brahmin* – not by birth but by knowing, by being. He said that everybody is born as a *shudra*, as an untouchable, the lowest – *brahmins* included. By birth nobody is higher and nobody is lower. By birth everybody is born as an animal. Then if you work, grow, seek and search and refine your consciousness, by and by, slowly, you move higher – from the *shudra* you become a *vaishya*.

A *vaishya* means a businessman. He is a little higher, has a few more values in life, thinks sometimes about music, sometimes about poetry. The *shudra* is one who thinks only of the body; he eats, sleeps – finished. Eat, drink and be merry – that is his whole circle of life. If you are doing only that you are a *shudra*, the lowest human being.

Everybody is born that way. You cannot expect a small child to be interested in music and poetry and philosophy and religion. When a child is born he is a hedonist, a *charvaka* an Epicurean. He sleeps for eighteen to twenty hours – what more can you expect? Whenever he feels hungry he awakes and cries and weeps – and finds food and nourishment. Then again he falls asleep. He eats, drinks and sleeps. Every child is a *shudra*.

By and by, when you start growing, new dimensions open in your being. You start becoming interested in things which are not only of the body. A little of the mind, a little of psychology enters into your being. You are no more just a physique. Then you are a *vaishya*. Then you are moving in the bigger business of life, you are a businessman. Not a very high state but better than the *shudra*.

Then comes the *kshatriya*, the warrior. He becomes a little more interested in higher things. He starts searching for truth, for beauty, for love. His interest is higher than the businessman's. And he is ready to stake his life, he is ready to lose his life for these higher values. He is ready to gamble, he is courageous. Courage enters him. The businessman is not courageous; if everything goes well he may enjoy music, he may enjoy poetry, he may sit in his home – centered, secure – and think about God too. But he will not undergo much danger, he will not take risks.

The warrior, the kshatriya, takes risks. He puts his life at stake. He becomes a gambler. The businessman is never a gambler. He thinks first about the profit and he goes only so far. He takes risks but only so far. It is a limited risk and he always thinks about what the profit will be and what the loss will be. He is always worried about profit and loss. The warrior risks all. He goes deep into life. That is the third stage.

And the *brahmin* is the highest, the one who goes deeper into the mystery of life, reality, existence. And he is never satisfied unless he comes to know what ultimate truth is. That is what *brahmin* means – one who comes face to face with the ultimate truth, the absolute truth.

Buddha said that these are not divisions of birth, these are divisions of qualities that one has to evolve. Everybody has to evolve from the *shudra* and everybody has to go to the brahmin. He destroyed the whole structure.

And he said that a sannyasin has nothing to do with age, has nothing to do with how old you are. Oldness has nothing to do with sannyas, it is not a chronological thing. If sannyas is not concerned with time how can it be concerned with age? Sannyas is a movement into the timeless. So anybody who is ready.... Sometimes a child will enter into sannyas. Shankara entered into sannyas when he was only nine years of age. If he had waited for the old Hindu concept he would have never become a sannyasin because by the age of thirty-three he was dead. Humanity would have missed something.

Buddha said that sannyas can be entered whenever somebody is ready. And there are different qualities of people, different intensities, different passions. At the age of nine somebody is more alert than most people ever are, even at the age of ninety. So you cannot decide outright by the age, you have to look into the inner intensity of the person. And it is your life. If you want to risk it, it is your freedom. You have to be allowed. Buddha allowed young people.

These two systems were the foundations of the Hindu society, and both were destroyed. And people were against him, naturally. He was always in danger. But he created a great revolution in human consciousness.

Buddha was passing through a village of *brahmins*. They gathered together and they insulted him very much. He listened silently. They pushed and pushed the buttons but nothing happened. So they became a little worried embarrassed – when you insult somebody and he stands there unperturbed, you become embarrassed. He seems to be beyond you. In fact, you cannot reach him because he is at such a height.

They asked, "Are you listening? Why are you standing silently? We are insulting and condemning you. Have you gone dumb? Have you gone deaf? Can't you speak? Can't you hear what we are saying?" Buddha said, "I can feel, I can see your worries, your embarrassment, but I am sorry. You should have come ten years before if you wanted me to react. Now it is too late. Now these buttons don't work. I have gone beyond."

It is as if a child is playing with a toy and you snatch the toy away and he cries and weeps. One day he will not be a child and then if you snatch his toy away he will not cry and weep. In fact, he will give it to you, he will present it to you and he will say, "You can take it, you can have it. I am finished with it."

That's what Buddha said. He said, "It is too late. I am finished with it. I have gone beyond."

This is knowing, real knowing. Knowing is a qualitative change in your being. It is a transformation of your being, it is a metanoia: you move higher, the altitude changes. With knowledge, the so-called knowledge, you remain the same except that you go on holding more. You know more but you remain the same.

The so-called knowledge is almost like money – you go on hoarding money. That doesn't change you. How can it change you? Your bank balance goes on growing but that doesn't mean you are growing with it. How can you grow with the bank balance? You may start collecting much money, you may hoard millions of rupees, but how is that going to help *your* growth? You remain the same. That's why you will see that even rich people remain beggars. Money is there but their inner beggary remains the same. They remain the same way – miserly. Sometimes they become even more miserly, because when you don't have you are not so worried about losing it. When you have, you become worried about losing it. Rich people become poorer, their poverty is tremendous. They cannot share. They are always afraid. Their inner poverty does not change at all, it remains the same.

It has to be so. If you are aggressive, just by changing your clothes you will not become non-aggressive. If you are an angry person, just by changing the style of your hair you will not become non-angry. So the amount of money you have does not make any difference to your inner being; you remain the same.

And in the same way the amount of knowledge you have makes no difference. You can go to the university, you can have all the degrees possible, you can have a Ph.D or a D.Litt, you can visit the libraries and you can go on reading and reading and reading and studying and you can collect much knowledge – but it will be just on the outside, on the periphery of your mind. It will be just in your memory, it will not change the quality of your consciousness. And unless your quality changes, nothing is attained.

So the first thing to be understood is that knowledge and knowing are different. Knowledge is information, knowing is understanding. Knowledge is gathered from the outside, knowing is a growth inside. Knowledge is borrowed, knowing is yours, authentically yours. Knowledge is learnt, knowing is not learnt from anybody.

You have to become more alert so that you can see more, so that you can feel more, so that you can be more. Knowing is being, knowledge is just a peripheral accumulation.

Another thing. When you are a man of knowledge, when you have hoarded much knowledge, your ego will be strengthened. You will think, "I know so much." And the ego is one of the barriers towards reality, it is not a bridge, it disconnects, it does not connect. When you are a man of knowing, ego disappears – because a man of knowing comes to know that there is nothing you can know. How can you know? Life is so mysterious, so tremendously mysterious, there is no way to know it really.

If you can know only yourself, that is more than enough, more than one can expect. If a small light starts burning in your heart and your inner being becomes lighted, that is more than enough. And that is what is needed. In that light you become aware that the reality is an ultimate mystery – that's what we mean when we use the word *God*. "God" means exactly what "nature" means with only one difference. In the concept of "nature" it is implied that if it is not known up to now it will be known later on – but it can be known. It is knowable. That is the intrinsic meaning of the word *nature*.

Just a few days ago an atheist was talking to me and he said, "Why use the word *God*? Why not use *nature*? The word *God* creates trouble." I said, "It can be used but then you will have to become more alert about what meaning you put on it." "Nature" means that which is known, or, if not known, that which can be known, is theoretically knowable. Science says "nature" because science says that we have known something of it, we know something of it, we will know something of it. But, basically, one thing is certain – that one day everything will be known. By using "God" we bring another dimension into it. We say that something is known and more will be known – more will always be known – but still something will always remain unknowable, something will go on being elusive. The mystery is vast, the mystery is infinite. And we are part of it so how can the part know the whole totally? It is impossible. The part cannot know the whole totally, the part can only know so far.

A man of knowing understands the mystery of life. That's why Buddha is silent about life. He does not say a single word about it.

Lao Tzu kept quiet for his whole life until he was forced, really forced, to write his experiences. He was getting old and he was moving towards the Himalayas and he wanted to disappear in the Himalayas but he was prevented at the last boundary post of China. The guards would not allow him to pass because they had received a message from the emperor not to allow Lao Tzu to escape out of the country unless he wrote a book about his experiences. So for three days, at that outer boundary post, he remained in a tent and wrote the book – because he wanted to get out of the country, he wanted to go to the Himalayas and disappear.

A beautiful place to die – the Himalayas is really a beautiful place to die. Where can you find a better place to die and disappear into God? Nowhere is there such a godly phenomenon. Watching those Himalayan peaks, that virgin snow with the sun shining on it, it is as if the whole world has become golden. Watching that, in that coolness, in that purified air, on that high altitude, what better space to die in? You cannot find a better graveyard. It is tremendously beautiful.

Lao Tzu was very old and he was in a hurry so he said, "Okay. If you insist, I will write." But the first sentence he wrote in the *Tao te Ching* is: "The Tao, the truth, that can be said is not the real Tao. The Tao that can be uttered or expressed is already false."

The truth cannot be said because you can say only things which have been really known, known totally, known perfectly. Then you can express it. Truth is never known totally. You feel it, you live it, you have great experiences of it, great visions; great mysteries open, but each mystery brings you to another mystery. As each door opens you see that a thousand and one doors are still there unopened. Each door brings you to new doors. So how can you express it?

A man of knowing will say "I don't know" or "I don't know the all, I know only a little bit. I know only myself." But that is enough, that is more than enough. That is the highest one can aspire to.

The man of knowledge goes on claiming that he knows everything – hence he proves his ignorance. Only an ignorant person says that he knows; the knower always says that he does not know. That is the sign, the indication, of real knowing.

One thing more. When you know something you divide reality into the knower, the known and the knowledge. The reality immediately becomes divided into three things. That's the meaning of the symbol of the trinity in Christianity. If you know, God becomes three. The moment you know, God becomes three. The one is no longer one. Knowledge divides. That is the meaning of the concept of the Hindi trimurti – God has three faces. The moment you know, he has three faces. Knowledge divides.

And now physicists say that they have come to know the fundamental of life, the fundamental of existence – electricity. Again they find it is divided into three: the electron, the neutron and the proton. It seems that three is very basic. It seems that if you dissolve into reality there is one but the moment you turn it over and look at it, it immediately turns into three. Certainly, because then you are separate, that which you know is separate, and between the two is knowledge – the knower, the known and the knowledge.

So knowledge divides – and that which divides cannot lead you to ultimate truth. Knowing unites. In knowing, one does not know who is the knower, who is the known and what is knowledge. That's why knowing, a man becomes a mystic; knowing, a man becomes one with reality; knowing, one loses all distinctions, differences, boundaries, definitions; knowing, one becomes undefined – as undefined as reality itself.

Now this parable.

> Lieh Tzu was studying archery, and hit the target.
> He sought advice from Kuan-yin who asked him,
> "Do you know why you hit the target?"

Each word has to be understood. Have the taste of each single word – because each single word is significant. These parables are not just to be read in one stroke and forgotten about, these parables were written to meditate upon. These are meditative devices.

> Lieh Tzu was studying archery...

Tao is the only religion which makes no difference between the sacred and the profane. All other religions make a distinction between the sacred and the profane.

Archery is a profane art – or swordsmanship, or cooking, or carpentry, or painting, or poetry. You cannot think of Buddha painting and you cannot think of Buddha as an archer. You cannot even think of Buddha composing poetry. These are mundane activities; Buddha is transcendental. Can you imagine Mahavira doing any ordinary day-to-day activity? No, he simply meditates. He remains in the purest sky. He walks on the earth but he does not belong to the earth. He walks on the earth but he never touches the earth. He is not an earthly being.

But Tao is something very rare and extraordinary. Tao says that any activity can be turned into a sacred activity – any activity whatsoever, even archery, even swordsmanship. In China and Japan there are schools of archery and swordsmanship but you will be puzzled to know that in the hall where the archer learns archery you will find a sign: *Meditation Hall.* People learn archery or sometimes wrestling – but the hall is known as the Meditation Hall. What type of meditation is this? People are fighting, wrestling, learning archery – murderous arts. What type of meditation is this? Why do they call these halls meditation halls?

Tao says that any activity done with full awareness becomes a meditation. Activity is not the real thing – how you do it, what consciousness you bring to it, is. You can pray in a very earthly way and then it becomes mundane – you know it. If you go to the temples and listen to people's prayers, you will know it. Their prayers are not real prayers. Somebody is asking for a lottery ticket; somebody is asking that his wife who is ill should be made well again; somebody is saying that his son has failed, next time God should please take care, somebody is saying that his daughter has become very grown-up and it is difficult to find a boy for her – help me. These are the prayers. They are very mundane activities. very ordinary. Why do you call them prayers? What is sacred about them? Nothing seems to be sacred about them. You may be sitting in a temple but that doesn't make much difference.

If your prayer can be profane then ordinary activities can be sacred. That is a Taoist contribution to the world. They say that activity is not the real thing, it is the consciousness you bring to it that is.

For example, you may be wrestling. The Taoist wrestler first bows down to the opponent. The Taoist wrestler first has to bow down to his opponent and meditate on the opponent as being God as being divine – not as the enemy. If he cannot meditate on the enemy as being God, as being a friend then he is not Taoist. Then it is ordinary wrestling. But if he can see the same God in his opponent as he feels in himself then wrestling is wrestling only on the surface; deep down it has become prayer.

Now, if you look from the outside, you will be very puzzled. Two swordsmen fighting with their swords first have to look into the other's eyes, into the window of the other's eyes to get the feel of the other's being. It is exactly like his own being. Then they fight but the fight is totally different. The fight is not aggressive, the fight is not egoistic, the fight is a play. And the wrestlers or the swordsmen are not interested in killing the other. They are not even interested in protecting themselves. They simply relax and go into a let-go. Then two energies are there, dancing. It is wrestling to you if you look from the outside but from the inside it is just a dance of two energies. It is almost a love affair, it is a meeting of two energies.

And, you will be surprised to know, if somebody is defeated he is thought to be one who is not yet in a let-go. He was still an egoist, that's why he was defeated.

Sometimes it happens that two Taoist wrestlers have been wrestling again and again for years and neither has been defeated – because both were non-egoists. How can you defeat a non-egoist? Both were non-aggressive. Both were in such tremendous love that neither could defeat the other.

Two swordsmen may fight for hours and neither gets hurt. This is the art. The whole art is to be so empty that the sword cannot cut anything. Now, if somebody hits you, you shrink; if somebody hits you, you resist. The Taoist art is: when somebody hits you, you expand. You take the attack into yourself and absorb it.

If somebody is throwing energy at you, don't fight with that energy, absorb it. He is giving you energy and you are fighting with it. Absorb it instead. Try it sometime. If somebody hits you or punches you, try one day to absorb it. Just go with it. Don't get hard, don't become stiff, let it be absorbed. You will be surprised. You will be surprised because there will be a totally new experience. If two fighters are there and one fighter goes on absorbing the other's energy – whatsoever he is throwing out the one who is throwing out energy will be defeated. It is not that the other has defeated him, he has defeated himself. He will become weaker and weaker and weaker and he will be defeated. And the other one will come out of it very radiant.

Each activity can be turned into meditation. Even these murderous arts of archery can be turned into non-violent arts. This is a great revolution.

The ego is hard and masculine. Tao believes in the feminine. The ego is aggressive, the feminine is receptive. Tao believes in the receptive. Tao believes in becoming a womb. The ego, the masculine ego is determined to penetrate rather than to be penetrated. The masculine ego is always trying to penetrate the other – just as in sex. In everything the male ego does there is a penetration, an effort to violate the other. And the feminine is absorbing – just as in sex. As in sex, so In everything.

Have you not watched it happening every day? You may not have thought about it in that way. Women are always the winners. Napoleon may be a great man outside his house, but when he comes back he is nothing. The woman may be tiny, a wisp of a woman, but that woman dominates. Every husband is hen-pecked. And I am saying *every*. If you can find a husband who is not hen-pecked then know well he is a Taoist. Then he is not masculine, that's why he is not hen-pecked. He is already feminine. Each husband has to be hen-pecked because the egoistic energy cannot win against the non-egoistic energy.

Have you not watched it? A woman crying is very powerful. You may have all the muscles of the world, you may be the great Mohammed Ali, but even Mohammed Ali, when his girl friend is crying, just does not know what to do. The tears seem to be more powerful. What is the power of the tears of a woman? She is so fragile, she is so vulnerable, she is so soft – from where comes the power of the woman? Why does she dominate? How does she manage? She manages without managing. In fact, she says that she is just dust unto your feet. That's how she manages. She massages your feet. That's how she manages. She takes care of you. She serves you in a thousand and one ways. And that's how she becomes the conqueror. She never tries to penetrate you, she never tries to conquer you – that is her victory. She is defenseless. But still some great strength comes from some unknown source.

Taoists say that this is the strength of the water element. Man is like rock and woman is like water. When the water falls on the rocks, the rock disappears, becomes sand – sooner or later. It is only a question of time. On the first contact of the water with the rock, the rock is so strong and the water is so soft that you cannot ever logically imagine that one day the water will destroy the rock, that it will disappear as sand and the water will still be there.

This is what Lao Tzu calls "the water-course way" – the strength of the feminine.

The energy of the masculine is that of the chopper, the wood-cutter. Have you watched a wood-cutter chopping wood? That is the energy of the masculine – destructive, aggressive, violent. The feminine energy is that of the surfer. The male wrestles with life rather than swimming with it; the feminine goes with it, swims with it, does not wrestle with it. The feminine is pliant and has suppleness, is more liquid.

If somebody is studying archery he can study it as a masculine energy. Then he will become technically expert but he will miss the deeper art of it.

Lieh Tzu was studying archery, and hit the target.

Now this is the man's understanding. If you hit the target you have learned the art. What more is needed? If out of a hundred you can hit the target all hundred times, a hundred per cent correctly, what more is needed?

In Japan a German professor, Herrigel, was learning archery with a Zen master. He became perfect, a hundred per cent perfect, not a single target was ever missed. Naturally he said to the master, "Now what more is there? Now what more have I to learn here? Can I go now?" The master said, "You can go but you have not learnt even the ABC of my art." And Herrigel said, "The ABC of your art? My target is a hundred per cent perfect now." The master said, "Who is talking about the target? Any fool can do that just by practicing. That is nothing much. Now the real thing starts."

Listen. When the archer takes his bow and arrow and aims at the target there are three things: the archer, the most fundamental and basic thing, the source, the innermost. Then there is the arrow which will pass from the archer to the target. And then there is the bull's eye, the target, the farthest-away thing. If you hit the target you have touched the farthest, you have touched the periphery. You have to touch the source. You can become technically expert in hitting the target but that is not much – not much if you are trying to get into deeper waters. You are an expert, you are a man of knowledge, but not a man of knowing.

The arrow moves from you but you don't know from what source the arrow moves, with what energy. How does it move? Who is moving it? You don't know that. You don't know the archer. Archery you have studied, the target you have achieved, a hundred per cent perfect was your aim, at a hundred per cent perfection level you have become efficient – but this is about the target. What about you? What about the archer? Has anything happened in the archer? Has your consciousness changed a little bit? No, nothing has changed. You are a technician, you are not a real artist.

Taoists say that the real thing is to see the source from where this aim comes, from where this aiming comes, from where this arrow takes the energy. Who is it who has succeeded? What is the energy? What kind of being is hidden behind you? That is the real target. If that is the target and sometimes you miss the outer target, nothing is wrong.

It is said about a great archer in Japan that he always used to miss his target. He was the greatest master but he was never able to aim rightly.

He must have been a man like me. Just a few days ago Priya put in a question which I have not answered yet. She asked: "Osho, can't you walk straight?" Never tried!

That master must have been a man like me – one who cannot walk straight. He must have been a drunkard. So he used to miss. He never succeeded, not for a single time in his whole life. But he was known all over Japan as the greatest master.

What was his mastery? His mastery was of a totally different kind. He had penetrated into the source, he had made the target his center.

The periphery is not the point. You may succeed or you may fail, but that is not the point at all. The real thing is: have you succeeded in getting centered in your being? Has that target been achieved?

To succeed with the outer target is masculine energy, to succeed with your inner source is feminine energy. To succeed with the outer source you have to be aggressive, ambitious, concentrated, attentive, outgoing, extrovert – the arrow will be going out, will be going farther away from you. It will be moving away from your being. The arrow will be going into the world.

To move into your center one needs to be feminine, passive, inactive, non-doing, non-interfering, *wu-wei*, meditative; meditation, relaxation, not concentration, is needed. One has to relax oneself completely and utterly. When you are not doing anything then you are at your center; when you are doing something you have gone away. When you do too much you are too far away. Coming closer means that you are dropping your activities, you are learning how to be inactive, you are learning how to be a non-doer.

Herrigel's master said to him, "You have become a doer, a perfect doer, but that is not the point. That you could have learned in Germany, there was no need to come to Japan. Masculine arts are available in the West, there is no problem. You can learn shooting. But if you have come to Japan, to the East, then please, now learn the real thing. Now you have to take your bow without being a doer; you have to pull your arrow without being a puller; you have to aim at the target without aiming. There should be no tension, no effort, no doing on your part. You have just to be passive. You have to let it happen rather than doing it. Then you will be centered."

Do you know the difference when you do a thing and when you let it happen? If you know the difference then you can understand this parable, otherwise it will be difficult.

Let me remind you, because you may not have noted it, sometimes, making love to your woman, you were a doer. Then you missed. Yes, there was a sexual release but it was not a true orgasm. Then sometimes it was not a doing, you allowed it to happen. Then it was a release, certainly, but with a plus. It was an orgasm. You had a feeling of expansion. You became enormous and huge, you touched the very boundaries of existence. In that moment you disappeared as an ego. You were not. You pulsated from one core to another core, you pulsated in all your layers, but you were not the doer. Bring the doer in and the pulsation stops. Drop the doer and the pulsation starts again.

Sometimes, swimming in a river, you started floating. Swimming is beautiful but nothing compared with floating. Sometimes, just lying in the river, not even making any effort, you started floating with the river. Then you will know a totally different quality of experience. The river takes you in her arms, the river supports you, the river and you are no longer enemies – there is a sort of inner connectedness. You have fallen en rapport with the river energy; your energy and the energy of the river are making love. Then there is an orgasm.

Sometimes, sitting silently, doing nothing, you have become aware of a let-go. And there is a benediction. Sometimes looking at the stars or at the trees suddenly it is there. You were not doing anything.

These moments come to everybody's life. Unasked for they come. They come only when you were not expecting, they come only when you were not – they steal in when your doors were open and you were relaxed Sometimes out of nothingness and from nowhere a great benediction comes. These moments come to everybody but you have not observed them, you have not noticed them. These are gifts from God. They are reminders that you are in a strange land – come back home. These are reminders. God goes on knocking on your heart again and again – whenever an opportunity is there, whenever you allow him to.

On a Sunday you can lie in bed and you are not in any hurry to go to the office and the children are awake and rushing around in the room and your wife is preparing the tea and there is the sound of the samovar, and the milkman and the traffic slowly moving outside, and you turn in your bed and you pull your blanket up again and there is no hurry and there is nowhere to go – it is Sunday. Christianity has given only one beautiful thing to the world – Sunday. Hinduism has no Sunday. Sunday is the greatest contribution of Christianity. You can dream a little more, you can still float into sleep again. There are vapors from the kitchen, the smells from the kitchen, the breakfast is being made and you are just in a state of relaxedness, not tense, untense – and suddenly you feel tremendously beautiful. Life has meaning. Something flowers in you. Something unknown enters you. These are the moments when you are feminine.

Rushing to the office you become male. You may go for a walk on the street along which you go to the office every day, but when you are going for a walk you are a female. When you are going for a walk you are not going anywhere in particular, you are just enjoying the birds in the trees and the wind and the morning and the morning sun and the children laughing and the children going to the school. You are enjoying and you are not going anywhere in particular, at any point you can turn back home; there is no target, there is no goal, you are simply enjoying a morning walk – and suddenly it is there that moment of let-go.

Watch these moments of let-go, because they are messages from God. Watch these moments of let-go, cherish them, taste them more. Welcome them so that they become more and more available to you. Receive the guest gratefully so that it starts coming more and more often.

Tao says that the real happens only when you are in such a state of diffused relaxedness that you cannot say I am. "I am" means you are tense.

> Lieh Tzu was studying archery, and hit the target.
> He sought advice from Kuan-yin who asked him,
> "Do you know why you hit the target?"

This Kuan-yin is a Taoist master and an archer. Lieh Tzu asked him about his archery and he said, "I have become an expert; technically, technologically, I have attained my goal. I have hit the target." The master asked, *"Do you know why you hit the target?"* From where? Who are you? Who is this one who has hit the target? Have you looked deep into the source of your energies? Forget the target and look at the archer. Archery you have learned, what about the archer? Now you have to learn the archer. And the processes are very different. You have to learn archery but if you want to learn the archer you will have to unlearn archery."

By learning, you know the world; by unlearning, you know yourself. By learning, you accumulate knowledge; by unlearning, you become a knower. By learning, you hoard; by unlearning, you become nude, empty.

The master asked, *"Do you know why you hit the target?"* Why? That's what Socrates means when he says to his disciples, "An unexamined life is not worth living. You may succeed, but it is not worth living if it has not been examined so deeply that you know the very source of it, the very foundation of it."

You see the flowers of a tree but that is not real knowledge unless you go deep and you know the roots. The flowers depend on the roots. The flowers are nothing but the innermost core of the roots come to be expressed. The roots are carrying the poetry, the source, the juice, which will become flowers, which will become fruits, which will become leaves. And if you continually go on counting the leaves and the flowers and the fruits and never go deep into the darkness of the earth you will never understand the tree because the tree is in the roots.

Where are the roots of the archer? You have succeeded in hitting the target – that is a flowering – but where are your roots? Do you know why you hit the target? Do you know why these flowers have bloomed? Do you know from where, from what source? The flower is the last activity, the most peripheral. The roots are the seed, the first primary activity, the most basic. The roots can exist without flowers but the flowers cannot exist without the roots. You can cut the flowers off and another flower will come; in fact, a far better flower will come. If you cut the flower the roots will take up the challenge immediately and they will send a bigger flower. They will say, "Let us see who wins."

I once had a gardener, a very rare man, a master-gardener, who used to win all the competitions in the city. Nobody was ever able to produce such big flowers as he – all sorts of flowers. And I asked him, "What is your secret?" He said, "This is my secret: I challenge the roots." I said, "What do you mean?" He said, "I go on cutting the flowers. I don't allow ordinary flowers to happen to the tree at all. If the tree can give a hundred flowers I allow only one. Ninety-nine I drop; I cut them off immediately because that is a wastage. And the roots get madder and madder and madder and angrier and angrier. And then comes the biggest flower – as if all hundred flowers are made into one. Finally the roots win. That is my secret I make them mad."

You can go on cutting the flower and it will come again, cut another and it will be replaced. But cut the roots and the tree is gone.

The master asked, "Do you know why you hit the target?" The disciple said, without any hesitation, without waiting for a single moment, *"No."* This is honesty. The disciple is really a disciple. It is Lieh Tzu himself, the man we have been talking about all these days. He said, *"No."* This is honesty.

If I ask you, "Do you know who you are?" only the very, very honest will say no. The dishonest will start thinking brooding. He will say, "Let me think." What are you going to think about? If you know, you know; if you don't know, you don't know. What are you going to think about? Thinking means you will try to manage an answer, you will try to manufacture an answer. If somebody asks you, "Do you know God?" have you ever said no? No, it is very difficult to find a man who can say no. And that is the man who can become a real disciple, that is the man who one day can know.

You will not say no. Somebody will say, "Yes, God is. I know" and somebody will say, "There is no God. I know" but both know. Nobody is able to say no.

The disciple said no – he is a real disciple, a true disciple, authentic. The disciple has to open his heart before the master the disciple has to be nude. He has not to hide anything – because if you hide from the master you will never grow.

Lieh Tzu said, *"No."* Then the master said, *"It won't do yet.* It is good, you have progressed. And your no is a good indication, but it won't do yet. You have to go further, still you have to go further."

He went away to practice and after three years again reported to Kuan-yin.

What did he do for three years? He had attained his target so what was he doing for three years? The parable does not say because this is a parable to be meditated upon. A parable is one which says only a few things and leaves many things unsaid. So you have to meditate and fill in the gaps. You have to find where the intervals are. And in those intervals is the real thing.

What did he do for three years? When you have hit the target then what more can you do? Now he was unlearning. Learning was finished, he had hit the target, learning was complete – so what else can you do? He was unlearning, or, he was turning his eyes inwards.

Watch. When an archer takes the bow and the arrow in his hand his eyes are on the target, naturally. But what was Lieh Tzu doing for three years? When he took up his bow and arrow he would look at the target but deep down he would look at himself. The target became secondary. The arrow of his consciousness became double-arrowed – that's what Gurdjieff calls self-remembering.

When you see me, you are seeing me; your consciousness is one-arrowed – arrowed towards me. If you change…. This you can do right now and it will be right to do it to understand You are looking at me, your eyes are arrowed at me. If you are really arrowed at me you will forget yourself This is a forgetfulness. Now make your consciousness double-arrowed Look at me and at the same time, simultaneously, look at yourself. Look at the looked-at and look at the looker-on.

When you are listening to me, listen, but always become aware of the listener too. The talker has to be listened to and the listener has to be listened to also. Then your consciousness has double arrows. Right now it is one-way traffic: you look at me and you are not looking at yourself. This is a sort of self-forgetfulness If you look at me and simultaneously become capable of looking at yourself, in that moment self-awareness happens. Buddha calls it *samyak smriti*; Kabir calls it *surati*; Gurdjieff calls it self-remembering. But it is the same.

What Lieh Tzu did for three years in the forest was a harder task. Learning was simple. He was male. Now he had to become female. First he was trying to penetrate the target outside, now he started moving inside into the womb of his own being. He became feminine.

Knowledge is aggression; knowing is passivity.

There are two types of minds talked of in Tao: one they call *mui* and the other they call *ui*. *Mui* means natural, relaxed, and *ui* means unnatural, tense, When you are fighting with life you exist as *ui*; when you are flowing with life you exist as *mui*. Swimming, you function as *ui*; floating, you function as *mui*.

When you are in a let-go it is the natural mind in tune with the whole, in tune with Tao. Then these birds singing here are not a distraction; on the contrary, they enrich. Then everything is allowed. All the doors are open. You are not resisting, you are not struggling, you simply are. That is the state of *mui*.

First Lieh Tzu learned and created the state of *ui*; he became very, very aggressive, extroverted, pointed towards the outside. It was ambition. He succeeded; he fulfilled his target. Then the master said this was nothing, he had to go further. Then what did he do for three years? He became *mui*; he relaxed. He would sit silently and feel the let-go. And by and by he would take his arrow and bow and shoot the arrow in a state of let-go. He would not shoot it – he would allow it to be shot. That is difficult. He would not shoot it – he would wait for it to shoot itself.

Herrigel tried with the master but could not succeed. Then one day, desperate, he said, "I don't think I will be ever able to succeed. I cannot understand what you call this *mui*, it is all nonsense. How can the arrow shoot itself if I don't shoot it? If I don't pull the bow how can things happen on their own? It is impossible."

We can understand Herrigel. That is the whole Western attitude: it is impossible.

The master said, "Then you can go." Herrigel said, "Will you give me a certificate?" The master said, "Impossible, because you have not learned anything. Whatsoever you have learned you could have learned anywhere else, so it is not a credit. You can go." He booked a flight, made the arrangements to leave, forgot all about everything. He had been there for three years – it was too long.

Then he went to say goodbye to the master but the master was teaching other disciples so he had to wait. He sat on a bench while the master was teaching and for the first time he was in a relaxed state because now he was no longer worried – he was leaving, finished – and he was no longer greedy. There was no effort. He just looked – and he could see that the master was not shooting. The master took the bow in his hand he pulled the bow with his hand – but the bow shot itself. He could see it. It was a vision. How he had missed it he could not believe. For three years he had been watching his master again and again but his own logical mind was an interference. It would not allow him to see. He said, "How can it be? He may be more expert but how can it be that the arrow goes by itself?" This morning he could see it. Now he was relaxed. Now he was not worried about attaining anything. When you are no longer in effort, in greed, in desire, you are relaxed.

He rushed to the master, touched his feet, and without saying anything took the bow from his hand and shot the target. And the master put his hand on his head and said, "You have done it. And you can have the certificate. And you can still go because now there is no need to wait. Finished. You have known it, you have tasted it."

Things can happen on their own. You were born – you did not manage it. You fell in love – you did not do it. Hunger comes, you eat, you feel satisfied. Thirst arises, you drink, you feel quenched. You are young, you will become old. One day you will die. Everything is happening. The doer is a false illusion. Be in the state of *mui*.

The society creates the state of *ui*. It makes you unnatural, tense, knowledgeable; it makes you cultivated, cultured – but it creates a hard crust around your heart and you lose your real nature, Tao.

> He went away to practice and after three years again reported to Kuan-yin.
> "Do you know why you hit the target?"

- again the same question –

> "I know,"

said Lieh Tzu.

Again it is simple, as simple as the first *"no"*. It is not a pretension. When a person pretends, he thinks before he says, "I know." He tries to rehearse in his mind – that's what you call thinking. The answer is without any thinking on Lieh Tzu's part. It is as it is. First he said simply, *"no."* Now, in exactly the same humble way – with no claim, remember – he says, "I *know*."

Many times you get too involved in words. The Upanishads say that one who says "I know" does not know. Right, but there can be a person who says, "I know" and does know. If you can say "I know, in a simple, humble way, with no claim, then there is no problem. When the Upanishads say that if a person says, "I know" he does not know, the emphasis of the Upanishadic seer is on the "I." When somebody says, "I know" the emphasis is on the "I" – "I" is underlined. When a person really knows and says "I know" – "I" is not underlined. The "know" is just a fact.

How can Lieh Tzu say something untrue? If he knows, he knows. He has to say it. But it is not a claim.

So don't get too burdened with words. People do get too burdened with words. For example, if a Vedantin reads this he will say, "He says 'I know' so he cannot know because of what the Upanishads say." Words are words and one has to feel the innermost core of the words, the heart of the words.

I say to you that when Lieh Tzu says, "I know," he knows. And his "I know" means exactly the same as when the Upanishads say "I don't know." His "I know" means exactly the same. It means exactly the same as when Socrates says, "I don't know a thing." By saying "I don't know a thing" Socrates is denying the "I." But by saying "I know" as a simple fact, as an ordinary fact, with no claim, Lieh Tzu is doing a far greater miracle because – listen to it – sometimes a pretender can pretend and say "I don't know" in the hope that you will think that he knows. Because the Upanishads say so and Socrates says so, a pretender can say "I don't know" and hope that you will think that he is a knower, that he is another Socrates. Mind is very cunning. So remember one thing: if a mind is simple, humble, and simply states the fact, then that is the truth – whatsoever the fact.

"It will do,"

said the master.

Very easily he said, *"It will do."* It is not a question of what Lieh Tzu is saying, it is a question of what Lieh Tzu is – the simplicity, the humbleness, the meekness of the person, the innocence of the person.

When you say "I know" a subtle ego arises. Just say the words "I know" and you will feel a subtle ego strengthening in you.

The master must have been looking into Lieh Tzu. Masters don't look at you, they look *into* you. They don't watch your face, they watch your heart. He must have looked into the heart when Lieh Tzu said "I know." Did something arise there? Did something integrate, become an ego? Nothing. The space remained untouched, virgin. He said "I know" and nothing happened inside him. The master said,

"It will do. Hold on to this awareness and do not lose it."

It is difficult to gain a glimpse of this let-go and it is very easy to lose it – because for centuries, for many lives, we have practiced doing. When those moments of non-doing come, our whole practice of many lives is against them, our whole habit is against them, our whole mechanism is against them. Their happening is a break-through and your past will struggle to close your doors again.

That's why the master says, *"Hold on to this awareness and do not lose it."* This is the treasure, the kingdom of God within you. This is the treasure – to be in a relaxed state and to allow God to function.

Now Lieh Tzu was not doing anything. Yes, he took the bow, he took the arrow, he aimed at the target, but *he* was not – it was God in him. This is the state Krishna, in the Gita, wanted Arjuna to be in – this is the state. Krishna wanted Arjuna to become empty like Lieh Tzu so that God could function. He wanted Arjuna to take his bow and fight the fight. If it had to be so, it had to be so.

Arjuna was bringing his mind in. He was saying, "How can I do it? It doesn't seem right." And Krishna was saying, "Who are you to think about what is right and what is wrong? Leave it to God. Don't come in. Just put yourself aside. Don't stand in the way." But Arjuna said, "How can I kill these people? It is violence." And Krishna said to him, "If you don't kill them then somebody else will kill them, because I can see that they are already dead. Somebody has to be instrumental in putting them into their graves – they are dead. If you are not going to become the instrument somebody else will, and you will miss an opportunity of becoming an instrument."

> This applies not only to archery but to ruling oneself: therefore the sage scrutinizes not the fact of survival or ruin, but its reasons.

This applies not only to archery but to ruling oneself. In fact, in Tao and Zen, archery is just a way to learn something about life. When somebody insults you, remember that the person who has insulted you is outside you, on the periphery, like the target; you are deep within yourself, the source. And between you and the insulter stands the mind – like the arrow.

If your mind is arrowed on the person who has insulted you, you will miss. Let it be arrowed towards the source. Rather than thinking that he has insulted you, look into your own being: you must be carrying some wound, that's why you feel insulted. Otherwise how can anybody insult you? If somebody calls you a fool and you feel insulted that simply means you think that you are very wise – nothing else. If you yourself think you are a fool you will hug the person. You will say, "Right! Exactly right! That's how I feel!" Then where is the insult?

If somebody says you are a thief and you feel humiliated that simply means that you have always been thinking that you are a great moralist, virtuous, this and that – but deep down you know also that you are a thief. He has hit the soft point in your being, the fragile point.

So now there are two possibilities: either you jump on him and prove that you are not a thief, or you look inside yourself. Always go to the source. In yoga, going to the source is called *pratyahar*. Mahavira calls this going to the source *pratikraman* Jesus calls it "repent."

Christians have misunderstood. "Repent" has nothing to do with repentance. "Repent" originally meant return, go back, go inside yourself. The Greeks have the right word for it: "metanoia" – turn into yourself, turn a hundred and eighty degree turn. You must have seen in some old ancient mystery books the symbol of a snake eating its own tail – that is metanoia.

Go back to yourself. Rather than going to the other, go to yourself, turn back. Let your arrow move in a circle and come back to the source from where it started. Somebody has insulted you and a turmoil arises. This is the beginning of the arrow. The arrow starts moving towards the other person. It wants to hit the other person, to insult the other person. Don't be deceived by it. Let it move in a circle. Let it come one hundred and eighty degrees back to you – to where it started, to where you felt the turmoil. Let it come back there; look there.

This can become the key of an inner transformation. A new being is possible.

Archery is just a device. Taoists have devised many devices. But in all the devices the basic thing, the essential thing, is to turn to one's own nature.

Meditate on this parable and start using it in your life. First, look for moments of let-go, wait for them, receive them with great welcome and rejoicing, invite them again and again, become more feminine.

Second, if any opportunity arises when your arrow starts to move outwards, remember immediately and turn it inwards. Turn it in. Rather than turning on, turn in. If somebody insults and you are turned on, if a beautiful woman passes by and you are turned on, sex arises – turn in rather than turning on. A beautiful woman passing by is not the real target, you have some sexuality in you. Go to the source. Let it be a great opportunity for meditation. Transform each ordinary opportunity into meditation and great will be the pay-off. Each moment will start becoming luminous.

And there is no mundane or profane activity. All activities can be turned into meditation – they have to be. This is my message too. Meditation has not to be something apart from life, it has to become the innermost core of it. Each activity, small and big, has to be luminous with meditative awareness. Then you will see that each activity brings you to God, each activity brings you home, each activity becomes a liberation.

Each activity has to fall back into the original source. The anger that arises from your being has to fall back into your being; the sex that arises from your being has to fall back to the source itself. There where the alpha and the omega meet, where the beginning and the end meet, where the snake turns to its own tail and starts eating it, you become complete, a whole circle. That's the stage of the sage. That's what sannyas is all about.

Enough for today.

CHAPTER #12

Stand in Your Son's Shoes

The first question:

> Osho,
> Once you said that Krishna was a brahmin, but really he was a kshatriya. Nobody is ready to accept him as a brahmin. Which is correct?

When I say something there is no need to ask anybody about it. Meditate over it.

When I said that Krishna was a *brahmin* I mean that he has known the ultimate truth, *brahma* is the ultimate truth. By knowing it one becomes a *brahmin*. When I say Krishna is a *brahmin* I mean Mahavira is a *brahmin*, Buddha is a *brahmin* – so is Moses, so is Jesus, so is Lao Tzu. I don't mean the caste *brahmin*. By birth nobody is a *brahmin*, nobody can be. I also know that he was a *kshatriya* a *kshatriya* by birth. That is meaningless. That is formal, accidental. I don't talk about accidents.

By accident I was born in India but I am not an Indian. By accident you may have been born in Germany but you are not a German. By accident you may be black or white but you are neither. The accident can only decide the form, not your being. Your being is beyond accident, beyond caste, beyond religion, beyond nation, beyond color. When I am talking I am talking about the innermost core.

So I repeat: Krishna is a *brahmin*. Even if the whole world says he is not, I don't care a bit. That knowledge is of no significance at all.

"It is surprising," said the professor to his wife, "how ignorant we all are. Nearly every man is a specialist in his own particular line and in consequence he is as narrow-minded as it is possible to be. He knows nothing of what other men are doing."

"Yes, dear," said his wife.

"I, for instance," he continued, "am ashamed of my failure to keep abreast of modern science. Take electric light, for example. I have not the least idea how it works."

His wife gave him a patronizing look and smiled, "Why, Herbert, I am ashamed of you too. It is simple. You press a switch, that's all!"

This wife thinks that by pressing a switch you know all about electricity. That's all. Simple. And she says she is ashamed of her husband – that he does not even know how electricity works.

You also know how electricity works. You press the switch, that's all. So simple. But has anybody really got any idea of how electricity works? And I am not talking about you and I am not talking about the professor. Even the man who worked miracles with electricity, Thomas Alva Edison, had no idea how it worked.

It happened once that he went to a summer resort where people did not know anything about him at least, nobody recognized his face. He was very happy – because famous people become very tired of being recognized the whole day, they are never at ease. So he was very happy, running on the beach, collecting pebbles. He had again become a child.

Somebody invited him to come to a high school exhibition. Looking at his childishness on the beach, at how he was running and playing with the foam and the pebbles and the sea-shells, somebody said, "Come to our high school. We are having an exhibition and the children have done many beautiful things." So he went. They had made an electric fan – Edison was the inventor of the electric fan – and a small boy was explaining how it worked. Edison became interested and he asked, "Do you know how electricity works? What is electricity?" And the boy said, "That I don't know. I will call my teacher."

So the teacher was called to explain – of course, he did not know who was asking the question. He was a graduate in science and he tried to explain the mechanism of the fan. But electricity itself? Electricity in itself is inexpressible. Nobody knows.

And Edison insisted, "Tell me, what is electricity? You are explaining how the fan moves, how the switch works, how the motor works, but I am not asking about the motor and the fan and the switch, I am asking about electricity, the power behind it. What is it?" And the man said, "You are asking a difficult question. I am just a graduate. I will ask my principal to come – he is a DSc. He will explain!"

The principal came and he tried hard to explain but Edison insisted. The D.Sc. principal was very puzzled about this man asking such a significant question, and he became very embarrassed because he could not explain. So he said, "Sorry, I will inquire from some higher people who are more in the know." Then Edison said, "I don't think anybody is going to help." He said, "What do you mean?" "I am Thomas Alva Edison and I don't know myself what electricity is, so from whom are you going to inquire?" He had invented one thousand things which worked through electricity – the radio, the gramophone, the fan and a thousand and one things – he was one of the greatest inventors of the world, but he said, I myself don't know what electricity is. I play with it, I manage it, it works. That's all we know how it works. But what it is, nobody knows. So don't be puzzled and don't feel embarrassed.'

You must have asked somebody who has the mind of this wife who says, "Why, Herbert, I am ashamed of you. It is simple. You press a switch. That's all." I also know that Krishna is a *kshatriya* but that is not what I am saying to you. I am not interested in the accident of his birth, in which womb he was carried for nine months. I am talking about his innermost experience – that experience makes him a *brahmin* because he has known the *brahma*. One who knows is a *brahmin*. One who does not know is not a *brahmin*.

The second question:

Osho,
"Don't do unto others what you don't want others to do unto you." Osho, I was meditating about it, but I feel stuck, I can't reach the bottom. Please can you tell me something about it?

The first thing: never meditate on anything negative. "Don't do unto others what you don't want others to do unto you." This is a negative message "Don't do."

If you don't want to get stuck then meditate on something positive. The same thing can be made positive: Do unto others what you would like others to do unto you. Then you will not get stuck.

When you move in a negative commandment you cannot move much. How can you move in a negative commandment? A negative commandment is like death. How can you meditate about death? You can start but you will be stuck at the very start. You can meditate about life, certainly. Life has so many things to meditate about – the flowers, the birds, the rivers, the stars, love, people, the beauty of it, the song of it. You can meditate about life infinitely and you will never get stuck – because vast is life, infinite is life, the whole universe is life.

In fact, when you meditate on life – meditating, meditating – one day you will come across death too because death is just a part of life. As other things are part of life – love, birth, joy, sadness, happiness – so is death. Death is not something against life, death is not something beyond life – death happens in life, death is an intrinsic part of life.

So if you meditate on life you will come to know death too, but if you meditate on death nothing will happen. What will you meditate on? You will simply feel darkness, and get stuck. How can you move in non-being? How can you think about nothing? You will go round and round and sooner or later you will wonder what you are doing. Chasing your own tail? Where are you going? There is nothing much to meditate on.

Meditation has to be about the positive. You can ride on the positive, you can go to the very source of existence – but on the positive, with the positive, in the positive. And of course, if you go with the positive, one day you will come across the negative too – but as part of the positive. And then you will know the negative too.

Listen...I would like it this way: Do unto others what you would like others to do unto you. Make it that way. Then you have a thousand and one things to think about.

And when you do unto others what you would like them to do unto you, naturally the negative part of it – don't do unto others – follows like a shadow. Remember, the negative is the shadow of the positive. The positive is the figure, the negative is the shadow. If you run, your shadow will run behind you. If you stop, the shadow will stop. But don't get too involved with the shadow otherwise you will get stuck. If you try to make the shadow run and then you want to follow it, it is impossible. Then you will feel very impotent. You will create a very crazy situation for yourself.

Look...all the Ten Commandments are in a way negative. If you go deep into Patanjali's Yoga Sutras you will not find a single negative commandment. Everything is positive. With the positive there is growth. Judaism has not grown at all. It remains stuck. In fact, it has not added anything to Moses. It is where Moses left it.

Hinduism has grown tremendously. It goes on growing. It is not a dead stone. And what is the reason for it, what is the secret of it? The secret is: it moves through the positive. If you get stuck with the negative then from the very beginning you are moving in a wrong direction – which will not allow you much movement. You are heading for trouble.

Judaism has not evolved any subtle religion. The Jews have remained the most irreligious people on the earth, the most worldly, money-minded, prestige-oriented. They have not developed anything deep in meditation or prayer; religion to them is just a formality. Religion is not something tremendous; it is not something that shatters you, uproots you, gives you wings; it is not something that destroys you and recreates you; it is not something that you become possessed with; it is not something that manages you – it is something that you manage.

Jews did not like Jesus because he became too possessed by religion. Jews did not like Jesus because he was too other-worldly. Jews have not liked any people born to Jewish families who became too possessed by religion. They have always denied and rejected them. They deny and reject all the messiahs because a messiah is a person who is almost in a passion. Religion is his love, it is not formality; He can stake his life for it. If crucifixion comes through it, he is ready to go to the cross.

The day that Jesus was ready to die on the cross he said that he was not a Jew in the ordinary sense. The Jews were puzzled. Why was this man so mad? Life is so beautiful, why be worried about things higher than life? Life is enough. Jews have lived in the merry-go-round of eat, drink and be merry – and, of course, sometimes go to the synagogue too. That is part of the social formalities.

Remember, if you start your meditations with a negative you will be stuck. And, another thing, if you think too much of the negative, you will become desert-like, you will not flower, you will become dry, your juice won't flow. The juice cannot flow in the negative – for that you need some positive passion, something alive, so that it can flower.

If you want to meditate, contemplate, good. But choose something positive. Meditate on a roseflower, it is positive. Meditate on the rising sun, it is positive. Meditate on the moon. Meditate on a child playing, laughing, jumping, dancing. Meditate on something which is flowering, opening unfolding, which is alive. Meditating on the negative is meditating on the desert – and you become that on which you meditate. You will become that on which you meditate so meditate on love, meditate on life, meditate on God.

And if something looks very beautiful to you but it is a negative statement, turn it into a positive statement. Each statement can be turned into a positive statement. And great is the change. When you want to say "no" try to say it in such a way that it has the form of "yes." Don't say "no." You can always find a way to say something in such a way that even if it is a "no" it comes in the form of "yes." And it will be helpful to you.

You must have come across people who are so addicted to the "no" that even sometimes when they want to say "yes" they find a negative way of expressing it.

The third question:

Osho,
Will you marry me?

Again? The day you became a sannyasin you got married to me. This question is from Dharma Chetna. To ask again means you have forgotten!

When he was very old somebody asked Immanuel Kant, the German philosopher, "Why didn't you ever get married? Did you never propose to anybody?" Kant brooded over it and said, "To think of it, yes, once I did propose to a girl."

The inquirer became very interested. He said, "Then what happened?" Kant said, "Something went wrong. I proposed a second time. I proposed one day and the next day I proposed again. And the girl got very mad."

Kant's memory was not very good – the girl had accepted

him the previous night. Can you marry a person who proposes a second time? This man is not reliable. After marriage he will come one day and he will say, "Who are you and what are you doing here?"

Sannyas is a marriage – but it is deeper than the marriage that you know about. In an ordinary marriage two bodies meet At the most, if one is very fortunate, two minds meet – that is rare. The marriage that sannyas is, is not of the body not of the mind, but of the souls. Two beings meet. To be with the master is to be in deep love with the master, to be surrendered, to be open, to go with him wherever he is going with gratitude, with trust.

You are married, Chetna. Keep alert. Don't go on forgetting.

The fourth question:

Osho,
My son has fled away from home and is here in the ashram. He is free to have any sort of thought, but first he should complete his graduation studies so that he can understand the world in a better way and take the right decisions.

I *can* understand the difficulties of a parent. Try to persuade your son, I am all in favor of it. Try to persuade him but don't force him, don't threaten him. Avoid subtle or gross threats. Just open your mind to your son, put your heart before him, tell him how you feel. What you are saying is not very meaningful, so leave the decision to him.

For example, you say: "My son has fled away from home and is here in the ashram." There must have been something wrong in the home otherwise why should one escape from home and come to this ashram? This ashram is another home again. Think about your home. What is wrong there? Something must be missing love, aliveness. Something must be missing. Watch it. Your son has given a signal that something is wrong.

Maybe the father and the mother are not in deep harmony and the house is a chaos. Maybe the children are neglected or maybe too much care is taken. Either way the child must be feeling suffocated – either by indifference or by too much love or too much care. Balance is missing.

Put your home right. Just taking the child back home will not help much because he will escape again. So think about it. Your child has given you an indication that something is basically wrong. That is the first thing.

The second thing – you say: "He is free to have any sort of thought but first...." You are just talking, you are not giving him freedom. What do you mean by "but"? Parents have that trick of talking. They say, "You are completely free, absolutely free, but...." That "but" is too big. It destroys all freedom.

And parents have an old habit of saying, "First grow up and then you will understand." But, excuse me, I would like to ask you if you have grown up. Have you seen any grown-up person? Maybe the person is well-educated, has graduated from the university, was on the merit list, has a good job, is married, has children – everything is going fine. But look deep is he grown-up? Has he really understood what life is? Has he any awareness? Or is he as ignorant of life as any child? Sometimes it happens that children are more alert than grown-ups because children have a fresher consciousness. Less dust has gathered on their mirrors. As yet they have not been poisoned by the society.

What do you call your university? It is an institution in the service of society. It poisons. It manipulates people. It forces people into the service of the society. It destroys people's individuality. Out of beautiful people it makes clerks, collectors, commissioners, *tahsildar*, station-masters, things like that. Out of beautiful people, out of beautiful children it creates ugly things, dead things. The whole education system is a way to destroy a person, his freedom; to destroy his consciousness; to destroy his aliveness; to make him usable – to reduce him to a means so that the society can use him in profitable ways, so that he becomes an instrument. Then he becomes a soldier in the army – kills and, is killed. Or he becomes a clerk in an office or a collector or a commissioner and wastes his whole life for something he cares nothing at all about and goes on doing things which he never wanted to do in the first place.

The closer and closer death comes, the more and more afraid you become – and fear cripples. And then you cannot change. It is very difficult for a person who is at the age of forty or forty-five to change, because now everything has settled – somehow. It has been a long struggle, things have settled, and now to change seems very difficult. Now one simply goes on waiting for death to relieve one.

You say: "But first he must complete his graduation studies so that he can understand the world in a better way." Do you think educated people understand the world in a better way? I have never come across it. Educated people are the worst because they have such a screen on their eyes. They may understand what is written in books but they don't understand what is there in life. An educated person has such a cultivated mind that he does not allow anything from the real to enter him. He looks in the books but he never looks into the faces of people, into the eyes of people. He never looks around. Even if God comes he will go on reading his Bible and he may even say to God, "Wait, wait outside, I am doing my religious meditation," or something like that.

There is a Hindu story about a very great scholar who used to do chanting every morning for three, four, five hours. From three o'clock in the morning he would start doing his chanting and prayers for years together. And he was a great scholar, a great Sanskrit scholar, a very learned man.

Then finally Krishna had compassion on him and one day he came to him. He stood behind the man, put his hand on his shoulders. The man looked up and he said, "What are you doing? Can't you see I am doing my prayers? Is this the time to disturb me?" And Krishna shrank back and disappeared.

Now this story looks very absurd. The man had been chanting *hari krishna, hari krishna, hari krishna* for years but when Krishna came he could not recognize him. He thought some intruder had come – some very foolish man who couldn't see that the scholar was meditating. This man may not even have taken his morning bath and here he was touching the scholar's body and spoiling the whole meditation. And the scholar had to go and take a bath again in the Ganges and again start his prayer. So he was very happy that he got rid of this foolish man. Who was this?

If Jesus comes to a Christian who is pondering on his Bible would the Christian recognize Jesus? If Mahavira comes to a Jaina who is on his fast and doing his mantra *namokar,* would he be able to recognize him? Impossible. To recognize truth you need naked, nude eyes – uncultured, uncultivated, uneducated.

I can feel you care for your child, that is true, but what you are saying is not true. I can understand and I would like your boy to go back home, I am all for it, but the reason you are giving is not right. I can feel your love for your child. You are worried about his future. You are worried what he will do, how he will earn his bread. I can understand, I am in total sympathy with you – but the reason that you are proposing is absolutely false.

You say: "…first he should complete his graduation studies so that he can understand…." Understanding never comes that way. For understanding to come one has to one day unlearn all that one has learnt. For understanding to come one has to become a child again, one has to wash off all that the society has done, one has to make his heart clean.

Once a man came to Buddha, a very cultured, educated man, a pundit. And he asked Buddha a question. Buddha said, "Please. Right now I cannot answer." The man said, "Why can't you answer? Are you busy or something?" He was an important man, well-known all over the country, and, of course, he felt offended that Buddha was so busy that he couldn't give a little time to him.

He said, "I have walked thousands of miles." In those days there were no trains, nothing, it was really difficult. It was dangerous to travel. He had walked far; he had come from the deep south.

Buddha said, "No, that is not the question. I have enough time, but right now you will not be able to receive the answer." The pundit asked, "What do you mean?" Buddha said, "There are three types of listeners. The first type is like a pot placed upside-down. You can go on answering, nothing will enter him. He is not available. The second type of listener is like a pot with holes in the bottom. It is not upside-down, it is exactly in the right posture, it is as it should be, but it has holes in the bottom. So it looks like it is being filled but that is only momentary. Sooner or later the water flows out and it is again empty. Only apparently, on the surface, does it look like something is entering – nothing really enters because it cannot hold anything. And then there is a third type of listener who has no holes in the bottom and who is not placed like an upside-down pot but is full of filth. Water can come into it but the moment water enters it, it becomes poisoned.

"And you are all three together, sir. So it is very difficult right now. You are filthy, filthy because you are so knowledgeable. Knowledge is filth. That which you have not known is filth; only that which you have known purifies, transforms, liberates. All that is borrowed is filth. You have stolen it, how can it purify you? Without knowing it you think you know. You are a pretender. You deceive. You are a hypocrite."

So when a man's head is like a pot which is full of filth, even if God comes and says something to him, the moment it enters him it will become poisoned. It will not be heard the way it has been told. It will be misinterpreted. It is very difficult to change a learned man because he has already got fixed ideas. He is hiding behind those ideas.

I have heard about a very shy man – a young man, very shy – who had never asked a girl for a date. His mother was very worried, naturally so. But one day the mother and father were both surprised because the boy said, "I am going on a date tonight." They were very happy. They helped him. They gave him money and they said, "Go and enjoy yourself."

He went out but came back within half an hour. They were again surprised and said, "So soon? Did you see the girl?" He said, "Yes, I did see her. And had I not been hiding behind the hedge she would have seen me."

Now what type of date is this? Hiding behind the hedge! He says, "I have seen the girl and had not I been hiding behind the hedge she would have seen me."

A man of knowledge is hiding behind hedges and more hedges. His understanding is less than ever even if his knowledge is more.

What do you mean, sir, when you say: "He will understand more?" He will be more knowledgeable, true, but he will not understand more. Right now he can understand more although even now it may be already too late. Had he come a little earlier he would have understood more.

Society can be transformed totally if small children start meditating. They are not serious so they are very ready for meditation. They are joyful, playful. They take everything in fun. Sometimes it happens that when a small child comes to take sannyas and I tell him "Close your eyes" he closes the eyes and he enjoys it as nobody else enjoys it. The very idea that he has been taken so seriously rejoices him. He sits silently. Sometimes I have seen grown-up people looking, just opening their eyes a little to see what is happening. But small children, when they close their eyes, they really close them. They close them very hard because they are afraid they will open if they don't do it hard. They really do it hard. They bring their total energy there because they know that if they are not doing it totally then the eyes will open and they will start looking to see what the matter is, what is going on. I have seen them really closing their eyes. And to see a child sitting silently is one of the most beautiful things you can come across.

Children can be taught meditation more easily because they are not yet spoiled. When you have been spoiled the hard work is to help you to unlearn.

I have heard that whenever anybody came to Mozart, the great composer and musician, he would ask, "Have you learnt music anywhere else before?" If the man had, then he would ask double fees. If he had not learnt music at all then he would say, "That is okay. Even half the fee will do."

People were very puzzled because this was illogical – "When a fresh man comes, who has not known anything about music, you say half the fee, and when somebody who has been working for ten years comes you say double the fee!" Mozart said, "There is a reason. First I have to clean the slate. That is the harder work. To destroy all that the person is carrying is harder than to teach."

Teaching is very easy if you are available. With a virgin heart, teaching is very simple – and a child is a virgin heart.

So I will not agree that your child will become more understanding of the world. He may simply become more worldly, as worldly as you are. Right now he is not so worldly, that's why he has come to the ashram and has become a sannyasin. He is other-worldly. He does not care a bit about money, power, prestige – all those trips. He is very other-worldly. You can see.

And you can see many young people here – ninety-nine per cent of my sannyasins are young people. Why? Why should young people be so interested in sannyas, and not the old people? Old people become cunning. counting, calculating. Old people become clever. They think in terms of profit and loss. They think of what is going to give them more, more profit, and they think of a thousand and one things. Except life they think about everything; except love they think about everything. They take care of all that is non-essential; the essential they don't take care of. They are worldly. What do I mean by worldly? I mean a man who thinks about the non-essential.

Mulla Nasruddin went to his boss one day and said, "Sir, can I have your car on the twenty-fifth of this month?" The boss asked, "For what? Why do you need the car, Nasruddin? You have never asked for it before." He said, "I am going to get married on that day." The boss said, "Certainly you can have it. One does not get married every day. You can have not only one car. You can have all of my three cars."

Nasruddin was very happy. And then the boss said, "Please tell me. Who is the fortunate girl?" Nasruddin answered, "I have not decided that yet. I thought I should first inquire about the car. If I can have the car, I can find a girl. That is not a big problem."

This is the worldly man. He thinks first about the non-essential: money, power, prestige, pull, car, house, bank, insurance. He thinks about these things first; security comes first. He is not at all worried about who you are. For whom is this security? For whom is this bank balance? For whom is this house and this car? For whom? You are disappearing, your life is slipping out of your hands – and you are worried about the non-essential!

The other-worldly man is one who thinks about the essential first. Your child is still other-worldly, non-worldly, hence he is here. And whatsoever you are saying is not very relevant, it is just an argument. If you have become more understanding then give proof of it. Then you tell the child, "You go home and study and I am going to become a sannyasin." That will be proof. And then, I think, the child will have to go because now he knows his father means it. That will be something.

I am ready to exchange. You be here and let the child go – and he will go happily because then his father really cares and understands and so whatsoever he is saying is meaningful.

One day an old Indian man came to me – he was seventy-five years old. Of course, in India, people are very much against me – bound to be, naturally – because they think that giving sannyas to young people is destroying their life. This man's young son had taken sannyas and he was very worried. He said, "What are you doing? This is against the scriptures. A person has to become a sannyasin only after seventy-five years of age. Give my son back. This is not the right time. First he has to get married." Just as you say your son has first to become a graduate, he said that first his son had to get married, experience life, have children, move into the work of the house-holder and then one day he could become a sannyasin.

The son was sitting by my side. "Okay, I can understand," I said to the old man. "Your son can go back but you sit in his place!" He said, "Why?" I said, "You are seventy-five, now the time has come. You have lived in the world. The scriptures say that after seventy-five one has to become a sannyasin. What do you say?" He said, "This is difficult." So I said, "Then what is the guarantee that your boy, if he ever becomes seventy-five – and who knows he may never become seventy-five – what is the guarantee that he will be able to take sannyas if you cannot take it? Give proof. You take sannyas and I will release your son and I will say, 'Go and get married.'" Since then that old man has never turned up and I don't think he will ever come again.

Just look at life. So many people are educated, particularly in the West. Everybody is educated now. Education is no more a value. In fact, the great thinkers of the West are thinking about how to de-school society. Ivan Illich has proposed a whole program of how to de-school society. And D.H. Lawrence used to say again and again that if man is to be saved all universities should be closed for one hundred years.

There are all those dreams and ideas that when humanity becomes educated, when everybody is educated, there will be paradise. That paradise has not happened. In fact, all paradise has disappeared because of education. Uneducated people are far more innocent, far more loving, far more beautiful than the educated.

The man of education becomes cunning, clever, exploiting. That's all that education is about – how to make you more efficient in exploiting people, how to make you capable of doing less and getting more. That is the whole technique of education. What else is it? What else is education but how to do nothing and get everything? Then you are the most educated person. The higher the education, the less the work – and the more the profit. The real man of education does not work at all. He simply exploits, he simply robs people.

No, education is not going to give him understanding or anything. Don't enforce anything on him; just put your mind before him and tell him that this is how you feel. Certainly tell him how you feel – it is your responsibility to tell him – but then your responsibility is finished. You told him, you made him aware of the situation, but if he decides to remain a beggar, let it be so. If he decides to remain a sannyasin and wants to live a dangerous life, let it be so. You have lived a very sheltered life. What have you gained?

When I came back from my graduation, from the university, my parents were very worried about my marriage. That is one of the most worrying problems in India – particularly for a person like me. My parents were very worried. It was time to get married and they were worried that I might say "no."

One night when I was going to sleep my mother came to me. She sat on my bed and told me that they were very worried. I said, "There is no need to worry. Tell me, what is the problem?" She said, "We are afraid you may say 'no.'" I said, "I can say 'yes' without asking what it is. You just tell me." She became very happy. She said, "We would like you to get married. You choose any girl – you choose, we are not concerned about that – but you get married." I said, "Okay, I have said 'yes' so I will follow it. There is just one thing – I will give you two weeks to think about it. Have you gained anything by marriage? After two weeks you simply tell me. You are my mother and I hope that you will not deceive me. Mediate over the matter for two weeks...if the chance was given to you again would you marry again or would you remain unmarried?"

My mother is a simple woman. Those two weeks were really hard on her. I saw her sitting and crying and weeping because the truth was coming to her again and again that it was simply meaningless. She had suffered her whole life. Marriage, twelve children, continuously taking care, this child is ill, that child is ill, poor family, twelve children, and all worries and worries.

After two weeks I asked, "What do you say?" She said, "You have put me into such trouble. No, I will not suggest that you get married but don't tell your father that I have said so."

I told her, "I will take care of him separately, you don't be worried. He is my father, he will also feel for me. What has he gained?" He never asked me. Never. He simply avoided the subject because he knew what had happened.

You have lived in the world, you are educated, you have lived a sheltered family life – what have you gained? Anything really? Anything really substantial? Can you really show that substance to your child? Can you say that you have lived wisely? Can you say that you are happy and that if God gives you another life you would like to live the same way you have lived? Just think, ponder over these things.

I can understand your love for the child. It is perfectly good. I am happy that you have come from so far to take your child back. You must be in deep love with him. But become a little more alert. Tell your heart. Tell what you have experienced in your life. Would it not be a great desire in your heart also that if you were born again and life was again given to you, you would like to start it as a sannyasin? Wouldn't it be good for a change, at least? Just think over it. If your boy becomes convinced by you, take him with all my blessings But if he is not convinced, don't go in anger. Then too go on loving him. Let him do what he wants to do. Let him have his own life experience in his own way. Who knows?

When Buddha left his palace his father was worried. And when he became enlightened and came back after twelve years his father was very angry – naturally. This was his only son born when the father was very old. He was a gift of God. He was the only heir to the kingdom and he had left the old man. To whom was this kingdom going to belong? There was nobody to look after it – and the old man was eighty years old.

When the son came back of course the father was angry. He came to the door and he said, "I am your father. I still feel for you although I know you have done a foolish thing. But you are not meant to be a beggar, a sannyasin, you are an emperor's son and you are meant to be an emperor. You come back. I am angry but I am your father, I can forgive you. You come back. Drop all this nonsense and disperse all these sannyasins, these mad people, who are following you. Their mothers and fathers must be suffering like me. I have not slept for twelve years. I could not sleep. It has been a nightmare. You have hurt me very deeply."

Buddha was standing there. The father was very angry He went on shouting at him until finally he cooled down a little Then Buddha said, "Sir, you don't see that I am not the same person who left the palace. Look at me. I am a totally new being. I am not the same person who left the palace, who used to be your son. My body may look the same but look deep into me. Something has happened. And I have come just to show my gratitude to you, to show I am happy that I was born to you, that you gave me birth. I have attained and I have come hare my experience with you. In your old age I would like you also to attain – because death is coming. I can see your legs are shaking, you cannot stand rightly Death is coming. Before death comes, know what truth is, know what life is. Before death comes, realize yourself."

The father looked. Certainly this was not the same man although he looked the same. This figure was luminous, a great light had happened to him. The father cooled down, he meditated over it, he thought about it again and again and he found that it was right. His reaction was just a reaction, an unconscious reaction. Finally he himself became a meditator. Eventually, before he died, he became a *bhikkhu*, he became a sannyasin.

Your responsibility is great, but don't just react out of unawareness. Give the boy a chance also. He may be right. Think from his side too. Always remember that truth is nobody's monopoly and truth has nothing to do with age. Sometimes a small child has it and sometimes an old man does not have it. And whenever you say something remember not to Judge.

Just a few days before, something happened. Old Paritosh had written a journal, a beautiful journal. I have looked into it and many other sannyasins have looked into it – and we have many talented people around here, authors, poets, published novelists. They have all looked at it and they liked it. So he sent it to a friend who is a publisher in England.

A few days before he received the journal back. By mistake, by some unconscious mistake, the letter that he had written to the publisher came back with the manuscript. The publisher must have given the manuscript to a reader – and on the letter the reader had written: "This man is boring".

First this letter should not have come with the manuscript. People go on doing things in a very deep sleep. Secondly, you cannot say: "This man is very boring" because the reader is supposed to talk about the book not about the man. The book may be boring but what do you know about the man? Thirdly, the reader was supposed to show his reaction, not to judge it. He should have said, "I am bored with this book" not "the book is boring." These are two different things. "I am bored with this book" – this is perfectly okay. This is my response – if I feel I am bored, I am bored.

But somebody else may be intrigued. When Vivek was reading the journal she was so interested she could not get away from it until she finished it, she had to finish it. She became very involved.

It depends on you. The person may be saying something about the journal but really he is saying something about himself. He may have felt bored. He may have no understanding about meditation, he may never have heard about sannyas. He may not know what is going on here. He may have felt completely unconnected. That is his response. But people work in deep sleep.

When I was looking at this letter and the reader's comment I remembered when Bertrand Russell was once traveling in America. He could not sleep the whole night because the train compartment had so many mosquitoes in it that they wouldn't allow him to sleep. In the morning he was very angry. You pay for a first-class carriage, air-conditioned, but what is the point if there are so many mosquitoes in it?

So he wrote a very angry letter to the director of the company.

Prompt came the reply by the next post. Bertrand Russell was very happy because the reply was very gratifying. The director said: "Sir, nobody has ever complained so we never knew about this. We are tremendously grateful to you that you took the trouble to inform us. Things will be put right. Next time you travel in our train this will not happen." He was very happy. And again and again the director had said: "We are grateful, grateful, very grateful, blah, blah, blah...."

Then suddenly Bertrand Russell became aware of a small slip in the envelope. He took the slip out. On the slip was a handwritten message: "Send this fool the bug letter." The director must have written that message to the clerk concerned – "Send this fool the bug letter." He was very shocked. And then he became aware that the letter was printed – so it was not the first letter. It was being sent to everybody.

But this is how things go. People are very unaware. You don't know what you are doing, you don't know why you are doing it, you don't know what will be the consequence, you don't know what the source of it is.

This is my suggestion to this father. You please meditate here, be here for a few days, see what your son is doing, try to understand from his side. Stand in his shoes for a little while. And then explain your heart to him. But you can explain only if you have understood him – what he is doing. Otherwise your understanding will be prejudiced, you will be a stranger. You will say something which may not fit. Try to see his view-point, what he is doing.

And who knows, you may be convinced rather than trying to take him back. You may start thinking about becoming a sannyasin or you may at least start thinking about meditating. Your son may have opened a door for you. Sometimes it happens that when old people have no courage then young people open the door. Young people are certainly dare-devils. They can do certain things which old people cannot do.

In the whole history of humanity it has always been because of young people that new things have happened – never because of old people. They cannot do new things because they are too efficient with the old.

Have you heard the beautiful parable about the clothes of the emperor?

It happened once that a cheat convinced an emperor that he could bring dress for him from heaven. Of course, the king became greedy. He said, "I am ready to pay. Whatsoever the cost, bring them but don't try to deceive me!" The man said, "I will never leave the palace because the way to heaven is not an outside way, it is an inner way. I have to go into my consciousness – from there I enter heaven. I know the key so I will bring the clothes for you. And remember, never before have God's clothes ever come on earth. This is the first time. You will be the first to have them, you will be a unique person. But millions of rupees will be needed." The king said, "Everything will be supplied."

The king put guards on the palace and the man was given a big room. And every day he asked for more money, more money, more money. The king became a little troubled – "What are you doing with so much money?" He said, "Bribery. The guards there in heaven and the ministers and the court people – it is a difficult thing to reach to God's clothes. But I am coming closer so you just go on supplying the money."

He took millions of rupees. Then the date, the cherished date came, and the man came out with a very beautiful box. He said, "These clothes should be received in a celebration." So a great celebration was arranged. The whole capital gathered. The court, the palace, everything was decorated. It was a rare thing. Never before had it happened. It was historical.

Then the cheat came to the king and said, "You come here, close to the box." He opened the box and he said, "There is one condition. These are invisible clothes."

Certainly – God is invisible so his clothes cannot be visible otherwise it would look very awkward, just shirts walking, coats walking. The clothes are invisible.

"But, said the cheat, one thing I inquired about when I was bringing these clothes. They said that they are invisible, but that people who are born, really born, from their own fathers, will be able to see them. Those whose birth is suspicious, doubtful, they will not be able to see them." He opened the box and he showed the king, "Look! How beautiful they are!"

Now the king thought, "If I say that there is nothing people will think that I am not born out of my own father. This is tricky." And then he called his court people and said, "Look, come here! See these beautiful clothes." And they all looked and they all said, "We have never seen such beautiful clothes." And they started praising the clothes like anything; they started competing with each other in praise. And the king said, "It was good I didn't say anything because everybody is seeing them." But everybody was thinking, "Everybody else sees the clothes, only I am suspicious, but it is better to keep the secret. What is the point?"

The cheat took up an invisible cap, gave it to the king and took the cap of the king and put it in the box. By and by the king's clothes started disappearing. He became afraid. When the last piece was going there was a moment when he started thinking, "Should I say the truth?" But now it was too late. All his prestige was at stake – not only his, his father's, his mother's, his whole heritage. And everybody saw and the crowd was shouting and became very excited. Nobody saw and yet everybody saw the clothes. So the king said to himself, "It is better this way. When everybody is seeing, why be worried? I only see myself as naked, everybody sees me as not naked."

So he took the last jump – his underwear also went. He was standing nude. And people were shouting and clapping and everybody saw that he was nude.

Then a small child, who had come with his father and was sitting on the shoulders of his father, said to his father, "But the king is naked." The father said, "You stupid! Keep quiet. You are not grown up yet. When you are grown up you will also see the clothes. Can't you see? Everybody sees the clothes."

Only that small child had seen the truth and was able to tell it. It has always been so. Only young people have been able to see the truth first – because they don't worry, they don't have anything to be worried about, they have nothing at stake. They can be courageous and daring.

So who knows? Your son may have seen the truth. Don't drag him back. Put your heart before him, talk to him, but in no way, subtle or gross, enforce anything. Just show how you are feeling and feel what he is feeling here. And don't say "When you are grown up and well educated you will be able to understand more."

The same thing was said by the father to the young child and he was the only one in that big crowd who was man enough to see the truth, to recognize the truth and to say it. But the father immediately hushed him. That's what fathers have been doing down the ages.

The fifth question:

Osho,
Why don't you hit me? I feel ready.

I don't accept your recommendation. If you feel ready it means you are not ready. This is your ego assertion that you are ready. One who is ready will never assert because readiness comes through non-ego. One who is ready will be humble and meek, one who is ready will stand at the back of the queue. He will not try to come first. Remember, those who are the last will be the first and those who are trying hard to be the first will be the last.

There is no need to come and propagate that you are ready. If you are ready I will know first, you will not know first. So leave it to me.

In fact, this is greed – and a very strange human mind. When I hit, people don't feel good. Ananda Prem felt terrible, so was the case with fat Veena – so-called fat Veena, she is not so fat. She cried the whole morning. And so was the case with Amida. When I was talking here she was feeling terrible. When I hit, you feel terrible.

But when I don't hit, you ask for it...because sometimes the mind is so cunning that it starts thinking that by being hit you will become special. That will be a proof that you are ready, ripe. That will be a proof that now you deserve to be hit.

This is ego. And ego is the only barrier. And it is the ego that doesn't allow you to change. I am not interested in little changes here, I am not interested in reforming you – I am interested in destroying you utterly so that something utterly new is born. Less than that won't do.

What you want is for your ego to be decorated with a few medals so that you can go out and you can say, "See, Osho has hit me – and harder than anybody has ever been hit before. I am special."

This desire to be special is a disease. And sometimes it happens that this desire to be special can lead you to become humble too. Because I say that those who are the last will be the first, you can start competing for the last place. Again you are competing for the first. Watch. Mind is really cunning. It can play game upon game upon game. It is like a Chinese box: you open one, there is another; you open that, there is still another. And they fit each other so perfectly. There is just a slightly smaller box inside and again a smaller one, and again a smaller one. Ego is a Chinese box. Watch it, otherwise you will never get rid of it.

And, let me repeat again: I am not here to reform you. Reform is an ugly word. Reform means that you remain the same with a few touches here and there – I paint you here and there. You remain the same, basically the same structure, the same gestalt, although perhaps a little more beautiful. No, I am not interested in that, I am interested in your utter disappearance – when you are no more.

When you are not, for the first time you will be virgin, innocent, fresh as the dew-drop in the morning. That's what God is. That freshness is God. That original happening is God. That entry of the new into the old is God. When that new enters, the old simply disappears, or, when the old disappears, only then the new enters. The entry of the new and the disappearance of the old are simultaneous. In a single moment they happen.

But I understand your trouble.

In a New England resort town there was a man so homely that he was the butt of every practical joke that his townfolk could think up. A plastic surgeon who visited the resort on a vacation was so touched by his ugliness that he offered to change the man's face without charge. "In fact," he said, "just for the heck of it, I will do some plastic surgery that will make you the handsomest man in New England."

Just before he put the man under the knife, the surgeon said, "Do you want me to change your face completely, totally?"

"No," answered the man, "not too much. I want the fellows to know who it is who is so handsome."

This is how the ego functions. You want the fellows to know who it is who is so handsome. You want the fellows to know who it is who is so meek, so humble, who it is who is standing at the back of the queue. If even that much desire is there the ego is completely alive, thriving. Nothing has changed. Only a total change is a change.

And you need not suggest to me what I should do. You leave it to me. When the time is ripe and I feel you need a hit on the head I will do it. I will never do it because you ask, I will do it when it is needed.

You cannot understand what is needed. Again and again you misunderstand your want as a need. Your want is not a need. I understand that you want it but you want it for wrong reasons. I will give the hit when you need it, not because you want it. And when all your wanting has disappeared you will need it – when you are not at all aware about it then it comes suddenly, it comes abruptly. Only then is it meaningful.

You have asked a question.... If you are waiting and I come there and hit you on your head it will be meaningless. You were waiting for it, you were expecting it, you will be thrilled, your ego will become a big balloon. You will go around with a big chest saying, "See what happened? I am ready."

God comes to you only when you are not expecting him at all. He comes in moments when you are completely oblivious of desire. He comes only in moments when there is no desire, when there is desirelessness. He comes abruptly, suddenly. When you expect is exactly when you remain closed. When you don't expect, you open.

Have you not watched it again and again in life? All that is beautiful happens only when you are not expecting it. When you expect, things don't happen. And even if they happen you don't get any blissfulness through them. All bliss is abrupt, unconnected with the past, discontinuous with the past.

So please wait. Wait without expecting. Wait oblivious of all desires. Whenever anything is needed, that is my business to do it, that is my responsibility. When you become a sannyasin it is your commitment and my responsibility.

The last question:

Osho,
It seems to me that I am becoming really mad.

You have always been mad it is not that you are becoming mad. You are becoming a little bit more alert about it.

Mind is madness. That's why you don't look within. If you look within, you will find a mad rush. Not only one mad person is there, there is a mad crowd. And the whole crowd is at each other's necks. That's why I go on saying "Look within." So says Socrates, so says Buddha, so says Jesus – "Look within. The kingdom of God is within."

Nobody is willing to look within. They listen, they say "Okay, sometime we will look." But nobody is ready to look. Why? Because when you look within, you don't see a kingdom of God, you see a madhouse. When you look within, you don't see the blissfulness of Buddha, you see just neurosis. You see the same thoughts repeating, repeating – as if a gramophone record has got stuck and goes on repeating the same, the same, the same. When you meditate you start becoming aware. When you become aware you feel you are becoming mad. No! If you are becoming aware that you are becoming mad, you are getting away from it, you are going beyond it.

A person who is aware that he is mad is already on the threshold of sanity. A mad person is never aware that he is mad. You can go to the madhouse and ask mad people. They will laugh. Nobody will be ready to say that he is mad. They think the whole world is mad except themselves. This is a criterion of a mad person – he thinks the whole world is mad except himself.

What about a sane person? Lao Tzu says, "The whole world seems to be very intelligent except me. The whole world seems to be very clear except me – I am confused. The world seems to have clarity, transparency of mind, I am muddle-headed. The whole world is clever and wise, I am an idiot." Look what Lao Tzu is saying. This is the indication of a sane man – the sanest ever.

So, Satisha – this is a question from Satisha – you are coming closer to sanity because you are becoming aware of your madness. Watch it. Don't get scared and don't rush out. Go into it. Look into it. Go into it and look into it. Persistent perseverance is needed.

Just remember one thing: the one who is aware is not the one you are aware of. The observer is separate from the observed. If you see a mad thought running, humming inside, you are not that thought – you are the witness that knows that it is there.

You say: "It seems to me that I am becoming really mad." Then there are two things: something is going mad and something is watching. That watcher is you. Mind is always mad, that's why we don't watch the mind. Watch the mind and you will start feeling what is happening. You never thought that you were mad, now you feel as if you are. It is a good sign, a good indication. You are coming closer to home.

An anecdote.

A man was charged with striking a woman fellow-passenger in a double-decker bus. The magistrate asked him what excuse he could offer.

"Well, Sir, it was like this," replied the culprit. "She sat on the seat beside me on the lower-deck of the bus. Then she opened her bag, took out her purse, closed her bag, opened her purse, took out a dime, closed her purse, opened her bag, put back the purse and closed her bag. Then she noticed the conductor was going upstairs, so she opened her bag, took out her purse, closed her bag, opened her purse, put in her dime, closed her purse, opened her bag, put in her purse and closed her bag. Then she saw the conductor coming down the stairs so she opened her bag, took out her purse, closed her bag, opened her purse, took out a dime and closed her...."

The magistrate could not bear it any longer. "Stop!" he cried. "You will drive me crazy."

"That's just what happened to me, Sir," said the man.

That is what is happening to your mind continuously. If you watch it, it feels as if it will drive you crazy, but watching is the only way to go beyond it. Otherwise whether you know it or not, you are crazy. Just by not knowing it you don't become a sane person.

Watch it, go into it, Satisha. And I know Satisha must be getting crazy. Today she asked almost three dozen questions. She must be going crazy! But it is good. In your becoming alert you are blessed. Hold on to this alertness. Get more centered in this alertness. The more alert you become, the further away the noise of the mind will go. When you are really centered the mind disappears – because it is the same energy that is involved in the thoughts which is used in centering. When the energy becomes centering, thoughts simply flop dead. They don't have any energy. They disappear.

Enough for today.

CHAPTER #13

Raise No Dust, Leave No Tracks

Duke Mu of Ch'in said to Po-lo: "You are getting on in years, is there anyone in your family whom I can send to find me horses?"

"A good horse can be identified by its shape and look, its bone and muscle, but the great horses of the world might be extinct, vanished, perished, lost. Such horses raise no dust and leave no tracks. All my sons have lesser talent – they can pick a good horse, but not a great one. But there is a man I know who carries and hauls and collects firewood for me, Chiu-fang Kao. As a judge of horses he is my equal. I suggest that you see him."

Duke Mu saw the man and sent him away to find horses. After three months he returned and reported to the duke, "I have got one, it is in Sha-ch'ui."

"What kind of horse?"

"A mare, yellow."

The duke sent someone to fetch it. It turned out to be a stallion, and black. The duke, displeased, summoned Po-lo. "He's no good, the fellow you sent to find me horses. He cannot even tell one color from another or a mare from a stallion. What can he know about horses?"

Po-lo breathed a sigh of wonder. "So now he has risen to this! It is just this that shows that he is worth a thousand, ten

> thousand, any number of people like me. What such a man as Kao observes is the innermost native impulse behind the horse's movements. He grasps the essence and forgets the dross, goes right inside it and forgets the outside. He looks for and sees what he needs to see, ignores what he does not need to see. In the judgment of horses of a man like Kao there is something more important than horses.'
> When the horse arrived it did prove to be a great horse.

Tao is the vision of the total, the vision of the whole. Parts don't matter; parts don't have any meaning in themselves. The meaning belongs to the whole, to the unity, tot he organic unity – if you look for meaning in the parts you will look in vain. Not only that, if you insist on looking for the meaning in the parts you will destroy meaning rather than finding it. It will be a destructive attitude.

For example, a poem does not exist in the words that constitute it, it exists somewhere beyond the words. It is transcendental. If you dissect the words, the sentences, the linguistic form, what are you going to gain? If you dissect a poem, if you dismember a poem, you are killing an alive unity. It is as if you are dissecting the body of a man – by the time you have succeeded in dissecting the body of the man the spirit is gone. Whatsoever you find will be a dead corpse. And you were searching for the man, not for the dead corpse. The man is in the unity, so is the poem.

If you dismember poetry you will find sentences; if you dismember the sentences you will find clauses; if you dismember the clauses you will find words; if you dismember the words, then the alphabet is left. But where is the poetry – the poetry that has thrilled your heart? Where is that beauty that has touched your being, that has given your wings? Where is that vision? In the alphabet there is nothing.

How did it disappear? Your approach was basically wrong. Your approach was basically destructive, violent. You dissected it. Poetry has to be seen in its totality. It has to be grasped as a whole. If you can grasp it as a whole then each word contributes to it; if you cannot grasp it as a whole then words don't constitute it. Words constitute only the body of a poem, not the heart of it. Yes, the heart cannot exist without the body but the heart is not the body.

Man cannot exist without the body, certainly, but man is not just the body. Man is far more. Man is far superior. Man is far higher. He is tethered to the body, living in the body, but not the body itself. The body is the temple and man is the God in it. Yes, if you destroy the temple the God will not have any abode; it will disappear, evaporate.

So disappears a poem. The poem is the God that resides in the words, the rhythm, the meaning, the beauty

Listen to a small haiku of Basho, the greatest master of haikus. It is a very small haiku, a few words.

The ancient pond....

When I say it, visualize it, because a haiku has to be visualized. It is a picture-poem. Only in visualization will you understand.

> The ancient pond
> A frog jumps in
> Plop.

Finished. You can visualize it, you can visualize it with your innermost eye – the ancient pond with moss on the *rocks*. You can almost touch it. You can feel the texture of it. It is a very ancient pond. Dry leaves are on the surface, dry leaves are on the banks. Old pine trees are standing on guard. You can visualize it. You can smell the smell of the pine trees, the fragrance, the coolness. Maybe the morning sun....

And the frog. You can see the frog alive. The frog jumps in. In Japanese the actual translation will be: a frog-jump-in – not jumps in. A frog-jump-in. The frog and the jump are not two things, you cannot dissect the frog from his jump. He is the jump. In the jump he is. In Japanese and Chinese the language is far deeper than other languages. But to put it rightly, in right

English, we will say *A frog jumps in* – as if he is doing something. To jump in is not doing anything for a frog, it is not an act. It is spontaneous.

A frog-jump-in
Plop.

The sound, the ripples on the surface of the old lake – and the silence.

Now, if you dissect this small poem – there are only thirteen syllables in it – what are you going to get? You will get a few words. Then dissect the words and you get the alphabet – linguistic elements. All meaning is lost. It is as if you go and see a beautiful painting and you dissect it into its colors. The painting is lost. Or, if I give you a beautiful lotus flower and you dissect it into its chemical constituents then the lotus is lost.

That's how science has destroyed all meaning in life. If people are feeling that life is meaningless in the West it is a by-product of their scientific endeavor. Science was trying to make life more intelligible – it has made life more intelligible, but all meaning has been lost.

Those people who had not much knowledge about life were far happier. Life had more meaning then. They had not dissected the lotus, they were enjoying the lotus. They were not worried about the constituents, the chemicals, they were not worrying about what beauty was – they were enjoying it, they were in it, they were swallowing it, they were swallowed by it. They were in tune with beauty, life, existence, and there was meaning.

Now science has made things much more intelligible, it has explained almost everything, and through explanations the whole beauty is destroyed. Explanation is in your hands but where is the mystery of life? If you go to a biologist and you ask him what love is, he will explain it to you. It is nothing but a hormonal thing. Some chemicals running in your veins, in your arteries, in your blood, some hormones released by your glands – that's what love is. Now tell a mother that the love that she has for her child is nothing but hormonal; tell a woman who has fallen in love with a man and is ready to sacrifice her whole life, is ready to die, will be happy to die for this man, tell her that it is just hormonal....

And you are not saying something wrong, you are perfectly true, you are perfectly right – but something is missing in your truth. Your truth is dead. Your truth is concerned with the lowest denominator. It is as if somebody asks you about the lotus and you say it is nothing but the mud. What is the lotus? Nothing but the mud – because it comes out of the mud. What is love? Hormonal – because it comes out of the hormones.

That's why Freud reduced all love to sexuality – then prayer too, then God too. Everything becomes sexual. The moment prayer, love and God all become sexual something is missed.

Tao's approach is just the opposite. Tao says rather than explaining the thing by the part, rather than explaining the hole by the part, try to explain the part by the whole.

For example, this haiku I told you....

> The ancient pond
> A frog-jump-in
> Plop.

Now, the word *frog* or the word *plop,* the sound "plop," can exist in a thousand and one contexts. In every context it will have a different meaning because the meaning will depend on the context. "Plop" itself does not carry the meaning. It depends. In Basho's haiku you suddenly know what it is because of the frog. The frog gives meaning to it, the ancient pond gives meaning to it. In a different context it will mean a different thing. The context, the whole, gives the meaning to the part.

The ancient pond.... The word *ancient* can be used in a thousand and one ways. You will find it used in many ways. In every context it will have a different meaning. So the meaning is not contained in the word *ancient,* the meaning is contained in the whole in which the word is used.

You can see it in your whole life. Everything has meaning

only because it is part of an organic unity which is higher than it, bigger than it. The meaning comes from the higher, the meaning comes from the bigger. The meaning certainly comes to the lowest, but the lowest is not the determining factor. Look at the different approach. If you ask the scientist he will say the lotus is nothing but the mud; if you ask the Taoist he will say the mud is nothing but the lotus.

The difference is tremendous. When you say that the lotus is nothing but the mud, the dirty mud, you have destroyed all beauty. Then only dirty mud is left in your hands and in your soul. Then you are left with a filthy life. Taoists say that if a lotus can come out of the mud then the mud cannot be just mud, it must be carrying the lotus, the possibility of the lotus. The fragrance, the color, the beauty of the lotus must be hidden somewhere in the mud. So don't call it just mud – it carries the lotus, it is the womb for the lotus. So even mud becomes beautiful. And you start looking for the meaning in the mud. It is there somewhere – you may be able to see, you may not be able to see, that depends on your clarity, your eyes. But condemnation disappears.

Freud says that all love is nothing but sex; even the love of God, even the love of Meera for Krishna, the love of Ananda for Buddha, the love of Mary Magdalene for Jesus, is nothing but sexuality. Can't you see how much beauty is destroyed immediately with a stroke? If you ask the Taoist he will say that even when a man goes to make love to a prostitute there is something of prayer in it, there is something of the divine in it.

Just few days ago I saw an article written by the Dattabal. He has put me with Freud, has said that we both say the same thing. There can't be any greater misunderstanding. I say sex is love, Freud says love is sex – and the difference is tremendous. I say that in sex also there is a glimpse of samadhi; I make sex also sacred. Freud says that in samadhi, in Ramakrishna's samadhi, there is nothing but repressed sexuality. He makes samadhi also profane.

Those who have no understanding can put me in one bracket with Freud. It is very easy, simple. They will say, "What is the difference whether you call love sex or you call sex love? There is no difference." Not much if you only think of the words. Then there is only the difference that I put sex in one place and love in another and Freud puts them just in the opposite places. So there is not much difference.

But can't you see the difference? The difference is tremendous, vital, and of great value. And much will depend on that difference.

The Taoist vision is to look at the part through the whole so that the whole can give a meaning to the part, can make it meaningful. Not otherwise. Your eyes are beautiful but taken out of your body they won't be.

It happened in the life of Vincent Van Gogh.... He was an ugly man, very ugly – a great painter and a beautiful soul, but a very ugly body. No woman ever fell in love with him. He was repulsive, he was horrible. And he suffered very much. At the age of thirty-three he committed suicide. If there is nobody to love you what is there to live for?

Once visiting a prostitute he said, "Nobody has ever said anything to me lovingly. Nobody has said that I am beautiful or I am nice or I am this or that. I hanker for it." The woman took pity on him, she must have had a very compassionate heart. She looked to find something that she could appreciate but she could not find anything. The face was ugly, the nose was ugly, the eyes were ugly, and everything was topsy-turvy – except the ears. So she said, "But you have beautiful ears." And she played with his ear.

He went home, cut off his ear and presented it to the woman. She could not believe it! He brought the ear with the blood flowing and he said, "You like it, so now it belongs to you."

But an ear cut out of the body is no longer beautiful – even the most beautiful ear will become ugly.

Take things out of their context and they lose all meaning, they lose all beauty, they lose all truth. Truth is with the whole, so is beauty, so is goodness. This is the first thing to be understood about Tao – it is a vision of the whole.

And the whole has not to be put together...this is the second thing to remember. There have been people who try to put the whole together. For example, Freud's psychoanalysis tried to dissect human mind, human psyche, into fragments – that's why it is called analysis, psychoanalysis. First he dissected the human mind into its constituent parts and destroyed much. Then came Assagioli and he created psychosynthesis. What Freud has done Assagioli tries to undo. He puts parts together again. Freud has destroyed but Assagioli has not been able to revive anything; he cannot.

This will be difficult but it has to be understood – because it will help you to understand the Taoist attitude. Freud does analysis. First he cuts off the limbs of the body and then he spreads all the limbs on the table and examines them. Then comes Assagioli. He puts all the limbs together again, binds them together, glues them together and thinks that now the man is whole. Both are wrong. Once you have killed something you cannot put it together. Life is so precious that once gone, it is gone forever. You cannot put it together.

If somebody takes all the petals of the rose apart and then Assagioli comes and puts all the petals together, pins them together and says that now it is a real flower, he is wrong. It is not the real flower. It only gives a false idea of unity. The unity is not there because the pins that are holding it were never part of it; the glue that is holding it was never a part of an alive rose. The alive rose was holding itself together – remember it. It was not being held together by something else, it was not dependent for its unity on something else, it was holding itself together. That is the spirit that keeps you together, that holds you together. It is not that your hands and your legs and your eyes are put together, no. Something in you exists which is keeping them together. Once that unity is destroyed even if you put things back it will not be the real unity.

So I am not in favor of Freud's analysis, neither am I in favor of Assagioli's synthesis. My attitude is exactly that of Tao.

What does Tao say? Tao says look for the unity that existed before analysis began. Go to the primordial, the primitive unity, the original. Go to the original. Synthesis comes after analysis, it follows analysis, it succeeds analysis. And the wholeness? The wholeness preceded analysis. It was before analysis destroyed it. The vision has to be total and you have to see things in their totality. You are not to put them together. If you put them together it will be a false unity, it will be a synthetic synthesis, it will be artificial, plastic. It will not be true.

Is it clear to you? Look at the tree. The tree is together. Look deep into the tree. The tree is together with the earth because it is joined together. If you look deeply, the earth exists together with the sun. Without the sun the earth cannot exist; without the sun the tree will not be green, will not be alive; without the air surrounding it, it will not be able to breathe. So it is joined together with the air, with the earth, with the sun, and with the stars – with everything. The whole existence is intertwined; we are intertwined with each other. I am in you, you are in me; we are in the tree, the trees are in us; we are in the earth and the earth is in us and we are intertwined. We are members of each other, we don't exist separately.

To look from this high standpoint of ultimate unity is what Tao is. And then things have a totally different color. Then your vision reveals to you things which cannot be revealed on lower planes. It is not a question of putting them together.

One day a Christian missionary came to me and he said, "I am happy that you are trying to put all the religions together." I said, "You have not understood me. I am not putting them together. I see them as one."

I am not putting them together, I am not making a synthesis. I am not in agreement with Mahatma Gandhi who was trying to create a synthesis by putting together Islam, Hinduism,

Christianity – a few parts from the Bible and a few from the Koran and a few from the Gita – and making something out of it. This is a hotchpotch, a *khichari*, it is not unity, it is not the total vision. I am not putting Christ and Mohammed and Mahavira and Krishna and Lao Tzu together. No, as I see them they are one. It is not a question of putting them together, I am not making any effort to put them together, I am not trying to find some synthesis in them. They *are* one – that is my experience. They are one. They have never been separate. The separation is not possible. They join together into truth. They know the same truth, they live the same life, they enjoy the same bliss. Their samadhi is one. I am not putting anything together, I am simply saying it is so.

The second thing: Tao is not interested in understanding anything in separation – because that understanding will be false, rooted in falsity. You cannot understand a thing separately because in that very separation, in that very definition, you have taken it out of its total context, out of its organic unity. Then you may have an explanation but no understanding.

Science explains; religion understands. Explanations are concerned with the parts; understanding is concerned with the total. Understanding is a very vague thing, liquid, cloudy; explanation is very clear-cut. Because it is clear-cut it is wrong. In life there is nothing clear-cut. Boundaries merge and meet.

For example, you see a woman. In the morning she may be a woman, in the evening she may become a man. You see a man, he is very angry. And within a moment he will become soft and may become a woman.

It happened last night. I hit hard on Yatri's head and he shouted and he screamed and he said, "I will cut off your head, Osho!" And I know him, he is a very feminine person. But he became very, very aggressive. Then he cooled down and fell at my feet. Now what to do? Rather than cutting off my head he fell at my feet. No, this is not the same person who was going to cut my head off. He puts his head at my feet. And the interval was not very big it happened within a few minutes. In one moment he was male, yang; then he became female, yin.

Boundaries meet and merge. The person who loves you can be angry: the person who is angry can love you.

In reality nothing is very clear-cut, and it is good that it is not very clear-cut. Look – the higher the being, the more vagueness there is; the lower the being, the more it is clear-cut. A rock has far more clear-cut definitions than a man. The rock remains a rock. You can go in the morning, you can go in the evening, you can go in the night – the rock remains the rock. But the man goes on changing, changing, changing. The higher the unity, the more delicate the balance; the lower the unity, the more fixed the balance.

When a person has really attained to the ultimate, he is very fluid, river-like. He is no longer like an ice-cube. He has melted. An ice-cube has definite boundaries, an ice-cube can be defined, but when you have melted, all definitions disappear.

Tao does not give any explanation but it understands; science gives explanations but it doesn't understand. And the very explanations become barriers to understanding. The moment you have explained a thing you have destroyed its mystery. Never say that something is completely explained – that means it is completely meaningless. Explain a thing and you have explained it away.

When the husband says that he understands his wife totally, love has disappeared. Now love cannot exist. Love can exist only when there is still mystery – when the husband still does not understand, when the wife still does not understand, when there is still a possibility that the husband may do something and the wife will be surprised, when surprise is still possible. This means that everything is not explained. Something remains unexplained, something remains elusive, something remains mercury-like. You go on grasping it and it continues to slip out – that's the beauty of life.

Tao says that the whole life is mercury-like. The total is so alive that no fixed explanation is possible. You cannot label anything because things change so fast. By the time you have labeled something your label is already false – the thing has changed. The moment you have said something the utterance is already meaningless because the reality is no longer the same. Explanation, Tao has none; understanding, it has tremendously. And it is one of the basic ingredients of understanding that life is a mystery.

The third thing: science tries to explain things by their causes and Tao tries to understand things by their ends. The difference is of tremendous value and has to be understood. Science goes into the causes, the "how" of things. Tao goes into the end, the ultimate flowering, the "why" of things. For example, if you fall in love with a woman or a man, science will ask "how" – how did you fall in love? It will go into the causes of it. Tao will ask "why." It will go into the end of it. Science moves towards the seed for its explanation and Tao moves towards the flower or the fruit for its understanding. Science goes into the past, Tao goes into the future. Science looks into the dead, Tao looks into the possibility and potentiality.

A Sufi mystic was sent to India by a great Iranian king as a messenger to the Indian emperor. Because of some conflict the Iranian emperor was a little worried. So he sent this Sufi mystic to put things right, to create some understanding between the two countries.

The mystic came to the Indian emperor, presented his credentials, and showed his appreciation of the Indian emperor by saying, "You are a full moon."

The news reached Iran that he had said to the emperor, "You are a full moon." When he had departed from Iran he had said to the Iranian king, "You are a new moon." The Iranian king was very angry. New moon? That means just the beginning, the first-day moon – you cannot even see it. Only on the second day does it become a little visible – on the third day a little more. Meanwhile he had said to the Indian emperor that he was the full moon. This was insulting. Let him come!

The king waited in anger. When the mystic came back he was caught immediately, brought to the court and asked for an explanation. He laughed. He said, "It is simple. A full moon is finished. It is already dead. A full moon is on its deathbed. It is ready to decline. It has a past but no future. Hence I said to the Indian king, "You are a full moon." You, I have called the first-day moon, the new moon. You have future, you have potentiality, you are growing. Maybe the Indian emperor's empire is great but it is dead."

Look – when something has a past it is already old. Science goes into the past, that's why if you go to a psychoanalyst he will go into your past. He will say, "Relate your whole past. What happened in the past? Start at your very childhood and go on from there." He goes into the past. If a man is mad and is brought to a psychoanalyst, the psychoanalyst goes into the cause – why did he become mad in the first place? He has to go there. He has to look into the past to find the cause there.

If you are brought to a Taoist he will not go into the past. He will look into the future. He will think of what purpose your madness can be used for. Just look at the approach. For what purpose can your madness be used? If you are mad can your madness be put to dancing, to meditation, to singing? Certainly a madman has more energy available – maybe that's why he is mad. His madness can be used in a creative way. There is no need to think of how to destroy it, the need is how to use it, how to be creative about it.

If you go to a Taoist he will look into your madness, he will try to figure out your future, your higher possibilities, and he will try to see how to use your madness for that future, how to make your madness serve your destiny.

That's what I am doing here. When you come to me you are mad, you are neurotic. I am not worried about it. My whole function here is how to make it creative. Madness is great energy. If you look into the past it is a problem, if you look into the future it can be used and can become a stepping-stone. Everything can be used.

Tao believes in doing exactly what a gardener does in using manure. You can hoard manure and it will simply stink and it will make your life impossible. But you can spread the manure on the flower-beds and the same stinking manure will become tremendously valuable perfume in the flowers. It has been used rightly. Manure is not to be collected, it has to be spread on flower-beds. Then the flowers grow bigger, with more color, with more life, with more fragrance, with more stability, with more zest and enthusiasm. And it is the same manure that may have become stinking, may have made life impossible.

What is madness? It is manure. What is anger? What is hatred? What is jealousy? They are manure. If you go on hoarding them you will go mad, certainly. It will be impossible to live with it. The Taoist approach is to spread it on the flower-beds. It can serve meditation, it can serve love, it can serve joy, it can serve happiness, it can serve God.

A madman can reach God faster than the so-called sane people because the sane people move very cautiously. They don't run, they don't rush. The sane people move only so far, and always think, doubt, hesitate, linger, wait. And they have many, many things that hold them back. A madman simply rushes. Nothing holds him. He is certainly mad. There is nothing to hold him. If he wants to do something he will do it.

If a madman becomes interested in God then it is sure that he is going to attain. If a madman becomes a painter his painting will have a certain quality. No sane person could ever paint like a madman because a madman will not only paint, he will put his whole life into it. Van Gogh was a madman, so was Picasso. In fact, all the great painters were mad people and all the great poets were mad people. In fact, all the great people who have existed on the earth were thought some day or other by someone or other to be mad. Madness has tremendous potentiality.

Everything is potential – look how it can be used. Look at the future. Never think in terms of being a full moon, always remain a new moon.

So the Tao approach is never for the cause but for the end. It is eschatological, it is not casual. And it is tremendously beautiful – because God is the end of the whole existence. That is the ultimate, where we are moving to, where we are going to. That's what we are going to be. Everything can be put in a right way so that we can reach that goal more easily more softly, more joyously.

The last thing before we enter into the parable: philosophy divides knowledge into two – the subject and the object. With the object you cannot have any dialogue. A rock is an object – you cannot have any dialogue with it. You can watch, you can dissect, you can observe, you can find a few clues about it, but you cannot have any dialogue because you don't believe that the rock is a person. It is an object.

The word *object* is beautiful. It comes from "objectum" – that which stands in your way, that which prevents you from moving, that which hinders your path. The object means that which stands in the way like a barrier, like a wall. If you believe that the whole world is objective – as science believes – then the whole world is a China Wall. There is no dialogue possible.

If you look at your wife as an object to be used sexually or financially or in some other way; if you look at your husband as an object, a security, or something like that, somebody to lean upon, somebody you can use, somebody you can depend upon, but as an object – then there is no dialogue. Between a husband and a wife the dialogue never happens because both think of the other as an object, as a means. They don't think of the other as a person.

Tao says everything is subject; even that which stands in your way has its own subjectivity. You can provoke a dialogue with a rock, you can provoke a dialogue with a tree. And what to say about human beings? You can provoke a dialogue with anything – with the universe itself, with the sky, with the wind – and then there is a relationship, you relate. When you think about things as things and not as persons, when you think about the world as objective – as science teaches you to do – then you can hammer out a few facts but truth remains unrevealed. Truth is revealed only when you persuade existence, when you seduce existence through deep love and sympathy, when you are en rapport with existence, when you touch the rock as you would like to touch a person – you feel the texture of it, you close your eyes, you create a sort of relationship with it. And, if you are ready, if you understand Tao, you will be able to create a relationship with the rock. It will start talking to you sooner or later; it will respond.

The whole existence is full of God. There is nothing that is dead, there cannot be. How can anything be dead? All is alive, thriving, throbbing. Listen silently and you will feel the heartbeat everywhere – in the rock too. And then the dialogue is possible.

In the old Indian scriptures it is said that the great science of *ayurveda* was found not by objective research but by subjective dialogue. The ayurvedic physicians would go to the trees, meditate with the trees, sit silently with the trees, and when they had fallen en rapport with the being of the tree they would ask, "Sir" or "Madam" – whatsoever the case may be – "Would you like to say something to us? I am searching for a medicine for a particular disease, would you tell me if your leaves can be of any help, or your fruit, or your roots, or your bark? Or else, for what use could they be? How can you help humanity? In what way?" And it is said – it is a beautiful story – that that is how ayurvedic herbal medicines were discovered. Not by objective research, not by dissecting a tree, not by chemical analysis, but by dialogue.

And the same thing is said about *unani* medicine. The greatest *unani* physician, Lukman, did the same thing. He went to herbs. He would put his ear to the roots of a tree and listen silently. He would fall in deep rapport, would become thoughtless, would silently be there, would listen to the heartbeat of the tree – and when the right moment came and the tree was ready to reveal its secret, he would take the secret.

And it seems that the stories cannot be just stories – because they had no instruments to find anything out. Instruments have not been found at all. And whatsoever they said about trees has been found to be true. So the stories seem to be literally true. Just one man, Lukman, has talked about half a million herbs. And there could have been no other way because no lab existed for such chemical analysis. And just one man? How could he find out all that? The way was not analysis, the way was not synthesis, the way was not mind – the way was through the heart, a dialogue. When you are in dialogue the tree becomes the "thou." You are "I" the tree is the "thou" and there is a possibility.

Explore this possibility. It will take time because your mind has been too conditioned by the objective. It will take time but it happens. You can develop this sensibility. And when this sensibility has grown you have become a Taoist.

No object is just an object. Every object is full of subjectivity because every object has a soul to it. Nothing is soulless. As you are full of soul, "interiority," so is everything else.

Now this tremendously beautiful parable.

> Duke Mu of Ch'in said to Po-lo, "You are getting on in years. Is there anyone in your family whom I can send to find me horses?"

In the ancient world horses were very important – just as nowadays fighter planes are. The horse was the very hub of the war and it was the fastest vehicle. Horses were valued very much. That was the only power that's why we still go on saying that the car has a five horsepower engine. That was once the only power, that was the only measurement. Still we go on saying, "How much power does this machine have?" Five horsepower? Ten horsepower?' The measurement still remains – at least in the language. The horses have disappeared by and by; they are no longer needed, their old utility is gone.

But in those days the people who could find a great horse were great masters. They were respected. Emperors would keep them, would pay them, would revere them – because everything depended on a great horse. And a great horse...we don't know what they meant by a "great horse" because that language has become almost useless for us. A horse is just an animal to us, to them it was not so. The horse is a very intelligent animal and sometimes the intelligence of the horse would be of tremendous value to the king. It could save a life.

This man, Po-lo, must have been an expert, a master-expert, about knowing what horse is good, what horse is bad and what horse is really great.

> "A good horse can be identified by its shape and look, its bone and muscle, but the great horses of the world might be extinct, vanished, perished, lost. Such horses raise no dust and leave no tracks. All my sons have lesser talent – they can pick a good horse, but not a great one. But there is a man I know who carries and hauls and collects firewood for me, Chiu-fang Kao. As a judge of horses he is my equal. I suggest that you see him."

This man, Po-lo, had become very old and now he could not go in search of horses. The Duke asked him if he could suggest somebody else.

First, his definition:

> "A good horse can be identified by its shape and look...."

By its characteristics. A good horse is a trained horse. Training never goes deep. It remains on the surface. A man of character is like a good horse. A moral man is like a good horse. He has been cultivated, he has been well brought-up conditioned rightly, has right values. Wrong values have been repressed and right values have been superimposed. A good horse has a character like a good man, but it is not a great horse.

Then what is a great horse? A great horse is one who has intrinsic qualities – qualities which are not imposed from the outside. A great horse is one who has in-born potentialities; he is not trained. A great horse is a natural power, is a born power. A good horse is a talented horse, a great horse is a genius.

Somebody went to Mozart, the great composer and musician, and said, "I would like to learn music and I would like to become as great a musician as you are. How should I start?"

The man was very young, not more than twenty years of age. Mozart said, "You seek a master." But the young man said, "I have heard that you never learnt from any master so why should I seek one? And I have heard that when you were just a kid of seven years old you started composing great music. I am twenty. Why should I go to a master?"

Mozart said, "Then it is up to you. But when I was seven – even when I was seven – I never went to ask anybody what to do about it. I did it. You have come to ask me. That simply shows that at the most you have only talent, you don't have genius."

Talents have to be learned. A talented man is imitative – he is imitating the genius. The genius is not imitative, the genius is original. A good horse is a horse who has been trained to look like a great horse. He does not have the soul of the great horse, he has just the character.

That's how it is in human life. A good man is a man who has been cultivated to look like a great man. A Christian saint is a good horse, Jesus is a great horse. The Christian saint has simply cultivated his character to look like Jesus. He is a carbon copy. So is a Buddhist monk – he is a good horse, certainly good, and it is better to be good than to be bad, I am not against the good. Relatively it is good. It is better to be a saint than a criminal – but it is nothing compared to being a sage, nothing compared to being a buddha. A buddha has not imitated anybody. It is his original face, uncultivated. It is how he is.

Then what is the difference? If somebody can cultivate a buddha and become a buddha by cultivation, why should we be against him? In ordinary situations he will be able to pretend but in extraordinary situations he will not be able to pretend. In ordinary situations he will look like a buddha but whenever there will be extraordinary pressure he will give in.

That is the difference between a good horse and a great horse. A good horse will look, pretend, jump, show that he is a great horse, but when the right moment comes, when the danger arises, when there is a challenge, he will give in. The carbon copy cannot go very far, the original is needed. Only the original can be depended upon. One can trust only the original.

When you are seeking a master always seek an original man. Don't seek a cultivated man. It is difficult to live with an original man, that is certainly true. It is very difficult because it is difficult to grow. And with an original man growth happens. It is very easy to be with an imitator.

You must have read Thomas a Kempis' very well-known book, *"Imitation of Christ."* That can create only a good horse. You can look almost like Christ but you cannot be Christ. The only way to be Christ is to be yourself. Buddha is a Christ, Christ is a Buddha. A Buddhist monk trying to be Buddha is not Buddha – but Jesus, who never tried to be a Buddha, was a Buddha. When you are yourself, true to your being, you are a great soul – whatsoever you are. If you just are a wood-chopper, there is nothing to be worried about – be an original wood-chopper, be a real carpenter. That will do. You will attain to buddhahood through it. That will be your door. There is no need to become a great poet, you can be a cook – but be original. Imitation is the greatest calamity.

The old man said:

> "A good horse can be identified by its shape and look, its bone and muscle, but the great horses of the world might be extinct, vanished, perished, lost. Such horses raise no dust and leave no tracks."

Look at the beauty of this sentence. These parables are not just stories. They have great insight. *"Such horses raise no dust and leave no tracks."* A great horse is one who has no past and no future, who lives in the moment. That is the meaning of the sentence, *"Such horses raise no dust...."* When a great horse is coming you will not be able to see that he is coming because he will not raise any dust; you will not see a cloud of dust being raised. Only when he has come right in front of you will you be able to see him – but then it is too late. Then you cannot make arrangements. And a great horse leaves no tracks. You cannot follow a great horse, he leaves no tracks. No footprints are left.

This is the quality of a Buddha, a Christ. This is the quality of the great man. He is in the present. He is unpredictable. You cannot say what he is going to do or say or be. Nobody knows. He is always a surprise. He leaves no track behind. He is like a bird flying in the sky – the bird flies and no track, no trace, is left behind – no footprints.

There is a book, a very famous one, called *"The Footprints of Buddha."* The title is ugly because a buddha leaves no footprint. There are many books like that which show misunderstanding. Buddha leaves no footprints. He walks so carefully and so alertly that he leaves no footprints. You cannot follow him. He leaves no signs, no indications, no maps otherwise you will become imitators.

There is a story of a great Zen monk, Bokuju. When he was dying he called his disciples to bring all his books and all that he had said and all that he had written. Everything was piled up but for a while they couldn't see what he was doing. And then he made a fire out of it.

And they started screaming and shrieking and they said, "What are you doing?" Because in those days there were no printing presses, there were only hand-written books. So they were lost, lost forever.

Bokuju said, "I am going and I want to leave no trace behind. I must not leave any footprints. Now whosoever wants to follow me will have to follow himself. Whosoever wants to understand me will have to understand himself. I am throwing you, all my disciples, to yourself. That's why I am destroying these books."

Another story of a Zen monk....

When he was dying on his deathbed a Zen master called his chief disciple to him and took out a book from underneath his pillow. Everybody was always curious about the book because he had never allowed anybody to see it. And during the night people had sometimes peeped through the keyhole and he was reading it.

"What book is that? Why does he protect it so much?" And the master never left his room unlocked and he would never allow anybody in his room alone. So nobody had seen what the book contained.

Then he called his chief disciple and said, "Keep this book. In this book there is everything that I have taught. Preserve it as you have seen me preserve it. This was given to me by my master, now I give it to you. It is a heritage." And the disciple threw the book into the fire.

All the others could not believe it. They were aghast. But the master put his hand on the head of the disciple and blessed him. He said, "You have understood. If you had preserved the book you would not have been my disciple at all. In fact, there was nothing in the book. It was empty. You have thrown it away – good. You have understood, you have understood my teaching that nobody is to follow anybody; everybody has to go into his own soul."

> Such horses raise no dust and leave no tracks. All my sons have lesser talent – they can pick a good horse but not a great one.

So he said, "I suggest a man, Chiu-fang Kao, he is a judge of horses, as competent as myself, equal to me."

> Duke Mu saw the man and sent him away to find horses. After three months he returned and reported to the duke,
> "I have got one. It is in Sha-ch'iu."
> "What kind of horse?"
> "A mare, yellow."
> The duke sent someone to fetch it. It turned out to be a stallion, and black.

Now this is absurd! The man cannot be a judge of horses at all. He cannot even judge whether it is a stallion or a mare. And not only that – he cannot even judge whether it is black or yellow. This man is a blind man, he does not know anything about horses.

These are simple things. Anybody knows. No master is needed to judge whether a horse is yellow or black. Naturally the Duke was very displeased.

> ...summoned Po-lo. "He's no good, the fellow you sent to find me horses. He cannot even tell one color from another, or a mare from a stallion. What can he know about horses?"

Now something has to be understood. This is the Taoist approach about things. A mare means the feminine, a mare means yin quality. The Duke could not understand the man. The man is not talking about the body, the man *is talking* about the soul, the man is talking about the whole. The whole quality of the horse is that of yin – passive, receptive, womb-like. The whole quality of the horse is round, shapely, soft, with no corners. The whole quality of the horse is that of a beautiful woman – non-aggressive, non-violent, loving, compassionate. That's what he means when he says that the horse is a mare. He is not talking about the body, he is not talking about the physical, he is not talking about the part – he is talking about the whole. The totality of the horse is feminine.

Have you not watched it many times? You see a man and he looks very feminine and sometimes you see a woman and she looks very masculine. These are qualities. A buddha is so feminine; a buddha is a mare, not a stallion. That's how Nietzsche has criticized him – he called him feminine. Nietzsche also criticized Jesus by calling him feminine. He has criticized these two men saying that they have destroyed the whole masculinity of the world, the manliness. His criticism is true in a way. These two persons brought the feminine into the world, the feminine grace.

That's why you will never see a mustache on Buddha's statue. Not that he did not have one, but those who know the quality of great horses know how to paint a buddha. The body has not to be painted, the innermost core has to come out.

Have you not noticed it? Mahavira has no mustache ho beard; Rama has no mustache, no beard; Krishna has no mustache, no beard; Buddha has no mustache, no beard. All the great sages of India, all the *tirthankaras avataras*, have no beards and mustaches. Do you think there was something hormonally wrong with them? Do you think that they were effeminate, that they were sexually missing something, that they were not man enough? No. They were great sages. They had beards, they had mustaches but the people who painted them knew the qualities of a great horse. It has to be looked at in its totality.

In that way Jesus is not so fortunate. He could not find a real painter. If he had been born in India he would have been painted without a mustache and beard. The people who painted Jesus must have looked from the outside, they could not see the inner quality, the inner quality of the feminine.

By saying that the horse was a mare, this man, Chiu-fang Kao, said something of tremendous value. The horse is non-aggressive and Taoists say that when a person is non-aggressive he is unconquerable. When a person is aggressive he can be conquered – because a person who is aggressive depends on his own energy. All energies are limited and when a person is aggressive he is wasting his energies in aggression. Sooner or later he will be weakened by his own aggression, he will be defeated.

How was Adolf Hitler defeated? He was too aggressive. That became his defeat. Don't you see? All the great aggressive people were always defeated eventually. What happened? They exhausted their energies themselves. Adolf Hitler or Mussolini or Napoleon or Alexander all died frustrated, failures. What happened to them? They exhausted their energies by fighting, by being aggressive.

A buddha dies a conqueror. Without fighting he conquers. A Lao Tzu is victorious. Without making any effort his victory is ultimate.

The great horse has the quality of non-aggressiveness. Nobody can defeat him. That is the meaning of "mare."

And the color yellow is also very symbolic. It stands for a few things. First, yellow is the color of gold, the costliest metal. Gold has always been used as the highest value. Gold became an alchemical symbol. Turning baser metal into gold means turning the lower into the higher, turning the devil into the divine, turning the gross into the subtle.

When he said that the horse has the color yellow he meant he is a gold, not a baser metal. He is not talking about the color of the body, that is irrelevant. What difference can color make? Whether the horse is black or white or yellow, the color of the body cannot make any difference. How can the color make a horse great or not great? Whether a person is a Negro, Indian, Chinese or American – black, white yellow – how does it matter? The color of the skin is just irrelevant to the being. It is just a very cheap pigment.

If you ask the scientist he will say that between the blackest Negro and the whitest white man the difference is only near about four annas worth of pigment. Nothing much. It is just that a certain pigment exists in the Negro which does not exist in the white man. So in fact the white man is missing something. The Negro is something more. The Negro needs the black pigment to protect him from the sun, from the heat. Naturally he is more powerful. He can tolerate more heat and remain cool. He does not need to go to the hill-station. Wherever he is, he is cool. The white man is in trouble. He cannot tolerate heat. His tolerance is very low, his body *is* not so resistant.

But there is not much of a difference. And how is this difference going to make any difference as far as greatness is concerned? Whether Jesus is a Negro or a white man, how does it make any difference? It is irrelevant.

That is why the old man did not talk about the body color. He was using the alchemical symbol, gold. It is the highest quality, the purest quality.

Secondly, the yellow is symbolic of the sun – vitality radiance, aliveness, youth, life. So he is saying that the great horse is very much alive – as yellow as the sun, as vital as the sun.

And thirdly, yellow is the color of death. That is why Buddha has chosen yellow as the color for his *bhikkhus* for his *bhikkhus*. Their robes were yellow. Why? Why the color of death? When a leaf dies it becomes yellow, when anything dies it becomes yellow. Yellow is death approaching close by. Yellow is the shadow of death.

But why should it be told to the Duke that the horse is yellow? Because only if somebody accepts death totally is he fearless, otherwise not. The Buddhist monk has accepted death, has accepted yellow, the color of death, with great gratitude, with reverence. He is ready to die any moment, hence there is no fear. All fear is of death; behind all your fears there is death. Sooner or later, if you go on looking, you will find death standing behind all fears. So unless one is completely in deep acceptance with death, in harmony with death, one cannot be fearless.

The old man says that the color of the horse is yellow. He says that he is just like a Buddhist monk – he does not worry about death, hence he is fearless.

> The duke sent someone to fetch it. It turned out to be a stallion and black. The duke, displeased, summoned Po-lo. "He's no good, the fellow you sent to find me horses. He cannot even tell one color from another, or a mare from a stallion. What can he know about horses?"
> Po-lo breathed a sigh of wonder. "So now he has risen to this?"

This is the beauty of Tao. They are absurd people, very paradoxical, but if you start loving them you will know that they have a certain quality which is missing everywhere else.

Po-lo breathed a sigh of wonder. He could not believe it, it was incredible – because this means the ultimate in Tao. *"So now he has risen to this?"* He does not even make a judgment about whether the horse is a mare or a stallion – these distinctions are only on the surface – and he has reached to the deepest core.

Are you a man or a woman in your deepest being? If I see you as a man then I don't see you. If I see you as a woman then I don't see you. The day I see you neither as man nor woman but as your innermost quality reveals you.

> "So now he has risen to this! It is just this that shows that he is worth a thousand, ten thousand any number of people like me."

Now it is a qualitative jump. No quantity can be compared… *"He is worth a thousand, ten thousand, any number of people like me."* First this old man had said that he was equal to him but now he says, "I am nothing I am just zero compared to him."

So he has risen to this insight? He cannot see that the horse is black, he just sees the yellowness of the horse. And he cannot see that the horse is a stallion, he just sees the hidden mare in it. He has become able to see the bodiless qualities, the spiritual qualities. Now he is incomparable.

> "What such a man as Kao observes is the innermost native impulse behind the horse's movements."

The body is just a surface, a moving surface – just as when you watch a lake and see the ripples on the surface Those ripples are not the real lake. To know the real lake you will have to dive deep. The body is just a surface – moving changing. You have to look into the innermost core, into the unchanging, the constant, the unmoving. That is what truth is.

> "What such a man as Kao observes is the innermost native impulses behind the horse's movements. He grasps the essence and forgets the dross, goes right inside it and forgets the outside. He looks for and sees what he needs to see, ignores what he does not need to see. In the judgment of horses for a man like Kao there is something more important than horses.'

So he is not just a man who knows horses, now he knows something more. He knows real Tao. He has the insight to see the whole and not to be worried about the parts. He can see the gestalt, the very pattern, the innermost pattern, of the horse – now he is not worried about the body, the color, male, female. He is not worried at all. These are accidental things, non-essential. He looks only for that which is essential because only the essential is meaningful. The meaning comes from the essential but we always go looking for the accidental.

When you see a very rich man you say, "How rich he is." Now can a person be rich just by having money? You cannot be rich just by having money. If that is how a man is rich then Buddha is not rich. And if Buddha is not rich, then who is rich? Is Alexander rich? Alexander is a poor man, a beggar. Hence in the East we have worshipped beggars and forgotten about emperors. We have not cared much about the emperors. They come and go – that is the surface of existence, non-essential.

Have you come to know that in the East we have not written history at all? The West is very surprised that in the East people have not written history. History is so important.

No, we don't write history – or, we started writing it only because of the impact of the West. We write myths, we write mythology, we write *puranas*, beautiful parables. We don't bother about history because history is concerned with the non-essential, history is concerned with politics day-to-day events, politicians, generals, wars, famines. History is concerned with the very non-essential, the moving, the flux. Myth, mythology, a *purana*, is concerned with the essential.

So there is trouble when a Western person starts reading the *Ramayana*. He becomes worried about when Rama was born. When? That is not said at all. We have never bothered about it. What does it matter? Any day will do any year will do. That is not essential. We look into the innermost, we look into the essential quality of Rama. What type of man was he? What greatness did he carry in his being, what fragrance? What song was his song – authentically his? We are not worried about the chronological we are worried about the spiritual. Time is irrelevant. We look into the timeless.

That's why Po-lo says, *"In the judgment of horses of a man like Kao there is something more important than horses."* He has become a sage himself.

What does he look for first? He grasps the essence and forgets the gross. Remember it. When you look at a man or you look at a tree or you look at a rock, always look for the essential, forget the gross. The gross is not the thing. But in the modern world we forget the essence and look at the gross. If a man has much money, we look. If he has a big car, we look; if he has a big house, we look. We forget the essential. We don't look directly into his heart. We don't have the eyes. In fact we don't believe that he has a heart, we don't believe that man has a soul. Man is just a body, a physical thing, and so is everything else.

So it is not a wonder that our life has become so dull. It has become a drag. There is no joy, no celebration. How can celebration exist without a soul? Celebration arises out of the soul out of the spiritual out of the essential. Joy arises out of your innermost core and we have denied that.

You don't look into yourself and you don't look into others. Only surfaces meet. In fact, it is not right to say, "meet" – they clash, because there is no dialogue. There is discussion but there is no dialogue. There is argument but there is no meeting, there is no love – because love can exist only between two souls. When two essential beings look into each other's essentiality, love arises. When you look through your essential core into the essential core of existence, God arises.

Don't ask where God is. God is a dialogue with existence, God is not a being, God is not a person. When you know how to be in a dialogue with existence, you know what God *is*. God is the meaning of existence, the meaning that permeates the whole. But it can be known only by moving through the essential. The essential is the door.

Kao looks and grasps the essence and forgets the gross. He looks into the innermost native impulses, he looks into the spontaneity of the horse, not at what has been cultivated in him.

Not in the character.... A man may be a saint or he may be a sinner. Don't look into the sainthood of a man and don't look into the sinnerhood of a man – look into the potentiality of his being. And then you will come to see that nobody is a sinner, nobody is a saint, everybody is a sage. Everybody is divine – sinners and saints, all. Then whatsoever a person is doing is not of much importance. Being is important. What you do is very irrelevant, what you are is relevant. Your acts are superficial, your being is fundamental.

"He looks for and sees what he needs to see." You don't look for that which you need to see. Whatsoever comes in front of you – the objectum – whatsoever comes in front of you, you look at it. You are not searching. Whatsoever accidentally comes in front of you, you look at it. You don't go deep, you don't explore any potentiality, you don't dive. You just stand outside. At the most you are a spectator.

But life can be known only through participation. Don't be a spectator. The whole modern world has become just a spectator, a crowd of lookers-on. Somebody dances, you look at it. What are you doing? How can you look at a dance? A dance has to be felt, a dance has to be danced. Somebody is singing and you look and you listen. To know the song and the beauty of it you have to sing, you have to participate. But this calamity has taken epidemic proportions. You go on looking at everything.

You rush to the movie – for what? Can't you live a beautiful life? Why do you have to go to see a movie? People are glued to their chairs in front of their TV's just looking at other people's living. And they are not even living, they are acting for you. They are acting for you and you are seeing those actors – and nobody is living. The dancer is not a true dancer, he is a professional and you are the audience. All is false.

Surfaces clash and the essentials are not meeting. Look for the essential. When you start looking for the essential you will become a participant. You will know. A dance has to be known in only one way – that is to dance. How can you know what swimming is if you just stand on the bank and you watch somebody swimming? You will see the strokes and you will see the man doing something in the water but how will you know the thrill that is happening to him, the kick that is happening to him, the sensation, the buoyancy, the joy? The feeling of the river, flowing with the river, dancing with the river – how will you know it by standing on the bank? Jump into the river, that is the only way to know life. Jump into the river. Never be a spectator. The spectator is the poorest man in the world. Participate. Through participation comes love, through participation comes truth, through participation comes beauty, through participation ultimately comes God.

> "In the judgment of horses of a man like Kao there is something more important than horses."

Yes, in this parable horses are not discussed, horses are just an excuse to talk about something tremendously important and significant.

> When the horse arrived it did prove to be a great horse.

You can also become great horses and you can also become knowers of great horses.

But remember, this parable is not about horses; horses are just an excuse. The parable is about the sage, the Taoist sage, the great sage.

Meditate over it. Let it sink deep in you. It will give you many insights, many more than I have talked about. You will get many more insights, because there are many which cannot be talked about at all. They will be revealed only when you meditate on it. You will get many more, because when you meditate you will certainly meditate in a different way – from your angle, from your vision.

I have just given you a few indications. These are not fixed rules. I am not an interpreter – remember always, I am not an interpreter. I love these stories and I try to share my love with you. It is not an interpretation. I am not a commentator Commentary is an ugly job – why should I comment? I am not commenting. I love these stories, I feel the fragrance of these stories and I like to share that fragrance with you.

Maybe through that fragrance you also become interested. Maybe listening to me a great desire in you arises to go deeper into the waters. If that is done then my effort has been fruitful.

So don't take my interpretations as rigid interpretations and don't think that I have done the job for you. I cannot chew for you, you will have to chew for yourself. I can simply seduce you.

These are seductions, not commentaries – just seductions so you become interested in a different dimension. And each Taoist parable opens a dimension, opens a new door. If you go into it, more doors will open and if you go into those doors, even more will open. It is a non-ending mystery.

Enough for today.

CHAPTER #14

The Ego on the Tip of the Nose

The first question:

Osho,
You say, "You can also become a great horse." Even though I am twenty-six I am seeking. Am I not trying to become a good horse? Can one become a great horse by seeking?

Never! Never can one become a great horse by seeking. Seeking is the only barrier to realizing your greatness. The very idea of seeking sends you away from yourself. Seeking means seeking somewhere else. Seeking means seeking outside. Seeking means you are looking everywhere else except in your own being. Non-seeking means not looking anywhere, just being centered in your being, just being there. When you are not seeking you are in your own being. In that very moment you are a great horse.

Everybody is a great horse – the good ones and the bad ones too. The bad ones have gone seeking along the bad lines and the good ones have gone seeking along the good lines. The bad ones have become criminals, immoral, and the good ones have become moral, saintly – but both are seeking. Both are always on the way. There is a goal in their life. And they are rushing away from themselves.

Everybody is born a great horse. When you become tired and frustrated with your seeking you drop all seeking to be good or to be bad. Then you just close your eyes and it is there, the great horse is there. It has been always there, it is your nature.

Nobody is born who is not great. Nothing else ever happens in this existence except greatness – because it is out of God. How can you not be great? You are great. Greatness will not be a real greatness – deep down you know that you are not great, deep down you know that you have practiced it, deep down you know that it is just on the surface, a mask. You are pretending that you are Alexander, pretending that you are Christ, pretending that you are a buddha, pretending this and that.

You can pretend, you can deceive the whole world, but how can you deceive yourself? You will always know who you are. You may be pretending to be brave but deep down you are a coward. You have hidden your cowardice by painting bravery on top of it. You may be smiling but hidden behind are tears. How can you deceive yourself?

So the first thing to remember is that nobody has ever come home by seeking. Seeking means going astray. Only non-seekers come home. But to become a non-seeker one has first to become a seeker. Seeking is a part, a part of attaining non-seeking. Even a buddha has to seek and go astray and suffer. That pain is a must. That is the price we pay. Then one day, when you have sought in every direction, in every dimension, and nowhere have you found anything that you wanted, when your frustration is utterly total, in that very moment of frustration all seeking drops. Suddenly you are back home. But to come home one has to knock on many doors.

So I am not saying you should drop your seeking – unless you are utterly confused, utterly frustrated. If you are still hankering, if there is still hope lurking somewhere in your mind that you can find by seeking, then seek, seek by all means – even though nobody has ever attained by seeking. I will say, "Seek. Seek by all means – so that you can be frustrated, so that you can recognize the hopelessness of the very effort." In that hopelessness is hope, in that frustration dances a totally new existence – the world of being. Seeking is the world of becoming.

To me you are already great horses. I have never come across anybody who is not a great horse. He may think he is not – that is his problem. He may think or even believe that he is not.... And people behave according to their beliefs. If you believe you are not a great horse you will behave in a way that is suitable to one who is not a great horse. If you believe you are bad you will behave in that way. If you believe you are good you will behave in that way.

But your pretensions are your pretensions, your acting. I see your original face, I see you as you are. The day I saw my own great horse, that very day all other kinds of horses disappeared for me. I look into every face, into every eye, and the great horse is there. The same horse that exists in me exists in you, there are not two horses – it is the same greatness. It is the same ocean that waves in you and that waves in me, that waves in a Buddha, in a Christ, in a Krishna.

But when you are seeking, you cannot look inside yourself. Seeking means you have moved into the future; seeking means you have already gone to the goal; seeking means you have already reached where you believe you have to be. It is a projection, it is a fantasy trip, it is a mind-journey. Non-seeking means that mind has stopped; non-seeking means that there is no movement inside you, you are not going anywhere.

> Sitting silently,
> Doing nothing.
> The spring comes
> And the grass grows by itself.

The second question:

Osho,
If groups are a safer and more stimulating place to begin to expand any conceivable, personal boundaries, why have you not encouraged the creation of Indian groups with Indian leaders?

This foolish question comes again and again so it is better to be finished with it.

The first thing: the East has developed a totally different kind of psychology than the West. The needs are different. Different medicines are needed.

In the West the psychology that has grown down the ages is extrovert; it is outgoing. The psychology that has been developed in the East is introvert; it is ingoing. For a real Eastern person growth groups are not needed. He needs meditations like *vipassana* or *zazen* – *zen* in which he can forget the whole outside world and just drown in his own being. He does not need any relationship. Relating is not needed. He needs only to unrelate himself from the world, to be in a state of total, utter aloneness. Deep solitude is needed.

Down the centuries the East has developed introversion; it is very natural for the real Eastern person to be introverted. I am saying the *real* Eastern person because it is very difficult to find a real Eastern person. The West has contaminated everybody. The Western education, the Western victory over nature, the Western domination of the East, has contaminated everybody. The real Eastern mind does not have any need to do any growth groups.

The growth group is needed because you have a tremendous need to relate, to love, to communicate. In the West the basic problem is how to communicate, how to relate. Many Westerners are here. When they come to me in darshan their problems are a hundred per cent relationship problems – how to relate.

Not even a single Indian has come who has said, "How to relate?" That is not a problem at all. He says, "How to be silent? How to be into one's own being?" His question is how to drop out of relationship. He wants to be non-attached, he wants to break all the bridges that exist. He wants to know how to live in the world and yet live in such a way that he does not live there, he is far away in the Himalayas. Even if one has to live in the world one wants to live in the world of the Himalayas – at least spiritually, inwardly. Not a single Indian comes who says, "This is my problem – how to relate to my wife, how to relate to my son, how to relate to my mother, how to relate to my friend." Relationship is a question of group dynamics. The Indian asks, "How not to relate? How to forget my wife, how to forget my children, how to forget my job, how to be just alone in my inner being – crystal-pure, clean, non-reflecting, with not even a shadow moving there?"

This is a different psychology. Both are ways to reach the ultimate: one is meditation, another is love. The East has developed the mind for meditation, the West has developed the mind for love. Love means relationship, meditation means non-relationship.

That's why I do not send Easterners to groups – except Japanese. I have sent a few Japanese because Japan is the most Western part of the East. I have sent Indians only once or twice – and these were only name's-sake Indians. They have been born in the East but their mind has not been developed by the Eastern concept, their mind is Western. They have been taught by Christian missionaries in Christian schools. Their whole education and up-bringing is Western.

This is the first thing to understand. The West will move through love easily and through love will come to itself. It is a longer way. Meditation is a short-cut. Love means: "I go into the other, see my face in the eyes of the other, encounter the other – and in encountering the other, I come to know about myself. And then I come back. It is via the other but I come back to myself." Love also comes to the inner solitude but it is a long way. It goes through the other. It is a big circle.

Meditation is a short way, it reduces everything to the minimum. You don't go to the other; you simply close your eyes and you drown yourself in yourself. You drop into your own being.

Both are perfectly right. It depends on the person – on what he needs. To a few Westerners also I don't suggest groups. When I see some Westerner who has no need to relate then I don't suggest groups, then I say there is no need.

But at least five thousand years of different psychological conditioning exists. That has to be taken note of. I cannot say the Easterner and the Westerner are just the same – they are not. At the innermost core they are, in their being they are, but in their minds they are not. Their approach is different. They need different methodology.

If a Westerner comes and I put him directly into *vipassana-like* methods he is simply at a loss, he cannot understand what is happening. It is a torture. He feels as if he is simply a masochist – why is he torturing himself? Why is he sitting in a *siddhasana* in a Buddha posture, with closed eyes? For what? The Western mind wants to move, relate, dance, sing, celebrate. The Western mind is dynamic. It wants some process – so that it can go step by step into things. One day the Western mind has to come to a silent, meditative state but it has first to go through growth groups. Then it becomes easier.

If he is sent to a growth group the Eastern person will simply be at a loss. Even Japanese are at a loss. There have been questions from Japanese like: "Osho, why do you send us to growth groups? You don't send Indians, why do you send us?" They don't feel good, they feel very worried. It is very difficult for them to relate the way a Western person can relate. They are not open that way. And they don't see the point of it. They don't see any point. Why go into it? When you know a short-cut then why go a long way? The East has known the short-cut always but in the West it has been different.

Here is a question: "What is the difference between an enlightened person, a Master, and a Messiah?" which is relevant to this question. An enlightened person is one who has come home, for whom all problems have disappeared, who has no problems to solve, who has just to live, whose life is no longer burdened by any question, whose life is absolutely weightless. But every enlightened person is not necessarily a master. Out of a hundred enlightened persons at the most one or two will become masters. An enlightened person is one who has come home and a master is one who has compassion for others and would like to help them. But a master is one who is interested only in individuals, he relates to individuals – one here, one there – he has no idea about society. This is a master.

A Messiah is one who has compassion for the whole society. He is not worried about individuals but takes the whole society as one unit. In the East enlightened people have existed and masters have existed but never a Messiah. The Messiah is not an Eastern concept at all. Buddha is not a Messiah, neither is Mahavira, nor Krishna. They are masters, perfect masters; their approach is to the individual, direct, personal. Jesus is a Messiah, so is Moses, so is Mohammed. Their approach is not individual, their approach is social, communal. They are interested in changing the whole lot of humanity. Judaism, Christianity, Islam, are all messianic; Hinduism, Buddhism, Jainism, are non-messianic.

All the basic Eastern religions say that the society does not exist – only the individual exists. And all the Western religions say that the individual is just a part of society; the real thing is the society, the group. The group exists, not the individual. The individual only exists in the group. Both are right in a way because both are half-right. The individual and society both exist – the individual cannot exist without a society nor can the society exist without the individual. Can you conceive of a society where no individual exists? There would be no society at all. Can you conceive of an individual who exists without a society? There would be no individual at all.

Even an individual who exists in the Himalayas, alone, even he exists in the society. He was born to a mother, he was brought up by a father, he lived in a society. Even the idea that one has to renounce all and go to the Himalayas was given by a particular society. Now sitting there in the Himalayas what is he doing? He must be meditating. That meditation was given by Patanjali or Buddha. What will he be doing?

He will be thinking of God, contemplating. That God comes from the society. And in the deepest core of his being he knows that the society exists. If he suddenly comes to know one day that the society he had left has disappeared completely from the earth, he will be shocked, he will be shaken, he will start trembling, perspiring. He will run back to the place to see what has happened to the society. Although he was living alone, in a subtle way he was still part of society.

No individual can exist without society; no society can exist without individuals. So both are true. But the approaches are different.

Jesus says that the whole society can attain to salvation. If people want to move in groups, in communes, they can attain to salvation. Buddha will say that is not possible. Each has to move alone, each has to move in his own, each has to reach God in solitude. No group can move. Hence all sorts of social philosophies have come out of Christianity but in the East no social philosophy has been born yet.

Communism comes out of Christianity. It is the same messianic idea. Although communism says there is no God and religion is the opium of the people, still it grows out of the same idea: that the society is important and can attain to a higher state. The individual is irrelevant. Fascism, socialism democracy, or other ideologies, are all born in the West they are all part of the same messianic ideal. The "Messiah" is a Western idea – that the society can have salvation, that the group can become enlightened as a group.

In the East, masters have existed but no Messiah. Jesus had a little tinge of politics in his utterances, maybe that's why he was crucified. Buddha was never crucified because the society was never much troubled with him. He was not talking about the society at all, he was talking about individuals. If you go on changing individuals the society can rest – there is nothing to be worried about. But when a person says he is going to change the whole society then there is fear.

Maybe that is the reason why Socrates was poisoned, Mansoor was killed, Jesus was crucified. No Buddha, no Mahavira, no Krishna was killed or crucified or poisoned. Why? There must be some reason. They were very dangerous people – more dangerous than Jesus, or at least as dangerous as Jesus, but their approach was individual. The society does not bother about individuals. If one individual becomes a meditator it doesn't change a whole society. It is as if a drop of water is changed in the whole ocean – who bothers? But Jesus had a program to color the whole ocean. Then the priest and the politicians all became afraid; their investment was at stake and they were being overthrown. They were being dethroned, they were being uprooted.

The Messiah naturally has something to do with politics; the master has nothing to do with politics. That becomes a problem. Christian missionaries used to come to me and say, "It is good to help people to meditate, but what about society? What are you doing for the society? People are hungry, starving, ill. Why don't you think about making more hospitals, schools? Why don't you help people to help others? Just meditating? Yes, it is good, a person becomes silent, but is it enough?" I can understand why they are asking the question. The question comes from the messianic ideal, the Messiah. A master has to be a Messiah.

In the East, no. In the East a master is simply a master. His approach is individual, his approach is meditative rather than political, personal rather than social. The East has one psychology, the West has a different psychology. This has to be understood once and for all.

"If groups are a safer, more stimulating place to begin to expand any conceivable personal boundaries, why have you not encouraged the creation of Indian groups with Indian leaders?"

That would not be possible. Even if I have to create a group for Indians the leaders would be Western. First: it would be difficult to find Indian participants and if I can manage that – because there are a few people who are no longer Eastern or only so-so – then too the leader has to be Western. It will be very difficult to find an Eastern group-leader because he will not have idea of it, he will not have the nuance of it, he will not have the real spirit of it. Yes, he can run a group but it will be mechanical. He will not be a Teertha, he will not be a Somendra, he will not be a Divya – he will not have that insight. He will not be Amitabh, he will not be Anam – no, he will lack the insight. Those insights take centuries to develop.

It is happening in other fields also. The scientist is basically a Western by-product. There are Indian scientists – one or two have even got a Nobel prize – but still I have never come across a real scientist in the East, never. The mind is not scientific. They learn, they put their intelligence to it, they learn all that can be learned, but the spirit is lacking. If you look into their personal life you will not find them scientific. Their approach will be non-scientific. When they are in their lab they may become scientific but when you go into their house you will find them doing *puja*, worshipping a statue, or saying a mantra and crying.

In the lab they may be objective but when they are in their home they are no longer objective. There they will be as superstitious as any ordinary person. They may even go and follow Satya Sai Baba, and think that miracles are possible. There are such people!

Now this is very unscientific. A scientist cannot believe that miracles are possible. No miracles are possible – that is a fundamental law of science. Everything is according to the law and a miracle is something which is not according to the law. So how is a miracle possible? A miracle means something is happening which should not happen. Science cannot trust it. If it is happening then it must be according to a law which has not been discovered yet. Then it is not a miracle. Or maybe there is some magic, some trick, some sleight of hand – it is simple, for the scientific mind it is simple. But you can find Indian scientists following Satya Sai Baba and believing that things are appearing out of nothingness.

Their mind is not scientific, their mind is centuries old – and the scientific layer is very thin. They have gone to the West, they have been to Oxford, to Cambridge, they have learned everything, they are intelligent people – but they are not scientific. They may have even discovered something, they may have been given a Nobel prize, but still they are not scientific. At the most they are technical – they know the technique. But if you look deep into them you will find the Eastern religious person who can believe in anything – a believer, gullible – you will not find real logic. All logic will be just superficial.

As far as their work is concerned they will be logical but as far as their life is concerned you will see them going to the palmist or to the astrologer. If their son is getting married they will not bother about any scientific approach towards it, they will go to the astrologer to inquire whether the marriage will succeed or not, whether the couple will be happy or not.

Now a scientific person should go to a scientist to inquire whether the blood specimens mix, whether the hormones go together. He should ask a computer. A computer should be fed with all the information about both the persons and the computer should show what is going to be the outcome of these two persons meeting. Will they suit each other? That will be more scientific than going to an astrologer who will look at their birth chart and who will think about stars and who will decide according to stars. And this scientist will never look at what is happening to the astrologer himself – at him and his wife. They are killing each other!

The Eastern mind is basically non-scientific. One can learn science but to be a scientist one needs a totally different spirit.

And something similar happens in the West. The Western person can become religious, can learn, can come to the East can become religious, but deep down the scientific approach persists. He goes on being logical. Sometimes it happens that books are written about Zen. Zen is an illogical approach, an absurd approach, fundamentally Eastern, and in the West books are written about Zen explaining the illogic in a logical way, trying to find out what the logic of this illogicality is! There must be some logic in it. They are trying to find explanations and they find them – when you insist you can always find. You can fill in the gaps, you can see things which are not there. Zen is simply illogical; there is no logic to it.

So if you read Western books written about Zen there is logic. They may say that Zen is illogical but then immediately they will explain why. They will always try to bring things to reason. Rationalization is the Western approach; the East is irrational.

So it is possible that we could train some Indian to be a group-leader but he would be just a phony group-leader, he would not be able to go deep into it. And he would not be able to be there authentically. Something would be missing.

And, moreover there are many who would like to go out of curiosity they go on asking again and again why Indians are not allowed. I can allow you but you will simply be disturbed. You will come out of it shaken, completely shaken, and there is more possibility that you will escape from me and you will never come back again because you will never be able to figure out what this is. You cannot relate it to religion at all.

Somebody is being angry and beating the pillow or beating the wall and getting mad. The Indian will sit there and he will say, "What is going on?" What is the point of it all? How is this man going to become meditative by being mad? These things have to be dropped. And for these things one must come to a group and pay for it? One can do these things at home. How is this man going to be helped by being so angry, so aggressive, so violent? The Indian cannot understand it because the Indian has not suffered two thousand years of Christianity. He does not know what Christianity has done to the West. Two thousand years of repression. That repression has gathered in the pit of the stomach, it is heavy there, it has not been allowed out. Everything has been forced.

When Vivek came here for the first time she was not even able to burp! Repressed, absolutely repressed. Burping is a beautiful thing but in the West you don't burp! From the very childhood a child has to be taught "Don't burp." What nonsense! In the East we have a totally different concept. If you are invited to a feast at somebody's house and you don't burp, it is insulting. That means you are not satisfied.

In my childhood I used to go with my father. He is a great burper. Whenever he went to somebody else's house he would burp loudly. So I asked him, "Why do you do it that much? You never do it that much at home?" He said, "It has to be done otherwise the people will think that we are not satisfied." The burp gives a satisfactory expression. It says the stomach is full and it is perfectly satisfied and it is happy. It is a physical expression.

I was reading one of Janov's books in which he gives a few certificates from his patients who have been helped by primal therapy. In one certificate one patient says, "I am very, very thankful to you because after primal therapy I began to burp for the first time in my life." He said that it was amazing. I also say it is amazing. Primal therapy is needed to help you to burp! Such a repression!

You don't know what a calamity has happened to the Western mind. Everything has been forced. You have to be loving and love has disappeared. You have not to be angry and anger has gone deep in the pit of the stomach – it is there solid like a rock. You have to go on smiling, you have to show a face to everybody – this is the etiquette. Falsity, phoniness has been taught. That phoniness has to be dropped before one can enter into meditation.

For the Eastern mind there is not such a problem. Phoniness has never been taught. So it is very difficult – if I send an Indian to the group he may even start being phony by trying to be angry. He will say, "Everybody is doing that so it has to be done." He will move to the other extreme – it has to be done because everybody is doing it and they are being helped and they are growing and they are enjoying it and they are feeling so ecstatic. "I will miss something if I don't do it" – and he will start doing it. He will be simply tired, exhausted. He will come out of it simply feeling spent, not expanded. That's why I have not allowed it.

And then he will go and start creating rumors all around – that is one of the basic curiosities. Again and again Indians ask why I am not allowing them to do the groups. Their curiosity is because they want to see what is happening there. If somebody becomes nude that will be something! The Indian will enjoy that nudity more than anything else. And he will go and spread the news all over and exaggerate as much as he can – in that, Indians are perfect masters! And that will create trouble for the groups, that's all.

The last thing: the West is how-oriented, the East is why-oriented. "How" means methodology, technique; "why" means no method, no technique, no effort. The West is effort-oriented, the East is effortlessness. The whole approach of the East is how to relax to know; the Western approach is how to strain, to concentrate to know, how to be more attentive to know. The Eastern approach is how to be so relaxed that there is nothing – a sort of euphoria, no concentration, a sort of vagueness, a cloudiness where boundaries disappear and distinctions are no more valid, where each thing meets and merges into each other thing. When all boundaries are blurred in that vague, void, distinctionless cloud, one comes to know. Methods are to clarify. The West has no vision of the "why" and the East has no provision for the "how."

But now things are getting mixed up. East is no more East, West is no more West. People are traveling, people are being educated here and there, people are coming to the East to learn religion, people are going to the West to learn science everything is meeting and merging.

You must have heard the famous lines of Rudyard Kipling: "West is West, East is East, and the twain shall never meet." They are meeting. In the days of Kipling it was almost certain that they would never meet. They are meeting. Things change. That which cannot be conceived becomes conceivable. East and West are meeting.

There is only one problem and only one fear – that Rudyard Kipling may prove right from the other side. The problem is the West can become so Eastern and the East so Western that again they may not meet. That's the only problem. The East may become West, the West may become East, and the twain shall never meet. That is possible. That's why there are not many Eastern people here. I am saying something that the East is no longer interested in. You will find many Eastern students at Harvard, you will find many Eastern students at Oxford, sitting at the feet of a scientist, learning from a scientist, but you will not find very many Eastern people sitting at the feet of a mystic and learning about meditation. And you will find Western people rushing there – a great pilgrimage has started.

You are coming from the West, dropping out of the Oxfords and the Cambridges and the Harvards in search of an inner space, and the Eastern young man is rushing towards the West to know more about technology, engineering, chemistry, physics, mathematics. There is a danger.

It happened once that in a small town there was a great atheist and a great theist. Both were great. And the whole town was disturbed and puzzled.

The atheist would prove to everyone that there was no God, and his arguments were superb. Then the theist would prove that there was a God, and his arguments were also superb. So the village was in a very difficult situation. What to decide? The whole village was confused. For twenty-four hours, day in, day out, these two persons were contradicting each other and the whole village came to a point where they started feeling they would go mad. Both the arguments were so superb it was difficult to decide. They were almost equal. They negated each other. But then the people were left with a vacuum.

Just to save their sanity the village decided to ask these two persons to have a great debate and convince each other. Either the atheist must become a theist or the theist must become an atheist – whatsoever they decide the village will follow. But it had to be decided. They had had enough of indecision.

So a great debate was arranged and the atheist proved that there was no God and the theist proved that there was a

God and by the morning a strange thing happened. The theist became convinced that there was no God and the atheist became convinced that there was a God. The problem remained the same and the village was still in confusion.

It is possible that the West may become East and the East may become West and again there will be the same polarity.

This has to be avoided. For the first time it has become feasible to create one world, for the first time it is practically possible to create one earth. For the first time it is possible to drop the concepts of East and West and create a new third psychology – I call it the "Psychology of the Buddha's." I am trying that.

But I have to look to your past. The whole goal here is to create a meditative space. How it is created is irrelevant. If you need group processes I will give you group processes, but the meditative space has to be created. If you don't need group processes, if you need simple meditations, I will give you simple meditations, but the meditative space has to be created. Only in that meditative space will the East and West disappear, will the Eastern and the Western psychology disappear, will the division disappear.

A great experiment is afoot. You may not be aware of how fortunate you are. You may not be aware that something of tremendous import is happening here, something which can become the door to a great synthesis. A great Tao can arise. We can attain to the primordial unity.

The groups are meant to destroy the Western psychology and the simple meditative techniques are meant to destroy the Eastern psychology. When both are dropped then you are human, neither Eastern nor Western. In fact, then you are just existential, with no mind. That no-mind is the goal.

The third question:

Osho,
I have decided to take sannyas although I don't know for what reason I am doing it. Can you throw some light on it?

If you have decided then what is the point of knowing the reason? If you have already decided to take sannyas then why this hankering to know the reason? Has there always to be a reason for everything you do? Is it really needed? Have you done everything in your life because of certain reasons?

This is again the Western mind, the Western psychology. There has to be a reason – otherwise why, why should you take it? Can't you take any step without a reason? If you cannot, you will not be able to live, because life is irrational it has no reason. Why are you here at all? Can you show any reason why you are here? Why were you born? Why do you breathe? Why do you love? Why are you happy? Why are you sad? For what?

Because of this "why," this constant hankering to know the reason, the West has become very suicidal. Then arises the problem of why to live at all. What is the reason? When you feel that there is no reason to live then why not commit suicide?

But I must tell you. There was a great Greek philosopher Xenon. He used to teach his people that there was no reason to live. But he lived to a very old age – eighty-nine years. He lived long. And it is said that many people committed suicide because of his teaching. He was saying, "There is no reason why you should go on living. Every morning getting up, again going to bed, again getting up…for what?" He puzzled many people.

If you really ask "why" deeply there is no "why." You will be left with only a very uneasy space within you – why? And Xenon was a great scholar and a great logician. He proved to people that there is no reason to live. Somebody asked him, "But why do you go on living?" He said, "I have to live to teach people that there is no reason to live. This is my reason."

When he was dying – at eighty-nine – somebody asked him on his deathbed, "It is very puzzling and confusing that you lived so long because for at least fifty years you have been teaching that there is no reason to live." He said, "That's true, but I could not find the reason to commit suicide either. For what?"

Now look at this man. His life must have been a tremendous misery. You have no reason to live and you have no reason to die.

I have heard.

A young man approached an old Jew. He was in love with the old Jew's daughter. He said to the old man, "Sir, I want to get married to your daughter."

The old man looked at him and, as Jews are prone to ask, he said, "But, young man, what are your reasons? Why do you want to get married to my daughter?"

The young man shrugged his shoulders and said, "No reasons at all. I am in love."

"No reasons at all. I am in love." Love needs no reason.

Sannyas should be a love affair. You should not ask for reasons otherwise sannyas will become very mundane.

When you go to the market and you purchase something, certainly there must be a reason for it. You go to the market to purchase a car. It is a commodity. There must be some reason for it. You need it. It is a utility. But if you fall in love with a woman or a man there is no utility. What utility has love? What use has love? You look at a roseflower and you are thrilled. What is the reason for being thrilled? What is there? You look at the moon and something in you simply gets connected with it, something starts changing in your being, you feel a coolness. What is the reason? If you look for the reason you will destroy all beauty, love, truth, God meditation – everything.

Please leave a few things in life which have no reasons. Let sannyas be one of those few things.

But I understand. The Western urge is to make everything rational, to find a reason for every act – otherwise you will feel uneasy. So you try to find some kind of rationalization. Reason there is none, but rationalization you can find. You can invent it. Why be bothered to ask me? You can invent a rationalization: it is because you want to search for truth, because you want to go in search of God, because you want to attain to self-realization or you want to become enlightened. These are all excuses, all rationalizations.

A stranger stopped at Mulla Nasruddin's store for cigarettes. On the wall was a sign: "This store will be closed on August 28th on account of the weather." As it was only August 15th, the man asked the Mulla how he could know what the weather would be like so far in advance. "Well," said Nasruddin, "if it rains lightly, I am going fishing. If it rains heavy, I am going to stay home and work on my tackle."

"But how do you know it's going to rain?" asked the man.

"Don't care if it rains or not," explained Nasruddin. "If it's sunny I will go fishing or work on my tackle anyway. All depends on the weather."

You can find something. "All depends on the weather." You can find a rationalization, an excuse.

If you have decided, let this decision be pure – uncorrupted by any reason. Look at the beauty of what I am saying. If you can do something without any reason it means you can do something without the mind coming in. If you can do something without reason that means you have done something out of no-mind. If you can do something without reason that means something has happened, you have not done it. Let sannyas be a happening. Why bother about reasons?

You must have fallen in love with my orange people. You must have fallen in love with me, you must have fallen in love with the space that is being created here. Let it be a love affair, don't bring reason in. And then your sannyas will go deeper. It can go very deep. It can transform you. With reason it will be superficial. It is for you to choose.

If you want a reason you can find one but my feeling is: try to be courageous, sometimes do something which has no reason at all. You could have avoided it, you could have managed not to do it, but still you allowed it to happen. Let something bigger than you happen to you. You cannot figure out what it is. Going into the unknown is sannyas. Going into the unfamiliar, the uncharted, is sannyas. Going into that without making arrangements about where you are going, for what, just going, as if pulled in by some greater power than you, is sannyas.

The fourth question:

Osho,
Does the man of Tao like to taste many women or does he stay with one until he is able to eat the master?

The first thing: for the man of Tao there is not many and one. For the man of Tao all women are one woman – because the man of Tao looks at the energy and not at the form. For the man of Tao one woman is different from another woman only because of the frame – the sky is the same. For the man of Tao there is feminine energy and masculine energy, yin and yang – whether you stand at one window and look at the sky or you stand at another window and look at the same sky makes no difference. So the first thing is that all women are one woman because there is only one feminine energy. It is one sky framed in different windows.

The second thing: for the man of Tao one woman is all women because when you look from a window into the sky if you are not too much obsessed with the frame it is the same sky, it is one sky. So one woman is all women and all women are one woman for the man of Tao – because a man of Tao thinks in terms, contemplates in terms of energies not of forms. He thinks in terms of the formless. When I look into you I am not bothered at all by the frame you exist in, I look at the painting, I don't look at the frame. The frames differ but the painting is the same. It is the one God, the same one sky.

And for the man of Tao, in fact, the man and the woman also start disappearing by and by. There is only one energy – call it xyz. Taoists call it Tao. It means nothing. It means x. There is only one energy, Tao. It functions in two ways, man and woman. It is the same energy. It has to create a polarity to function otherwise it will not be able to function at all.

These two hands of mine are same energy. I am in both. But if I want to clap them I can clap them, I can put them against each other. I can hit my right hand with my left, or I can love my left hand with my right. But I am flowing in both hands. I am Tao. The right hand is yang, the left hand is yin. You are Tao. The masculine is your right hand, the feminine is your left hand. Now you can create either a clash between the two or you can create a harmony between the two. But whether it is a clash or a harmony, the energy remains the same.

The man who has attained to Tao has gone beyond man and woman. He is Tao.

The fifth question – and now for the bombshell:

Osho,
Lieh Tzu never existed, right?

Whether Lieh Tzu existed or not does not matter. Right or wrong, it does not matter at all. Western scholars have been very puzzled about Lieh Tzu – about whether he ever existed or not. There are great treatises. They worked hard for years to find out whether this man really existed. To the Eastern mind this whole scholarship looks stupid because it does not matter whether he existed or not. If you ask me whether he existed or not I say it is all the same. Whosoever wrote these beautiful stories was Lieh Tzu – whosoever. One thing is certain: somebody wrote these beautiful stories. That much is certain because these stories exist.

Now, whether somebody of the name of Lieh Tzu really wrote these stories or somebody of some other name wrote them, how does it make any difference? It will not add anything to the stories, they are perfect. It will not take anything away from the stories, nothing can be taken away. Whether Lieh Tzu was a historical person or not, how is it going to affect these stories? These stories are so beautiful, they have intrinsic value. One thing is certain: somebody wrote them – but why be bothered about what his name was, whether it was Lieh Tzu or something else?

It is possible that they were written by many people then too there is no problem. Whosoever wrote one of these stories must have touched the consciousness of Tao, otherwise they could not have been written. One man may have written them or many men, but whenever these stories were written somebody had penetrated in to the Tao consciousness, somebody had understood what life is, somebody had had a vision.

In the West this is very significant. People go on writing books and books about whether Shakespeare ever existed or not. As if it makes any difference. The plays that Shakespeare wrote are so beautiful – why not look into the plays and love and enjoy them? This seems to be going astray to ask whether Shakespeare existed or not. And the problem arises because it is thought that Shakespeare was an uneducated man so how could he write such beautiful things? Have you ever known very educated men to write beautiful things?

It is thought that it was not Shakespeare but Lord Bacon who was the real author. But I cannot trust this because I have read Lord Bacon's other books – they have nothing to compare with Shakespeare. Lord Bacon is just ordinary. He may have been a very learned man, he may have been a great scholar, but his books are ordinary, rubbish. Just because he is Lord Bacon and a very famous name, who is deceived? Have you ever heard the name of any book by Lord Bacon? Who is bothered? How could Lord Bacon write these Shakespearean plays? Under his name he has not written a single masterpiece so how could he write one under a pseudo-name? And if he can write such beautiful plays as the Shakespearean plays are, under a pseudo-name, then what was he doing when he was writing under his own name? It doesn't seem right.

So whether Shakespeare was known as Shakespeare or not is not the point. Some consciousness certainly existed which gave birth to these beautiful plays. What is wrong in calling that consciousness Shakespeare?

The same is true about Lieh Tzu – there is suspicion. There is no suspicion in the East, we have never bothered. In India we have many books written by one man, Vyasa. *The Mahabharata* is enough. To write a book like *The Mahabharata* is enough for one author. It is an *Encyclopedia Britannica*. It will make one man famous for ages to come. And that is only one of the books that he has written – there are hundreds of books in his name.

Now Western scholars cannot believe that one man can write so many books. I can understand. It does not seem possible. And these books are not written in one age – one book was written five thousand years ago, another book three thousand years ago, another book two thousand years ago. So this man existed for thousands of years?

But in the East we have never worried about it. Don't we see the problem? We can also see the problem but our approach is different. We say, "What does it matter who wrote them?" The books are beautiful, very beautiful, tremendously significant. We have enjoyed them down the centuries, we have loved them, we have contemplated over them. The authorship is irrelevant.

And why one man? In fact, the case is this. Once Vyasa's name became famous then other authors simply did not bother to write their own name. They said, "It will do. Vyasa's name is good and it is a well-known name, it will do." So down the centuries anybody who wrote a beautiful book and thought that it was worthy of a Vyasa, signed it Vyasa. It was worthy of the man who wrote *The Mahabharata.* SO how could he sign his own name? That would not look right. In fact, it was so beautiful that only Vyasa could write it – so the author signed with the name of Vyasa.

These people were beautiful, they had no egos of their own. They were just vehicles. In fact, later on the name "Vyasa" became synonymous with "the author." "Vyasa" means "the author" – written by the author. It does not mean anything else. In the East we know that when a book is written by Vyasa it means: written by the author. Naturally, every book has to be written by the author. "Vyasa" became synonymous with "the author."

Lieh Tzu is suspicious. He does not seem to be a historical person at all, he has not left any trace. Either he was not a historical person or he was a great horse. My preference is for the second. He was a great horse who never raised any dust and who never left any track behind. He effaced himself completely. Only this small book exists – the book of Lieh Tzu – with these small parables. It says nothing about Lieh Tzu.

But why should one bother? This is going into the non-essential, this is looking at the color of the horse. The color of the horse was black and the man of Tao reported it as being yellow. And the horse was a stallion and the man reported it as being a mare. Lieh Tzu may have been a woman, he may not have been a man. Who knows? He may not have been a Chinese, he may have been a Tibetan. Who knows? He may not have been at all. It does not matter. But these parables matter. These parables are doors.

So please don't go into the non-essential. Look into the spirit of the essential. Don't be bothered by the gross, go into the subtle.

The sixth question:

Osho,
The earth seems to be shaking beneath our feet and our faces reflect some imminent cataclysmic event. What is happening?

Don't be worried. It has always been so. Every age and every generation has thought that something great is happening to them, because every generation has a great ego. How is it possible that something great is not happening while you are here? No, something cataclysmic, something great, something really final is going to happen.

This has been so from the very beginning.

I have heard that when Adam and Eve were thrown out, expelled out of the Garden of Eden, the first thing that Adam said to Eve was, "Darling, we are passing through a great revolution."

Since then man has always felt the same – again and again and again down the ages. It is nothing new. A six-thousand-year-old stone has been found in Babylon with four or five sentences inscribed on it. When these sentences were deciphered people were puzzled. If you read those sentences you will not believe that they are six thousand years old, they look as if they are part of the editorial of today's *Pune Herald*. The first thing that inscription says is: "Where are those old golden days? The new generation has become very corrupt. The children don't respect their parents...." Six thousand years old! It has not used the word "hippie," right, but what is the difference? "Children don't obey their parents. There is no respect left. Love has disappeared. Wives don't love their husbands, husbands don't love their wives. It is the most immoral age ever." These are the sentences. "The most immoral age...."

But the ego feels satisfied. Our age is the most immoral age. Nobody else can compete, nobody else can compare. And every age has always felt that it is passing through a very critical moment. Sir, it has been always so. Don't be worried. Rest and go to sleep. Let the earth shake, it has always been shaking. It is nothing new.

On the earth almost everything is old and ancient. There is a saying in India that there is nothing new under the sun. And in a way it is very significant. Only forms differ, everything is the same – the same anger, the same hatred the same war, the same violence, the same inhumanity, the same madness, the same neurosis. Nothing is new under the sun.

Don't waste time about it. Just go within yourself and find out that which is eternal, find out that which is your reality. These outer things have remained the same, changing a little bit here and there but basically repeating the same gestalt: the politics, the politicians, the war amongst nations, the religions and the churches and their violent struggle to survive and crush each other, the greed of man and the aggressiveness of man, and the inhumanity of man towards other human beings.

The last question:

Osho,
Please summarize what the ego is.

An egotistical lover met a girl in a drugstore and asked her "How would you like to sleep with me tonight, baby?" The girl, insulted and angry, used her knowledge of judo and swung him out of the door. Jolted and jilted, the egotistical lover returned. "But baby," he said, "You haven't answered my question!"

That's what ego is – the greatest stupidity. You can't see it because you are it. You can always see it in others, you cannot see it in yourself.

A Jew suddenly became very rich and he wanted to show it off to everybody. So he and his wife went to the costliest restaurant dressed in the costliest dresses. The wife was wearing diamonds and emeralds and all that money could purchase – and they had really become very rich. She was looking very ugly with all those diamonds and emeralds because she had no taste. You can become rich suddenly but you cannot gain taste suddenly. You can become rich suddenly but you cannot become cultured suddenly.

And sometimes, when you suddenly become rich, all your ugliness comes to the surface. You purchase all that ugliness with your richness – you can afford it now. Up to now it had been hidden but now it comes to the surface.

They sat down in the restaurant and looked at the menu. But as the menu was in French they could not read it – they did not know anything about French and they did not want to admit it to the waiter. So the wife asked, "What are you going to order now?" He told her not to be worried and said to the waiter, "Bring me one hundred dollars' worth of salami sandwiches – one hundred dollars' worth."

The ego is just absurd. Asking for one hundred dollars' worth of salami sandwiches!

The waiter could not believe it. He said, "You are both going to eat them all?"

It is difficult to look at your own ego. The ego is something that everybody is aware of except yourself. Whenever others say something about you, ponder over it, meditate over it. There is every possibility that they will be right. When others say something about your ego, don't deny it, don't reject it. There *is* every possibility that they will be right. There is a ninety-nine per cent possibility that they are right – because others can very easily see your ego even if you cannot. And you can see other egos very easily; it is there just exactly on the tip of their noses. In everything they do – walking, talking sitting, listening – it is there. It is so apparent, so obvious to everybody – except to the person himself. He hides behind it.

The actors were out of work when they met in Lindy's one day. "Say, I got an idea," 'said one. "Why don't we team up? Do an act together."

"Sounds good," said the other. "What kind of an act you got in mind?"

"Well, I come out and sing. The curtain comes down. Then it goes up and I come out and dance. Then it comes down. Then it goes up again and I come out and juggle. Then…."

"Hey, where do I come in?"

"The curtain don't go up and down by itself!"

That's what ego is. You are the emperor and everybody is a servant. You are the end and everybody is a means This is the basic ingredient of the ego, the very center – that you are the center of the whole existence and everybody is here to serve you, to be used by you. If you are using people you are an egoist. If you think of yourself as the center and everybody else as your periphery then you are an egoist.

If you think that everybody is an end unto himself, then the ego starts disappearing. If you don't put yourself higher than others or lower than others then the ego disappears. Remember, you know that to put yourself higher than others is to be egotistical but I am saying that to put yourself lower than others is also egotistical. It is ego standing on its head but it is ego all the same. So don't put anybody higher than you and don't put anybody lower than you. We are one. We are one existence. Nobody is lower, nobody is higher. Nobody is superior, nobody is inferior. There are not two gods so how can there be inferiority or superiority? It is one unity. Ego makes you feel separate; non-ego joins you to existence. To feel one with the cosmos is to get out of the ego; to feel separate is to be with the ego.

Ego is what Tao is not; and Tao is what ego is not. If you are in the ego you will never taste Tao, if you want to taste Tao you will have to drop the ego. Dropping it, you come home; dropping it, the benediction is there.

Enough for today.

Information About
The Original Audio Series

Books by Osho are transcriptions from discourses given before a live audience. All Osho discourses have been published in full as books and are also available as original audio recordings. Information about the audio recordings and the complete text archive can be found at the OSHO Library at www.osho.com.

About the Author

Osho defies categorization, reflecting everything from the individual quest for meaning to the most urgent social and political issues facing society today. His books are not written but are transcribed from recordings of extemporaneous talks given over a period of thirty-five years. Osho has been described by *The Sunday Times* in London as one of the "1000 Makers of the 20th Century" and by *Sunday Mid-Day* in India as one of the ten people – along with Gandhi, Nehru and Buddha – who have changed the destiny of India.

Osho has a stated aim of helping to create the conditions for the birth of a new kind of human being, characterized as "Zorba the Buddha" – one whose feet are firmly on the ground, yet whose hands can touch the stars. Running like a thread through all aspects of Osho's talks and meditations is a vision that encompasses both the timeless wisdom of the East and the highest potential of Western science and technology.

He is synonymous with a revolutionary contribution to the science of inner transformation and an approach to meditation which specifically addresses the accelerated pace of contemporary life. The unique OSHO® Active Meditations™ are designed to allow the release of accumulated stress in the body and mind so that it is easier to be still and experience the thought-free state of meditation.

OSHO International Meditation Resort

Every year the OSHO® International Meditation Resort™ welcomes thousands of people from over 100 countries who come to enjoy and participate in its unique atmosphere of meditation and celebration. The 28-acre meditation resort is located about 100 miles southeast of Mumbai (Bombay), in Pune, India, in a tree-lined residential area, set against a backdrop of bamboo groves and wild jasmine, peacocks and waterfalls, The basic approach of the meditation resort is that of Zorba the Buddha: living in awareness, with a capacity to celebrate everything in life. Many visitors come to just be, to allow themselves the luxury of doing nothing. Others choose to participate in a wide variety of courses and sessions that support moving toward a more joyous and less stressful life, by combining methods of self-understanding with awareness techniques. These courses are offered through OSHO® Multiversity™ and take place in a pyramid complex next to the famous OSHO® Teerth Park. ™

People can choose to practice various meditation methods, both active and passive, from a daily schedule that begins at six o'clock in the morning. Early each evening there is a meditation event that moves from dance to silent sitting, using Osho's recorded talks as an opportunity to experience inner silence without effort.

Facilities include tennis courts, a gym, sauna, Jacuzzi, a nature-shaped Olympic-sized swimming pool, classes in Zen archery, Tai chi, Chi gong, Yoga and a multitude of bodywork sessions.

The kitchen serves international gourmet vegetarian meals, made with organically grown produce. The nightlife is alive with friends dining under the stars, and with music and dancing.

Online bookings for accommodation at the OSHO® Guesthouse which is inside the meditation resort can be made through the website below or by sending an email to: guesthouse@osho.com

Online tours of the meditation resort, how to get there, and program information can be found at: http://www.osho.com/resort

For detailed information to participate in this meditation resort please contact:

OSHO INTERNATIONAL MEDITATION RESORT
17 Koregaon Park, Pune–411001, MS, India
Phone: +91-20-66019999 Fax:+91- 20-66019990
Email: resortinfo@osho.net Website: http://www.osho.com

Books by Osho in English

EARLY DISCOURSES AND WRITINGS

A Cup of Tea
Dimensions Beyond The Known
From Sex to Super-consciousness
The Great Challenge
Hidden Mysteries
I Am The Gate
The Inner Journey
Psychology of the Esoteric
Seeds of Wisdom

MEDITATION

The Voice of Silence
And Now and Here (Vol 1 & 2)
In Search of the Miraculous (Vol 1 &.2)
Meditation: The Art of Ecstasy
Meditation: The First and Last Freedom
The Path of Meditation
The Perfect Way
Yaa-Hoo! The Mystic Rose

BUDDHA AND BUDDHIST MASTERS

The Book of Wisdom
The Dhammapada: The Way of the Buddha (Vol 1-12)
The Diamond Sutra
The Discipline of Transcendence (Vol 1-4)
The Heart Sutra

INDIAN MYSTICS

Enlightenment: The Only Revolution (Ashtavakra)
Showering Without Clouds (Sahajo)
The Last Morning Star (Daya)
The Song of Ecstasy (Adi Shankara)

BAUL MYSTICS

The Beloved (Vol 1 & 2)

KABIR

The Divine Melody
Ecstasy: The Forgotten Language
The Fish in the Sea is Not Thirsty
The Great Secret
The Guest
The Path of Love
The Revolution

JESUS AND CHRISTIAN MYSTICS

Come Follow to You (Vol 1-4)
I Say Unto You (Vol 1 & 2)
The Mustard Seed
Theologia Mystica

JEWISH MYSTICS

The Art of Dying
The True Sage

WESTERN MYSTICS

Guida Spirituale (Desiderata)
The Hidden Harmony (Heraclitus)
The Messiah (Vol 1 & 2) (Commentaries on Khalil Gibran's The Prophet)
The New Alchemy: To Turn You On (Commentaries on Mabel Collins' Light on the Path)
Philosophia Perennis (Vol 1 & 2) (The Golden Verses of Pythagoras)
Zarathustra: A God That Can Dance
Zarathustra: The Laughing Prophet (Commentaries on Nietzsche's Thus Spake Zarathustra)

SUFISM

Just Like That

Journey to the Heart
The Perfect Master (Vol 1 & 2)
The Secret
Sufis: The People of the Path (Vol 1 & 2)
Unio Mystica (Vol 1 & 2)
The Wisdom of the Sands(Vol 1 & 2)

TANTRA

Tantra: The Supreme Understanding
The Tantra Experience
The Royal Song of Saraha (same as Tantra Vision, Vol 1)
The Tantric Transformation
The Royal Song of Saraha (same as Tantra Vision, Vol 2)
The Book of Secrets: Vigyan Bhairav Tantra

THE UPANISHADS

Behind a Thousand Names (Nirvana Upanishad)
Heartbeat of the Absolute (Ishavasya Upanishad)
I Am That (Isa Upanishad)
The Message Beyond Words (Kathopanishad)
Philosophia Ultima (Mandukya Upanishad)
The Supreme Doctrine (Kenopanishad)
Finger Pointing to the Moon (Adhyatma Upanishad)
That Art Thou (Sarvasar Upanishad, Kaivalya Upanishad, Adhyatma Upanishad)
The Ultimate Alchemy, Vol 1&2 (Atma Pooja Upanishad Vol 1 &2)
Vedanta: Seven Steps to Samadhi (Akshaya Upanishad)
Flight of the Alone to the Alone (Kaivalya Upanishad)

TAO

The Empty Boat
The Secret of Secrets
Tao:The Golden Gate (Vol 1&2)
Tao:The Pathless Path (Vol 1&2)
Tao: The Three Treasures (Vol 1-4)
When the Shoe Fits

YOGA

The Path of Yoga (previously Yoga: The Alpha and the Omega (Vol 1)
Yoga: The Alpha and the Omega (Vol 2-10)

ZEN AND ZEN MASTERS

Ah, This!
Ancient Music in the Pines
And the Flowers Showered
A Bird on the Wing
Bodhidharma: The Greatest Zen Master
Communism and Zen Fire, Zen Wind
Dang Dang Doko Dang
The First Principle
God is Dead: Now Zen is the Only Living Truth
The Grass Grows By Itself
The Great Zen Master Ta Hui
Hsin Hsin Ming: The Book of Nothing
I Celebrate Myself: God is No Where, Life is Now Here
Kyozan: A True Man of Zen
Nirvana: The Last Nightmare
No Mind: The Flowers of Eternity
No Water, No Moon
One Seed Makes the Whole Earth Green
Returning to the Source
The Search: Talks on the 10 Bulls of Zen

A Sudden Clash of Thunder
The Sun Rises in the Evening
Take it Easy (Vol 1 & 2)
This Very Body the Buddha
Walking in Zen, Sitting in Zen
The White Lotus
Yakusan: Straight to the Point of Enlightenment
Zen Manifesto : Freedom From Oneself
Zen: The Mystery and the Poetry of the Beyond
Zen: The Path of Paradox (Vol 1, 2 & 3)
Zen: The Special Transmission
Zen Boxed Sets
The World of Zen (5 vol.)
Live Zen
This. This. A Thousand Times This
Zen: The Diamond Thunderbolt
Zen: The Quantum Leap from Mind to No-Mind
Zen: The Solitary Bird, Cuckoo of the Forest
Zen: All The Colors Of The Rainbow (5 vol.)
The Buddha: The Emptiness of the Heart
The Language of Existence
The Miracle
The Original Man
Turning In

OSHO: On the Ancient Masters of Zen (7 volumes)*

Dogen: The Zen Master
Hyakujo: The Everest of Zen– With Basho's haikus
Isan: No Footprints in the Blue Sky
Joshu: The Lion's Roar
Ma Tzu: The Empty Mirror
Nansen: The Point Of Departure
Rinzai: Master of the Irrational

**Each volume is also available individually.*

RESPONSES TO QUESTIONS

Be Still and Know
Come, Come, Yet Again Come
The Goose is Out
The Great Pilgrimage: From Here to Here
Invitation
My Way: The Way of the White Clouds
Nowhere to Go But In
The Razor's Edge
Walk Without Feet, Fly Without Wings and Think Without Mind
The Wild Geese and the Water
Zen: Zest, Zip, Zap and Zing
From Bondage To Freedom
From Darkness to Light
From Death To Deathlessness
From the False to the Truth
From Unconsciousness to Consciousness
The Rajneesh Bible (Vol 2-4)
Beyond Enlightenment (Talks in Bombay)
Beyond Psychology (Talks in Uruguay)
Light on the Path (Talks in the Himalayas)
The Path of the Mystic (Talks in Uruguay)
Sermons in Stones (Talks in Bombay)
Socrates Poisoned Again After 25 Centuries (Talks in Greece)
The Sword and the Lotus (Talks in the Himalayas)

The Transmission of the Lamp (Talks in Uruguay)

OSHO'S VISION FOR THE WORLD

The Golden Future
The Hidden Splendor
The New Dawn
The Rebel
The Rebellious Spirit

THE MANTRA SERIES

Hari Om Tat Sat
Om Mani Padme Hum
Om Shantih Shantih Shantih
Sat-Chit-Anand
Satyam-Shivam-Sundram

PERSONAL GLIMPSES

Books I Have Loved
Glimpses of a Golden Childhood
Notes of a Madman

INTERVIEWS WITH THE WORLD PRESS

The Man of Truth: A Majority of One

For any information about OSHO Books, please contact:
OSHO Media International
17 Koregaon Park, Pune – 411001, MS, India
Phone: +91-20-66019999 Fax: +91-20-66019990
E-mail: distribution@osho.net
Website: http://www.osho.com

Full Circle is a distinguished publisher of non-fiction, and classic and contemporary fiction. Known for quality publishing and production, Full Circle continues its commitment towards providing good reading at great value.

We are dedicated towards creating a peaceful and harmonious inner and outer world ever mindful of our connection with the divine human spirit.

Our fine books are available at leading bookstores across the country and the Full Circle Bookstores below: